ENVIRONMENTAL POLICY

Environmental Policy

Objectives, Instruments, and Implementation

Edited by
DIETER HELM

OXFORD
UNIVERSITY PRESS

OXFORD
UNIVERSITY PRESS

Great Clarendon Street, Oxford OX2 6DP

Oxford University Press is a department of the University of Oxford.
It furthers the University's objective of excellence in research, scholarship,
and education by publishing worldwide in

Oxford New York

Athens Auckland Bangkok Bogotá Buenos Aires Calcutta
Cape Town Chennai Dar es Salaam Delhi Florence Hong Kong Istanbul
Karachi Kuala Lumpur Madrid Melbourne Mexico City Mumbai
Nairobi Paris São Paulo Shanghai Singapore Taipei Tokyo Toronto Warsaw

with associated companies in Berlin Ibadan

Oxford is a registered trade mark of Oxford University Press
in the UK and in certain other countries

Published in the United States
by Oxford University Press Inc., New York

© *Oxford Review of Economic Policy*, 2000

British Library Cataloguing in Publication Data

Data available

Library of Congress Cataloging in Publication Data

Data available

ISBN 0–19–924136–8 (Pbk)
ISBN 0–19–924135–X (Hbk)

1 3 5 7 9 10 8 6 4 2

Printed in Great Britain
on acid-free paper by
T.J. International Ltd.,
Padstow, Cornwall

Contents

Contributors

Giles Atkinson
Giles Atkinson is Lecturer in Environmental Policy at the London School of Economics and Political Science, and Honorary Senior Fellow at the Centre for Social and Economic Research on the Global Environment (CSERGE), University College London and University of East Anglia.

Scott Barrett
Scott Barrett is Professor of Environmental Economics & International Political Economy at the Paul H. Nitze School of Advanced International Studies, Johns Hopkins University. He has published widely on the strategy of negotiating international environmental agreements and received the Erik Kempe Prize for this work. He was a lead author of the second assessment report of the Intergovernmental Panel on Climate Change and has also advised a number of international organizations on the problems of negotiating a climate change treaty.

Inger Brisson
Inger Brisson is a lecturer in Resource and Environmental Economics at the Institute of Ecology and Resource Management at the University of Edinburgh. One of her main areas of research is the economics and policy of waste management, with particular emphasis on externalities. She contributed to research which informed the setting of the UK landfill tax. Dr Brisson has also been involved in waste-policy-relevant research for the European Commission, and she has assessed the validity of the waste hierarchy using cost–benefit analysis.

Simon Cowan
Simon Cowan is a lecturer at Oxford University and Wigmore Fellow in Economics at Worcester College, Oxford. He is the author, with Mark Armstrong and John Vickers, of *Regulatory Reform: Economic Analysis and British Experience*, published in 1994 by the MIT Press, and is Managing Editor of *Oxford Economic Papers*.

Dieter Helm
Dieter Helm is Fellow in Economics at New College, Oxford, and a director of Oxford Economic Research Associates (OXERA) and of OXERA Environmental. He is a member of the Department of Trade and Industry's energy advisory panel and chairman of the Department of the Environment, Transport and the Regions' academic panel. He is editor of *The Utilities Journal* and an Associate Editor of the *Oxford Review of Economic Policy*.

Anthony G. Heyes
Anthony Heyes is Professor of Economics at Royal Holloway College, London University. He has degrees from Cambridge and McGill Universities and was previously a Fellow of the Oxford Institute for Energy Studies and Nuffield College, Oxford. His research interests span regulation, environmental policy, and the economics of law.

Ian Hodge
Ian Hodge is the Gilbey Lecturer in the Department of Land Economy, University of Cambridge. He has previously taught at the Universities of Queensland and Newcastle upon Tyne. He has research interests in the areas of environmental management, rural development, and land use. He is the author of a number of publications, including *Countryside in Trust: Land Management by Conservation, Amenity and Recreation Organisations* (with Janet Dwyer, Wiley, 1996), and *Environmental Economics: Individual Incentives and Public Choices* (Macmillan, 1995).

David Macdonald
David Macdonald is Director of Oxford University's Wildlife Conservation Research Unit and A. D. White Professor at Cornell University. He is also a Fellow of Lady Margaret Hall, Oxford. His training is in behavioural ecology, with especial emphasis on mammals. Recently he has established various forums in which decision-makers can discuss policy at the interface of biodiversity, business, and politics.

Chris Nash
Chris Nash joined the Institute for Transport Studies at Leeds University in 1974 as BR Lecturer in Rail Transport, and became Professor of Transport Economics in 1989. He is currently Director of the Institute. He is author or co-author of four books and around a hundred other published papers. He has managed many European, Research Council, and industry-financed research projects, particularly in the fields of rail transport, public transport economics, and project appraisal.

David Pearce
David Pearce is Professor of Economics at University College London. He is the author or editor of some fifty books, mainly in the areas of environmental economics and cost–benefit analysis. He is a recipient of the 'Global 500' award of the United Nations for services to the global environment.

Jane Powell
Jane Powell is a senior researcher at the Centre of Social and Economic Research on the Global Environment (CSERGE) in the School of Environmental Sciences at the University of East Anglia. She has a first degree in environmental sciences and a Ph.D. in the environmental evaluation of energy from waste systems. Dr Powell has extensive research experience in waste management and energy systems, particularly in policy issues and the development and use of life-cycle assessment techniques and multi-criteria evaluation.

Stephen Smith
Stephen Smith is Professor of Economics at University College London. His main research interests are in the fields of public finance and environmental economics. He was previously Deputy Director of the Institute for Fiscal Studies. Professor Smith is, in addition, a member of the Department of the Environment Academic Panel on Environmental Economics, of the HM Customs and Excise Academic Panel, and of the Treasury Panel on Public Services.

Preface

DIETER HELM

The twentieth century probably witnessed more pollution than the total for all of previous human history. It was the century of population explosion and the burning of fossil fuels, resulting in major biodiversity loss and climate change. Yet it was only in the closing decades that the full extent of the environmental damage was beginning to be recognized, and the environment was transformed from a narrow sectional interest and moved to the centre stage of governments', companies', and individuals' decisions. Where once environmental issues were a minority interest, they now command the attention of prime ministers, chief executives, and the general public. Party manifestos proclaim the greenness of politicians, companies produce glossy environmental reports, and shoppers have begun to opt for organic products.

The fact that environmental issues have risen up the policy agenda is not entirely motivated by the desire to win over voters. Throughout developed countries, governments face constraints on their ability to raise further revenue from conventional taxation. Yet the demands for health care, pensions, and social security continues to rise faster than economic growth can finance. Raising revenue by taxing pollution becomes an attractive option when compared with increasing income tax or VAT. It is, for example, unsurprising that the broadly social democratic governments in the UK, Germany, and France have all seen the merits of new energy taxes.

Paralleling the new green enthusiasms, there has been an explosion in research, both scientific and economic. Whereas the case for action in the 1960s and early 1970s—most famously set out in Rachel Carson's *Silent Spring* (Carson, 1963) and in the *Club of Rome* report (Goldsmith *et al.*, 1972)—were accompanied by calls for relatively crude prohibitions and direct government action, the current concerns find a much richer literature on the evaluation of environmental impacts and the design of policy instruments. This time around, the case for market-based approaches, using economic instruments rather than command-and-control mechanisms, is much better understood. Cost–benefit analysis uses data on people's preferences, eliciting their willingness to pay for environmental improvements, and green taxes and tradable-permit schemes are designed to confront polluters with the costs they impose, and to make sure pollution reduction is achieved at least cost.

The coincidence of demands for greater environmental protection with the supply of the tools to address them has created a major opportunity to improve the quality and efficiency of policy formulation and implementation. It is not, however, without its critics. The very ideas that the environment might by given a monetary value, that the optimal level of pollution is rarely zero, and that companies might be granted permits to pollute — these all deeply offend many environmentalists and excite much political opposition.

In consequence, the potential for economic analysis to contribute to environmental policy has not been fully realized. There are, as yet, few well-designed environmental taxes or permit schemes in operation, and several which purport to be are — as we shall see — far from ideal. The so-called climate-change levy, for example, fails to distinguish between carbon and non-carbon sources of energy production, while the fuel-price escalator has had much more to do with raising revenue for government than confronting motorists with the full environmental costs of the car.

These failures tend to give economic instruments a bad name, but they are largely political in origin. Environmental improvement is typically costly, and extra costs are rarely attractive to those who have to pay them. It is better politically to disguise the costs, and to tax industry rather than consumers. Regulation has the great political advantage over taxes that the impact on prices to customers is almost always implicit rather than explicit. The costs do not, however, go away. Indeed, the costs of traditional command-and-control regulation are often (but not always) greater than those of taxes.

But the fault also lies with the design of economic instruments. Too often, the context is only crudely modelled, and the problems of transition poorly taken into account. Companies and consumers are typically conditioned by the prices and costs of a polluting environment, and sudden tax shocks fail to take account of the need to adapt. The perfect tax is often the enemy of the good. Furthermore, the economists' concern with the substitution effects of instruments can neglect the powerful income effects from taxing what are often inelastically demanded goods — especially where these are essential inputs to household and company costs, such as water, energy, and transport. While it is important to get the principles right — and to explain why economic approaches may often achieve more for the environment at lower costs than traditional approaches—this is merely a first step. Careful attention to the design of instruments and their application is essential if progress is to be made.

This volume is an attempt to address these practical issues of policy design. It is structured in three parts—the principles and concepts, the policy context, and sectoral applications. It is intended that these parts fit together, to help to understand how environmental policy might be improved.

The central organizing principle of environmental policy, following the Rio and Kyoto negotiations, is 'sustainable development'. Almost every developed country pays lip service to it. But although it excites warm feelings among politicians, the media, and the general public, it is a tricky concept to put into operation. In the hands of British politicians, it has been transformed from a primary focus on environmental matters, to encapsulate wider political aspirations. The Major government added on economic growth—in part in response to the priorities of the early 1990s recession—while the Labour government after 1997 added on the social part. It is now, in the hands of politicians, a largely meaningless concept, as I show in chapter 1. Indeed, so pliable is the concept, that Peter Mandelson, when Secretary of State for Trade and Industry, could claim that protecting the British coal industry—one of the most polluting industries—was consistent with it, once due weight had been given to the non-environmental factors.

This abuse of the concept need not, however, undermine it. Giles Atkinson shows in chapter 2 that the sustainability concept has been the subject of a major amount of economic work. The ideas of substitutability between man-made and natural capital, the requirements of intergenerational equity, and the discounting of future costs and benefits have greatly enriched our understanding of the appropriate objectives of policy. Failure to follow a path of sustainable development is not for lack of economic guidance; the guidance is there, but it has not been followed.

The concept of sustainable development necessitates measurement. We need to know what the environmental costs and benefits of alternative policy options are. This is primarily an economic matter, and the techniques of cost–benefit analysis are designed precisely with these requirements in mind. David Pearce sets out the arguments for cost–benefit analysis in chapter 3, and in chapter 4 he shows how the traditional command-and-control technique, BATNEEC (best available technology not entailing excessive cost), has—and has not—integrated considerations of costs and benefits into what is essentially a technical/engineering appraisal methodology. I set out the more general arguments against command-and-control regulation, as developed in the UK, in chapter 1.

Economic instruments are not, however, confined to taxes and permit schemes. Many pollution problems require an element of standard setting and monitoring of compliance. Anthony Heyes, in chapter 5, sets out the economics of enforcement and compliance and shows how fines and penalties need to be carefully designed to take account of the marginal costs—and hence the incentives—of the polluter. Attention to this rich literature has the potential greatly to increase the effectiveness of policy design.

Part Two of the volume concentrates on the policy context, and in particular on the two 'great' environmental problems—global warming and biodiversity loss. Global warming is complicated in that it creates not only the conventional economic problems of designing policy instruments in the face of uncertainty, but its global nature requires international cooperation. The Kyoto process illustrates this: how to get nations to cooperate in reducing emissions, when it is in the interest of each for the others to reduces theirs while it continues to pollute. With these classic 'prisoner's dilemma' characteristics, the task is to create credible international protocols and agreements. Scott Barrett, in chapter 6, sets out the requirements which need to be met, and shows how difficult it is to make agreements like Kyoto stick.

Biodiversity loss is also a global problem, but unlike climate change it is typically played out on a very local scale. There are no general instruments, such as carbon taxes and tradable permits, to address biodiversity: it is much more clearly concerned with specific habitats. Species tend to be interdependent, and there is no escape from tying up environmental policy with detailed ecological study. The ecological perspective is here provided by David Macdonald in chapter 7. This specificity does not, however, make biodiversity loss an isolated and separable problem: it is caused by population pressure, climate change, and, above all, land-use policies.

Part Three provides a series of sectoral applications, showing how environmental policy has, in practice, been applied—or, too often, misapplied. It is in these practical examples that the problems of tailoring good economic tools to specific contexts are illustrated, as are some of the reasons why their application to date has been disappointing.

The most recent example is the climate-change levy, which was promoted as an economic instrument to help achieve the Kyoto target and the more demanding domestic aspiration to reduce CO_2 emissions by 20 per cent from their 1990 levels by 2010. Stephen Smith, in chapter 8, shows how the competing requirements of general taxation and the specific nature of the problem interact with the important income effects of such taxes. The political constraints (avoiding explicit consumer taxes and protecting the coal industry) have produced a tax which is badly designed on environmental grounds, being confined to industry and failing to distinguish between carbon and non-carbon sources.

Simon Cowan, in chapter 9, considers how economic instruments might be applied to the water industry, and, in particular, looks at the problem of abstraction rights and the scope for trading. The localized nature of water sources and pollution emissions heavily constrains the policy options, and it is unsurprising that, after nearly a decade of active consideration, such instruments have yet to be applied.

Agricultural policy suffers from similar location-specific character-istics. Ian Hodge, in chapter 10, describes how attempts have been made to 'green' the Common Agricultural Policy (CAP), by tinkering at the edges to create incentives for environmentally benign practices. These efforts are, however, dwarfed by the central flaws in the CAP, and it remains doubtful whether a substantial improvement can be made in the absence of a major reform of the policy.

Transport and, in particular, the integrated transport policy, was designated as the flagship of environmental policy in the 1997 Labour manifesto. The explicit objective was to induce a switch from private to public transport. At first glance, this is an area where the prospect of economic instruments is extremely promising. Yet, as Chris Nash explains in chapter 11, the practical realities of transport policy have proved major obstacles to progress. It is hardly surprising that the policy pressure in the manifesto has not so far proved easy to deliver.

The final example is more encouraging — the landfill levy. Inger Brisson and Jane Powell describe in chapter 12 how this concept was developed and how it has been applied in practice. It is an example of a specific tax, where the externalities have been properly considered, and where the scope for substitution to more environmentally benign practices is considerable.

These case studies provide no more than glimpses at the potential to apply economic concepts to environmental policy. Yet, in each, the scope for achieving objectives at lower cost is readily apparent. As the scale of environmental damage grows, so will the costs of mitigating it. The 'low hanging fruit' — the obvious and cheap opportunities for environmental improvement — will become rarer. As the costs grow, so will the political difficulties of addressing the problems. There will be a growing premium on efficient, least-cost solutions. Cost–benefit analysis can help to identify them, and economic instruments will help to induce appropriate supply- and demand-side responses.

Part One: Principles

1

Objectives, Instruments, and Institutions

DIETER HELM*

1. Introduction

The current approach to environmental policy in the UK dates from the 1990 White Paper, *This Common Inheritance*, which set the prime object-ive as sustainable development. Though neither the concept nor many of the themes in the paper were new, it marked a significant break with the past, in that it recognized for the first time the pre-eminence of global pollution and, in particular, global warming and biodiversity loss. It also recognized that these 'new' problems were of a different scale and importance. From 1990 onwards, governments would take environmental matters much more seriously.

Taking the environment seriously is a necessary but not sufficient step towards an environmental policy. To provide coherence, the policy requires clear objectives and targets that derive from them. It also requires an appropriate set of instruments and a set of institutions capable of implementing it.

In theory, the overarching sustainability principle provided a clear guide to policy formulation. All government policy was to be subject to this test, with the consequence that the piecemeal, *ad-hoc* treatment of each individual environmental problem which characterized the British approach for most of the century would be replaced by a tough, predict-able, and measurable set of coherent policies. Where there was scientific doubt, the precautionary principle dictated a risk-averse approach.

In practice, although there has been significant legislation, the impact of the sustainability policy has been somewhat muted. The recession of the early 1990s dampened political enthusiasm, and succes-sive governments failed to give any precise definition to the concept.

* New College, University of Oxford. The author is grateful to Nick Hartley, David Pearce, Ronan Palmer, Chris Riley, David Slater, Robin Smale, and Janet Wright for helpful comments. The usual disclaimer applies.

Targets were adopted without much regard to it, except by way of lip service, and many of these were relatively easy to achieve. The definition of sustainable development was widened, first by the Conservatives to include economic growth and development, and then by Labour to include social considerations, leaving the inevitable trade-offs with the environment ambiguous.

With the exception of the social component, the 1997 General Election has not yet fundamentally affected the broad thrust of environmental policy.[1] Labour's White Paper (DETR, 1999a) added a host of targets and indicators, from the level of crime to wild birds, but did little to explain how these might be achieved. Of the major decisions facing the Labour administration in its first years in office, four have illustrated the political and practical difficulties of applying the sustainability concept. The transport White Paper, *A New Deal for Transport, Better for Everyone* (DETR, 1998a) was perhaps the most environmentally driven, but had to balance the desirability of a switch to public transport against the practical obstacles to the use of hypothecated charges on road-users to pay for it. The decisions on water quality (DETR, 1998b) required balancing perceived customer hostility to rising water bills with the costs of improving water quality and sewerage treatment, and signalling the need to conserve water resources through the price mechanism. Perhaps most difficult, the politics of coal led to explicit intervention to slow the decline of its market share through the energy White Paper, *Conclusions of the Review of Energy Sources for Power Generation* (DTI, 1998), despite the major environmental problems created by its mining and burning. Finally, the Department of Environment, Transport and the Regions (DETR)'s housing plans have had to reconcile the need to protect the green belt, while providing for changing social needs and economic development (DETR, 1998e). All are claimed to be examples of sustainable development in action, but just how these policies 'protect and enhance our environment so that the country we hand on to our children and our grandchildren is a better place in which to live' (Labour's Manifesto, p. 29) has not been explained. Making sustainable development an operational concept which enables policy choices to be made requires these sorts of hard trade-offs. Such explicitness is already proving as hard for this government as for its predecessors.

There are problems, too, in implementing policy — in setting targets and choosing instruments. Economics offers tools to assist, but, as with the sustainability concept, there is a reluctance to use them. An example

[1] Labour's manifesto simply reaffirmed the sustainability principle and claimed that an integrated transport policy was the most important component. The only explicit commitment was to a parliamentary environmental audit committee.

is provided by the commitment to a 20 per cent reduction in carbon-dioxide emissions from their 1990 level by 2010. While a tough target might be represented as 'environmental leadership' in Europe and globally, just why this number is more sustainable than the Kyoto target (12.5 per cent of a basket of greenhouse gases) or some other number, say, 30 per cent, is far from clear.[2] Although government is committed to taking account of the costs and benefits of environmental policy, for major decisions such as these, there is little evidence that it has done so.

On policy instruments, the 1990 White Paper again marked a turning point,[3] and both the Conservative and Labour governments in the 1990s have supported the principle of greater use of economic instruments, such as taxes and tradable permits, to ensure that the polluter pays. The current government has come forward with major new initiatives—notably in energy, with the climate change levy, and the prospect of trading green credits for renewables—but formidable obstacles remain to their effective implementation. Proposals for pesticide and aggregate taxes have proved politically even more difficult.

The gulf between the potential for greater use of economic techniques and current practice provides a major opportunity to improve resource allocation and hence achieve environmental goals at lower cost. But there are considerable barriers to further take-up of such opportunities. Some of these are *technical*, many of which can be overcome. Some are political, and need to be explicitly incorporated into policy design, if there is to be any significant progress. First-best economic policies rarely pass such tests, especially when there are significant distributional consequences. (See Goulder, 2000, on the second-best context, and Smith in chapter 8 of this volume.) Finally, there are institutional barriers, which need to be addressed if the environmental concerns are to be fully incorporated in policy design. This chapter provides a critique of current environmental policy and considers the scope for improving resource allocation.

2. The Sustainability Objective and the Global Context

(a) *The Origins of Sustainability*

While the concept of environmental stewardship has a long history, rooted in agricultural practices before the age of artificial fertilizers,

---

[2] The climate change consultation paper (DETR, 2000) provides no further illumination of the rationale for the 20 per cent number.

[3] Annex A to the White Paper (pp. 271–8) provides a concise case for the wider use of economic instruments.

herbicides, and pesticides, as the 1990 White Paper recognized, the modern idea of 'sustainability' has grown out of concerns about global environmental pollution and degradation. In its simplest form, sustainability is a recognition that without intervention, the global environment will not be able to provide a reasonable standard of living for future generations. In the now famous Brundtland definition, sustainable development is 'development that meets the needs of the present without compromising the ability of future generations to meet their own needs' (World Commission on Environment and Development, 1987).

That definition has a 'warm glow' to it, which helps to explain why so many governments and individuals have felt able to sign up to it and why it has been so effective as a means of rallying public support for environmental causes. It can be made to fit with a wide range of ethical standpoints on rights, equity, and (possibly) efficiency. To it have been married a number of subsidiary notions—the use of 'best science', the precautionary principle where uncertainty arises, and the 'polluter pays' principle in assigning costs.[4] All find ready political and public approval, but the relationship between the general good intentions and the specific implications is less clear. As Solow (1993) aptly put it: 'the less you know about [sustainability] the better it sounds . . . [it is] an essentially vague concept.'

The reasons for this divergence are multiple, but two broad difficulties can be identified. First, the science remains far from settled: the global problems and their consequences are only weakly understood. Scientists cannot tell us with much precision what levels and types of economic activity are 'sustainable', because the global environment and its reactions to pollution are of immense complexity and the interdependency between its constituent parts poorly understood. 'Best science' is therefore a very uncertain basis for policy. Second, the politics and economics are hotly contested: the trade-offs between economic growth and development now, and the environment now and in the future, are hard to define, given that there is no consensus about whether economic growth is consistent with environmental protection and, if so, in what form and at what level, and because the political process is inherently more short-termist than the scale of environmental problems.

---

[4] These factors are explicit in the (substantial) 1994 White Paper, *Sustainable Development: The UK Strategy* (HMSO, 1994).

(b) *The Global Problem: Biodiversity, Global Warming, and Population Growth*

Recognizing the uncertainty of scientific evidence is important in policy design. As we learn more, policy can be better directed. But there is a cost to waiting, and the trade-off depends very much on the sources of the uncertainty. It is, therefore, helpful to set out some of the broad parameters — or what economists might describe as stylized facts — upon which sustainability is to be grounded. First, on biodiversity, the total number of known species of plants, animals, and micro-organisms is estimated to be of the order of 1.4 million, give or take 100,000 (Wilson, 1992, pp. 124–5), but the total is likely to be many times greater. Thus it is hardly surprising that, if most species are not even yet known, the rate of species loss is very uncertain. Wilson has suggested that by 2022 'a 20 per cent extinction in total global diversity, with all habitats incorporated, is a strong possibility if the present rate of environmental destruction continues' (p. 226). It is thought that this rate of species loss is sufficiently fast to rank among the four or five great species extinctions of geological history. The recovery times from previous extinctions are estimated to be in the range 10–100 million years: new species creation, notwithstanding advances in genetic engineering, is not relevant to human historical time spans.

On global warming, a few scientists still dispute the direction of temperature change, but an element of consensus has been built up around the work of the Intergovernmental Panel on Climate Change (IPCC), which suggests that, in the absence of any intervention, global temperature would rise between 1 degree and 3.5 degrees Celsius by the end of the twenty-first century. The UK Climate Impacts Programme (UKCIP, 1998) reports for the UK an 0.5 degrees Celsius warming in the twentieth century, and presents four scenarios of climate change for the next century, with rates of warming between 0.1 and 0.3 degrees Celsius per decade. Its main findings are that warming will be greater in the south-east, with wetter winters in all regions, and that changes in climate variability and extreme events are likely to be more important than simple changes in average climate.[5]

Biodiversity loss and climate change are linked by a more fundamental trend — the growth of the world population. Cohen (1995) summarizes the statistics as follows. Until 1750, global population growth rates never exceeded 0.5 per cent per annum. Since 1950, they have never fallen below 1.6 per cent per annum, with a peak of 2.1 per cent between 1965 and 1970. The result is a current population of around

[5] See Carson (1996) for a non-technical summary of the science.

6 billion, increasing at around 100 million per year. Cohen points to the implausibility of these trends being physically sustained by quoting UN projections to the effect that:

> if human populations continued to grow, in each major region of the world, at the rate presently observed in each, then the population would increase more than 130-fold in 160 years, from about 5.3 billion in 1990 to about 694 billion in 2150. . . . A clear conclusion from the United Nations' conditional prediction is that population growth rates must decline very substantially in some parts of the world within the next century and a half, or people must learn to eat without growing plants that transpire water back to the skies. (Cohen, 1995, p. 15)

Though the arithmetic is relatively straightforward, we know much less about the causes of population growth. As Dasgupta (1995) notes, a general theory of fertility behaviour is not currently available. But even if we had such a theory, changing the causes of population growth would be a very long-term project, and hence the next doubling is almost inevitable, and the depletion of biodiversity and increasing fossil-fuel burning are likely to continue for some time to come. The global environment is bound to get worse, even if it eventually gets better (and that is far from certain).

Among environmentalists, there are two broad responses to these trends. For some policy optimists, population growth is a serious but essentially transitional problem. On this view, the falling death rates will eventually be matched by falling birth rates, allowing the world population to stabilize during the course of the next century. Energy production can gradually be made independent of greenhouse-gas emissions, through technological switching to non-fossil fuel sources. Eventually, as population growth slows, so too will energy demand, while supply-side technical substitutions will ameliorate the emissions. Biodiversity loss will also slow down with the population trend, and better science will enable more of the existing biodiversity to be salvaged in reserved areas. On this view, the task of policy-makers is to design instruments that encourage the supply-side substitutions and preserve as much as possible of natural habitats,[6] so that, in the new stable world, environmental damage can begin to be reversed. It might even be possible to use advances in genetic science to help to re-establish endangered species.

The second response is more pessimistic. On this view, the convenient assumption (for which there is limited evidence) of population

---

[6] For an analysis of species protection policies — and, in particular, the US Endangered Species Act — see Brown and Shogren (1998).

stabilization through declining birth rates is questioned, and the economic growth — and, hence, energy demand — of the developed nations is traced through to greater use of natural resources. With the USA producing one-quarter of the world's carbon-dioxide emissions, and showing no clear signs of a significant switch from fossil fuels, and with China and India's population growth projections for the next century and their associated fossil fuel development plans, the environmental pessimists emphasize a scenario in which greenhouse-gas emissions continue to rise, global warming raises sea levels, birth rates hold up, and, eventually, the Malthusian check applies to humans as it does to animal populations.[7] The policy task is then more fundamental — to reassess the desirability of economic growth and to adjust to lower consumption levels now, to head off disaster in the next century.[8]

(c) *The Environment, Economic Growth, and Sustainability*

The scientific uncertainty is unlikely to be quickly or suddenly resolved. But even if it were — even if we knew for certain the relationship between greenhouse-gas emissions and climate change, the impact of climate change on the environment, and the consequences of biodiversity loss — that in itself would not determine the appropriate national or international environmental policy response to these formidable threats. Science is a necessary but not sufficient input. Environmental policy also requires that trade-offs between competing (economic) ends are defined, and between generations. Sustainable development purports to be the central organizing principle to internalize and resolve both of these.

That it cannot provide an easy answer is hardly surprising. There are both theoretical and practical reasons for this. Let us begin with the theory. What does the concept of sustainable development tell us? There are numerous definitions, but little consensus. Economists have, unsurprisingly, attempted to reconcile the concept of sustainable development with the framework of welfare economics. The conventional approach was to rely on the discount rate to connect generations.[9] Modern approaches regard sustainability as adding something 'new' to

[7] Kennedy (1993) discusses the prospects for a Malthusian check in the next century.

[8] These have been variously stylized as strong vs weak sustainability arguments in the economic literature, and their advocates as 'dark' and 'light' greens in the political literature. There is much confusion in the politics and economics literature on the definitions of these terms.

[9] Beckerman (1994) discusses the merits of this traditional optimizing approach in comparison with sustainability. See also Dasgupta and Heal (1979) for the standard treatment of exhaustible resources, and chapter 2 Atkinson in this volume.

the optimization framework, by introducing additional intergenerational constraints. Where these constraints are binding, they can act as 'trump cards' in policy debate. Thus, while all market failures need to be taken into account, some (environmental) ones are to be given more prominence, with the implication that other policy interventions are subsidiary to environmental concerns, which must be met first.

The most obvious way of capturing the Brundtland Commission's intuition is to require that consumption in future is at least as great as at present. The limiting case is constant consumption, and the conditions required have been developed by Solow (1974) and Hartwick (1977, 1978a). These turn on the assumption made about the substitutability between different types of capital, in particular renewable and non-renewable resources. Put simply, non-renewable resources (both physical and biological) can be used up provided they are converted into renewable (productive) capital efficiently enough.

It is important to bear in mind that the substitutability of the natural environment is an *assumption* in the Solow–Hartwick literature: consumption (and hence utility) can be sustained through either type of resource, and there is no overriding limitation to growth as nonrenewable resources are depleted. In principle, then, the loss of biodiversity and depletion of fossil fuels can be compensated for by other forms of produced capital. Science can enrich the concept further by building in physical feedback mechanisms and the interdependencies within the environment. The economic literature tries to incorporate these features by distinguishing between use and non-use value, existence values, and irreversibility.[10] Not surprisingly, this is a complex and controversial area: in part because the economic distinctions are at best crude approximates of the rich complexity of the environment, and in part because they are only weakly understood. The sharpest controversy relates to biodiversity: can the welfare benefits of biodiversity be substituted for by anything else? Or is it unique? If it is, then the Solow–Hartwick approach defaults to a much harder constraint.

More radical approaches to defining sustainable development rest upon a rejection of the concept of Pareto optimality as the basis of welfare economics, by arguing that welfare judgements should be based upon wider informational sources, and that these are relevant to the design of environmental policy. Additional information on equity, rights, and capabilities then bears upon the policy evaluation. On this view, our obligations to protect and conserve the natural environment

---

[10] The concept of total economic value (TEV) attempts to link the science to the economics.

go beyond our own narrow interests, to incorporate the rights of others, and its value cannot be expressed merely in terms of the ability to generate utility.

Much of the philosophical literature on the environment takes this line, and as a consequence, debates between environmentalists of this persuasion and economists on policy matters are often a dialogue of the deaf. The differences are fundamental, and hence do not easily admit of policy trade-offs. Some philosophers widen the informational base to incorporate the idea that nature itself has intrinsic value and, hence, there can be cases where no trade-off between produced and natural (non-renewable) capital is sanctioned. Elliot (1997), for example, argues that we cannot 'fake' nature, and hence its destruction represents a permanent loss.

From a policy perspective, the problem with the philosophical literature is that there are a very large number of alternative welfare bases, and there is a dearth of well worked-out implications from this literature for operationalizing the sustainability criterion. Policy-makers want to know how resources should be used, and hence how trade-offs are to be made. Much of the philosophical literature motivates our concern for the environment, providing reasons why it should be valued. However, it gives little guidance as to *how* it should be valued, and which actions should be taken.[11]

It is clearly beyond the scope of this chapter to summarize the voluminous literature upon which these approaches are based.[12] However, two main points emerge: first, the further one travels towards the view that sustainable development reflects something 'special' about the environment, the more demanding it becomes as a policy objective; second, that the more demanding definitions typically include the more conventional ones. Thus, it is almost always relevant to know which outcome is the most economically efficient, even if it is to be trumped by additional constraints, and where non-utility information is used, it is useful to know the efficiency cost of pursuing these other concerns. This leads directly into the question of measurement and the role of cost–benefit analysis (CBA), the traditional efficiency tool, which we consider below in section 3. But before turning to this, let us first note how the UK has chosen in practice to interpret sustainable development in environmental policy.

---

[11] This is also true for much of the political literature. See, for a survey, Goodin (1992).

[12] For a succinct recent survey of the economic literature, see Atkinson *et al.* (1998, ch. 1) and chapter 2 below.

(d) *The UK Approach*

Since the 1990 White Paper, successive British governments have
wrestled with how to turn the sustainable development concept into an
operational tool for policy design. It has been a process of broadening
the scope in response to political and practical pressures. The environmental enthusiasm of the 1990 White Paper was tempered by- the
recession of the early 1990s. The Major government was concerned to
show that economic growth and environmentalism were not incompat-
ible, and in its substantive 1994 White Paper, *Sustainable Development:
The UK Strategy* (HMSO, 1994), took a pragmatic line. It claimed that

> sustainable development does not mean having less economic development:
> on the contrary, a healthy economy is better able to generate the resources to
> meet people's needs, and new investment and environmental improvement
> go hand in hand. Nor does it mean that every aspect of the present environ-
> ment should be preserved at all costs. What it requires is that decisions
> throughout society are taken with proper regard to their environmental
> impact. (p. 7, para. 12)

This approach has the merit of flexibility. It takes the environment
seriously but avoids prescriptive rules. The environment is a resource
to be properly incorporated in the economic calculus. In consequence,
the priorities are to ensure that it is properly accounted for in national
income accounts,[13] to introduce environmental assessment into all
major policy processes, and to design instruments (often based upon
price, following the 'polluter pays' principle) and institutions to implement the outcome of assessments.

But even the Major government's definition does not grant complete
freedom of action. Having 'proper regard' to environmental impacts is
hard to reconcile with many politically sensitive activities. Taking
policy decisions is not just about economic optimization, but also about
the political reality of pressure groups, lobbying, party funding, and the
process of making policy within a party system. Hence, it is unsurprising
(as we shall see in the next two sections) that there has been less
progress on economic assessment and economic instruments than many
economists might want, and that politicians have sought to widen the
definition of sustainable development to help justify decisions *ex post*
which at first glance apparently fail to have such regard.

For Labour, the social dimension was given emphasis in the party's
manifesto, and in consequence the definition was widened further:

---

[13] The concept of net national income has been an important theoretical input, and
the Office of National Statistics has grappled with the practical measures, not wholly
successfully (see Atkinson *et al.*, 1998, ch. 3).

sustainable development is about ensuring a better quality of life for everyone, now and for generations to come. . . . The government's vision of the goal is based on four broad objectives:
- social progress which recognizes the needs of everyone;
- effective protection of the environment;
- prudent use of natural resources; and
- maintenance of high and stable levels of economic growth and employment. (DTI, 1998, para. 9.1)

Explicitly adding social factors on top of economic growth adds yet more flexibility, and in the absence of clarity about the weights on the components, allows many more policies to pass the test. With enough ingenuity, almost anything could be defined as 'sustainable'.

To give an example, with the 'right' weights, support for the coal industry and limits on gas-fired electricity generation are claimed to be consistent with sustainable development. Notwithstanding the environmental benefits of gas compared with coal, in this case, the requirements of security and diversity of supply took precedence. As the consultation paper on the UK Climate Change Programme (DETR, 1998c) stated:

We inherited a situation which had exaggerated the advantages of gas-fired plant, and which took little concern of the need for security and diversity of supply. As a consequence, changes in the fuel mix for electricity made a disproportionate contribution to meeting the 2000 target [for carbon-dioxide reductions], relieving pressure from other sectors such as transport to reduce emissions. (para. 24)[14]

Even if the premise were correct (which it is not—see Helm, 1998a), there has been no overall *economic* (as opposed to physical) assessment of the contributions from different sectors, as the climate change consultation paper shows.[15] The inescapable general conclusion is that the objectives of energy policy overrode those of environment policy, and that, in particular, within energy policy the interest of coal miners has been given more weight than the environment (or even competition).[16] To describe the outcome as consistent with sustainable devel-

[14] See also DTI (1998, paras 2.47–2.53), where relaxations on sulphur controls and plans for further flue-gas desulphurization units (FGDs) are presented as part of the government's strategy to achieve 'sustainable energy supplies'.

[15] The paper is designed 'to stimulate a national debate on how we might meet our targets', providing a number of illustrations of possible quantity reductions, but presents virtually no information on costs, except for combined heat and power and energy efficiency. See also DETR (2000).

[16] It has been suggested that the energy White Paper merely provided for a longer transition towards the closure of the coal industry, and therefore a slower path of declining emissions. The paper does not, however, indicate that coal cannot hold on to its output. Indeed, that is precisely why it is argued to provide an option for longer-term security and diversity of supply.

opment might meet political imperatives, but is hard to reconcile with *any* of the approaches in the theoretical literature discussed above.

A further White Paper, *A Better Quality of Life*, was published in 1999, identifying the priority areas for action, as well as a set of indicators and targets (DETR, 1999*a*). The lists are long and varied, and any explicit attempt to aggregate the components into an index or measure of sustainable development is explicitly rejected. Sustainable development now incorporates anything from 'qualifications at age 19', 'the level of crime', and 'homes judged unfit to live in', through to 'populations of wild birds' and 'emissions of greenhouse gases'. The 1999 White Paper thus completed the transition of sustainable development from a primarily environmental concept capable of assessment, to a wish-list of things that government would like to achieve.

These domestic policies have been set within the context of internationally agreed objectives and targets which successive governments have signed up to. Notable among these has been the Rio 'Earth Summit' (1992) and Kyoto (1997). Rio saw the UK sign up to conventions on biodiversity and climate change, as well as to Agenda 21 on sustainable development.[17] Kyoto saw the adoption of targets for greenhouse-gas emissions for developed countries.

The form and content of such agreements are open to considerable question as means towards achieving sustainability at the global level. They are—as Barrett notes in chapter 6—the outcome of political negotiations largely in the absence of international institutions to ensure implementation and compliance (see also Barrett, 1991). As with the domestic policies discussed above, the tangency between the international targets and sustainable development is obscure: given the projections for biodiversity loss, climate change, and, above all, population growth, it is hard to see how Rio and Kyoto can be considered tough enough to be consistent with the Brundtland definition which motivated the agreements.

To summarize the argument so far, the environmental policy role of the concept of sustainable development has grown up as a reaction to major trends in the global environment, notably climate change, biodiversity loss, and, above all, population growth. At the physical level, the population growth rate cannot be sustained, in the sense that there are no good reasons for believing that there will be enough resources to feed all the mouths created, and that possibly before that point of physical saturation is reached, climate change and species loss may have (very) serious consequences for economic welfare. There is

---

[17] On the Rio biodiversity convention, see Swanson (1997) and Macdonald, chapter 7 below.

considerable dispute about the science, and about the appropriate policy response. Sustainable development *could* act as a guide to policy only insofar as it can be defined, measured, and then related to actual policy decisions. Although much progress has been towards an economic operational definition, the current literature remains a long way from providing an overarching and readily usable tool for policy design. These very real theoretical and empirical difficulties have not, however, stopped successive UK governments from broadening the definition to the point that it is in danger of becoming largely meaningless as a policy objective, or from adopting broad policy targets and commitments on climate change and biodiversity.

This rather unsatisfactory state of affairs is neither inevitable nor irreversible. Governments, having adopted the concept, now face the challenge of injecting it with more content—and, in particular, more empirical information. Fortunately, cost–benefit analysis (CBA) provides a set of tools which is not only a necessary input into sustainable development but also helpful in its own right.

3. CBA, Optimal Pollution, and the Efficiency Approach

Before environmental policy became global and the sustainability criterion was developed, the traditional economic answer to the objective of environmental policy was to maximize social welfare by correcting for the market failures which environmental problems represent. Pigou (1920) defined the optimal level of pollution consistent with maximizing social welfare, where the marginal costs of abatement equal the marginal benefits. On this view, environmental policy is about the pragmatic business of measuring marginal costs and benefits, and then using appropriate instruments—taxes, property rights, and regulation—to internalize the externalities. Each case is to be judged on its peculiar merits, and the application of policy depends upon the context. It is piecemeal, rather than guided by general rules.[18]

Optimal pollution is calculated by the application of CBA, which in essence has two fundamental components: the monetization of costs and benefits to create a common calculus to approximate utility; and reliance on consumer demand information to establish valuations. Neither of these has been widely accepted in environmental policy. Many non-economists adhere to the view that environmental assets

[18] The standard exposition in the Pigouvian tradition is Baumol and Oates (1988). Interestingly, Baumol and Oates do not mention sustainability at all in their textbook. See also Helm and Pearce (1990).

cannot be monetized: that they are strictly priceless. Habitats and species, it is argued, cannot be placed in a common calculus with factories, equipment, and offices. As noted above, this view is held by those who regard utility as too narrow a basis for measuring welfare,[19] and those who go beyond the informational argument to claim some intrinsic value to nature. Many scientists (and others) argue that to rely on consumer preferences is to devalue (superior) scientific knowledge. An additional objection is that, since future generations are not yet born, we cannot in any event know what their preferences will be.

While there are important ethical issues raised by these various critics, none undermines the use of CBA as an *input* into the setting of environmental targets. Those who reject monetization on ethical grounds often misconstrue the purpose of CBA. It (ethically) is not concerned with establishing the 'right' level of pollution, but only the efficient or 'optimal' level. The fact that the optimal level of pollution happens to be defined as one point does not imply that that is the 'right' level of pollution. It remains possible to choose inefficient outcomes. Whereas a change which is consistent with sustainable development is claimed to be desirable, one which passes the CBA test is merely more efficient than one that does not.

But more striking, perhaps, is the fact that, in making a choice, policy-makers are ranking alternatives, and that such rankings can be interpreted in cost–benefit terms. For example, when it was decided as part of an international negotiation to end the dumping of sewage at sea, an implication could be that the costs of the alternative do not exceed the environmental gain and, hence, it is worth expending resources on alternative methods of disposal.[20] To take another example, when it was decided not to build a tunnel under Twyford Down as part of the M3 extension, but instead to carve it in half to build a motorway, an implication could be that the Down is not worth the cost of the tunnel. The fact remains that those who oppose monetization necessarily make choices over the use of (scarce) environmental and other resources and, at least *ex post*, these can be monetized. The point holds too for the plethora of quasi-CBA techniques used in environmental appraisal, which frequently rely on using expert judgements, but fall short of monetization.

There are other more instrumental objections to CBA, many of which are documented by David Pearce in chapter 3. Notable among

[19] See Williams (1992) for a moral philosophy critique.

[20] International agreements pose special problems for such *ex-post* exercises, since agreements in a particular area may be necessary to gain advances in other areas. Nevertheless, even if this were the case in this example, it is still worth evaluating the efficiency consequences of the decision.

these at the policy level are two broad ones which have surfaced in British policy debates: that CBA often produces very uncertain answers, which are sensitive to small changes in assumptions (in particular, that consumers' valuations are extremely sensitive to new information), and that CBA studies are costly.

Each of these can be met. The fact that a valuation is uncertain is itself informative to policy-makers, and helps to clarify the specific characteristics of the problem. It is particularly helpful to know whether the major uncertainties lie on the cost or the benefits side, since this may influence the choice of instruments used (as Stephen Smith points out in his chapter in this volume; see also section 4 below). The problem of new information has led to innovations in the design of questionnaires, interviews and repeated sampling.[21] The costs of CBA studies relative to the project size will influence the scope and extent of the exercises, but do not undermine the rationale.

There remain many technical questions about the best way to conduct CBA (see again Pearce in this volume, and Johansson, 1993). These can be classified into three broad domains: those related to the valuation of non-market goods; those related to correcting for distorted prices, in the presence of other market failures; and discounting. Most of the CBA literature has focused on the first of these, and the techniques involved—mainly hedonic pricing, contingent valuation, and travel cost—represent a variety of different ways of trying to approximate people's valuations. Less attention has been paid to the presence of other market failures and, in particular, the counterfactual—what would have happened in the absence of other distortions in the particular market under consideration. Thus, for example, in considering a possible carbon tax as an instrument to abate air pollution, the monopoly elements in the electricity generation market need to be taken into account.[22] Establishing the 'correct' price of electricity before estimating the tax is not straightforward. Water regulation provides a further example: with the water price level set artificially low relative to the value of the assets employed, and, for many, price being unrelated to quantity consumed, consumer information on the desirability of higher water and effluent standards is likely to be distorted.[23]

Finally, the discount rate remains contentious and links the CBA debates with the concept of sustainability discussed in the previous section. Some—notably philosophers—object to discounting *per se* (e.g.

[21] See, for example, Arrow *et al.* (1992).

[22] The Marshall Report (1998) largely neglects this central issue.

[23] See Cowan's chapter in this volume for a general analysis of the regulatory issues.

Parfit, 1984; Broome, 1992). Others debate the rate, questioning in particular the extent to which market costs of capital should be used and endeavour to open a gap between individuals' and society's time preferences.

These technical debates will rumble on, helping to refine the estimates which provide an input into environmental policy formulation. Notwithstanding the difficulties, CBA helps to identify the efficient level of pollution: it is, in Pearce's words, the only show in town. To summarize: it is not a decision-making tool, but rather makes explicit the monetization, which is, in any event, implicit in virtually all environmental policy decisions. It builds upon consumer sovereignty as the fundamental component of valuation, and the practical problems that CBA encounters do not invalidate the technique.

Why, then, somewhat contrary to Pearce's view, has the application of CBA to the setting of environmental targets been largely the exception rather than the rule? Very few key environmental targets — in air, water, or land — have been subject to formal CBA scrutiny. To return to earlier examples, although a great deal of effort has gone into gathering information on carbon-dioxide emissions, no CBA has been conducted to support the claims that the 20 per cent carbon-dioxide target, and the interventions in the electricity industry to support coal are 'sustainable'.

In the cases where CBA has been used, the spur has been partially provided by the general requirement for the Environment Agency and the European Commission to take account of costs and benefits, and partially by political expediency. In the latter regard, a form of *à la carte* CBA is in danger of emerging, with the technique being used to justify targets already set, or which can easily be met, or to undermine the case for expenditure on public projects that might otherwise pass normal Treasury investment tests. It has also been used to assist in supporting revenue-raising environmental taxes, such as the landfill and the aggregates levies. CBA has not, however, frequently been used as an *ex-ante* tool on policy analysis to assist policy formulation.

This failure is as much political as economic. CBA is radical in the sense that it forces ministers to be explicit about the economic rationale for policies and, in making information transparent and public, can undermine the case for supporting sectional and lobbying interests. In the above energy example, CBA would probably not support the outcomes ministers have chosen: the 20 per cent target is essentially arbitrary; coal generation is environmentally much worse than gas; the flue-gas desulphurization (FGD) technology is not the most efficient method for reducing sulphur-dioxide emissions, and, indeed, makes other emissions worse.

To avoid the misuse of CBA, the appropriate response is to make a general rule, requiring its use for all major policies and projects, to become part of the standard menu, rather than remain *à la carte*. Some progress has been made in this area, through government guidelines for the conduct of environmental appraisal.[24] However, these have generally fallen short of the full endorsement of CBA, frequently relying on more subjective and qualitative approaches, based upon scoring and weighting (see below). There is considerable scope for further initiatives in this area, notably building on the requirement on the Environment Agency to take account of costs and benefits. Some economies of scale might be reaped by setting up a unit specializing in such studies to avoid the duplication of effort that has sometimes characterized existing approaches.

4. Instruments

Once the optimal level of pollution has been defined (or at least approximated), and targets set, environmental policy is then concerned with selecting appropriate instruments. The traditional and still over-whelmingly dominant approach is command-and-control regulation. Pollution 'experts' from the various institutions set maximum discharges through licensing processes, based on the application of top-down or bottom-up targets. These limits typically have had a strong technological content, being based on local environmental quality and on the best available technology (BAT). These should not entail excess cost (NEEC) but only where a transitional period is required to reach the BAT (see chapter 4 by Pearce in this volume). The licensing regime has been predominantly source-based and the current form derives from the Environment Act 1990, and in particular Integrated Pollution Control.

The problems with the traditional regulatory approach are numerous and well documented (Helm, 1993*a*, 1994). The regulators have their own interests, within an institutional framework, and will tend to adopt their own definitions of the public and environmental priorities. Technical capture and the advocacy of particular preferred solutions may give insufficient scope for new concepts. Regulators cannot know what best available technology is, and in any event, 'availability' itself depends on regulators' behaviour. For example, FGDs are, as noted above, economically inferior, but they were an 'available' technology.

[24] See DoE (1991*a*), and, for a review of subsequent guidance, DETR (1998*d*, Annex 1).

Forcing their application to coal-fired power stations altered the
incentives to invest in combined-cycle gas turbines (CCGTs). Risk-
aversion may lead to over-burdensome regulatory controls, and it is
unlikely that least-cost solutions will be forthcoming. These difficulties
are compounded by the problems of monitoring and enforcement. As
Anthony Heyes, in chapter 5, argues, the design of optimal enforcement
mechanisms is very different from the practice. Where there is regular
interchange of personnel, regulatory capture may exacerbate such
problems.

Economic instruments avoid many of these problems. The crucial
difference is informational: economic instruments fix a price (taxes) or
a quantity (permits) and then leave the market to sort out the response.
The presence of uncertainty is essential to their rationale: if information
was perfect, then command-and-control would, in principle, be at least
as good. Economic instruments are themselves *information revelation
mechanisms*: by setting the price or quantity, we can then observe the
market effect, and adjust the instrument accordingly. The initial level
of a tax need only be approximate, and, indeed, may be set fairly low
to overcome the inevitable political difficulties. CBA can help to give an
initial idea of the level and extent of uncertainty by testing the
robustness of estimates to small changes in assumption. The choice
between taxes and permits turns on whether it is the costs of abatement
(taxes) over which we require greater control or the pollution level
(permits).[25]

A second – related – advantage of economic instruments is the avoidance of the supply-side bias of command and control. Economic
instruments set prices or quantities which encourage richer responses
on both demand and supply sides, and allow the market to sort out the
relative contributions of each, both in the short and the longer run. A
carbon tax would, for example, encourage consumers to save on
electricity and gas, and *also* encourage producers to switch to non-fossil
fuels for generation. Research and development programmes would
also respond.

Yet, despite an increasing recognition of the failures of traditional
environmental regulation, and many official statements and reports on
economic instruments, there have been few examples of the implementation of explicit mechanisms. The main ones have been the landfill tax
and recycling credits. Water abstraction and pollution charges (DETR,
1997*a*), aggregates, and pesticides have all been proposed, but not yet
implemented (Environmental Audit Committee, 1999).

---

[25] The classic treatment of prices and quantities is Weitzman (1974).

More progress has been made on *implicit* economic instruments. Most notable are taxes on petrol and the unleaded differential. Such taxes are, however, developed primarily for other reasons, notably raising revenue. As a consequence, their design does not map the shape of externality taxes, with the result that substitution effects are imperfect. The carbon-dioxide example illustrates this point well. Petrol is heavily taxed. Coal has been implicitly subsidized for the period 1990–8 by artificial contracts with the electricity industry to hold price and output up, paid for by electricity customers. As noted above, this support is being implicitly extended, and investment in gas-fired power stations has been, at least temporarily, halted. Nuclear power has been subsidized, as have renewables. In this confused context, the Marshall Report (1998) proposed an energy tax, along with a pilot tradable permits system, within the context of its restricted terms of reference— limited to the business sector, excluding domestic customers from any tax which might remotely resemble VAT on domestic fuel.[26] The subsequent tax—the misnamed Climate Change Levy—is based upon energy, not carbon. The confusions of objectives for the levy (protecting coal, supporting non-fossil fuels, maintaining competitiveness of large industrial firms, and avoiding tax increases on households) and the multiple existing interventions makes the design of environmental economic instruments a complex matter.

Why has it proved so difficult to introduce economic instruments? The reasons are partly related to the income effects and partly institutional. Polluting activities are frequently ones for which demand, at least in the short term, is price inelastic. Hence, to introduce an instrument that will have a significant impact on the level of pollution, the tax rate needs to be relatively high. For example, to persuade motorists to switch to public transport appears to require very sharp rises in petrol prices. Such high taxes on inelastically demanded goods will have substantial income effects, and it is typically impossible to prevent the burden falling on domestic customers. The political consequences are immediate, while the impact on pollution is longer term.[27]

Where many of the polluting activities also arise in the context of basic social primary goods, such as heating, lighting, water, and transport, there is inevitably a politically difficult trade-off between social and environmental policy. Thus, VAT on domestic electricity and gas proved difficult to impose, and, as noted above, subsequent

[26] The new energy tax in Germany, following the 1998 Federal elections, has some similar features.

[27] It is notable that the Conservative party has recently adopted a more pro-car policy stance in response to increases in petrol taxes and proposals for parking charges.

attempts to design an energy tax have been set within the context of explicitly excluding domestic customers.

In principle, the conflict between social and environmental policy can be solved by using two instruments—the environmental and the social—with economic instruments dealing with the former, and adjustments in social security addressing the distributional consequences. However, in practice, the macroeconomic constraint of the public-sector borrowing requirement has typically been binding—for both Conservative and Labour governments. Hence, the social security adjustment has not (politically) been an option, and the policy conflict has to be addressed directly when setting the environmental policy.[28] Widening the definition of sustainable development explicitly to include social considerations enables politicians to present such compromises as consistent with environmental policy.

Environmental taxes are highly visible to the electorate, so it is hardly surprising that the government has been reluctant to opt for large-scale experiments when there are less visible alternatives. The use of regulation has the political merit that the economic incidence is much more opaque. Regulations act to drive up costs of the polluting activity, with the result that prices rise (in the absence of substitution on the supply side). These price rises represent implicit taxes, but are rarely linked back to environmental policy. If the price of paint, for example, goes up because the licensing policy on paint producers is toughened, few consumers are likely to link this to government action.

A politically attractive way of using implicit taxation for pollution abatement is through the regulation of privatized utilities, whose activities are closely associated with the main forms of pollution (energy and transport with air pollution; water with river and marine pollution). By placing additional environmental obligations on utilities, the costs can be passed through to customers in the form of disguised taxation. In effect, it is a form of regulated tax hypothecation. The 2000 utilities legislation provides for explicit guidance on social and environmental matters to be given to regulators, and it has included incorporation of the concept of sustainable development, as well as renewables policy and energy efficiency.

This opportunity is particularly politically attractive where the underlying costs of the basic utility services are falling owing to productivity improvements. Thus, where a utility can finance its functions with *real price reductions* matched by increases in efficiency, but consumers will accept *constant real prices*, a 'political' tax wedge emerges between the costs (RPI – X) and constant real prices (RPI – 0), as set out in Figure 1.

---

[28] An exception was the partial social security offset of VAT on domestic fuel.

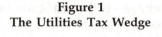

Figure 1
The Utilities Tax Wedge

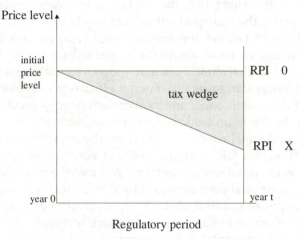

Regulatory period

Given that the energy and water companies are closely associated as intermediaries in polluting activities, the *formal* incidence of pollution abatement expenditures on these companies can also be presented as being consistent with the 'polluter pays' principle. (The economic incidence depends upon the regulatory regime, but in practice is mainly on consumers.)

The most graphic illustration of the implicit tax wedge is in the 1999 water periodic review, where the Environment Agency encouraged a programme of environmental capital expenditure consistent with RPI – 0, as against the economic regulator's demand for substantial initial price cuts (Ofwat, 1997; Environment Agency 1998b). The DETR wanted both price cuts and extra environmental expenditure (DETR, 1998b). Though the two services provided by water companies—the standard utility provision and the environmental programme—could be separately addressed through utility charges and pollution pricing respectively, the economic instruments for pollution charging have not been implemented, despite numerous studies, as Simon Cowan shows in chapter 9. Thus, the approach has been to specify the required capital expenditure (command and control) and then consider what customers can afford as part of the monopoly pricing of water services.

Although politically expedient, such implicit taxation is likely to be economically inefficient in comparison with explicit economic instruments: by setting pollution prices, the market is left to sort out the most efficient solutions, whether on the supply or demand side.[29] A further

[29] Water companies have complex incentives on capital expenditure (see Helm and Rajah, 1994).

example — mentioned above — is the reduction in carbon-dioxide emissions to meet the 20 per cent target. A tax on carbon would elicit two responses: in the short run, the capital stock (cars, power stations, industrial plant, the transport infrastructure) is given and, hence, the main effects will fall on demand, through reduced use and energy efficiency measures. However, in the longer term, a supply response is to be expected from technical change. Indeed, as the global population grows and living standards rise, energy efficiency is unlikely to prove sufficient to cap emissions, and non-carbon energy production techniques will be the main vehicle to emissions control.

Two related conclusions emerge from the experience of economic instruments in the UK: that the political constraints are at least as important as the economic advantages; and that the incidence effects of many of the proposed pollution taxes tend to fall on domestic customers and, hence, create political obstacles to their application. These constraints are often ignored in the economics literature, but cannot be avoided in environmental policy design.

They give rise to two parallel responses: to refine the case for economic instruments, and to tailor such instruments to meet the multiple objectives, notably revenue raising and social equity. Whereas the economics literature focuses heavily on the substitution effects, the policy design needs to pay at least as much attention to the income effects of the instruments.

Although hypothecation of revenues would not necessarily be first best, there is considerable scope to utilize such approaches *within* sectors. Thus road charges may be used to subsidize rail transport. This sort of redistribution is to be sharply distinguished from recycling of revenue to polluters — i.e. within-industry hypothecation. Giving money back to polluters undermines some of the output adjustments the instrument is designed to bring about. It is not surprising that large energy companies favour permits over taxes to address carbon-dioxide emissions, where the grandfathering of initial permits limits such income effects, as compared with energy taxes. The income effects will be more easily absorbed if their introduction is gradual, and hence affected parties have time to adjust. This is a further reason for initial low levels of taxes — over and above the informational revelation rationale discussed above.

Most of these measures to accommodate political constraints weaken the efficiency of the economic instruments. However, the counterfactual is frequently not some ideal economic instrument, but command and control regulation, or even no intervention. An imperfect economic instrument may be second best, but still be much superior to current practice. And, once introduced, it can often be gradually improved, while at the same time providing practical examples encouraging more widespread uses of such instruments.

5. Institutions

The design and implementation of any policy is conditioned by the institutional context. This institutional context has helped to shape British environmental policy and hence is in part responsible for the two major weaknesses identified above in sections 3 and 4 — in the setting of targets and standards with too little regard to costs and benefits, and the strong bias towards command-and-control regulation over economic instruments. Neither CBA nor economic instruments has yet prospered in the British institutional setting.

There are two broad reasons why the design of British environmental institutions has led to this state of affairs. The first is historical, concerned with the administrative style of regulation developed since the creation of the Alkali Inspectorate in the late nineteenth century. The British approach to pollution control can be characterized as piecemeal, pragmatic, technically driven, and conducted by experts largely free from the reach of the courts. Put simply, in the UK, regulation is conducted by inspectors, directors general, and chief executives charged with pursuing general and ill-defined broad objectives. These individuals have traditionally sought out what they deem to be 'best available technologies' and, more recently, 'sustainable' solutions. There has been a high degree of interdependency between the polluter and pollutee, with the latter frequently recruiting its staff from the former. It is a classic example of what has been described in another context as 'good chaps regulation': provide a flexible and broad public-interest objective, and rely on selecting individuals with 'good' judgement. The corollary is that the quality and shape of regulation depends heavily on the personalities involved.[30]

The second reason for the reluctance to use CBA and economic instruments is more proximate, and lies in the design of the Environment Agency — in particular, the failure to merge the separate water, air, and land domains along functional lines, and the failure to focus on policy, regulation, and enforcement, rather than production activities.

When the then Conservative government endorsed the concept of integrated pollution control (IPC) in the 1990 White Paper (DoE, 1990a),

[30] These aspects of British environmental regulation are explored in Helm (1993a) and the parallel with utility regulation in Helm (1994). For a summary of the UK approach to pollution control, see Gouldson and Murphy (1998).

it considered the case for creating a new body which would be responsible for considering all the pollution media—land, water, and air. In July 1991 the government announced the intention to establish an Environment Agency, and a Green Paper was published in November 1991. The process of integration turned out to be a fraught one. There was an intense debate as between two main models for the Environment Agency: the functional model of Her Majesty's Inspectorate of Pollution (HMIP) (the successor to the Alkali Inspectorate), which was a small, tightly focused regulatory and enforcement body; or on the sectoral model of the National Rivers Authority (NRA), a large, federal, and broadly based producer, regulator, and enforcer.[31] Whereas HMIP had some 400 staff, the NRA had over 6,000, many of them engaged in flood defence and river basin management.[32] After a protracted debate, the solution adopted was to corral HMIP, the NRA, and the Waste Regulation Authorities together to create a major new institution, now with around 9,000 employees and a budget of over £500m, and to leave it to the Environment Agency to carry out the integration process *ex post*. In practice, the NRA dominated, with its Chief Executive succeeding to the leading position in the Environment Agency, and the Environment Agency has become predominantly an enlarged NRA.[33]

Since the Environment Agency is the body responsible for environmental regulation, the ways in which its structure and incentives have influenced its conduct are of great importance. One main weakness revealed has been a lack of managerial focus—given the conflicting pressures of a large operational work-force, the day-to-day business of pollution licensing, river basin management, the regulatory functions, monitoring pollution, enforcement and prosecution, and engaging in policy debates. The Environment Agency is responsible for such diverse activities as managing locks on rivers, prosecuting polluters, dealing with environmental emergencies, setting industrial emissions constraints, and advising the Secretary of State on the appropriate capital expenditure by water companies (Environment Agency, 1996). In economic terms, it is the loosely configured agent of many different principals whose objectives conflict, and, in consequence, it has had considerable freedom to develop its own agenda and managerial interests, under the general duty to promote sustainable development.

[31] See DoE (1991*b*, 1994*a*) and also Helm (1992). The Green Paper actually had four models, but the functional versus federal distinction was the most important.

[32] In 1996/7, the successor Environment Agency had around 3,500 staff classified as working on environmental protection, and over 5,000 on water management (3,400 of whom on flood defence, representing 45 per cent of expenditure).

[33] Eleven of the top 15 posts in the new Environment Agency went to officials from the NRA (*ENDS Report*, August 1995).

It is not, therefore, surprising that there have been a number of high-profile criticisms of its conduct, ranging from its performance over sulphur regulation through to the way it crisis-managed the floods in spring 1998. The Select Committee on Environment, Transport, and the Regions reported in June 1998 criticism of staffing and resources, inspection, and prosecution.[34]

The Environment Agency has been somewhat resistant to the use of CBA and has played little direct part in developing economic instruments. Although the Environment Act 1995, which set up the Environment Agency, required that it should take account of the costs and benefits of its activities,[35] in practice, the Environment Agency has not given such assessments a central role, and its senior staff have tended to reflect scientific and engineering interests, rather than economics. This reluctance has been reflected in the fact that, among the 10,500 employees, currently only about five are professional economists.

A recent example of this reluctance has been the Environment Agency's contribution to the 1999 periodic review of the water industry. Under pressure to justify water capital expenditure, it has recently developed its own multi-attribute technique (MAT) (see Environment Agency, 1998a,b). This technique relies upon the application of a scoring or rating system to predicted impacts, which are then weighted on the basis of the importance of one impact category over another, and the weighted scores then aggregated into an overall measure of impact. It is a somewhat belated attempt to assess the benefits of environmental expenditures which could be financed through the tax wedge discussed above, as a response to the challenge from Ofwat (Ofwat, 1997). Although there has been some attempt to use values from other CBA studies,[36] in practice, MAT continues to rely heavily on weights and scores provided by its own experts, rather than data from consumers. Making these expert judgement explicit has some obvious advantages, but it remains to be seen how far in practice it is used to justify the Environment Agency's preferred options, and how far it genuinely challenges them. For further insight into the Environment Agency's thinking on this, see *Guidance Note No. 29* (Fisher *et al.*, 1999).

[34] See DETR Select Committee 6th Report, 17 June 1998. For a critique of its regulatory practice, see ENDS (1998a).

[35] Clause 39(1,b) requires that the Environment Agency 'shall, unless and to the extent that it is unreasonable for it to do so in view of the nature and purpose or in the circumstances of the particular case, take into account the likely costs and benefits of the exercise or non-exercise of the power or its exercise in the manner in question'. This is then hedged by 39(2) which excludes its obligations and requirements placed upon it otherwise than in this section.

[36] Pearce, in chapter 3, notes that this has not always been appropriately conducted, particularly in regard to the Darent study transfers to the Kennet exercise.

The Environment Agency's reluctance to embrace CBA and economic instruments is not an accident: it reflects the incentives of the
Environment Agency's management and employees. Scientists and
engineers are unlikely to welcome the idea that pollution licences
should be subject to detailed scrutiny of costs and benefits, and that
economic valuations might help to determine the optimum level of
pollution. Many current activities and decisions might be consequen-
tially questioned. More threatening still are economic instruments,
since their application removes much of the role of the experts in fixing
and revising regulation, and would make the activities of some employees redundant.

Thus, at the heart of environmental policy is a principal–agent
problem: the government's agent, the Environment Agency, has its
own internal incentives, and the extent of the differences of objectives
between government and the Environment Agency has been greatly
exacerbated by the way in which the Environment Agency's institutional architecture built upon that of the NRA rather than HMIP. The
implication is that reform of the Environment Agency's structure may
be a necessary condition for the more widespread adoption and
development of CBA and economic instruments. The detailed nature of
these reforms is beyond the scope of this chapter, but suffice it to note
that a separation between operational production activities (such as
flood defence) from regulatory and enforcement functions would
greatly alter the size and managerial focus of the organization, and in
separating out around 5,000 of the employees, the producer-orientated
incentives would be weakened.

However, if the structure of the agency is imperfect, then so too is
that of its sponsoring government department. The Department of the
Environment has been, since its inception in 1970, an amalgam of
functions. It was created from the Ministries of Housing and Local
Government, to which transport was added, and then subtracted in
1976.[37] After the general election in 1997, this large amorphous department became even bigger, with transport returning, and the regions
added. Its Secretary of State, therefore, has to weigh up matters related
to three sectors of the economy — housing and construction, transport,
and water — oversee a host of quangos, as well as considering practical
environmental issues. By contrast, energy, which is at least as environmentally sensitive as transport, resides at the Department of Trade and
Industry, while agriculture has its own ministry. With, on the one hand,
so many different sectors and interests to address, but, on the other,
without energy or agriculture, the DETR is neither fully integrated to
internalize environmental decisions, nor narrowly focused enough for

---

[37] See Hennessy (1989) for the historical detail.

the environment to have overriding dominance. The confusion between vertical, industry-driven and horizontal, policy-driven structures at the DETR mirrors the problems with the design of the
Environment Agency discussed above. Vertical industry ministries are
more prone to capture by the producer interest, whereas horizontal
ministries are able to focus on policy. In the former case, the Ministry
of Agriculture, Fisheries, and Food's capture by farmers' interests is
perhaps the clearest example.[38] This might not matter too much if
sustainable development could provide an overarching — and hence
integrating — focus. But, as argued in section 2 above, it does not as yet
do so.

A functionally designed Department of the Environment might be
more likely to provide the appropriate focus for environmental policy
within government in a consistent fashion across sectors than would the
existing institutional architecture. Thus, from the perspective of environmental policy, the creation of the DETR can be argued to be a step in
the wrong direction: rather than adding transport and the regions to
the existing functions, it may have been better to subtract many housing
and local government activities, and to focus the department around
the core environmental policy activities.

6. Conclusions

The promise of the 1990 White Paper has proved harder to deliver than
its authors can have expected. It promised a coherent environmental
policy, based upon a recognition of the gravity of global environmental
threats, and built upon a thoroughgoing use of economic techniques
and markets, and new institutions. Almost a decade later, it would be
hard to argue, notwithstanding Rio and Kyoto, that the global environment is in better shape: that the Brundtland ambition has been met.
Biodiversity loss is probably accelerating, and emissions of greenhouse
gases continue to rise at the global level.

The central organizing principle of environmental policy in the UK
is the pursuit of sustainable development, at a global as well as national
level. That concept has had two political advantages. First, it is capable
of engendering wide support without, second, greatly exposing government to public scrutiny for failing to implement policies consistent
with it. Almost any policy — including even supporting the coal industry — can be claimed to be consistent with sustainability, since the

[38] These problems of institutional design are not confined to environmental policy.
Recent debates about merging economic regulatory bodies into sectoral bodies, or
even one large body, raise many similar issues.

definition has been stretched by government to be sufficiently wide to be practically almost meaningless. And without an organizing concept and a clear objective, environmental policy in practice collapses into a series of *ad hoc* measures, driven as much by the relative political weight of other considerations, as by environmental concerns.

This policy vacuum could be filled in one of two ways: either the government could give sustainability content by explicitly addressing the trade-offs between the environment, social issues, and economic growth and development; or the concept could be abandoned in favour of a more conventional economic optimality framework, concentrating on correcting for environmental externalities and public bads.

Developments in measurement techniques hold out the promise of empirical tests of policy options, and green national income accounts may help to demonstrate whether the environment is getting better or worse over time. As an efficiency concept, sustainability can be given a fairly precise set of definitions, and it can help to encourage a better understanding of the relationship between the science and the economics. But, as yet, the temptation of politicians to stretch its definition to bask in the concept's 'warm glow' has proved too seductive to permit hard tests to be applied to environmental policy design. The 1999 White Paper added lots of targets and indicators, but did not facilitate rigorous analysis. It is still not possible to say whether the government's transport, energy, water, and housing policies meet the criterion or not.

But whichever course is adopted, there is a strong case for using CBA to increase understanding of the efficiency characteristics of policy, and to harness the market through economic instruments to minimize the resource costs of improving environmental quality. Policy should not, of course, be restricted to efficiency considerations, and other wider welfare considerations clearly have a place. But where policy departs from economic optimality, it is at least worth knowing the price.

The fact that government and policy-makers have so far failed to harness the full potential of these economic tools is partly due to technical problems in their development and application. But these technical difficulties can easily be overstated: the more challenging task is to incorporate political constraints into environmental policy design. Having proper regard to the income effects of economic instruments, adopting gradualist approaches, and focusing on those areas where public concern is greatest, is more likely to be conducive to enlarging the role of such instruments. But to make much progress will require an element of institutional reform. It is a necessary condition towards the development of a more efficient design and implementation of environmental policy and it is here that we should start.

2

Sustainable Development and Policy

GILES ATKINSON*

1. Introduction

The call for countries to pursue policies aimed at achieving 'sustainable development' was established both in the Brundtland Report and at the Earth Summit in 1992. Sustainable development has since been adopted as an over-arching goal of economic and social development by international agencies, individual nations, local governments, and even corporations, and, further, has generated a huge literature. While there are legitimate questions about what these bodies have signed up to, the focus on sustainability broadly embodies the goal that development policy deliver improvements in the prospects of people both now and into the future. However, what really matters, once terms have been defined, is what has to be done to secure this. One decade after the early formulation of the problem, there have been great advances in the theoretical aspects of sustainable development. Much of the ongoing debate has focused on the need to manage sustainably a portfolio of diverse assets and, within this portfolio, on which assets merit 'special attention' with regard to the conservation of critical stocks. The continuing weak versus strong sustainable development controversy embodies many of these issues. This has also led to significant and parallel advances being made on the ways in which sustainable development might be indicated. Indeed, this indicator work often has been at the forefront of much of the broader debate. Alerting decision-makers to the underlying 'true' trends in the economy and to the way in which their policies may affect those trends is a prerequisite to informing decision-making that is not systematically biased towards environmental degradation and over-extraction of resources. Formidable challenges confront policy-makers who have publicly stated their commitment to sustainable development and many governments have begun to respond to this responsibility primarily by the development of numerous indicators by which rhetoric can be judged against the reality of performance. However, because sustainable development is such an all-embracing concept, there has been a natural tendency for governments to define it to include all possible and desirable policy themes, making it more difficult to distinguish between those aspects of the debate that are relevant and those that are not. Hence, it is only by reference to a well-grounded concept of sustainable development that progress (or otherwise) can be properly evaluated.

2. Achieving Sustainable Development

(a) *Definition of Sustainability*

It is over a decade since the early shaping of the sustainability problem in the Brundtland Report. In that time, substantial progress has been made in clarifying the many controversial issues that have emerged. The concept of sustainable development itself has been defined in a number of ways. The Brundtland Report defined it as 'development that meets the needs of the present generation without compromising the ability of future generations to meet their own needs' (WCED, 1987, p. 43). Economists have tended to reinterpret this as a requirement to follow a development path where human welfare or wellbeing does not decline over time (see, for example, Pezzey, 1989). Arguably, this has led to a consistent 'story' about sustainable development: what it is, what the conditions are for achieving it, what might have to be sacrificed to obtain it, and how it can be measured. Nevertheless, interest in sustainable development represents a 'broad church' and it is far from clear that there is consensus about our obligations to the future. Increasingly, it is argued that, in order to accommodate these diverse views, what is required is a 'pluralist' approach (Farmer and Randall, 1998). For example, Barry (1999) argues that sustainability should be seen in terms of not allowing development *opportunities*, rather than welfare, available to future generations, to decline, while Howarth (1997) views future generations as having rights that must be protected. Some contributions appear to require a dramatic change of emphasis, most notably those definitions that focus upon procedural concerns such as the requirement for greater public participation in decision-making (Toman, 1998). However, Pearce (1998a) argues that the broad *conditions* for sustainable development are invariant with the definition, if the conditions are couched in terms of opportunities, capacities, and so on, in addition to welfare consequences: i.e. sustainable development becomes an *enabling* concept rather than solely a particular path of change.

Discussion of the meaning of sustainable development is clearly important if we are to understand what it is that policy-makers are striving to achieve. Nevertheless, some aspects of the debate do not require a thorough dissection of the concept itself. The most notable is the proposition that policy for 'sustainable development' will require an economy-wide focus in addition to the traditional focus on relatively narrowly conceived environmental and resource policies. That is, the compatibility of environmental targets with economic goals in addition to how economic development affects the environment. This also extends the policy agenda in the direction of wider aspects of micro- and macroeconomic policy that previously might have been perceived to have little, or even no, connection to the environment. For example, economic policies that are not usually designed for environmental purposes may have substantial effects on the level and quality of environment-related activities. Acknowledging these often complex linkages represents an important step towards constructing future policies that take into account undesirable outcomes, such as degrada- tion of the environment (Munasinghe and Cruz, 1995).

The distinguishing feature of the sustainability debate is, however, its focus on the living standards of future generations. Indeed, the appropriate 'coefficient of concern' to guide policy-makers, in principle could lie somewhere between a few generations and, in the limit, infinity (Atkinson *et al.*, 1997). For example, problems such as global warming refer to impacts that could be felt up to 100–200 years into the future, while the temporal dimension of biodiversity loss appears to be largely unknown at present. Even projecting 'concern' a few decades on, policy-makers are faced with the problem of how to predict the future, including the contribution of technological change in determin- ing what activities are currently unsustainable (Weitzman and Löfgren, 1997). Similarly, properly determining the weight to assign to costs and benefits that occur in the future relative to the present is crucial in evaluating projects and policies in a way that captures concern for sustainability. For example, relatively high discounting of future costs is likely to lead to significant costs being passed on to future genera- tions. It is important to note that the issues go beyond debates, familiar in the literature, as to whether to 'discount' or 'not discount' (Beckerman, 1993). Interesting recent contributions have emphasized the impor- tance of non-conventional procedures, such as hyperbolic discounting, which give greater weight to the future than conventional discounting (Mourato and Swierzbinski, 1998; Weitzman, 1998).

More recently, there has been much discussion of 'social sustainabil- ity', which can be traced to the Brundtland Commission emphasis on the role of the essential *needs* of the world's poor. What this suggests is that distribution *within* the current generation is also relevant to the policy-maker's problem, perhaps because proposals to achieve sustainable development, to the extent that these imply sacrifices, now place a disproportionate burden on developing countries or the world's poor (Martínez-Alier, 1995). If so, then this requires that policy-makers follow a more specific requirement to prohibit not only current development, which was at the expense of the future, but also increases in welfare for the better off in society which came at the expense of those who were worse off. A distinct issue is the recent attention directed towards the link between 'social capital' and sustainability (see, for a discussion, World Bank, 1997). Putnam (1993) speaks of social capital as comprising certain features of social organization—norms of behaviour, networks of interactions between people and between institutions, and trust between people. This could be important for sustainability in several ways. First, it is argued that there is an 'economic pay-off' from social capital, whereby conditions favourable to economic growth are fostered by a climate of trust between agents (Knack and Keefer, 1997). Second, there could also be an 'environmental pay-off' whereby, for example, strong community ties help enforce ownership regimes and management systems for common property. The argument is that, other things being equal, the stronger the social ties, the less likely the management system is to collapse.

(b) *Theory of Sustainable Development*

It is clear that many see sustainable development as serving many goals—economic development, a better environment, a particular concern for the poor, a requirement for community participation in decision-making, and so on (Pearce and Atkinson, 1998; Toman, 1998). Of course, delivering all goals simultaneously is probably beyond the capabilities of policy-makers. In other words, sustainable development cannot deliver all desirable policy objectives now and into the future and, in practice, we would expect there to be trade-offs among competing goals such as sound economic policies to foster growth and a better environment. Furthermore, this also raises fundamental questions regarding the costs of policies to achieve sustainability. As long as there are costs involved, there is no overwhelming reason why sustainable development should be elevated to some overriding goal for economic, social, and environmental policy (Nordhaus, 1995; Beckerman, 1995). Indeed, if these costs are large then it is possible that a sustainable world could be a very undesirable one. Some proponents do appear to imply that the sacrifice required is potentially high, arguing that what is being witnessed, with global problems such as ozone-layer depletion, climate change, tropical forest loss, and so on, is the ultimate 'limit to economic growth'. This amounts to a requirement, according to this view, to restrict the physical scale of the economy by controls on the resources used as inputs to production and by reducing the amount of goods that people consume (Daly and Cobb, 1989; van den Bergh and Hofkes, 1998). Others dispute this claim, arguing that not only are such radical policy responses undesirable, but that they are also unnecessary in achieving sustainable development (see, for example, Pearce *et al.*, 1989).

If current patterns of resource use and environmental degradation are thought to be unsustainable, then the sacrifice required by the present generation, committed to sustaining development, depends on the scope that exists for adjusting and adapting this behaviour. Defining sustainability as non-declining welfare, for the sake of simplicity, achieving a sustainable development path will imply a reduction in current welfare only if that flow of welfare cannot be reproduced for each successive generation. By examining theories of sustainable development, specifically with reference to the distinction between weak and strong sustainability, competing claims regarding the sacrifices required to make good our obligations to the future can be scrutinized. Although these theories are derived from very different worldviews, common to both is an emphasis on environmental resources (e.g. commercial resources, clean air and water, biodiversity, etc.) as a component of wealth — i.e. natural assets (or 'capital') — and a concern with thresholds beyond which assets are run down. In addition, proponents of both theories agree that development policy in the past has not paid sufficient attention to this particular component of wealth. However, the two frameworks differ in the type of thresholds they examine, which in turn reflects very different views of the world. For weak sustainability, the relevant reference point is one where, on balance, assets are neither created nor destroyed. Strong sustainable development derives more of its foundations from ecological science and, as such, stresses 'limits' to the deterioration of certain natural assets.

For *weak sustainability* (WS) any one form of asset can be run down provided 'proceeds' are reinvested in other forms of assets. Put another way, it is the 'overall' portfolio of wealth that is bequeathed to the future that matters. Hartwick (1977) showed that achieving sustainability required as a 'rule of thumb' that some of the proceeds (specifically, the total rents) from the exploitation of non-renewable resources be reinvested in produced assets. Now known as 'Hartwick's rule', this suggests that sustainable development is feasible, in principle anyway, even if there is an initial reliance on non-renewable resources, a result that can also be extended to consider the role of renewable resources and changes in environmental liabilities (Hartwick, 1978b; Mäler, 1991). Finally, Solow (1986) has shown that Hartwick's rule amounts to holding the aggregate stock of capital intact and treating consumption as the interest on that stock. It is by following this rule that the basic requirement for WS, that the change in the (real) value of assets should not be negative in aggregate, is fulfilled. Put another way, there is no specific focus or special place for the environment and, as such, there are no particular things that we owe to future generations. It is by passing on some generalized productive potential, broadly construed, that we will ensure that future welfare is sustained (Solow, 1993).

Ecologists and ecological economists take a rather different approach: *strong sustainability* (SS). SS stresses 'discontinuity' and 'non-smoothness' in ecological systems and hence in the (economic) damages to which ecological impairment gives rise (Pearce *et al.*, 1996). The basic idea is that that development is currently unsustainable because environmental limits are being exceeded. This places a greater emphasis on the conservation of natural assets within the broader goal of prudently managing a portfolio of assets over time (see, for example, Victor *et al.*, 1998). It is worth noting that WS does not eschew conservation and is also informed by ecology. To the extent that society is, for example, over-consuming natural assets, i.e. in excess of socially efficient levels of use, proponents of WS would advocate more conservation than currently prevailed. This remains, however, a different stance to that taken by advocates of SS; it is the physical protection of absolute levels of ecological goods, rather than the balancing of costs and benefits at the margin, that is a prerequisite for sustainability. The rationale underlying this embodies both the complexity of ecosystems and the absence of substitutes for functions, such as waste absorption and ecological system maintenance (Norton and Toman, 1997). Hence, it is argued that natural assets are characterized by important thresholds that, if exceeded, lead to large-scale and irreversible ecological losses. There are several variants on this proposition. Very few supporters of SS argue that all natural assets must be conserved. More usually, it is argued that there are *critical* natural assets, crucial for human welfare, that have no substitutes and therefore cannot be traded off for other forms of wealth (Pearce *et al.*, 1989). A related concept is 'resilience' — the ability of an economic, ecological, and social system to 'bounce back' from shocks (such as outbreaks of disease in agricultural systems) and to persist despite continuous stresses (Common and Perrings, 1992). Arrow *et al.* (1995) argue that the loss of biological diversity (via species loss or the increasing trend towards monoculture in agricultural production) is associated with losses in resilience and that, in turn, a less resilient system is also less sustainable.

A world characterized by WS suggests that fears of sustainable development as an instrument for depressing current and immediate future standards of living is generally, but not totally, lacking in foundation. The conflict between welfare now and into the future can be reconciled by prudent management of a nation's portfolio of assets and by bringing the private costs of economic activity in line with its wider social costs. If, on the other hand, there are genuine 'limits' on use of critical natural assets, this suggests a greater sacrifice may be required if we are not to confer massive social costs on future generations. In such a scenario, more stringent limitations such as quotas and direct controls could also have their role to play (Pearce and Atkinson, 1998). It is important to note that there are a number of complications in both theories. If, for example, (developed) countries can import sustainability from (developing) countries by importing their own resource needs, while leaving their own resources intact, a global perspective may be additionally useful (Martínez-Alier, 1995). Moreover, many natural assets are not owned nationally and better management necessitates that complex issues of international cooperation are successfully brokered (see, for example, Barrett, 1998). There are various concepts to be considered in addition to wealth, including, for example, population change. As population expands, this both leads to more people over whom welfare must be sustained, and may threaten sustainability as human populations place further pressure upon assets, as, for example, forests are cut down or burned to make way for agriculture, urban expansion, and roads (Dasgupta, 1993; Pearce, 1998a).

The dichotomy between WS and SS creates a problem for policy-makers by suggesting a two-tier approach to achieving sustainable development. Clearly, the key question is how demarcations of the tiers are to be identified in practice (Norton and Toman, 1997). Specifically, there is likely to be uncertainty, which scientific evidence is currently unable to resolve, regarding which policy regime should apply: i.e., which natural assets are critical and which are not. Many policy choices faced in the real world are considerably more complex than suggested by the distinction between WS and SS. Hence, there exists no straightforward choice between running down the stock of a resource or conserving that stock at some level. This has led to proposals for decision-making rules as the precautionary principle, entailing the conservation of certain resources without full scientific knowledge of the consequences (Perrings, 1991). Similarly, Farmer and Randall (1998) propose a safe minimum standard (SMS) whereby policy-makers follow standard cost–benefit rules unless there is a compelling reason not to, for example to conserve a critical natural asset. However, this conservation rule can itself be overridden if its costs are 'intolerable'. Clearly, however, there will be disagreement, among both experts and the public, as to when this policy switch should be made, introducing an arbitrary element to two-tier approaches to sustainability policy. However, Woodward and Bishop (1997) demonstrate formally that it is precisely this disagreement that motivates decision rules such as SMS, in the face of this uncertainty, as rational criteria for decision-making.

3. Measuring Sustainable Development

The policy process cannot begin unless we have some idea of *why* unsustainable development occurs. This leads to a number of questions, such as why are natural resources being depleted too rapidly or why does environmental degradation occur at its present rates. The focus on 'sustainability' helps to explain what has gone wrong with past development decisions because it reminds us, for example, to monitor and evaluate the impacts of policy on those assets that will sustain future welfare. Hence, almost as important as identifying driving forces, are efforts to find indicators to measure sustainable development, for otherwise it will not be possible to say whether an economy is on or off a sustainable development path. If it is the case that societies are increasingly financing consumption by liquidating environmental assets, then identifying this using indicators provides policy-makers with new and useful information. Even so, the debate about what should be measured and how is, if anything, even more beset with controversy than those surrounding the theory of sustainable development.

First, the SS paradigm dictates indicators that focus primarily on ecological assets, functions, and processes. In turn, such indicators tend to stress 'limits' to the deterioration of natural assets. Indicators in this category include: (i) *resource use*, e.g. energy and material throughputs to a system (Daly and Cobb, 1989); (ii) 'distance to goal' approaches in which deviations of ambient pollution concentrations from 'sustainability targets' are aggregated to derive an overall performance indicator (Hammond *et al.*, 1995). A monetized counterpart of this is offered by Hueting *et al.* (1992) and is couched in terms of the costs of reaching these goals; (iii) biological diversity, since resilience is assumed to be a function of diversity (Arrow *et al.*, 1995; Common and Perrings, 1992).

Second, the WS paradigm, on the other hand, emphasizes the substitutability of assets and hence focuses on aggregate measures such as better measures of national income saving (Mäler, 1991; Hartwick,

1993; Hamilton, 1996). In the main, these indicators are intended to measure performance at the national level, but it is as well to note in passing that the distinction between WS and SS also affects microeconomic indicators, in particular, it affects cost–benefit measures (Barbier et al., 1990).

Lastly, there are numerous other examples of frameworks which are not underpinned by any particular theory of sustainable development (i.e. providing the rationale for interest in indicators). This has characterized most 'official' responses to the measurement problem (e.g. Department of Environment (DoE), 1996; for an exception, see World Bank, 1997).

(a) Background to the Measurement Debate

Interest in quantifying environmental change emerged in the 1980s. This period saw a proliferation of environmental indicators such as air quality indices and water quality classifications. While being a first step, these indicators had limited policy uses as policy-makers typically could not make direct use of environmental data that were voluminous, difficult to aggregate, and not connected to other policy variables: e.g. economic indicators (Atkinson et al., 1997). At the same time, there was a growing appreciation that decision-making made on the basis of economic data alone ignored broader quality-of-life issues. Focal to this debate was the perceived inadequacy of the main indicator of economic activity, gross domestic product (GDP), or more specifically its growth rate, to address a growing number of policy questions relating to the environment. This suggested two activities for the government statisticians who oversee the compilation of environmental indicators and the national accountants responsible for the provision of economic data. The first asks how environmental information could be made more relevant to the economic and social domains of decision-making. Although, there is disagreement about what these indicators actually measure, these have become known as 'sustainability indicators'. The second asks how economic data (specifically, the economic or national accounts) can complement environmental data in order to improve decision-making by taking account of the impact of economic activity on the environment: i.e. 'green accounting'.

(i) 'Sustainability indicators'

The evolution of 'sustainability indicators' from environmental indicators is evident from the continuing influence of the 'pressure–state–response' (P-S-R) framework on this work (e.g. OECD, 1994a). This basic structure focuses upon measures of pressures or 'stresses' on the environment, in turn, linked to measures of the state of the environment and then to policy responses. Although applying the P-S-R framework additionally to the socio-economic domain stretches its original intent, many governments have settled on an augmented P-S-R as a starting point for constructing indicators. For example, the UK Department of Environment, Transport and the Regions (DETR) has been among the leading international players in establishing indicators as a component of its Sustainable Development Strategy (DoE, 1996). Whether that resulting package of indicators actually measures 'sustainability' remains unclear, in that it is only loosely pinned to a meaningful concept of sustainability (that of 'ensuring better quality of life for everyone now and for generations to come'; DETR, 1999a). Certainly this work is not based on any theory of sustainable development. However, some of these indicators do at least encompass many of the concerns articulated within that debate.

The UK approach itself is based on a 'menu' of indicators currently made up of around 150 grouped under various themes. Selecting indicators is no easy task in that there will always be criticism that those chosen are 'too many' or 'too few' or convey the 'wrong emphasis'. But, to complement this potentially bewildering collection of data, the DETR has attempted to boil these indicators down, or rather select from their menu 15 headline indicators (DETR, 1999a).

Table 1 outlines these indicators, which correspond broadly to aspects of economic, social, and the environmental policy identified as central to the government's Sustainable Development Strategy. While this has been viewed as a useful step forward, several issues as to how these indicators will be used remain to be clarified. We deal in detail with the more important of these below. However, it is worth noting that DETR (1999a) does not elaborate on how these indicators will be evaluated simultaneously and how trade-offs will be explored. For example, GDP growth is typically reported annually or even quarterly. For other indicators, the most obvious example being populations of wild birds, reporting over this time period arguably will not yield useful information. Insofar as this indicator is influenced by policy, this impact will only be apparent over the long term.

(ii) Green accounting

The background to the focus of green accounting is the national accounts, which consist of a large body of information confined primarily to observable marketed transactions. Hence, the goods and services that get counted are those which pass through the market and the costs of provision of certain services, such as state education,

Table 1
Proposed Headline 'Indicators of Sustainable Development' in the United Kingdom

Policy theme	Indicator
Economy	
Economic growth	Gross Domestic Product
Investment	Total and public investment
Employment	People of working age in work
Social	
Health	Expected years of healthy life
Education and training	Qualifications at age 19
Housing quality	Homes judged unfit to live in
Crime	Level of crime
Poverty	Change in numbers living in poverty
Environment	
Climate change	Emissions of greenhouse gases
Air pollution	Days of air pollution
Transport	Road traffic
Water quality	Rivers of good or fair quality
Wildlife	Populations of wild birds
Land use	New homes built on previously development land
Waste	Waste and waste disposal

supplied by government. From this mass of economic data, most attention is given to the aggregate measure of income or product, i.e. GDP, resulting from the accounting process. Its primary use, along with a small number of additional indices, such as the unemployment rate, inflation rate, and balance of payments, is to characterize the state of the economy in the past and to forecast prospects for the near future. The national accounts have been widely criticized for their failure to account for the environmental side effects of economic activity: i.e. this framework is well-suited for recording the 'goods' created by economic activity but not the 'bads', such as, for example, pollution. Hence, by adding an explicit environmental component to these accounts, it was hoped that a better balance would be achieved. In addition, it was hoped that this would serve other related functions, such as persuading government departments and the public of the need for environmental policies: e.g. by raising awareness that wealth is reduced when the environment is harmed (Hamilton *et al.*, 1994).

Green accounts differ from 'sustainability indicators' in that the focus is on identifying links between economic activity and the environment using relatively detailed data. The practice of accounting, with the discipline that this entails (e.g. via accounting identities) is well suited to make sense of these data. Although interest in the practical use of green accounts has developed in response to different focal policy concerns there is an overarching international dimension to these efforts laid out by the United Nation's Statistical Office (UNSTAT) (United Nations, 1993). UNSTAT's Satellite Environmental and Economic Accounts (UN SEEA) is, in turn, an *adjunct* to the conventional UN System of National Accounts (SNA). Hence, it does not alter the core structure of the accounts but is intended as a complementary tool. It is worth noting that while the SEEA provides the potential for international comparability, it embodies a wide enough range of activities and methods to permit countries to develop green accounts according to their particular policy concerns. Within the UK, the Office for National Statistics (ONS) is responsible for the environmental accounts in its role as data provider to the government and its departments. To date, the ONS has developed and published air emissions, environmental expenditure (e.g. on pollution abatement), and water accounts, and natural resource balances for UK reserves of oil and gas (ONS, 1998).

Statisticians, working on the construction of green accounts, are clearly responding to a political objective—namely, how to raise environmental issues in ways which decision-makers will notice. Indeed, the range of policy uses associated with green accounts, if properly exploited, is large, and hence the challenge for the future is how these accounts will be *used* in policy-making. Therefore, it is surprising that many official green accounting programmes were initiated with very little discussion of end-uses. Addressing this shortcoming is crucial if current efforts are to be more than an elaborate but largely symbolic gesture. Case-study evidence suggests that the development of clearly mapped-out policy uses highlights the importance of institutional relationships in creating links between data providers and policy-makers, which are typically lacking (Hamilton *et al.*, 1994). An exception to this is Norway, which has the longest history in the development of green accounting, allowing the cultivation of an explicit linkage between account development and policy uses. A related feature of the Norwegian work is the active role of Statistics Norway (SN) in economic analysis, research, and modelling, making it a natural bridge between the Ministry of Finance and the Ministry of Environment in analysing environment–economy linkages.

The potential challenges for policy development in the UK can be illustrated with reference to emissions accounts. These accounts describe the physical flow of emissions of pollutants (e.g. tonnes of carbon dioxide) by production and final demand sector (e.g. electricity generation and households) in the (monetary) input–output (I/O) accounts. In the published accounts (ONS, 1998), this physical flow of emissions is described in a summary table of 12 sectors with a more detailed break-out account of over 30 sectors complementing this. With links to the I/O tables, these accounts lend themselves naturally to policy model-ling. For example, the UK government currently is contemplating the introduction of a 'carbon levy' in order to facilitate compliance with its commitments agreed under the Kyoto Protocol. The UK emission accounts could inform the design of any proposed tax in two ways. First, economic models using emission accounts can be used to estimate the approximate size of the levy required to achieve a given policy goal. Second, measuring the burden of a proposed policy is an important element of its design. Models based on emission accounts can be used to estimate the impact (on output and profits, for example) of environ-mental tax proposals.

(b) *Valuation and Green Accounts*

The common feature of both sustainability indicators and green ac-counts is that the predominant emphasis is on presenting data about the natural world in physical terms. However, while physical indicators are essential inputs into decision-making, in themselves they do not contain information for appraising whether an economy is on or off a sustain-able path of development. First, what this work indicates is pressures on the environment rather than the impacts that these burdens cause. Any approach based on physical indicators needs to be augmented by a focus on socio-economic impacts of environmental change such that emerging issues, such as pollution-related human health impacts, can be properly monitored and evaluated. Second, it is sometimes proposed that physical indicators are attractive in that they appear to be more 'objective' than weighted indicators and have an obvious link to the SS paradigm which stresses the importance of natural assets (Rennings and Wiggering, 1997). However, this appeal is superficial unless under-pinned by a satisfactory theory of strong sustainable development (i.e. providing the rationale for interest in the change in physical indicators) and, typically, this foundation is lacking in this work. In general, decision-makers require indicators to be weighted in order, for ex-ample, to gauge the *importance* of environmental damage, or a specific environmental issue. More generally, expressing these weights in common units is one means whereby the trade-offs between different policy goals can be determined.

Obviously nothing is achieved if the set of weights intended to gauge relative importance is largely arbitrary. Nevertheless, weights, or measures of importance, could be derived from several sources, including public opinion, implicit market weights, or expert judgement (Atkinson *et al.*, 1997). Of course, public opinion and expert assessment of what is important are often two very distinct things and it may be that some 'mix' of expert and public assessment is required. That is, the role of the expert being one of conveying information to individuals as the ultimate arbiters of what they, as the constituents of society, actually want (Pearce and Atkinson, 1998). A related view is that such a mix is ultimately best achieved through the monetization of preferences. Establishing the foundation for sustainable development, such as exists for the evaluation of costs and benefits of individual projects and policies, is essential. For some, however, this is an almost insurmountable obstacle. Custance and Hillier (1998), for example, argue that this places a far greater degree of judgement on the part of statisticians and national accountants than is reasonable.

Some of this scepticism is understandable. In particular, the problem is to value these changes systematically for a whole country, whereas most of the methods used by economists to value environmental goods (see, Bateman and Willis, 1999) are concerned with specific projects or assets. Determining how to add up values for a nation is a formidable problem, although considerable progress is being made in the appraisal of social costs of energy generation (European Commission, 1999; Markandya and Pavan, 1999). It is interesting to note, however, that many of the building blocks required are already in place. That is, once statistical offices have compiled pollution emissions accounts these can be used as the required input for 'downstream' models of dispersion and impact. Furthermore, if impacts on health, living resources, produced assets, and natural ecosystems can be estimated, valuation of these impacts becomes possible. This implies that the net benefits of policies, for instance, can be estimated, which could lead to adjustments of such policies in order to maximize benefits. There remains a significant, but realizable, challenge in determining how future statistical work can be informed by an explicit understanding of societal preferences for the economy–environment trade-offs.

(c) *Green Alternatives to GDP*

A compelling corollary to valuation in green accounts is the construction of national accounts aggregates adjusted to reflect resource depletion and environmental degradation. These alternatives to GDP are among the most comprehensive and integrated of all such measures and, with appropriate caveats made, promise to be superior indicators for guiding sustainable development policy. Much of the motivation for this arose as a result of empirical efforts that appeared to suggest that conventionally measured growth diverged from what might be considered to be sustainable (see, for example, Repetto *et al.*, 1989). In response, many critics argued that retaining GDP as an arbiter of development perpetuates a bias against the environment (or social aspects of wellbeing) in decision-making. There may be a point here, but these same commentators have sometimes suggested that until GDP is replaced by a completely new concept, development will never begin to be sustainable. This is claiming too much. However, considerable progress has been made in developing the empirical counterpart of the theory of sustainable development.

The fundamental idea is that the asset boundary in the national accounts should be expanded to include natural resources and environmental liabilities in the form of pollution stocks. Thus, the use of resources and the environment represents asset consumption, i.e. depreciation of natural assets, a concept ideally suited to treatment within the national accounts. Alternatives to GDP attempt to approximate 'net' or 'sustainable' income — income in excess of asset consumption, a definition that goes back to Hicks (1946). Thus, green net domestic product (gNDP) is defined as GDP net of asset consumption. That is, net of the depreciation of produced assets, depletion of resources, and accumulation of environmental liabilities. Efforts to estimate this green alternative to GDP have led to a burst of activity over the past decade resulting in a plethora of studies in the developed and developing world (see, for a review, Hamilton and Lutz, 1996). While, in principle, gNDP is a better measure of income than GDP, for a variety of reasons, attention has shifted away from it, at least insofar as in its role as a indicator of sustainability (see, for example, Hamilton, 1996).

The primary criticism is that gNDP measures only *potentially* sustainable income. Hence, this does not in itself answer the question of whether the rate of saving is sufficient to maintain this income indefinitely. It is the saving rate that informs the question regarding whether a country is over-consuming at the expense of welfare in the future. Hence, a more promising indicator, in this respect, is the rate of 'genuine' saving, or net savings less the value of both resource depletion and the net accumulation of pollutants. If genuine savings are persistently negative, then eventually welfare must decline (i.e. negative genuine savings lead to non-sustainability) (Hamilton and Atkinson, 1996). The genuine savings rate is a one-sided indicator of sustainability in that it is only negative savings that permits us to make a judgement as to non-sustainability. Hence, the measurement of a positive genuine savings rate at a given point in time is not sufficient to lead to the conclusion that the economy is on a sustainable path (Asheim, 1994). However, the policy prescription arising from measuring a negative genuine savings rate is clear: continuing dissaving is not sustainable and must be rectified (Atkinson *et al.*, 1997). An analysis of savings rates in countries shows that there were a considerable number that displayed negative genuine savings in the mid-to-late 1980s (Atkinson *et al.*, 1997; World Bank, 1997). Hamilton and Atkinson (1996) show that, in the UK, genuine saving was negative over much of the period 1980–90. Of course, these data carry 'health warnings' in that they rely on estimates of the value of depletion and pollution that could be contested. However, they also provide a potentially alarming signal for governments committed to achieving sustainable development.

This framework also leads naturally to a range of direct policy concerns (Atkinson *et al.*, 1997). For example, the generation of royalties from natural resources also raises the question of public and private investment — since the rule of thumb for sustainable development is to re-invest resource rents. Prudent government policies would aim to ensure, for example, that investment at least matches the value of depletion of natural resources as negative genuine savings rates imply, by definition, excessive consumption whether by governments or households. Moreover, because increments to pollution stocks are analogous to the depletion of natural resources, there is the need to see that investments in other assets offset these increments, as well as to implement policies to achieve (socially) efficient levels of pollution emissions. In addition, attention should be paid to the effectiveness of investment. Investments may be in produced assets, as has traditionally been the case, or they may be, say, in pollution control, decreasing the size of the pollution liability to its efficient level. Typically, returns to investments in environmental assets will be non-marketed and hence it is likely that countries will under-invest in these assets and over-invest in environmentally damaging activities. Again, this reiterates the message that one important aspect of policies for sustainable development is the demonstration of values of environmental assets at the local, national, and the global level.

An important feature of the genuine savings rate is that it is tied to a theory of sustainable development that offers clear guidance regarding the measurement of the relevant resource and environmental flows. In contrast, many contributions to the debate appear to be only loosely connected to a rigorous, or even adequate, understanding of the concept itself. It is notable that this includes contributions from official sources including DETR (1999*a*). The resulting tendency is for public pronouncements on sustainable development to include each and every aspect of policy believed to be important at a given point in time, giving the impression that the concept is just another way to package existing policies. Arguably, this is contrary to much of the original spirit of the concept and its subsequent elaboration.

Evaluation of the concepts underlying sustainable development has progressed significantly since the expositions of, for example, the Brundtland Commission. Notions of weak versus strong sustainability, while remaining useful for illustrative purposes, have been superseded by a much sharper focus on changes in the real value of assets. This does not mean that the focus of policy-makers, concerned with establishing a firm foundation for statements regarding sustainability, need be unduly narrow. Thus, using this framework is entirely consistent with a concept of sustainable development that retains the wide base as envisaged in the Brundtland Report and other policy statements encompassing social, economic, and ecological dimensions. However, it is desirable that this consistency is achieved within reasonably clear bounds. Thus far, most progress has been made in the integration of resources and environment into economic frameworks. Indeed, this has contributed much to the debate on the measurement of sustainability. Yet, there is no reason why future contributions should not strengthen the representation of the social and ecological dimensions. For example, heavy weather has frequently been made by those who attempt to distinguish between those indicators pertinent to worlds characterized by either weak or strong sustainability. To an extent this debate has been misdirected: sustainability most probably requires both an avoidance of persistently negative genuine savings and declines in stocks of critical natural capital. This gives a particular impetus to efforts to provide understanding of the 'two-tier' approach to decision-making described above. Specifically, determining what actually constitutes critical natural capital and the threshold levels of the stocks that must be held is a crucial test of whether strong sustainability is more than just rhetoric. It is in this way that, combined with the above-mentioned social and economic dimensions, a coherent and consistent programme for sustainability will emerge from seemingly disparate strands.

4. Conclusions

Sustainable development has undoubtedly emerged as one of the political buzzwords of the past decade. Indeed, such is its appeal that observations of the term 'sustainable' prefixed to numerous and disparate policy objectives are now commonplace. This often makes it difficult to distinguish those aspects of the policy debate which are

meaningful from those that are not. However, given that most governments, the UK included, have signed up to the goal of sustainable
development, decision-makers face considerable challenges not only in
understanding what they have committed themselves to, but also in
constructing credible policy responses and frameworks to monitor
progress.

Numerous policy implications have emerged from the sustainability
debate of which the following five points are among the most important.

(i) A concern for future generations is the defining feature of this
discussion, despite the increasing complexity of the way in
which policy-makers interpret the concept. The argument is that
past policy decisions have too often neglected, for example, the
wellbeing of near or far-off future generations. To correct this
bias, policies need to be more forward-looking, whether this be
to encourage saving for the future in general or to conserve
particular natural assets. In addition, this discussion is not
divorced from the social side of policy-making, as the recent
focus on social capital indicates.

(ii) Increased attention to economy–environment linkages has
enabled policy-makers to move away from dealing with environmental concerns as a collection of individual issues and
conceiving environmental and resource policies as having little
connection to the economic (or social) world. This understanding works both ways. Economic policies also have important
impacts on the environment.

(iii) There are costs and benefits to policies to attain sustainable
development. Policy-makers tend to interpret sustainable development as serving many goals – economic, environmental,
and social. It is debatable whether all these goals can be achieved
simultaneously. Furthermore, there will also be trade-offs between sustainable development and other goals that have little
or nothing to do with sustainability but represent comparably
desirable objectives for society. On the whole, advocates of
sustainability have not made a detailed examination of these
trade-offs, but it is clear that, in order to enhance policy
relevance, this shortcoming needs to be addressed.

(iv) The construction of frameworks whereby sustainability can be
evaluated and measured promises to be a crucial input into
decision-making. This is particularly true of green accounts, the
construction of which could be important in design of, for
example, environmental taxes. On a negative note, the lack of
discussion of the policy uses of green accounts so far has been

disappointing. An interesting question is whether these accounts may, in the future, be used to construct indicators that could provide a synopsis of sustainable development. Green national accounting aggregates, such as genuine savings, are obviously incomplete in terms of satisfying all criteria of the broader sustainable development debate. Yet, there is nothing in this approach that excludes the possibility of separately accounting for, say, changes in the level of crucial natural assets for which substitution possibilities are low and aspects of social capital thought to be important. Indeed, it would be surprising if any single indicator is capable of providing all the answers that policy-makers apparently require.

(v) Policies for and measurement of sustainable development should not be divorced from a proper understanding of the concept itself. While this requires a focus on changes in the real value of assets, it does not entail ignoring social, economic, and ecological dimensions. However, contrary to notable policy statements, it does not mean that sustainable development must embody any policy thought to be desirable. Some problems are relevant to the sustainability debate and others are not. Nevertheless, there remains a challenge to strengthen the representation of the social and ecological dimensions within this framework.

3

Cost–Benefit Analysis and Environmental Policy

DAVID PEARCE*

1. Introduction

The theoretical foundations of cost–benefit analysis (CBA) are well established, although no practitioner should pretend that all the problems are resolved. Essentially, CBA compares the gains and losses associated with an investment project (a road, railway line, port, urban expansion, etc.) or with a policy, e.g. the setting of an environmental standard. Gains and losses are defined in terms of increments and decrements of human wellbeing (or welfare, or utility) and, in turn, these are measured as follows: individuals' willingness to pay for a gain or willingness to pay to avoid a loss; or individuals' willingness to accept compensation to tolerate a loss or to go without a benefit. These willingness-to-pay and willingness-to-accept concepts correspond to the measures of consumer surplus formalized by Hicks (1943).

Historically, the origins of CBA lie in the appraisal of investment rather than policy, but in recent years in the European context it has come to be used more for policy appraisal. CBA is widely practised. Why then does it remain so controversial, and especially so in the context of the environment? This paper outlines the use made of CBA in UK environmental policy and offers some explanations for the continuing controversies. But, while the debates continue, they should not be construed as meaning that CBA is not widely used in British government. CBA has entrenched itself in policy appraisal far more than ever before in UK history in the sense that more CBA-type appraisals are conducted. However, there remains a gap between

* CSERGE, University College London.

I am very much indebted to Ian Bateman, Andrew Jordan, Dieter Helm, Ken Willis, and Nick Hanley for comments on the earlier draft which appeared in the *Oxford Review of Economic Policy*, vol. 14, no. 4, Winter 1998, pp. 84–100. I take sole responsibility for the views expressed here.

conducting CBA and CBA affecting actual policy decisions. The reasons for this lack of correspondence between practice and influence are explored.

2. A Brief History of CBA

Cost–benefit analysis has a long history. Its origins probably begin with the work of the French engineer and economist Jules Dupuit (1844, 1853). Efforts to claim earlier origins with US Secretary of the Treasury Albert Gallatin in 1808 (Hanley and Spash, 1993) do an injustice to the profound intellectual effort produced by Dupuit. Dupuit established the foundations of what today would be called 'marginal analysis', defined the way in which benefits and costs should be measured, and firmly embraced the principle that an investment decision, such as a building, road, or bridge, should meet a criterion that benefits exceed costs. The exact meaning of benefits and costs is explored below. While the theoretical foundations of marginal analysis were greatly expanded and developed in the late 19th century, little happened to apply these principles in practice. In 1936, however, the United States Flood Control Act stated that water projects in the USA should proceed 'if the benefits to whosoever they accrue are in excess of the estimated costs', embracing the idea that all gainers and losers should be considered. The stimulus was public and political concern over the effects of major hydro-power construction. The formalization of these notions continued after the Second World War: in 1946 a subcommittee of the Federal Interagency River Basin Committee was set up to consider benefits and costs, and in 1950 the subcommittee produced the 'Green Book' of guidance on the benefit–cost appraisal of water projects. Circular A-47 of the Bureau of Budget produced further guidance in 1952. In hindsight, all of these efforts were rudimentary and lacked proper theoretical foundations. None the less, they were catalytic in effect.

At the same time as the practical guidelines were being drawn up in the water sector, considerable attention was being devoted to 'efficiency in government', especially military spending, by bodies such as the Rand Corporation. In 1958 three seminal works appeared: Otto Eckstein's *Water Resource Development*; John Krutilla and Otto Eckstein's *Multipurpose River Development*; and Roland McKean's *Efficiency in Government Through Systems Analysis* (Eckstein, 1958; Krutilla and Eckstein, 1958; McKean, 1958). The feature of these works was the synthesis of practical concerns with the theoretical 'welfare economics' literature that had emerged in the 1930s and 1940s, and notably the work of Kaldor and Hicks (Kaldor, 1939; Hicks, 1939, 1943). The essential step here was the justification for the benefit–cost principle: justifying projects or policies on the basis that benefits exceed costs is wholly consistent with there being losers, i.e. those who suffer the costs. The Kaldor–Hicks criterion established that projects were none the less justified because gainers *could* compensate losers, such that losers would be no worse off and gainers would still have a net benefit. This implies that, provided the compensation takes place, no one is actually worse off, thus meeting the long established 'Pareto criterion' for an improvement in overall wellbeing.[1] However, *actual* compensation need not occur: it is necessary only that it could take place.

By the 1960s, then, the economic basis for CBA was almost in place. Almost, because two things were missing. First, there appeared to be no way to deal with the socio-economic distribution of benefits and costs. *Who* gains and loses did appear to matter as much as the overall net benefit, whether it is a matter of different income groups, ethnic groups, regions, or even broadly defined stakeholders (producers and consumers, for example). Second, there was no mechanism for bringing what were then called 'incommensurables' into the picture with the same measuring rod as other costs and benefits, i.e. money. In the early days, incommensurables were thought to include human health effects, accidents, and, only marginally, the environment. Since environmental awareness was still in its infancy, it seems fair to say that few people thought these omissions were major deficiencies.

The distributional issue was perhaps never fully resolved. Those who wanted to integrate it into CBA found the answer in 'distributional weights', weighting factors applied to a benefit or a cost to reflect the income of the individual affected. The theoretical foundations for such adjustments already existed with the idea that the wellbeing an individual got from an extra unit of income was higher the lower the income in question (declining 'marginal utility of income'). Such adjustments became commonplace in the literature dealing with CBA in developing economies, mainly because income disparities were thought to be higher there (Marglin *et al.*, 1972; Little and Mirrlees, 1974; Squire and van der Tak, 1975). Later, however, distributionally adjusted CBA went out of fashion, perhaps because of the data-intensity of the

---

[1] The Pareto criterion is named after Vilfredo Pareto (1848–1923), the Italian economist and sociologist. In its simplest and most impractical form the Pareto criterion declares that 'society' is better off if at least some individuals in society prefer the new situation to the old, and no one 'disprefers' it. The rule is impractical because virtually all change involves someone being a loser. The benefit–cost compensation rule, therefore, replaces the rule with the modified form introduced by Kaldor and Hicks, i.e. that society is better off provided gainers can compensate losers and still have net gains.

approach, but more probably because of the feeling that distributional issues were not best addressed through project investments. This second view had in fact defined the position of many from the start — see Mishan (1975).

The issue of 'incommensurables' grew to be the single most controversial issue in CBA, and it remains so today. The environmental movements of the 1960s and 1970s forced the realization that environmental problems were not minor deviations from the workings of a beautifully competitive economy. They were pervasive at the local and transnational level, and in the 1980s their global nature also became apparent.[2] Since many of these effects had no market — peace and quiet is not directly bought and sold, any more than is clean air — the challenge was to find monetary values in contexts where markets failed to exist. Massive US Environmental Protection Agency research programmes in the 1970s pushed back the frontiers, especially on air and water pollution. The first set of procedures for finding money values are what today would be called 'revealed preference' techniques. While there are no direct markets in many environmental effects, there are markets in related commodities, such as housing or transportation. Clean air tends to raise house prices relative to contexts where there is not clean air. People spend money getting to a recreational site so that their expenditures must be related in some way to the benefit they get. And so on.

The 1980s witnessed the emergence of questionnaire-based approaches, or 'stated preference' techniques, although they had already been used sparingly in the 1970s, particularly by the consultancy, Social and Community Planning Research. These approaches adopt a market research stance, directly asking people for their monetary valuation, or asking questions in such a way that those valuations can be inferred from the answers given. While all 'monetization' procedures are controversial to some, questionnaire-based approaches have remained the most controversial.

3. The Basics of Cost–Benefit Analysis and the Current Theoretical Debate

As indicated above, cost–benefit analysis (CBA) is a procedure for evaluating the social worth of investment projects, programmes, and

---

[2] The pervasiveness of environmental problems and, therefore, potentially the pervasiveness of externality had in fact been demonstrated back in the 1960s with Kenneth Boulding's seminal 'spaceship earth' essay, followed by explorations into the materials balance principle — see Boulding (1966) and Ayres and Kneese (1969).

policies. Its essential features and the nature of the current debate about CBA are set out below.

A benefit is defined as any gain in human wellbeing ('welfare' or 'utility') and a cost is defined as any loss in wellbeing. Wellbeing is anchored in human preferences, so that, crudely put, if any individual prefers A to B, his or her wellbeing is said to be higher with A than with B. The way in which these preferences are observed is through the market place, whether directly, as in an exchange of money for goods, indirectly, by observing how the good in question affects the price or quantity of another good, or through the response to a question about preferences. Thus, the economic value of air-pollution damage is not directly observable because there is no market for clean air. But it can be observed indirectly by looking at the effects of air pollution on, say, the output of crops or on health expenditures. And it can be inferred from questions about the willingness to pay of individuals to avoid the adverse consequences of air pollution, for example on their health. The consistent theme in all cases is that preferences count, that preferences determine choices, and choices 'reveal' wellbeing through the medium of willingness to pay. In turn, willingness to pay can be observed in markets, surrogate or associated markets, or 'created' hypothetical markets. Most analysts would accept that the accuracy of willingness to pay as a measure of wellbeing is highest where real markets exist and lowest in the hypothetical market case. Considerable efforts are therefore made to test the accuracy of the measures of wellbeing in each market context.

In the early days of practical CBA the *motives* for these preferences were not considered worthy of much discussion. It was typically assumed that preferences were 'selfish', i.e. that A was preferred to B because A contributed more to the individual's own interests. The neglect of motive has perhaps created more confusion in the debate over CBA than anything else. If individuals are motivated by self-interest alone, then CBA would appear to be potentially unethical in its application to public policy. Public policy should, presumably, reflect what is in society's interests. Most critics of CBA tend to take this stance. Recent work has focused on the philosophical underpinnings of CBA in order to explore this apparent contradiction.

Milgrom (1993) has argued that since CBA is based on self-interested motivation, preferences that are motivated by other concerns—such as altruism, moral commitment, and 'citizenry'—cannot legitimately be included in CBA. However, the criticism suffers from the straw-man syndrome: what is being criticized is a view that few, if any, cost–benefit analysts would hold. The view that most analysts would hold is that motives do not matter, not that only self-interested motives matter.

A more subtle questioning of the role of preferences argues that motives do none the less matter. Each individual is assumed to have a *utility function*, a numerical representation of a preference ordering by the individual. Some critics question whether it makes sense to make this assumption, an issue discussed below. The more immediate question is whether individuals' utility functions are unique. It has long been suggested that individuals may have (at least) two such functions: one in which they order preferences for themselves, and one where they order preferences 'on behalf' of society (see, for example, Harsanyi, 1955; Sen, 1977; Margolis, 1982). Effectively, individuals behave schizo-phrenically, in the sense that their choices appear contradictory or inconsistent. They have a utility function based on self interest and another utility function—effectively an individualized 'social' welfare function—where they judge preferences as if they were deciding what is best for society as a whole. This view has been emphasized by some political philosophers as well (Sagoff, 1988). The language needs careful definition. Traditionally, economists have distinguished individual utility functions, and a social welfare function (SWF) which is some aggregation of the utilities of all individuals. A SWF is assumed to be something that politicians, rather than individuals, maximize because they might, for example, want to make some individuals' utility count more than others. Put another way, one would 'weight', say, the utility of the poor more than that of the rich, even though this would not be the strict result of adding up the utilities of the rich (as the rich see it) and the utilities of the poor (as the poor see it). On this traditional view, individuals have utility functions and someone judging on behalf of society, best identified as a politician, has a social welfare function. On the Harsanyi–Sen–Sagoff approach, however, it is individuals who have both functions: a self-interested utility function and a SWF which is invoked when they act as citizens rather than individuals.

While these distinctions may seem trivial, it has been argued that they matter when it comes to aggregation. Recall that CBA is about aggregating preferences. But which set should be aggregated? Should it be the individual utility functions, or the individual SWFs? The answers may be very different, and if they are, which should be used? Those who argue that motives do not matter might respond that we should aggregate whatever preferences are revealed, whether they are self-interested or 'citizen' preferences, or some mixture of both. The neoclassical approach to economics is entirely consistent with weak anthropocentrism, i.e. values that are necessarily 'of' people but which may be 'for' any number of objects of concern. Even if it is true that hypothetical questionnaire approaches to willingness to pay elicit not self-interested preferences but 'warm glow' or 'moral satisfaction' (Kahneman and Knetsch, 1992), this is not an argument for calling such values 'non-economic', an observation that has been made repeatedly in the economic literature—see Arrow (1951), Becker (1993), and Harrison (1992).

Sagoff (1988) argues that environmental assets tend to be *public goods* in the sense that environmental improvement affects everyone (though not necessarily equally) and the relevant preferences for public goods must therefore be citizens' preferences. If so, what should be aggregated is individuals' SWFs, not their self-interested preferences. Thus, while we should allow purely self-interested motives to determine the allocation of *private goods*—goods that when consumed by one person cannot also be consumed by someone else—the very 'publicness' of the environment means that decisions must be left to individuals only if they exhibit public preferences.

The problem, of course, is how we are to know what the motives are for preferences. The spectre of social engineering looms large. Preferences for public goods would be 'allowed' if they exhibit citizenry but not if they exhibit self-interest, and it is far from clear how one would know which was which. It would be just as easy for any individual to insist they were behaving as citizens as it would be for politicians to reject public opinion because it is self-interested. This is clearly one more example of the age-old conflict between politicians deciding what is 'good' for society and reflecting people's preferences, however they are formed. Ultimately, the issue seems to reduce to being sure that we know people are informed about the context of their choices. It is true that few questionnaire-based approaches to eliciting willingness to pay explore the full context of a public good. They tend not, for example, to explain that the good in question will benefit everyone, and they rarely intimate that, in expressing a preference, respondents should take account of this fact of public benefit (Nyborg, 1996).

The issue of citizen versus individual preferences does seem to involve some issues about the design of questionnaire-based approaches to willingness to pay. It is not clear that it involves more than this, although it has been suggested that citizen preferences can be motivated by moral concerns which render not just aggregation impossible, but the monetary valuation of individual wellbeing impossible as well. It seems likely that individuals have very well-defined preference orderings over some states, but cannot compare those states with others. The 'preference set' is effectively compartmentalized into 'mental accounts'. One set of mental accounts may hold the moral views of the individual and these may not be traded off against goods that are in other 'accounts'. On the face of it this might explain the responses sometimes given to questions in stated-preference valuation approaches. Some people appear not to be willing to 'trade' the environment against other goods, or, stated differently, they refuse to cite a money value for an environmental good. The good in question is thought to have some moral dimension, or 'intrinsic value', that makes it 'non-tradable'.

Notions such as animal rights, rights of natural things, moral obligations to future generations, stewardship of the Earth, and so on, are invoked. In economic language the issue is one of 'lexical preferences': a particular good is preferred over all others and no amount of the other good can be substituted for it. The essential feature of lexicality is that it is not then possible to define the utility function of the individual. If so, WTP is a redundant concept and cannot be measured. Since CBA rests on the idea of trade-offs, lexicality undermines CBA as well.

But the evidence for lexicality is not as persuasive as might be imagined. It comes from questionnaire approaches where individuals appear to be refusing to trade-off the environment against money. Such refusals appear to confirm the view that people often act 'as citizens', i.e. take a moral view, when answering questionnaires. Some surveys have found that a minority of respondents have indicated intrinsic value as their motivation while simultaneously being unwilling to pay anything at all for conservation (Stevens *et al.*, 1991; Fredman, 1994; Hanley *et al.*, 1995). Thus, the Stevens *et al.* study suggested that 70 per cent or more of respondents agreed with the statement 'all species of wildlife have a right to exist independent of any benefit or harm to people'. Yet around 60 per cent of respondents refused to pay anything, and 25 per cent of these said wildlife values should not be measured in dollar terms. The objects of value in this study were salmon, bald eagles, wild turkeys, and coyotes. Seventy per cent of respondents in the study by Fredman, of white-backed woodpeckers in Sweden, suggested that rights to existence defined their motivation for positive willingness to pay. The Hanley study also suggested that some 23 per cent of respondents were unwilling to trade off conservation of Caledonian pinewoods against money. But these studies could be criticized for not making the trade-off context as real as possible. Interestingly, a later study by Hanley and Milne (1996) found that 99 per cent of respondents thought that wildlife and landscape have a right to exist. But this percentage fell to 49 per cent when it was suggested that conservation costs money and jobs, and to 19 per cent when the cost was translated to be 25 per cent of the respondent's income. While the authors of this study see the remaining 19 per cent as a salutary reminder that not all individuals are willing to trade off conservation against other things, it is interesting that 80 per cent of respondents lost their belief in a rights-based approach as soon as the reality of trade-offs was presented to them. Arguably, rights may be easily assigned and defended when they cost little. Additionally, there are doubts as to the validity of ascribing lexical preferences in these studies. Foster and Mourato (1998) suggest that there are preference orderings which are consistent with the appearance of lexicality: effectively the individuals concerned are prepared to make a trade-off, but at a high price for surrendering the environment.

CBA, then, has philosophical underpinnings which have been re-peatedly questioned in the literature. Another current issue relates to the distinction between willingness to accept compensation (WTA) and willingness to pay (WTP). WTA seems appropriate when the policy or project in question involves a loss, and WTP is relevant when the context is one of gain. This is consistent with Hicks's original measures of consumer surplus. Two problems arise. Any potential gain can be measured by either WTP or WTA since we can always ask what someone is WTA to forgo the gain. Which should be used? The broad answer is that it is a matter of property rights. WTP is relevant when the person concerned does not have the property rights, and WTA is relevant when they do. In the former case we are seeking WTP for something to which they have no legal right. In the latter case we are obliged to compensate them for the loss of something to which they do have a right. But this broad answer may not be very helpful in the environmental context where no one may have 'rights'. For example, there are often rights to clean water defined in law, but no rights to clean air. There seem to be no rules for choosing between WTA and WTP for clean air. The issue gets even more complicated for globally shared environmental assets, such as the earth's climate. There are no 'rights' to the global atmosphere so it is not clear whether anyone should compensate anyone else for the effects of global warming or ozone-layer destruction. In practice, some of these ambiguities are reduced, though not eliminated, by legal agreements, e.g. the Frame-work Convention on Climate Change in the case of climate, and the Montreal Protocol in the case of ozone-layer depletion. Choosing WTA or WTP may be resolvable to some extent by looking at legal rights, but environmentalists tend to argue from a wider concern about moral rights, leaving ample scope for disagreement about what they are. Finally, choosing between WTP and WTA would not matter if, as was traditionally assumed, they do not differ. But the findings of many questionnaire-based approaches that have used both measures suggest that WTA is often markedly higher in size than WTP.

Benefits and costs stretch out over time. Since individuals tend to prefer the present to the future, and since human preferences are paramount in CBA (see the discussion on motivations above), this 'present orientation' has to be accounted for. Future benefits and costs are therefore discounted at some 'discount rate'. The resulting sums are 'present values', i.e. sums of discounted benefits and costs. The benefit–cost rule then becomes that the present value of benefits must exceed the present value of costs. A perennial issue on CBA is the choice of the discount rate, and it seems fair to say that it is no more a resolved issue today than it was 30 years ago.

There are two concepts that may be subject to discounting:

(i)   future *consumption* may be discounted because of some judgement that it will generate less 'wellbeing' than current consumption. This is consumption discounting;

(ii) future wellbeing may be discounted because people simply prefer their pleasures (benefits) now and their costs later. This is utility discounting.

The *social time preference rate* (STPR) incorporates both elements of discounting with the result that

$$s = \delta + \mu.g$$

where: s = social time preference rate of discount; δ = 'pure time preference', i.e. the rate at which wellbeing is discounted; μ = elasticity of the marginal utility of consumption schedule, i.e. the rate at which marginal utility declines as consumption increases; g = the expected growth rate of consumption *per capita* in the economy.

The second main candidate for estimating the social discount rate is the social opportunity cost of capital (SOC). The argument then is that investment will yield a rate of return, r, such that £1 invested today will yield $(1 + r)$ in one year's time, $(1+r)^2$ in two years' time, and so on. How much, then, is £1 in one year's time worth now? The answer must be that it is worth $1/(1+r)$ now since this sum growing at r per cent will be £1 in one year's time. The rate of return, r, is the marginal productivity of capital. A project yielding z per cent rate of return is not attractive unless z>r, so that r per cent becomes the discount rate against which actual returns are compared.

Cost–benefit appraisals often relate to public sector investments and public decision-making. The value of r could then be the marginal product of capital in the public sector, but it is more typically the marginal rate of return in the private sector. The rationale for using a private-sector rate of return to discount public-sector costs and benefits is that public investment is likely to be at the expense of the quantity of investment in the private sector. This usually reflects a judgement about the effects of 'crowding out' private-sector investments.

In a world of perfectly competitive markets $s = r$ (see Pearce, 1986). In practice, s and r diverge for various reasons, but notably because of the presence of taxation. Consider company taxation. Shareholders will expect a rate of return at least equal to s per cent, their own time preference rate. Companies have to pay a tax rate t per cent on their profits. Hence to provide shareholders with s per cent, companies must earn $s/(1-t)$ per cent. But this is the return on investment, i.e. the marginal productivity of capital. Hence SOC cannot equal STPR.

Pearce and Ulph (1999) estimate a social time preference rate for the United Kingdom. They divide the rate of time preference, δ, into two components. The first is the rate of 'pure' time preference, or utility discount rate, which we will denote by ρ. The second is any increase (or decrease) in the risk to life. Let L be the rate of growth of life chances. If life chances get worse through time, then this makes for a higher rate of time preference, whereas if they get better then this is an argument for a lower rate of time preference. Thus we have the following relationship:

$$\delta = \rho - L$$

so that the formula for the STPR becomes:

$$s = \rho - L + \mu.g.$$

Substantial debate surrounds each component of this formula, ranging from discussion about how to project the growth rate of *per-capita* consumption, to more philosophical concerns, such as whether it is morally correct to discount future utility at all. After a careful literature review, Pearce and Ulph conclude that 'central' values for the components are:

$$\rho = 0.3$$
$$L = -1.1$$
$$\mu = 0.83$$
$$g = 1.3$$

so that $s = 2.4$ per cent, with a credible range of 2–4 per cent.

How might r be estimated? The value of r might be estimated as the weighted average of returns to debt and equity in the private sector.

Debt could be represented by government bonds where relevant, or by interest rates on bank loans and advances. Rates of return in the private sector will be higher than in the public sector, owing to the fact that the private sector has to pay tax, as noted previously. This 'tax wedge' puts private rates of return above the rate of return to government bonds. In the United Kingdom, for example, it is suggested that the difference is between 3–4 per cent on government borrowing and 4–6 per cent for the marginal rate of return in the private sector.

While the debate continues, the calculations above suggest that the current government discount rate of 6 per cent is too high and that rates of perhaps half this would be justified.

An excellent treatment of the logic and practice of CBA can be found in Boardman *et al.* (1996).

4. Cost–Benefit Analysis in the USA

In the space available it is possible to provide only the briefest insight into the use of CBA in the USA. None the less, some reference is essential to set the scene for the UK analysis.

In the USA, CBA developed beyond the 1950s focus on water resources, extending into most areas of public policy, including education and health. A major impetus to CBA came with the Reagan Administration. Within weeks of taking office in 1981, President Reagan issued Executive Order 12291 required a CBA for all new major regulations. The order required, among other things, that 'regulatory objectives shall be chosen to maximize the net benefits to society', and that, for given regulatory objectives, 'the alternative involving the least net cost to society shall be chosen'. As Smith (1984) notes, this did not mean that CBA was carried out consistently or universally. Substantial areas of regulation are not subject to CBA. Indeed, some regulations explicitly forbid an appraisal of costs and benefits. Court rulings have also established that where the original enabling legislation does not mention costs and benefits, agencies may not consider them (for a detailed description of which environmental legislation is subject to CBA, see Morgenstern, 1997). None the less, CBA plays a significant role in regulatory assessment. In contrast, as we shall see, there has been a cautious trend in the UK towards a general requirement for *some sort* of regulatory CBA, but nothing as precise as the US legislation.

Much of the stimulus to CBA in the USA came, as it had in the 1950s, from a concern about efficiency in government. But whereas the earlier concern related to a real scarcity of government funds and political concerns with major *investments*, the 1980s and 1990s focus was on *regulation*. In particular, there was a political backlash against perceived excessive regulation and against clear inconsistencies and irrationalities in public controls. In the view of those concerned about regulation, CBA would help to prevent over-regulation. In the environmental arena, several attempts had already been made to test the consistency of environmental policy with a cost–benefit test. Freeman (1982) found that air and water pollution controls resulted in unrecorded gains in the US GNP of a little over 1 per cent. Put another way, the US GNP was understated by 1 per cent because of unmarketed gains. Portney (1990) suggests that US air-quality control policy had benefits in excess of costs in the early 1980s. Freeman (1990) found water-pollution control to have costs in excess of benefits for the mid-1980s. By far the most detailed benefit–cost assessment of US regulation has been produced by Robert Hahn (1996). Hahn first uses the regulatory agencies' own numbers to see which 1990–5 regulations pass a cost–benefit test. He concludes that around 50 per cent of final and proposed regulations would pass such a test, i.e. about 50 per cent would fail. Focusing on the Environmental Protection Agency regulations, Hahn finds aggregate net benefits of some $70 billion across 40 final regulations, and $18 billion across 21 proposed regulations. But only 12 out of the 40, and nine out of the 21 pass a benefit–cost test. More-detailed analysis suggests that only regulations relating to clean air and safe drinking water have benefits greater than costs. Turning to the quality of the estimates of benefits and costs, Hahn considers that agencies have an incentive to exaggerate benefits, while some regulations quite explicitly forbid a balancing of costs and benefits, thus providing no incentive to consider a CBA test. Some costs might be overstated, however. On balance he concludes that, if the estimates were to be recomputed by a 'neutral' economist, they would significantly reduce net benefits.

It is interesting to note these several attempts to compare costs and benefits across the whole of regulatory activity. No such exercise can be found elsewhere, and certainly not in the United Kingdom or Europe generally. Indeed, such an exercise would be immensely difficult precisely because no formal requirements existed to carry out a CBA prior to enactment or *ex post*. Sporadic assessments have taken place, but usually at the behest of Parliamentary Select Committees (e.g. see House of Lords (1994–5) on bathing water quality).

The other stimulus to the use of CBA in the USA came from legal actions for damages. The USA has a greater proclivity to use the courts than in Europe. Monetary valuation of damages is a natural means to determine court settlements and they have been widely used for this purpose, ranging from liability assessments under the 'Superfund' legislation (which deals with clean-up of hazardous waste sites) to probably the most well-known settlement for pollution damages, the *Exxon Valdez* case of 1989, in which an Exxon tanker spilled oil into Prince William Sound in Alaska (Carson *et al.*, 1995). In contrast, Europe has only some environmental liability legislation and there is no tradition of 'taking CBA to court' (Kopp and Smith, 1989).

5. Cost–Benefit Analysis in the UK: The Emergence of Regulatory Appraisal

CBA has had a chequered history in the United Kingdom. Its first application was project-based and was to road transport. Britain's first motorway was the M1 from London to Birmingham. The application of CBA was, in fact, experimental rather than an integral part of the assessment. Had the CBA shown excess costs, the motorway would still have proceeded. Costs of construction were compared with the benefits in terms of working and non-working time saved, reduced accidents, and changes in fuel consumption and vehicle wear and tear (Coburn *et al.*, 1960). A little later the London Victoria underground railway was evaluated in CBA terms (Foster and Beesley, 1963), an interesting study because the line was not justified in purely financial terms, but was found to be profitable from a social standpoint once all time savings had been included. A consistent feature of these early studies was the total neglect of environmental impacts. The (then) Department of Transport Manual—'COBA'—for using CBA (Highways Agency, 1997a) continues to exclude environmental impacts, although these are treated in extensive detail in non-monetary terms in a separate extensive publication (Highways Agency, 1997b).

The past resistance of the Department of Transport (now merged with the Department of the Environment) to extending CBA to environmental impacts has never been easy to explain, not least because the revealed and stated preference techniques required for monetizing environmental impacts—which are excluded from COBA—are the same as those used to value travel time savings and accidents, which are included in COBA. The Standing Advisory Committee on Trunk Road Assessment (SACTRA), which advises the Department of Transport, consistently advised against monetization, sometimes on the basis of curious arguments and limited appreciation of the literature (e.g.

SACTRA, 1992).[3] None the less, opposition to the use of monetization has slowly eroded. The merger of the Department of Transport and the Department of the Environment in 1997 also posed a problem of consistency: Transport was not committed to monetization, whereas much of Environment was.

Part of the slow progress in transport was probably due to an unwillingness to embrace these techniques in contexts where political opposition at public inquiries was likely to be highest. In part, this reluctance was reinforced among the older generation of civil servants by the experience of the massive public inquiry — the 'Roskill Commission' — into the siting of London's third airport in 1969–71 (Commission on the Third London Airport, 1971). A government-appointed research team concluded that an inland site was preferred on cost–benefit grounds. Most significantly, apart from savings in air and ground travel time (which together dominated the analysis) the team attempted to value noise nuisance and disamenity through an estimation of impacts on house prices (the hedonic property-price approach). By today's standards, the study was primitive, but it was the first significant attempt to estimate environmental impacts in monetary terms (for a subsequent formalization of the noise model, see Walters (1975)). Environmental opposition to the study was intense and it is easy to see why, when, according to the Commission, environmental costs amounted to less than a half of one per cent of total social costs at the preferred site, and only 1.5 per cent at the 'worst site'. Moreover, the CBA took place against a totally contrary political back-drop since the Commission's *least* preferred site, Foulness on the coast, was the only one supported by any of the county authorities. The Commission was subject to some ridicule for allegedly placing a fire insurance value on an historic Norman church at one site. In fact this was only a suggestion at one stage, and never appeared in the final report, despite continuing erroneous comment that it did — see, for example, Grove-White (1997). None the less, the damage was done. Not only did the Commission's least preferred site become the government's chosen site, but CBA suffered consequently from the adverse criticism (for a full discussion see Pearce, 1970; and Dasgupta and Pearce, 1972).

[3] Similarly, the UK Royal Commission on Environmental Pollution (RCEP), dominated by scientists and with little expertise in environmental economics, has never strongly favoured monetization of environmental impacts, the closest support coming in its 18th report on road transport (RCEP, 1994). But an entire report on soil degradation never once mentions the economic cost of soil erosion (RCEP, 1996). While governments are obliged to take account of and respond to Royal Commission reports there is little evidence to suggest that the Commission affects mainstream thinking.

As in the USA, CBA began with project applications, reflecting the way in which the underlying theory itself developed, and only later came to be applied to policy. Other areas where CBA had an influence on project decisions include the following.

(i)   The Aldburgh sea flood defence wall. The significance here was that this was the first use of contingent valuation results commissioned by the Ministry of Agriculture and accepted by HM Treasury. The Treasury had always shown scepticism towards the results of questionnaire-based approaches (Turner *et al.*, 1992).

(ii) The conservation plan for the Norfolk Broads. The economic valuation study commissioned by the Ministry of Agriculture notably included an assessment of non-use values which were shown to dominate the overall valuation of benefits. Aside from the controversy over contingent valuation, there is a separate debate about the 'relevance' of non-use values to CBA (Bateman *et al.*, 1992; Bateman *et al.*, 1995; and Bateman and Langford, 1997).

(iii) A cluster of local authority issues such as local sea defence schemes.

Turning to CBA and *policy*, although some bodies, such as House of Lords Select Committees, had for some time been putting pressure on government to indicate the costs and benefits of European Directives, the modern period of CBA in British government dates from the late 1980s with the first effective environment 'White Paper' (DoE, 1990*a*).[4] While there had long been pressure to put environmental concerns further up the political agenda, most of the argument has been along traditional conservationist lines. In 1987 the United Nations had produced the 'Brundtland Report' on sustainable development (World Commission on Environment and Development, 1987). The report was extremely influential. While failing to recognize many of the inevitable trade-offs between environment and economic development, the Commission none the less established environment as a key element of economic policy. Basically, all economic activity affects environment, and many environmental policies positively affect the economy, for example, through improved health and productivity. While these were

---

[4] My attention has been drawn to an earlier White Paper under the Wilson government of 1970.

familiar messages to environmental economists, they secured a world-wide platform with the Brundtland Commission's report. Since countries were obliged to respond to the report, the UK Department of the Environment commissioned a report to interpret the meaning of sustainable development and to define the outlines of a coherent environmental strategy. The resulting 'Pearce Report' (Pearce *et al.*, 1989) secured massive media coverage for its emphasis on market-based instruments, especially pollution taxes, and on monetization of environmental impacts. The report was (generally) sympathetically received within government, in part, because it is evident now that some internal efforts had been made several years previously to secure adoption of a similar agenda.

Why did these changes occur? Several factors were at work, some of which were not peculiar to environmental policy.

First, the sheer 'weight' of research in applied environmental economics had grown to such proportions in the late 1980s that it would have been difficult for anyone to ignore it. Arguably, policy would have had to respond sooner or later.

Second, there was a renewed emphasis on efficiency in public expenditure in an effort to meet overall macroeconomic objectives of controlling public expenditure generally, and because of continuing publicity over waste in local and central government. As in the USA, CBA appeared to hold out the prospect of delivering some of that efficiency.

Third, there was the continuing underlying theme of deregulation in an effort to reduce the perceived costs of regulation on business and on competitiveness. Indeed, 'deregulation units' were subsequently established in government departments, with a central unit in the Cabinet Office, and guidance was issued on regulatory appraisal. A Deregulation Task Force recommended in 1995 that:

> no regulatory proposal affecting business should be entertained by a Minister without a proper CCA [compliance cost assessment]. Ministers should be required to personally sign off all CCAs and risk assessments. No regulatory proposal should be considered collectively by Ministers without a certificate signed by the responsible Minister that he has read both the risk assessment and CCA, and that he believes that the balance between costs and benefits has been appropriately struck. (Cabinet Office, 1996)

Echoing Presidential Executive Order 12291 in the USA, regulatory appraisal became a requirement for all regulatory proposals affecting business. Such appraisals might include a risk assessment (construed as an assessment of uncertainty) but would always include a compliance cost assessment (CCA) indicating the costs to UK industry of complying with the regulation. In fact, since April 1993 CCAs had been required for all legislation that might have an impact on business. In 1994 this was extended to the impacts on small businesses. Essentially, what began as a narrowly focused exercise, estimating only the costs to business, was broadened in 1996 to include economy-wide costs and some effort at estimating benefits.[5] It remains the case that regulatory appraisals vary substantially in the information they contain and few would qualify as a comprehensive cost–benefit appraisal.

Fourth, and perhaps less significantly, the European Commission had begun to embrace formal cost–benefit appraisal of proposals for Directives and Amendments to Directives. This it had done in light of Article 130R(3) of the Single European Act which, while not explicitly referring to CBA, clearly mandated some form of cost–benefit appraisal. The UK probably cannot be thought of as a 'follower' in this respect, however, since it had been instrumental in getting the clause included in the Act because of growing concerns about the cost of regulations. The decision contrasts with an earlier refusal by the Commission to estimate costs and benefits, despite an explicit request from the European Parliament to do so (ENDS, 1980). The background to the Commission's decision is documented in Pearce (1998a).

Fifth, as we have seen, environmental issues had risen up the political agenda because of the stance adopted towards sustainable development. One of the central features of sustainable development is the pervasive role of environment in all decisions. Environment had therefore to be treated seriously and formally: there was a need to know how it could be incorporated into decision-making. The advances in project appraisal and monetary evaluation of environmental impacts held out considerable promise in this respect.

6. Cost–Benefit Analysis in the UK: Official Guidance on Environmental Appraisal

One outcome of these changes was *Policy Appraisal and the Environment* (Department of the Environment (DoE), 1991a). This document sought to give guidance on environmental appraisal techniques for project and policy evaluation, and the guidance includes monetary evaluation,

---

[5] From 1993 to 1995 the focus appears to have been on compliance costs only. In 1996, new guidance asked departments to estimate benefits where possible (Department of Trade and Industry (DTI), 1996). Risk assessment is construed to mean that uncertainties in estimates are addressed. CCA combined with risk assessment (RA) is referred to as CCRA. Actual CCAs are listed in formal Cabinet Office statements to Parliament and full CCAs are available from individual departments.

along with risk assessment (which was the subject of separate subsequent guidance, see DoE, 1995a), and multicriteria analysis. Although
unstated, there was a presumption that monetization and cost–benefit
analysis were more favoured. This is consistent with guidance from the
UK Treasury which had long published a 'Green Book' for guiding
government departments in their appraisal work. The latest issue (UK
Treasury, 1997) is couched mainly in terms of monetized costs and
benefits, although explicit attention is paid to situations where
monetization is thought not to be possible. In 1997 the then Department
of the Environment issued a discussion paper on costs and benefits in
the context of environmental policy and competitiveness (DoE, 1997a).
This signalled a concern not to identify environmental regulations only
with 'drag' effects on the economy, but with opportunities as well, for
example in the abatement technology sector.

Some indication of the commitment to more rigorous approaches to
policy was the follow-up to *Policy Appraisal and the Environment*.
Consultants were hired to see how far the guidelines were being
implemented. The indications were the guidance was too long and
detailed for those who need to provide rapid guidance on the environmental implications of policy initiatives and too short for those requiring technical guidance (Department of the Environment, Transport and
Regions (DETR), 1997b). An investigation into what guidance was, in
fact, available revealed that there were numerous 'manuals' and
guidelines on CBA for sectoral use, especially in the water sector
(EFTEC, 1998), but most related to projects rather than policies. Policy
appraisal might differ because of the scale and pervasiveness of the
effects of policy — errors could be catastrophic politically, whereas
project failure can usually be confined. Policy appraisal also faces many
more uncertainties than project assessment, although the problems are
far from fatal as the US experience shows.

Brief guidance on policy appraisal was issued by the DETR in 1998
(DETR, 1998f). It advises that several steps are required to assess the
possible environmental impact of a policy: (a) impacts can be broadly
assessed by 'screening'; (b) only significant impacts matter and significance should be tested with the screening process; (c) screening
involves checklists based on the likely implications of the policy for the
consumption of natural resources — water, greenfield land, materials,
energy; the creation of waste; the creation of emissions to air and
effluent to water; and the increase in global pollutants; (d) attention
should be paid to second- and higher-order impacts: e.g. the creation
of one effect may exacerbate another effect (e.g. loss of greenfield sites
may increase biodiversity loss); and (e) costs and benefits should be

quantified where possible. While the guidance reaffirms the role to be played by formal assessment techniques, and by CBA in particular, it offers no guidance on how a 'significant' impact is to be measured or what significance means. More to the point, the guidance is little more than the bare bones of any rational approach to policy-making. The fact of its issue suggests that the need to impose some sort of elementary order on decision-making is still needed, despite the decades of work on cost–benefit and other appraisal procedures.

7. Cost–Benefit Analysis in the UK: The Record

The 1997 consultants' report on the use of the *Policy Appraisal* guidelines revealed that there was a long way to go before CBA was widely adopted across government departments. This is especially true in contexts where policy is primarily non-environmental but has environmental consequences. For overtly environmental policy, however, CBA has secured a much stronger foothold. Table 1 attempts to list major policy decision areas and the input from CBA studies. It should be noted that full cost–benefit studies are rare: most deal either with the cost side or the benefit side. Only studies that were directly requisitioned for policy advice or which are cited by government sources as informing decision are included. There are many other cost–benefit studies. *Project-based* CBAs and documents containing guidance only are also excluded. There are numerous benefit-estimation studies of individual habitat protection and river-flow schemes—see Bateman *et al.* (1994) for an overview. Wetland schemes are reviewed in Brouwer *et al.*, (1997). However, a number of guidance documents for the water sector do contain recommended unit values for damages/benefits; these are included. In one or two cases, such work is not government-financed but has quasi-official status.

Table 1 suggests the following conclusions:

(i) in some areas, notably waste, monetary-benefit estimation has been extremely influential in determining policy. Notably, the initial setting of the UK landfill tax was based on monetary estimates of environmental costs;

(ii) benefit and damage studies are also being used to inform decisions on other possible market-based instruments, notably a pesticides tax and a tax on extraction of aggregates from quarries;

Table 1
Cost–Benefit Appraisals in Support of UK Environmental Policy
(relevant studies listed under environmental sectors)

Air quality

National air quality strategy, 1997 (DoE, 1997*b*). Used to 'inform' the policy but not to set objectives:

Sulphur dioxide: AEA (1996*a*) – compliance costs only; ApSimon *et al.* (1997) – benefits only.

Volatile organic compounds: AEA (1996*b*) – abatement costs only; ERM (1996) – abatement costs only.

(Low-level) ozone: AEA (nd1) – health, crops, and materials benefits.

Particulate matter: Pearce and Crowards (1996) – health benefits; Tinch (1996) – benefits; AEA (nd2) – compliance costs only.

Nitrous oxides: AEA (nd2) – compliance costs only; ApSimon *et al.* (1997) – benefits only.

Agricultural externalities

RPA (1997) – costs and benefits to farmers from policies aimed to reduce pesticide risks; ECOTEC (1997) – exploration of wider costs and benefits of pesticide reduction (extension in process); RPA (1995) – risks and benefits of reducing agro-chemicals.

Solid waste and minerals

CSERGE *et al.* (1993) – estimated environmental costs of landfill and incineration; basis for the landfill tax; London Economics (1998) – first estimates of damages from aggregates extraction; Mourato and Pearce (1998) – critique of London Economics (1998); EFTEC (1996) – costs and benefits of alternative uses of dredged harbour material.

Energy pricing

CSERGE (1992) – monetary value of externalities from electricity; CSERGE *et al.* (1994) – monetary values of externalities from renewable energy systems.

Chemicals

HSE carries out numerous CBAs of controls on various substances, mainly relating to occupation exposure, including propylene oxide, PCBs, platinum soluble salts, O-Toluidine, Iodomethane, cotton dust, softwood dust, azodicarbonamide, antimony, triglycidylisocyanurate (TGIC), and wool process dust.

Water

Foundation for Water Research (1997) – guide on unit values for benefit estimation; Garrod and Willis (1996) – benefits of low-flow alleviation; EFTEC *et al.* (1998) – guide on unit values; NERA (1998) – guide on unit values; RPA (1998) – guide on unit values; Georgiou *et al.* (1998*a,b*) – evaluation of benefits of complying with EC Bathing Waters Directive.

Forestry

Forestry Commission (1991); Pearce (1994).

Wildlife, habitat, and landscape

Numerous studies exist but their influence on policy appears to have been negligible – see Hodge and McNally (1998) and Garrod and Willis (1998).

Cultural heritage

Allison *et al.* (1996). Synopsis of studies showing that cultural heritage has significant economic value.

(ii) the setting of environmental standards is still determined by considerations unrelated to benefit estimates, e.g. critical loads, avoidance of health impacts, etc. None the less, CBA is being used indirectly to substantiate those targets and to help determine the time-paths for their achievement;

(iv) some agencies, such as the Health and Safety Executive (HSE) and the Forestry Commission, routinely use CBA. This use extends beyond project appraisal to the role of costs and benefits in setting risk standards (HSE) and in the justification of afforestation in terms of non-timber benefits (Forestry Commission);

(v) the Environment Agency has shown considerable interest in CBA, reflecting the requirements of the Environment Act of 1995 to take into account the likely costs and benefits of its actions, and to be excused from this requirement only if it is 'unreasonable' to do so. While the requirement does not formally mandate any particular form of CBA, considerable effort in the EA has gone into devising guidelines on the use of unit monetary values for assessing schemes and policies based on 'benefits transfer', i.e. the 'borrowing' of money values from one context for application in another context;

(vi) overall, substantially greater use is made of CBA and benefit estimation than is probably realized.

8. Obstacles to the Further Use of CBA

If CBA and benefit estimation are more widely used than is realized, it remains the case that there is substantial ambivalence both within government and among regulatory agencies towards their extended use. The sources of this resistance are several.

First, there continue to be doubts about the reliability of CBA studies, and especially about benefit estimation. There is substance to these doubts in the very nature of the environmental economics research process in Europe. The formal requirements to engage in CBA are not rigid, as with the Environment Act's mandate on CBA to the Environment Agency, or the new Regulatory Appraisal process for government departments. As such, CBA has developed from a mix of studies prepared unilaterally by academics for research interest, and by academics and consultancies for individual agencies and government departments. While the number of studies is surprisingly large, it is not large enough to provide a statistical base for benefits transfer. Combined with the fact that the science of economic valuation has evolved and still is evolving, uncertainty is endemic in the estimates. This uncertainty presents government with several problems. First, if policy was directly related to benefit estimates, then it is conceivable that the policy could be subject to legal challenge. This prospect is discounted by some experts because policy is, ultimately, whatever politicians decide it is. Only judicial review relating to unreasonable behaviour could challenge it. None the less, there is some explanation here for the distancing of policy from CBA results.

Second, there is outright hostility within some parts of government to some aspects of CBA, whatever the official guidance. Some of the traditional arguments against monetization are often emotive and irrational, but some coherence is afforded to these views from the belief that environmental assets are somehow 'different' and should not be subject to trade-offs. Academic studies which claim that individuals do not trade off environment and other goods—so-called 'lexical preferences' discussed in section 3—give some comfort to this view. Some hostility arises because it is thought that the use of a money metric 'debases' the environment, making it appear as if it is as saleable as a supermarket good. Interestingly, most discussions in the environmental ethics literature do not mention the notion of economic cost. Yet environmental conservation is not costless and any cost is a forgone benefit since the resources that make up cost could have been used elsewhere. In turn, forgone benefits embrace potential rights or obligations: perhaps the right to a livelihood, the right to work, the right to health care, etc. (Beckerman and Pasek, 1997). Opportunity costs, therefore, 'embody' rights and obligations, so that the correct ethical context is one of trade-offs between rights and obligations. Far from 'debasing' the environment, the use of the money metric is there to establish the fact that the correct context is one of trade-off, whether that is expressed in terms of costs and benefits, or competing ethical values. Only if the environment has some higher-order moral status than, say, helping the poor or the elderly, can there be a moral justification for ignoring cost.

Third, it is often argued that CBA is not 'transparent'. Highly varied and different costs and benefits are 'reduced' to single numbers, giving the impression of a 'black box' approach to policy. This is a valid criticism which could be surmounted by showing the sensitivities of the CBA outcome to various factors and by showing clearly which stakeholders gain and which lose. Sensitivity analysis tends to capture most of the former, but the latter is not a feature of most modern CBAs and should be. This may also help overcome the reasonable objection that most CBAs fail to identify the incidence of costs and benefits on different groups when, in most cases, this could easily be done. Trying to build a consensus among stakeholders about a policy change clearly explains the divergence of many policy outcomes from what would appear to be 'rational' on CBA grounds. This also explains some of the emphasis on 'process' which, taken to the limit, implies that, so long as the main stakeholders are assembled round a table, whatever is the outcome is for the best. Arguably, however, CBA reaches stakeholders who tend to be excluded from process—not everyone has a well-organized lobby or voice.

Fourth, and perhaps a cynical interpretation, CBA tends to present results in a reasonably cut and dried manner, subject to the uncertainty of the estimates. Benefits exceed or do not exceed costs. But decision-makers may place as much importance on flexibility of decision. A CBA that, in effect, removes that flexibility will not be welcome. At its worst, this view says that politicians will do whatever they want, and that they do not want to be troubled by cost–benefit studies that might produce the opposite answer: CBA 'crowds out' flexibility.

Fifth, as noted previously, CBA works best when the goal of policy is economic efficiency. Distributional considerations can be accounted for, as noted above, but their incorporation probably raises the level of discomfort that critics feel. Other goals, such as employment creation, protection of competitive position, and the desirability of the *process* of decision-making, tend to be omitted from CBA studies. While calling for more use of CBA in Europe, Navrud and Pruckner (1997) argue that the more formalized use of CBA in the USA owes more to the tradition there of emphasizing economic efficiency when compared to Europe. This may be true, but raises the issue of how best to accommodate multiple objectives if that is the desired goal. It is far from clear that other approaches fare any better than CBA. CBA is readily supplemented with an analysis of effects on competitiveness and employment, and modern practitioners of the contingent-valuation approach emphasize its role in securing public participation. None the less, these broader concerns may explain the current interest in the UK in multi-criteria techniques which have been popular for some time in the Netherlands. The Environment Agency has experimented with multi-criteria techniques for ranking project options. The, albeit limited, focus of multi-criteria approaches does reflect the fact that CBA is efficiency-oriented, whereas policy goals are often wider than efficiency alone. This offers one explanation for the apparent 'gap' between the current widespread practice of CBA and the fact that decisions appear not to be heavily influenced by CBA. If decision-making is rational, and efficiency was the only goal, then CBA should show up as being influential. But efficiency is not the only goal, nor are decisions always made rationally. It would, therefore, be surprising if CBA dominated actual decisions.

Sixth, the science of benefit estimation changes very rapidly. It is hard enough for academics specializing in the subject to maintain pace with the large published and even larger 'grey' literature. Busy civil servants are even less likely to be at the cutting edge of developments. Understandable ignorance of the literature does account for some continuing hostility to monetization.

Finally, CBA is practised with varying degrees of sophistication. If it is poorly executed, critics will use poor practice as a basis for criticizing the technique *per se*. The risks of poor practice are highest in benefits transfer, since the temptation to use existing studies to provide estimates for 'new' sites is a strong one: it saves the costs of an original study and is highly suited to approaches based on guidelines and manuals of practice. An interesting illustration of the problems arose with the public inquiry into Thames Water Company's proposal to extract borehole water from near the River Kennet. The proposal was opposed by the Environment Agency on the grounds that the abstractions would affect the flow of the Kennet which is a valuable chalk stream, is located in an Area of Outstanding Natural Beauty and is a Site of Special Scientific Interest. The Agency chose to use benefit assessment as its main case against Thames Water, adopting economic valuations recorded in a 'benefits manual' prepared by the Foundation for Water Research (FWR, 1997). No original study was carried out with respect to the Kennet. Since the issue was the effects of low flow on users and non-users, the relevant part of the FWR manual was that relating to studies of low-flow alleviation. In this case there was only one such study, and it related to the River Darent in Kent (Willis and Garrod, 1995; Garrod and Willis, 1996). The Darent study was itself of interest because non-use values, i.e. willingness to pay for flow improvement by individuals who did not visit the Darent at all, amounted to just under 90 per cent of the total benefits. The public expenditure part of the Darent low-flow alleviation was not fully authorized by government, even though it had received the Darent benefit assessment study which showed benefits greatly exceeding costs. Garrod and Willis (1996) speculate that failure to secure the full authorization arose from scepticism about the non-use value estimates in the Darent study. Despite this experience, the Environment Agency borrowed the Darent study estimates for both use and non-use values and applied them to the Kennet. The risks in such an exercise are considerable, and the problem was compounded by multiplying the individual non-use values per person by an arbitrary population defined as the population served by the Thames Water company. The end result was that Thames Water's appeal against the Agency's original restriction on abstraction was upheld by the public inquiry. The Inquiry Inspector reduced the non-use value component of the Kennet benefits by 98 per cent to just £0.3m compared to £13.2m as estimated by the Agency. The adjustment reflected the reduction of the 'affected' non-use population from the 7.5m people in the Thames Water area to just 100,000.

For some, the Kennet decision was a serious blow to CBA (e.g. see ENDS, 1998*b*). But an alternative view is that the Agency was pursuing a risky misuse of CBA by borrowing figures from a manual which in turn had to rely on just one, albeit well-executed, study of a single river. Benefits transfer is controversial in its own right and few practitioners adopt it without serious reservations (Brouwer and Langford, 1997). Misusing benefits transfer is not a criticism of CBA in itself. The proper course of action in the Kennet case should have been an original benefit assessment. But the controversy has focused attention on an important issue of how to define the relevant population for non-use values, an issue that is debated in the literature (Bateman and Langford, 1997).

9. Conclusions

CBA has gone through cycles of favour and disfavour in the UK. Currently, it is in favour. This may not be obvious from a casual inspection of government and regulatory agency activity, but it is clear that CBA studies are multiplying and that they are exerting some influence. There are more studies than might be thought, and they are also having more bearing on individual pieces of legislation than might be expected. But their role should not be exaggerated. There is a much smaller tradition of using CBA for regulatory appraisal and for damages settlements in Europe than there is in the USA. In the UK, notable developments that are leading to a change in that situation are the development of formal regulatory appraisal for all new regulation, and the requirements upon the Environment Agency to use CBA. In mainland Europe, a similar stimulus has come from Article 130R of the Treaty on European Union (Pearce, 1998*a*). If damage legislation were ever to develop in Europe, there would be further stimulus to benefit estimation. One area where benefit estimation could be expected to develop is in the public inquiry process. Surprisingly, few public inquiries are informed by benefit estimates, an issue that requires a separate explanation on some other occasion.

Obstacles remain. Monetization is controversial. Much of the controversy is misplaced and reflects on poor understanding of what monetization is about, but some of it has substance and needs to be addressed. In some cases, the obstacles can be overcome by improving the way in which CBA is presented and carried out. In other cases, the ethical debate is to the fore, and in many cases it raises many pertinent issues. Arguably, advocates of CBA have overstated their case, making it sound as if CBA substitutes for decision-making. It can, at best, inform decision-making and it is important that it does so since economic efficiency is all too easily forgotten in the political process. Finally, the issue is whether we have anything better as a decision aid. Here there has to be doubt. CBA still seems the 'best game in town'.

4

The Economics of Technology-based Environmental Standards

DAVID PEARCE*

1. Introduction

All environmental standards, however implemented, impose costs on the regulated party. This is true of emission or ambient quality standards, environmental taxes, tradable emission permits, and standards based on the 'best available technology'. Not surprisingly, therefore, all environmental regulation is, to a greater or lesser degree, the outcome of some political balancing of costs and benefits. Part, at least, of the initial cost is passed on to final consumers (the extent depends on the price elasticity of demand), which is consistent with the *polluter pays principle* (OECD, 1975). The *costs* of regulation are therefore borne by society as a whole. The *benefits* of regulation are also shared by society as a whole, although some groups in society may benefit more than others and, where trans-boundary pollution is involved, different *countries* will receive variable benefits.

While there has been some transition to market-based instruments in OECD countries, such as environmental taxes and tradable permits (Stavins, 2000), most environmental legislation is still based on standard setting, and most of that is, in turn, based on some form or other of a best available technology (BAT) prescription. In essence, BAT requires that individual sources of emissions should adopt that emissions control technology which affords the highest level of environmental protection, subject to the 'availability' of this technology. As we see shortly, however, even this definition is open to several different interpretations. Additionally, most legislation has attenuated the 'best technology' concept by making reference to some notion of cost, such that a technology that is both 'best' and 'available' may none the less not

* Centre for Social and Economic Research on the Global Environment (CSERGE), University College London.
This paper extends and updates an earlier paper, Pearce and Brisson (1993).

be prescribed because it is 'excessively costly'. Again, the notion of excessive cost is open to several interpretations, so that concepts such as 'best available technology not entailing excessive cost' (BATNEEC) are far from being unambiguous.

Effectively, then, BATNEEC, and similar cost-attenuated concepts, imply that the highest possible levels of environmental protection may not be worth achieving. The implicit process of balancing costs and benefits can be identified in a number of environmental standards. The result is a welter of acronyms for standard setting, none of which can be defined in any precise sense. This lack of precision is deliberate since unambiguous language would inhibit the flexibility of regulators, and polluters, to set standards according to professional judgement. The scope for judgement defines the 'bargaining space' between regulator and polluter. In turn, this bargaining space is what brings regulator and polluter together in what Helm (1998b) describes as: 'a classic example of . . . "good chaps regulation": provide a flexible and broad public-interest objective, and rely on selecting individuals with "good" judgement. The corollary is that the quality and shape of regulation depends heavily on the personalities involved' (Helm, 1998b, p. 14).

Given this regulatory culture, it is unsurprising to find equally fuzzy definitions for standards such as 'best practicable means' (BPM), 'best practicable environmental option' (BPEO), 'as low as reasonably achievable' (ALARA – used in radiation protection contexts), 'prudent avoidance' (PA – used in the context of electromagnetic radiation contexts), and the 'precautionary principle' (PP). The precautionary principle is embodied in the Treaty on European Union and in international agreements such as the Framework Convention on Climate Change. Yet its practical meaning has been widely interpreted by governments to include some reference to the costs of taking precautionary action.

Surprisingly, there is only a very small literature on the economics of technology-based standards, perhaps because economists have generally regarded them as part and parcel of traditional 'command and control' approaches to environmental legislation. Much of the literature has been concerned to demonstrate the superiority of market-based approaches over command-and-control approaches, thus neglecting any detailed examination of what constitutes command and control. This chapter seeks to redress the balance by looking closely at one of the 'cost-attenuated' concepts of technology-based controls, BATNEEC. As implied above, the findings can be applied to other, similar concepts where a technology standard is recommended. The context for discussion will be the changes in UK environmental regulatory legislation in the last decade, and the perspective is that of economics, because economic analysis has particular insights to offer.

2. BATNEEC in UK Legislation[1]

Technology-based standards have a long history in the UK. The National Society for Clean Air (NSCA, 1996) dates the concept of 'best practicable means' (BPM) to an 1842 law in Leeds which enabled fines to be imposed on anyone not using BPM to abate smoke nuisance. The Alkali Act of 1863 became the first wide-ranging control on air pollution, and an 1874 Amendment required the use of BPM to abate emissions from alkali works. It is clear that, from the outset, the term 'practicable' referred to the financial cost of introducing the control measure, and that the relevant cost is the cost to the emitting industry, not the cost to the nation. We see later that this focus changes as the legislation develops. The Alkali Acts were subsequently extended to all major industrial processes and consolidated in the Alkali etc. Works Regulation Act of 1906. The Alkali Inspectorate had powers to fine or even close down non-complying sources. The Inspectorate issued 'BMP Notes' advising polluters of the available technologies. The Inspectorate was renamed as Her Majesty's Industrial Air Pollution Inspectorate in 1983, and in 1987 a unified inspectorate system was created as Her Majesty's Inspectorate of Pollution (HMIP). HMIP covered air pollution, hazardous wastes, radiochemicals, and some serious water pollution. At this stage, BPM was still the prevailing standard-setting philosophy. Anyone meeting any established emission limits was assumed to be employing BPM, even though BPM might, technically, achieve lower emissions. Note that BPM or BAT always implies an emission limit since the choice of technology will determine the emission levels. The sequence, however, is not from desired emission limits to choice of technology, but from choice of 'best' technology to the implied emission limit.

A major change came in 1990 with the Control of Pollution Act.

The first change was the introduction of 'integrated pollution control' (IPC) which was designed to deal with the problems arising from controlling emissions to a single receiving environment. Effective evasion of control was possible if processes were changed to emit to other receiving media. IPC therefore regulated cross-media emissions such that the emitting source had to demonstrate the use of the 'best practicable environmental option'. BPEO had been introduced as far back as 1976 by the Royal Commission on Environmental Pollution (RCEP, 1976) as a term requiring that the *total* impact on the environ-

---

[1] We have ignored the distinctions between England and Wales, and Scotland for ease of exposition, but separate legislation is involved.

ment was minimized in a multi-media pollution context. The Commission had also recommended a unified pollution inspectorate embracing air, water, and waste, but the recommendation had not been accepted by the UK government. The Royal Commission returned to the BPEO concept several times, in its 10th, 11th, and 12th reports (RCEP, 1984, 1985, 1988). While a unified inspectorate remained excluded from the Control of Pollution Act, HMIP's powers were extended, though waste remained largely under the control of local authorities, and water pollution under the control of the National Rivers Authority (NRA).

The second change under the 1990 Act was the introduction of BATNEEC to replace BPM. The Department of the Environment (DoE) declared that the change was 'for the sake of international consistency of terminology' (DoE, 1988). In other words, BPM and BATNEEC were not distinct. BATNEEC had actually already been introduced at the European level in the Air Framework Directive of 1984 (84/360/EEC). The Directive refers to BATNEEC in terms of '*technology*' whereas the Environmental Protection Act of 1990 makes the 't' refer to '*techniques*'. The difference is significant since technology tends to imply end-of-pipe solutions which can easily conflict with any requirement to minimize the costs of compliance on emitting sources, while technique embraces wider compliance mechanisms, e.g. managerial and organizational change, energy conservation etc. Thus the 1990 Act was already broadening the nature of technology-based standards. While the notion of cost still appeared to refer to the costs borne by the emitting source, some ambiguity was beginning to enter the advice given by government and regulators about BATNEEC.

Guidance issued by the then Department of the Environment (DoE) and the Welsh Office (1993) offered some definitions of BATNEEC. 'Best' means the most effective technique for reducing and rendering harmless polluting emissions. 'Available' means that the technique is generally accessible to emitters, regardless of whether it is available in the UK or outside it, and regardless of the competitive conditions under which it is supplied. 'Technique' refers to technology but also to factory lay-out, staff qualifications, working methods, training, etc. 'NEEC' is given two contexts: new processes and existing processes.

For *new processes*, the cost of BAT must be weighed against the environmental damage done, although nothing is said about how this comparison is to be carried out. But, the greater the damage, the higher is the cost burden that would be allowed before it is regarded as being 'excessive'. In other words, BAT here has an effective cost–benefit interpretation, although benefits are not interpreted in monetary terms. The bigger the harm, the bigger the cost of control that can be justified. If serious harm remains even after the application of BATNEEC, an authorization can still be refused. For *existing processes* the same considerations apply, but in the context of a timetable to bring the process up to BATNEEC standards. A subtle ambiguity thus creeps into the BAT/BATNEEC concepts. On one interpretation the NEEC concept appears to refer to the costs to the emitting sources rather than the costs to the nation as a whole. On a second interpretation, the focus moves to costs commensurate with the environmental damages in question, i.e. big damages justify big costs of control and without reference to the impact of the costs on industry cost structures.

In 1996 further changes occurred. The Environment Act of 1995 provided for the HMIP, the NRA, and local-authority waste regulators to be combined in one organization—the Environment Agency (EA), finally bringing about the Royal Commission's recommendation of some 20 years earlier. Nearly all regulatory activity was thus under one authority, exceptions being the Drinking Water Inspectorate and regulation of discharges to sewers. Significantly, the Agency must take into account likely costs and benefits of its actions, although precisely what this means was not defined. Moreover, this duty to consider costs and benefits must be observed unless it is 'unreasonable' for it to do so. The 'cost–benefit' requirement was the subject of extensive debate during the passage of the Environment Bill that preceded the Act of 1995. It remains the case to this day that the precise meanings of the cost–benefit requirement and the meaning of 'unreasonable' are unclear. The Agency has embraced cost–benefit analysis in a significant number of activities, notably the regulation of the water companies, but has interpreted the concept broadly in other contexts to embrace some form of multi-criteria analysis ('scoring and weighting') or cost-effectiveness analysis. At no stage does the Agency appear to have linked the cost–benefit requirement to BATNEEC, even though it is obliged to adopt both concepts in its regulatory stance.

The final piece of legislation of relevance is the European Commission's introduction of the Integrated Pollution Prevention and Control Directive of 1996 (Directive 96/61). IPPC and IPC are conceptually the same but IPPC extends beyond IPC in terms of the range of activities to which it will apply. The industries covered include energy production (above 50 MW rating), metals production and processing, minerals, chemicals, waste management, and 'other' industries including pulp and paper production, tanning, textiles, food processing, and intensive livestock production. The UK Department of the Environment, Transport and the Regions (DETR) estimates that 5,600 installations are covered by IPPC, an additional 440 by (UK) IPC, and 11,500 further installations are covered by UK local air pollution control (LAPC)

(DETR, 1999c). Integrated permits are required in keeping with the integrated pollution control philosophy, and issues also covered include waste minimization, energy efficiency, resource utilization, accidents, and site restoration. New or substantially modified installations must apply IPPC from October 1999 and existing installations no later than October 2007.

The focus of IPPC also moves away from emissions to source reduction, i.e. the avoidance of emissions rather than their end-of-pipe treatment. Thus energy must be used efficiently. Most importantly, for current purposes, is the fact that BATNEEC (with t = technology) is not adopted. Instead, BAT is favoured (but with t = techniques). The NEEC element common to earlier legislation has thus disappeared, but the use of the term 'technique' suggests that the focus on emission control technology has also given way to wider options for preventing emissions at source through management regimes and general environmental 'good practice'. IPPC does not, however, set aside national legislation. Its compatibility with other EU legislation has been the subject of some discussion, e.g. the extent to which IPPC BAT would overrule any less strict standard embodied in specific EU legislation (Emmott, 1999).

Once again, the BAT in IPPC is defined vaguely. This remains the case even though the European Commission will issue 'BAT reference notes' showing how emission limit values have been derived in various member states. These notes are seen more as exchanges of information within the EU rather than prescribing what BAT is. What then of the NEEC component? According to the UK Department of the Environment, '(technology) upgrading requirements are not expected to change as a result of the change in terminology from "BATNEEC" to "best available techniques" ' (DETR, 1999c). In other words, the new BAT is equivalent to the old BATNEEC.

The compatibility of IPPC with some market-based instruments, especially tradable permits, has been questioned. By definition, a technology-based standard, if met by all relevant installations, leaves little room for the trading of emissions through a tradable-permits regime. If BAT is not overly rigorously defined, however, then trading could take place to the mutual cost advantage of the participants. Similarly, if the unit of control — the 'installation' — is broadly construed to be a *set* of installations, then at least intra-site trading might take place without breaching IPPC standards. As it happens, carbon dioxide is not listed as a controlled pollutant in the IPPC Directive. This suggests that carbon trading could occur provided the requirement to use energy efficiently is not narrowly defined to be applicable to each and every installation. A broader approach involving negotiated agreements has been entertained (DETR, 1999d). On this option, a negotiated agreement covering a whole sector could be presented as ensuring overall sector compliance with IPPC, i.e. on average, an IPPC standard would be met. But since the compliance relates to an average achievement, some installations would under-comply and some would over-comply, opening the way for a trading regime. Unfortunately, the legal basis for this solution is not clear and the reaction of the European Commission is, at the time of writing, unknown. The issue is of fundamental importance to the nature of the Climate Change Levy (CCL) regime in the UK whereby an energy-cum-carbon tax is being imposed and where emitters can secure exemptions if they negotiate a successful self-regulation scheme with the government. Tradable-permit regimes are one of the features of the agreement packages.[2]

This potted history of legislative developments in the UK in the last decade serves to illustrate several things. First, despite all the changes in terminology, the notion that the cost of introducing cleaner technology is a reasonable defence for not securing the highest environmental standards has remained embedded in the legislation for over 150 years. Second, while the notion of cost appears throughout to be confined to the cost to the polluter from purchasing some technology or making some change in 'technique', the idea that bigger environmental damages would justify bigger cost impositions suggests that cost is being more widely construed. The implied idea is of the cost to the nation as a whole, since justifying large costs because of high pollution shifts the focus away from the cost to the industry in terms of its financial viability. Third, there has been a distinct and welcome shift from 'best technology' to 'best technique', making the regime more flexible than when originally introduced. Fourth, the regime has shifted from media-by-media controls to cross-media controls. Fifth, technology-based standards have been introduced and extended without due thought for the problems they create for potentially cost-saving measures such as tradable permits. Sixth, while never explicit, cost-attenuated technology standards can be shown to be consistent with cost–benefit thinking, i.e. bigger benefits from control justify bigger costs of control.

We now turn to a more detailed economic analysis of technology-based standards.

---

[2] Although at the time of writing it is not clear that trading itself will result in any exemptions from the CCL. The government appears to see trading as profitable in itself.

3. The Economics of Technology-based Standards

It is widely recognized that technology-based environmental standards have the potential for being *economically inefficient* (Ackerman and
Hassler, 1981; Førsund, 1992). This is because, as Helm (1992) states,
BATNEEC 'is a classic command-and-control instrument of regulation
. . . Regulators decide, on the basis of a case-by-case analysis, and after
detailed discussions with the firms concerned, what the right answer
ought to be'. There are three types of inefficiency.

First, depending on how 'technique' is defined, BATNEEC will
involve a choice of technology or management options which need not
coincide with the *least-cost* option for controlling emissions. 'BAT' tends
to refer to 'end-of-pipe' options—e.g. a flue-gas-desulphurization
plant—whereas a menu of technologies and techniques is usually
available—e.g. fuel switching, energy conservation, environmental
taxes, output adjustments, etc. If BAT or BATNEEC is not the least-cost
option, then adoption of technology-based standards gives rise to a
form of 'X-inefficiency' (Leibenstein, 1966) in regulation: a higher cost
of control than is necessary per unit of emission reduction (see Figure
1 and Table 1). Førsund (1992) shows that BAT/BATNEEC is necessarily inefficient in the cost sense since it fails to account for output changes.

Figure 1
The Potential Inefficiencies of BATNEEC

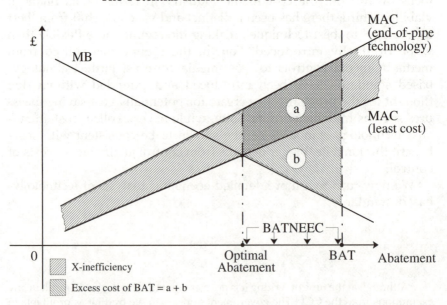

Note: (a) is X-inefficiency beyond the optimum; (b) is cost of not specifying the
optimum correctly.

Table 1
Empirical Studies of Air Pollution Control

Study	Pollutants covered	Geographic area	CAC benchmark	Ratio of CAC cost to least cost
Atkinson and Lewis	Particulates	St Louis	SIP regulations	6.00[a]
Roach et al.	Sulphur dioxide	Four Corners in Utah, Colorado, Arizona, and New Mexico	SIP regulations	4.25
Hahn and Noll	Sulphates	Los Angeles	California emission standards	1.07
Krupnick	Nitrogen dioxide regulations	Baltimore	Proposed RACT	5.96[b]
Seskin et al.	Nitrogen dioxide regulations	Chicago	Proposed RACT	14.40[b]
McGartland	Particulates	Baltimore	SIP regulations	4.18
Spofford	Sulphur dioxide	Lower Delaware Valley	Uniform percentage regulations	1.78
	Particulates	Lower Delaware Valley	Uniform percentage regulations	22.00
Harrison	Airport noise	United States	Mandatory retrofit	1.72
Maloney and Yandle	Hydrocarbons	All domestic Du Pont plants	Uniform percentage reduction	4.15[c]
Palmer et al.	CFC emissions from non-aerosol applications	United States	Proposed emission standards	1.96
London Economics	Sulphur dioxide	United Kingdom (excl. Northern Ireland)	Separate emission quotas for the electricity industry	1.16

Notes: CAC = command and control, the traditional regulatory approach; SIP = state implementation plant; RACT = reasonable available control technologies, a set of standards imposed on existing sources in non-attainment areas.
[a] Based on a 40 µg/m^3 at worst receptor.
[b] Based on a short-term, 1-hour average of 250 µg/m^3.
[c] Based on 85 per cent reduction of emissions from all sources.
Sources: Adapted from Tietenberg (1991) and London Economics (1991).

BAT is typically defined to be the 'practical limit' of control — i.e. it is not effectively possible to do better than the emissions level dictated by BAT. BAT then becomes a specific point on the firm's cost function. It effectively *fixes* the output level at whatever corresponds to that point on the cost function. This can only be optimal if optimality coincides with maximal emission control (see Figure 1).

Second, *even if* BAT or BATNEEC is the lowest-cost solution, it cannot be guaranteed that it will produce a 'socially optimal' level of emissions or ambient concentrations. 'Socially optimal' here means that level of emissions which maximizes the difference between the social benefits of control (i.e. reduced environmental damage) and the costs of control (abatement costs). Unless BATNEEC is deliberately chosen on the basis of cost–benefit analysis, it is only by chance that it will produce emission levels corresponding to the optimum (Figure 1).

Finally, BATNEEC will not be efficient if there are multiple sources of pollution. Efficiency in that context requires that the marginal abatement cost be equal for each source in order that aggregate compliance costs be minimized. But the concept of 'best technology' will vary by source so that marginal costs are not likely to be equated. This observation can be regarded as a variation on the first deficiency.

As we show later, the second source of inefficiency in technology-based approaches can be minimized if, indeed, the 'BAT' in BATNEEC is chosen so as to maximize environmental benefit, and the 'NEEC' qualification is construed in terms of the total resource cost of applying BAT. That is, BATNEEC effectively becomes a compromise between the social costs of control and the social (environmental) benefits of control. The first source of inefficiency can be minimized by construing 'technology' to embrace 'technique' (see section 2), and construing 'technique' to embrace all policy options for reducing emissions, as appears now to be the case, at least in intent, with recent legislative change. Only if *both* these interpretations are applied can BATNEEC *approximate* efficient environmental regulation.

4. Two Interpretations of BATNEEC

Environmental regulation works on the basis that expenditures on pollution control are generally financially disadvantageous, i.e. the implementing company secures no financial gain in terms of turnover, profits, or competitive advantage. The issue is how large this financial loss is from the standpoint of:

(i)   the company or industry—which we will call the corporate economic burden;

and

(ii) the nation relative to the gains in environmental quality achieved, which we will call the national economic burden.

A measure of both of these burdens is potentially relevant to the determination of 'excessive' cost in BATNEEC. That is, a regulatory cost may be 'excessive' with respect to some yardstick of acceptable profitability of the plant, company, or industry, or it may be 'excessive' from the national standpoint if the corporate economic burden is not more than offset by gains in the national environment.

Both interpretations involve computing the actual cost of BAT, but the former expresses this cost as some proportion of corporate profitability, while the latter ignores the corporate burden and compares the cost to some measure of national environmental gain.

The distinction made in BAT-type regulations between new and existing plants raises the question whether existing plants will be kept in operation long after their 'natural life' has ended, simply because of differential requirements. Whereas new plants may be expected to be fitted with BAT, existing plants 'only' have to install BATNEEC. The BATNEEC applied to existing plants will most likely provide less pollution control than the BAT fitted in new plants. Thus, if operating existing plants fitted with BATNEEC is cheaper than building new plants which must install BAT, the outcome could be that plants that would otherwise have been replaced by new will continue operating and thus cause more pollution than if this distinction did not exist.

With respect to 'excessive costs', BAT guidance after 1990 appears to construe them *both* in relation to environmental benefits to be achieved *and* in relation to the economic burden on the industry/plant. A statement by HMIP says of applications for authorizations to emit pollution:

> The application may identify a selected process that is not the best option in terms of effect on the environment. If the applicant has selected such an option he must justify this on the ground that the selection of the best option would involve entailing excessive cost. The applicant will be expected in that case to present information on both the cost of the product produced by his selected option and the best available technique. It is not sufficient to describe excessive costs in absolute terms without reference to the cost of the product. The applicant must be able to demonstrate that the increased cost of the product produced by the best available technique is grossly disproportionate to any environmental benefit likely to accrue from that method of production. The extra cost must represent a significant fraction of the cost of the finished product. (HMIP, 1991)

This extract suggests some ambiguity. It can be read to embrace the corporate cost-burden approach (here expressed as a proportion of the cost of the product made with BAT) or the national economic-burden approach (comparing the costs of implementing BAT with environmental benefits). It is also unclear whether the term 'cost of the product' refers to product *price* or to production *cost*. The distinction between price and cost burden is quite important. The installation of pollution-control techniques can affect production costs significantly. But whether product prices will reflect this very much depends on the economic situation, and the position the company in question holds in the market. As a price-taker in a depressed market, a company might be forced to sell at prices which do not cover production costs in order to maintain market shares. Internationally competitive industries do not 'make' prices. They tend to be determined by the international price, which, in turn, is heavily influenced by the lowest-cost producer.

Reference to the corporate burden concept being measured by *price* changes is simply a misunderstanding. The only meaningful burden concept is one relating to overall costs of production or profitability. This is consistent with the very limited amount of theoretical literature on BATNEEC (Ramchandani and Pearce, 1991; Førsund, 1992). More formally, the corporate cost-burden approach must involve some assessment of the effect of the cost of BAT on socially 'acceptable' rates of return to capital. If BAT forces rates of return below the socially acceptable level, then the cost of BAT can be said to be 'excessive'. Clearly, this raises formidable problems of defining socially acceptable rates of return. A methodology for determining socially acceptable rates of return could be developed, based on the experience of regulated industries. At the theoretical level, a minimum acceptable rate of return corresponds to the economist's concept of 'normal profits' (see Førsund, 1992).

Essentially, if

$$BAT > (\Pi - \Pi_n)$$

where BAT = cost of BAT; Π = profits; Π_n = 'normal' profits, there is 'excessive cost'.

Identifying 'normal' profits is, of course, problematic. If the industry is regulated then normal profitability could be held to coincide with the regulator's assessment of a 'fair' or 'reasonable' rate of return. But there is no necessary coincidence between companies regulated for competitive purposes and companies regulated for environmental purposes. The former will tend to be a subset of the latter. Hence there will be a large number of environmentally regulated firms for which no estimate of normal profits will exist. This imposes an unusual burden on the environmental regulator—namely, estimating fair rates of return. Typically, environmental regulators have neither this capacity nor a disposition to make such assessments.

Note also that BAT is typically applied to *processes*, not *firms*. Yet the concept of a fair return on capital will tend to be firm-based, not plant-based. Moreover, a poorly managed firm may have a low value of Π so that the BAT > $(\Pi - \Pi_n)$ condition for excessiveness could easily be met. This is why discussions of BAT as corporate burden tend to relate to 'representative' firms, not specific firms.

Another problem of interpretation relates to the term 'significant fraction'. The HMIP *Manual* (HMIP, 1991) states that excessive costs will be incurred if the extra cost represents a significant fraction of the cost of the finished product. But no indication has been provided as to how much would constitute a 'significant fraction'.

The second interpretation of excessive costs relates the costs of installing BAT to the environmental benefit to be achieved. The argument in this context is that, if the potential environmental benefits are greater than the costs of installing BAT, then it should be installed regardless of the corporate cost burden. If benefits are less than costs (or perhaps if they are not significantly greater), then BAT should not be installed. In the UK context this interpretation of BATNEEC in 1990 would have been novel. As Helm (1992) notes, detailed assessment of costs and benefits was not at that time given primary importance, a situation that is, however, now changing.

The next question is: what costs and what benefits?

Obviously we should consider the costs incurred by the company in question in relation to installing the technique. Costs here should include not just the 'end-of-pipe' technology costs, but all the implications of installing BAT for other costs in the corporation. For example, some BAT will increase energy costs (e.g. flue-gas-desulphurization equipment) and the additional energy costs should legitimately be included in the total cost of BAT, as should additional management costs, any downstream costs, costs of waste disposal from add-on equipment, etc.

With respect to environmental benefits, the problem, aside from measuring them, relates to geography. Should one only look at local or national benefits, or is it necessary also to include international benefits? This can be illustrated with the example of abatement of acid rain pollutants, of which the effect might be fairly limited locally and nationally, but which could result in significant benefits in other countries owing to the trans-boundary transport of such pollutants.

Table 2
A Matrix of BATNEEC Possibilities

	Net benefit to nation	Net benefit internationally but net cost nationally	Net costs internationally and nationally
Low cost to company	Implement BAT	Probably reject BAT	Reject BAT
High cost to company	?	Very probably reject BAT	Reject BAT

Table 2 summarizes the matrix of possibilities associated with the dual interpretation of BATNEEC. In this matrix more weight has been assigned to national environmental benefits than international environmental benefits, and more weight has been assigned to the national economic burden argument than to the corporate burden argument. If this analysis is correct, it clearly matters a great deal that the corporation seeking to claim excessive cost as an argument against BAT should be able to demonstrate low national environmental benefits relative to the corporate cost burden. Note, however, that the context in which there is a high corporate burden and high environmental benefit to the nation is not resolved. Hence, a methodology to determine environmental benefits is important.

Is the cost–benefit interpretation of BATNEEC more likely than the corporate-burden approach? The reasons for favouring the cost–benefit interpretation are as follows.

(i) The corporate-burden approach necessarily involves assessing acceptable rates of return. This is an extremely difficult exercise, even for those industries that are regulated and where such calculations are an integral part of the regulator's task. Environmental regulators are rarely in a position to make such assessments across so many authorizations (although, strictly, the calculation is necessary only where 'EEC' is claimed).

(ii) What little legal opinion there is on BATNEEC, suggests that the cost–benefit approach is more likely. Bigham (1992) notes that in the absence of any clear guidance, 'the primary meaning of a word should be adopted'. This, he suggests, means that an interpretation along the lines of 'excessive' as 'being in greater amount or degree than is beneficial or right' (*Oxford English Dictionary*) will apply. In such a case, BAT is justified according to its environmental benefits, although Bigham cautions that the

other factors—such as employment impacts—may still be relevant considerations.

The cost–benefit interpretation is also more consistent with economic efficiency, as we have argued. But this does not mean this
interpretation prevails. The problems with the cost–benefit interpretation lie in (a) the long tradition of interpreting 'practicable' and now
'excessive' in terms of the cost burden on the company and (b) the
credibility of the benefit estimates. It is worth asking why BAT-type
controls remain popular when, as is widely acknowledged, they are, as
currently interpreted, inefficient. One response is that, as we show,
BATNEEC (but not BAT) *could* be approximately efficient if it were
suitably interpreted in the cost–benefit sense. BATNEEC could then be
seen as a transitional instrument between old-fashioned command-
and-control and the coming wider use of market-based instruments
and optimally designed standards. But this may be an over-generous
interpretation of the evolution of environmental policy. A political
economy interpretation is that, provided the 'NEEC' qualification
remains, BATNEEC permits some degree of regulatory capture by
polluters (Helm, 1992). The case-by-case approach permits negotiations
and bargains. A strict application of BAT does not. Neither does the
market-based approach.

5. Conclusions and Summary

We have argued that there are two potential interpretations of
BATNEEC:
  (i)   the corporate-burden concept, where the cost of BAT is ex-
        pressed relative to some indicator of company costs or profits;
  (ii) the national-burden concept, where the cost of BAT is compared
        to the environmental benefit obtained from BAT, regardless of
        any indicator of burden this cost may impose on the company.

It seems clear that interpretation (i) defined the early experience
with BAT and BATNEEC, and that it is still very important today. The
corporate-burden concept is consistent with the more general command-and-control philosophy which, in turn, has facilitated some
regulatory capture by polluters. Regulatory capture fits the general
regulatory culture of the UK. The corporate concept also fits the
preoccupation of governments with regulations that may impair competitiveness. But the corporate burden interpretation came under
attack because of its economic inefficiency and its general inconsistency
with more centralized standard setting by the European Community.
That is, the case-by-case approach of BATNEEC was threatened by

economics and by the need to harmonize environmental regulation. The cost–benefit interpretation, in which 'technology' is more broadly interpreted as 'technique', and 'excessive' is measured against environmental benefits, is more consistent with economic efficiency. More importantly, it reduces the threat of regulatory capture since polluters would now have to prove their case for exemption by demonstrating that the cost burden is excessive relative to environmental benefits. As we have also argued, a systematized cost-burden approach to BATNEEC, in which cost burdens alone are the criteria, forces the environmental regulator into assessments of 'fair' or 'normal' rates of return, an activity for which they are ill-equipped. The cost–benefit interpretation replaces the rate-of-return assessment with a different yardstick: 'cost per unit of pollution reduced'. Finally, a cost–benefit focus forces cost-minimization to the fore and this should ensure that greater consideration is given to making BAT–type regulations more consistent with cost-reducing measures, such as permit trading.

Overall, the national-burden concept of BAT appears to have entered into some of the guidance and legislation on IPC, but without it being explicit. Some guidance has been ambiguous and regulators appear on occasion to have been using both cost-burden concepts simultaneously. The case therefore remains for being more explicit about the meaning of BAT and cost-attenuated BAT concepts. Since BAT appears to be endemic to environmental regulation, as the recent developments in integrated pollution control show, it should at least be as efficiently designed as possible. The cost–benefit interpretation would greatly improve the efficiency of BAT (or greatly reduce its inefficiency). It would be nice to think that environmental regulators should be more comfortable with this interpretation.

5

Making Things Stick: Enforcement and Compliance

ANTHONY G. HEYES*

1. Introduction

Environmental regulations are only useful if firms comply with them. Since compliance is generally costly, regulations have to be enforced if they are to work. Since enforcement is itself costly, enforcement is usually incomplete, meaning that some firms get away with non-compliance. Only by taking account of this sort of leakage can the success of a regulatory programme be assessed accurately.

While enforcement is an important dimension of any regulatory programme, the problems involved in enforcing environmental regulations are particularly pronounced. Ignoring enforcement issues in policy design and assessment here is likely to lead to particularly misleading results.

Non-compliance with many environmental regulations is commonplace and *effective* regulatory standards diverge substantially from the *nominal* standards of published legislation and agency directives. By its nature, evidence on non-compliance is scant, but some authoritative studies do exist. The US Government Accounting Office (GAO), for example, estimated that 65 per cent of regulated sources may be in violation of air pollution emissions limits (reported in Russell, 1990, p. 255). In the UK, the Environment Agency estimates that, depending upon region, compliance rates of trade dischargers with numerical discharge limits is 48–83 per cent, with an average of 74 per cent (see Department of the Environment (DoE), 1998). In most countries pub-

* University of London.

I am grateful to Tim Leunig, Chris Riley, Stephen Smith, and Dieter Helm for very helpful advice.

lished rates of compliance with key environmental standards is less than full, often substantially less.[1]

In section 2 we present the standard economic theory of compliance and enforcement. The usual approach is to treat 'cheating' as a gamble such that the standard theory of choice under uncertainty can be applied. In the following sections we outline some of the ways in which the basic model can be extended to make it a more useful tool for policy design. These include taking account of self-reporting, criminalization of non-compliance, and the scope for the involvement of private citizens in enforcement.

The focus throughout is on general principles. While we draw on the USA and EU for examples to illustrate general points, it is not our aim to give detailed account of the institutions or procedures of enforcement in any particular country. Most of the principles presented apply across instruments, and through most of the discussion we take the choice of instrument (standards, permits, etc.) as given. We also ignore the fact that sensible policy-makers will calibrate their instruments in anticipation that there may be 'leakage' at the implementation — focusing on the enforcement process *per se*.

2. Understanding Compliance

The first step to saying anything useful about enforcement strategy is to understand the way in which firms respond to enforcement incentives.

The model we will set up here is necessarily a very stylized one and it is worth noting that the relevance of any particular model of enforcement will depend crucially on the particular type of regulation involved. There is likely to be a world of difference between the types of programmes needed to ensure compliance with process, emissions,

---

[1] True compliance rates — which are what really matters — are likely to be even less impressive. When official data say that 70 per cent of firms are compliant, what that really means is that for 70 per cent of firms the inspection agency has not established non-compliance. Given the inadequacy of most inspection programmes this is, obviously, a much less compelling statement. In one well-known study of the US Environmental Protection Agency (EPA) by the US GAO, conducted in 1979, it was found that of those sources which the EPA had designated as compliant with air emissions standards *only 3 per cent were actually compliant*. The distinction between actual and published non-compliance also gives rise to the paradoxical likelihood that as the intensity of any inspection programme is *reduced*, published rates of compliance will go *up*. A general principle in this field is: do not take published compliance figures too seriously.

and environmental quality standards. Fly-tipping and other local misdemeanours in the waste field are very different from breaches of integrated pollution control (IPC) authorizations, for example.[2]

How do firms decide whether or not to comply?

It is conventional for economists to model the compliance decision of a firm as a choice under risk — a gamble — with monitoring essentially a random process.

Suppose there exists some regulation requiring a firm to execute action a (e.g. to install a particular piece of abatement equipment, to stop emissions of a particular substance from a particular discharge pipe). If the cost to the ith firm of complying with that regulation is c_i, the probability of non-compliance being detected is π and the penalty for non-compliance is P, then it is apparent that — in the absence of other consideration — a profit-maximizing and risk neutral firm will comply if and only if

$$c_i \leq \pi.P. \tag{1}$$

The right-hand side is the expected penalty for non-compliance, the left-hand side the firm's cost of compliance. Only those firms that find compliance sufficiently cheap will comply — the rest will take the risk of being caught and fined.

What matters in environmental terms is the compliance rate across all firms. It is plausible to think that in most settings firms will differ in how costly they find it to comply. This might reflect differences in skills, corporate structures, plant locations, or technologies. If c is distributed according to some cumulative distribution $F(c_i)$, then the compliance rate across the industry as a whole (which we will call g) can be expressed as a function of the enforcement policy parameters[3]

---

[2] When operators must in practice install the equipment required to meet process standards, the non-compliance issue relates more to accidents — for example, resulting from inadequate quality control or process maintenance. The simple model developed here relates most closely to deterministic polluting technologies — though it can straightforwardly be generalized. There is an interesting related issue about how to design a regulatory system, with appropriate monitoring and enforcement regimes, that will ensure average discharges are acceptable while permitting periodic peaks. Stochastic pollution process throws up a number of tricky policy-design issues of this sort.

[3] A cumulative distribution measures cumulative probability mass. In other words $F(x)$ tells us the proportion of firms for which $c_i < x$. It is apparent that $F(.)$ must lie between zero and one and must be everywhere (weakly) increasing in its argument.

$$\gamma = F(\pi.P). \tag{2}$$

It is obvious from looking at the inequality in equation (1) that raising the probability that non-compliance will be penalized and/or raising the size of the penalty will make compliance more attractive to the firm and so increase γ. The size of that increase—how effective raising π or P would be—will depend mainly upon the 'shape' of F.

What of the cost–benefit efficiency of the induced pattern of compliance? Assuming social welfare to the unweighted sum of industry costs and environmental damage, compliance decisions will be first-best if and only if the product $\pi.P$ happens to equal the marginal expected environmental damage caused by non-compliance. Such an expected penalty serves to internalize the externality due to the non-compliance and can be referred to as a 'Pigovian penalty'. For any *given* population compliance rate it is worth noting that the *distribution* of compliance effort between firms is efficient—it is always those firms with the lowest compliance costs that comply.

In a model of this sort the agency maximizes compliance (i.e. minimizes environmental damage) by setting both π and P as high as possible. It will only be able to ensure full compliance, however, if it can set them such that $\pi.P$ exceeds the upper bound of c. In most cases this will not be possible—budgetary, legislative, and other constraints almost invariably put limits on how high expected penalties can be raised.

While this sort of set-up makes modelling relatively easy, it is not particularly realistic. It assumes that the compliance decision faced by each firm is a binary one—a firm chooses either to comply or to violate, there is no 'halfway' option. Most real compliance decisions are, in fact, 'continuous' in character. This is true not just in the environmental setting but in many others. A motorist does not just choose between the options of 'speeding' and 'not speeding' but, rather, chooses exactly how fast to drive. A firm does not just choose whether or not to violate—it will typically have to choose a level of pollution which is an inherently continuous variable.

Suppose, to capture this, that firm i is subject to a regulatory standard which forbids it from discharging effluent e_i beyond some level S. Assume that the expected penalty for exceeding the standard is some increasing function $P(e_i - S)$ of the size of the violation,[4] and costs

---

[4] If the enforcement programme is prone to type I errors (falsely determining compliant firms to be non-compliant) then $P(e_i - S)$ may be positive even if $e_i < S$, i.e. even if the firm is complying (see Segerson, 1988).

are increasing in environmental cleanliness according to a function $c(e_i)$. Then the firm's problem is to choose a level of emissions to minimize

$$c(e_i) + P(e_i - S). \tag{3}$$

The solution to this problem (which we will call e_i^*) is implicitly defined by the associated first-order condition:

$$c'(e_i^*) = -P'(e_i^* - S). \tag{4}$$

The firm pollutes up to the point at which the marginal cost of further abatement equals the marginal saving in terms of expected penalties.

It is an important point to note that to solve equation (4) we do not have to know anything about the *level* of penalties (i.e. the value of $P(e_i^* - S)$), only about their properties at the margin. Once the decision to violate has been taken, the size of the violation depends only on the *marginal*, not the *average* properties of the expected penalty function — it is not the size of penalties that matters, but rather the 'speed' with which they increase with the degree of violation. This is the 'theory of marginal deterrence' (Shavell, 1992).[5]

Average and marginal penalties do not always move together — one enforcement regime may involve harsher penalties but have a 'flatter' penalty structure — and this can throw up some paradoxical results.

(a) The Optimal 'Amount' of Enforcement

Compliance models provide a link between changes in policy instruments and environmental performance. Equation (2), for example, describes a causal relationship from penalties and inspection probabilities to population compliance rates.

While very little empirical work has been done in the UK, a number of attempts have been made to operationalize models of this sort in the USA. Gray and Deily (1996), for example, use data on individual steel mills to study the relationship between EPA enforcement of air pollution regulations and firms' compliance decisions, while Cohen (1986) estimates the impact of US Coast Guard patrols on the frequency and severity of oil spills in US waters. Similar work has been done by Magat and Viscusi (1990) on pulp mills' compliance with water pollution regulations, by Feinstein (1989) on enforcement of safety regulations at

---

[5] This is rather like the firm's choice of output level in industrial economics. To find that level we go to the point at which the marginal cost and marginal revenue functions cross. Fixed costs (and by implication total costs) do not have an impact on this decision because they do not affect anything *at the margin*.

Figure 1

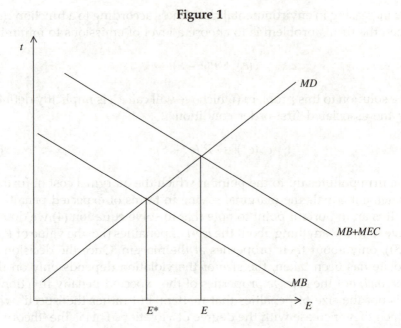

US commercial nuclear power plants, and by Epple and Visscher (1984) on marine pollution.

The aim of each of these studies is to answer a question of the form: 'By how much will violations fall if enforcement parameter X is increased by 1 per cent?' Enforcement activity is (in most cases) costly, however, so cost-efficient policy design will require the balancing of the environmental benefits from enforcement (of the sort that such empirical studies characterize) against its costs.

In Figure 1, E on the bottom axis is the total discharge of some pollutant by an industry. The marginal damage (MD) and marginal industry benefit (MB) functions are drawn in the usual way, giving an optimal pollution level of E^* at the point where they intersect:[6]

$$MD(E^*) = MB(E^*). \qquad (6)$$

But achieving reductions in E implies not just costs to industry but also enforcement costs, EC. Adding marginal enforcement costs (MEC) to the diagram means that the optimal level of pollution—that which the enforcement agency should target—is E', the level which ensures that

[6] The MB slopes down under the assumption of diminishing marginal returns to abatement effort—the 100th unit of emission is less costly (in terms of spending on technology, or forgone production) to get rid of than is the 90th, and so on. Most classes of pollutant impose increasing marginal damage.

$$MD(E') = MB(E') + MEC(E'). \qquad (6)$$

It makes sense that E' is greater than E^*—taking account of the enforcement costs associated with implementing a given outcome leads the policy-maker to 'water down' his or her objectives. In terms of the diagram, those increments of pollution between E^* and E' are socially inefficient according to standard cost–benefit criteria, but the administrative cost (in terms of a greater enforcement effort) of implementing a policy to remove them is excessive.

Taking account of enforcement costs, then, implies a 'distortion' in policy objectives away from that suggested by conventional analysis which tends to abstract from transactions costs. In some cases the regulatory agency may be prevented from optimizing its enforcement programme in this way:

> Sometimes the search for the optimum in enforcement priorities is blocked by statutory dictates: all establishments of a certain kind, the law might say, shall be inspected once every so often. Such directives may reflect legislative responses to catastrophes or scandals or may simply reflect notions of equal treatment. Either way, they can be very inefficient. (Bardach and Kagan, 1982, p. 165)

How great any such distortion might be will depend upon how sizeable those enforcement costs are in a given context, but it may be substantial. It is much more difficult to estimate *marginal* — as opposed to average — costs in this sort of setting, and this makes empirical optimization of enforcement programmes notoriously complex.[7,8]

A classic empirical analysis of the optimization of an enforcement programme is Cohen's (1986) study of the prevention of oil pollution in US coastal waters (Figure 1 here corresponds with Figure 1 in Cohen's paper). He uses detection-adjusted regression techniques to estimate the marginal costs of oil-spill prevention. The key results are summarized in Table X (p. 185) of that paper. The estimated *marginal* cost of preventing the release of one gallon of oil is estimated (all in 1986 dollars) to be \$5.50. Of this, however, only \$3.98 is the cost to the

---

[7] In most areas of economics average things are easier to estimate than are their marginal counterparts. Think of a firm's costs of production, for instance. Average cost is simply total costs divided by total output, both of which can be observed directly. Marginal cost, on the other hand, is not based on observables and involves coming up with an answer to the hypothetical question 'by how much would my total costs have gone up had I chosen to produce one more unit of output?'

[8] Sometimes the costs or benefits need to be adjusted to account for particular industry circumstances — Gray and Deily (1991), for example, look at the considerations particular to the environmental regulation of a declining industry.

industry associated with additional preventive efforts (i.e. $MB(E)$ = 3.98). The remaining \$1.52 (or 27.6 per cent of the total) is the enforcement cost associated with the US Coast Guard having to operate more frequent patrols (i.e. $MEC(E)$ = 1.52). Clearly any attempt to set an optimal pollution target using cost–benefit criteria but ignoring MEC— given that it is so substantial — is likely to be well off the mark.

In the case of 'Superfund' in the USA — a programme designed to collect money from polluters of land to fund clean-up — a study by the Washington-based think tank, Resources for the Future, conjectured that for every dollar collected from polluters and used to clean up damaged land, as much as 50 cents could go on enforcement and transactions costs (principally the cost of tracking down those responsible and extracting the appropriate money from them). Even more alarmingly, Porter and van der Linde (1995, p. 115) quote a study that estimates that '88 per cent of the money spent by insurers between 1986 and 1989 went to pay for legal and administrative costs, while only 12 per cent was used for actual site clean-ups'.

It is also important to note that enforcement considerations could and should have an impact upon the choice of regulatory instrument — with the costliness of enforcement being anticipated at the point at which an instrument is selected, not just at the point at which a given instrument is calibrated.[9]

3. Beyond the Basics

The type of model that we have developed here describes compliance behaviour — with its implication for enforcement strategy — in the simplest possible regulatory settings. The analysis is essentially borrowed from the more general economic analysis of law initiated as long ago as 1968 by Becker.

While the results of such work provide a useful bench-mark, the analysis needs to be extended. The simple model has a lot of unrealistic features and some of the more restrictive assumptions need to be relaxed if it is to be of much use in policy development. Some are purely technical — though none the less important to resolve — such as taking account of risk aversion in modelling the behaviour of both firms and

---

[9] It is instructive to note that the combination of a particular enforcement regime with some regulatory instrument A may come to yield a hybrid instrument which has the incentive properties more akin to some other regulatory instrument B. Thus a (non-binding) emissions limit s combined with an expected penalty p per unit of violation comes to mimic — in terms of its incentive properties — a linear emissions tax regime with $t = p$.

regulators, taking account of the fact that firms may depart from naïve profit-maximizing behaviour, and so on. Some are more substantive.

(a) *Self-reporting*

Most environmental enforcement programmes do not simply involve the regulatory agency conducting random inspections of would-be polluters but, rather, include an element of self-reporting: 'Self-reporting is becoming an increasingly common feature of enforce-ment, particularly enforcement of pollution standards' (Livernois and McKenna, 1997, p. 1).

In this case understanding incentives can be quite a bit more complicated. The firm has to decide not just how much to emit, but also how much of any emissions to report (there can be no presumption that the firm will necessarily report honestly). The agency will no longer conduct inspections randomly but can, rather, condition those inspec-tions on the content of the paperwork it gets from each firm, in very much the same way as the Inland Revenue can target its income tax audits on the basis of individual tax returns.

A number of authors have shown that such self-reports can greatly help effective enforcement. Harford (1987), Livernois and McKenna (1997) and others have shown that a number of the 'conventional wisdoms' generated by standard models do not necessarily carry over once account is taken of the strategic role of self-reporting. (Livernois and McKenna, for example, show that raising pollution penalties can increase pollution rates by interfering with the incentives for honest reporting.)

Of course, the reality of enforcement models with self-reporting is more complex than stylized models of this sort might suggest. A company's incentives are mixed — the raw data they hold are auditable, as is (in most cases) their compliance data process. Such failure might not only affect their public image, but would also expose them to additional penalties.

(b) *Noisy Monitoring*

The 'gamble' model of the type sketched in section 2 is often motivated by the joint assumption of random inspection plus accurate inspection technology. In reality, monitoring equipment is likely to yield only a noisy estimate of actual emissions from a particular source such that the enforcement process is likely to be characterized by both type I and type II errors (i.e. with some actual violators being miscategorized as compliers and vice versa).

Recognizing the possibility of type I errors—that some firms may be deemed to be violators even when they are really compliant—leads to the possibility of 'more than full' compliance in settings where the regulated firm faces a continuous decision problem. That is, once firms have cut emissions down to the permitted level they may choose to abate even further to reduce the chance of being mistakenly prosecuted. This can be a source of 'regulatory chill' whereby regulations have greater than anticipated impacts and may even dissuade firms from operating in some sectors.[10] The risk of type I errors—the false prosecution of the innocent—is one of the most substantial arguments against the popular view that it would be desirable to force everyone to comply by setting penalties arbitrarily high (along with being one of the key reasons why legislators and courts are unwilling to allow regulatory agencies to impose draconian penalties).

Russell (1990) and others have argued that improving the accuracy of monitoring technology should be a key priority of environment agencies, and engineering research in this area has received increased agency funding in recent years.

One interesting possibility is that in many contexts there may be things that polluters can do to make themselves 'difficult' to inspect, making 'inspectability' a strategic variable for the firm.

In the USA a firm's constitutional right to privacy (under the 4th amendment) means that inspectors are obliged to conduct at least the initial rounds of their work from outside the firm's perimeter fence using remote-sensing devices. If the accuracy of such equipment decreases with distance, the firm can invest in uninspectability simply by buying more land—putting greater distance between the source of the pollutant and the nearest point from which detection can legally be attempted (see Strock, 1990). Alternatively, a firm might establish 'sanitized areas'—operationally redundant 'dummies' established for the benefit of inspectors. If the inspection process is seen as a sampling game in which the inspector tries to find a non-compliant part of the plant (the illegally set effluent outlet among the 20 properly set ones, for instance) then the firm can decrease the likelihood that he or she does so simply by increasing the number of sanitized areas. Linder and McBride (1984, p. 339) provide evidence of this and other sorts of 'attempt to change operations or employ idle capacity in order to pass on-site inspections'.

Heyes (1993) provides a formal model in which firms can avoid expected penalty by investing in 'uninspectability' as an alternative to

---

[10] Of course a smart regulatory agency might anticipate this and take account of it in calibrating the regulation.

spending on pollution control. A key result of that analysis is that because increasing the frequency of inspections encourages firms to switch towards less easily inspectable choices of technique, agencies should conduct *less frequent* but *more detailed* inspections than suggested by existing studies.

In a similar spirit Kambhu (1989) constructs a model in which a non-compliant firm can—by spending money on high-powered lawyers or in other ways—erode the penalty paid for a violation of given magnitude. In his model actual environmental performance can, intriguingly, be *negatively* related to the stringency of the regulatory requirement in place.

The uninspectability problem is probably less in the UK—where the Environment Agency has substantial rights of access and inspection— than it is in the USA.

(c) *Penalty Structures*

While the simple, continuous framework described in equations (5) and (6) is rather general, it belies the difficulty in specifying the penalty function adequately.

In many cases the penalty function $P(.)$ can reasonably be treated as exogenous—not at the discretion of the enforcement agency. In others (such as is the case with the EPA in the USA) the agency exercises quite substantial discretion over the penalties levied and it is useful to think about what the optimal specification of $P(.)$ would be.[11] In the USA the penalty levied is explicitly broken into a component chosen to recover any economic gains from violation and a 'gravity' component, designed to be purely punitive.

EPAs in most countries, including the USA and Britain, are constrained—in some settings quite tightly—by legislation or the judiciary in how heavily they can fine non-compliant firms. It is not necessarily the case, however, that compliance-maximization will involve penalizing all violators to the fullest extent possible. More subtlety is required in specifying a profile of penalties which has good 'marginal deterrence' properties. The penalty faced by a firm following a minor infraction must not be so great that the firm has no incentive to prevent any release into the environment from escalating. Shaffer (1990) and others have done extensive and interesting work in this area.

---

[11] In the UK the regulatory agencies bring prosecutions, but fines are imposed by the Courts. As such, the UK Environment Agency has no scope to vary penalties— and hence to devise penalty structures with good marginal deterrence properties—though it may canvas the Courts. The possibility of introducing administrative fines—at the discretion of the Agency—could usefully be looked at further in the UK.

In one recent paper, Heyes (1996) adapts the basic deterrence model to take account of the fact that pollutants differ in the extent to which their impacts are 'persistent'. Firms choose how much effort to exert in preventing an accidental spill, but, if a spill occurs, have also to choose whether or not to admit that it has happened and instigate clean-up. The instigation of clean-up is especially important if the pollutant is highly persistent (such as oil in the ocean, or radioactive pollutants with long half-lives).[12] The penalty regime needs to be harsh enough to ensure adequate incentive for prevention, but at the same time 'forgiving' enough to ensure that the firm responsible party does not skulk away once an accident has actually occurred. An interesting feature of Heyes's model is that the optimal penalty turns out to be *non-monotonic* in the persistence of the pollutant being regulated—with the highest penalties being reserved for firms discharging pollutants of 'medium' persistence.[13]

(d) *Judgement Proofness*

In setting penalties it is not just higher powers that may prevent penalties being set as high as EPAs might like. It has often been noted by agencies and observers that a firm's asset base constitutes an upper bound on the penalty that can be levied—bankruptcy offers an escape hatch which means that a firm cannot be fined for more than its net worth. Shavell (1986) coined the term 'judgement proof' to describe such firms. This is likely to be a particularly worrying problem in two contexts: (i) where the regulated industry is populated by small firms (or, more accurately, by firms with comparatively small net worth) and (ii) in sectors where the type of environmental damage done is infrequent but catastrophic.

If the *effective* maximum penalty is restricted by the bankruptcy constraint, then the incentive properties of any particular enforcement regime can be compromised.[14] Where this problem is particularly

[12] An example of a completely *unpersistent* pollutant would be something like noise which has only an impact effect and offers no meaningful opportunity for clean-up. The nature of biological pollutants is particularly interesting—the scope for breeding may mean that, rather than diminishing, the size of their impact actually grows through time.

[13] A *monotonic* relationship means that as one thing goes up so does the other. Non-monotonic in this context means that as we increase the persistence of the pollutant in question then, other things being equal, the optimal penalty at first rises then falls.

[14] This is not that unusual—very many firms in high-tech sectors, for examples, may have the potential to do environmental damage of much greater value than their monetary net worth. Small biotech firms handling biological pollutants or haulage firms engaged in the transportation of hazardous waste provide examples.

pronounced the Agency may wish to compel firms to carry liability insurance.

The extent of judgement proofness, however, is likely to be anything but fixed—with firms recognizing the benefits of 'being small' when operating in particular sectors. The burgeoning rate of environmental penalty and litigation in the 1980s and 1990s has led to what Ringleb and Wiggins (1992) refer to as 'strategic subsidiarization', whereby large firms hive off environmentally sensitive components of their overall operations into independently incorporated subsidiaries with small asset bases, thereby protecting the assets of the parent company from exposure to environmental risk.[15]

(e) *Multiple Polluters*

Most early analysis of environmental enforcement—following its antecedents in law and economics—has assumed a single polluter.

In fact, in many settings several polluters will share an outlet. Many firms may, for example, discharge effluent into a particular stretch of river, or polluters may emit into the air in the same vicinity. This makes the task of inferring the contribution of a particular source from ambient measures difficult, in some cases impossible. In these cases the enforcement agency may be obliged to adopt 'second best' instruments and to regulate and monitor other signals of environmental performance, such as the consumption of polluting inputs by source (see Segerson (1988) for some discussion of these issues).

Even when not linked by pollutant-recipient, firms may be strategically linked through the enforcement process itself—e.g. if the agency is budget-constrained and only has the resources to pursue the worst 'tail' of polluters.

(f) *Criminalization*

One of the most high-profile developments in environmental enforcement in the USA since the mid-1980s—one not followed in the EU—has been the increased use of *criminal* sanctions.

The type of analysis presented in section 2 above has effectively treated penalties for environmental infractions as being pecuniary and

---

[15] Ringleb and Wiggins (1992) provide compelling evidence of the occurrence of strategic subsidiarity in the USA. There remains some doubt over the efficacy of the strategy. Courts may choose to 'pierce the corporate veil'—penalize the parent for the actions of the subsidiary—if the subsidiarization is judged to been a ploy purely designed to avoid legal sanction. There is, as yet, insufficient case history to predict to what extent—and in what sorts of cases—courts will be willing to do this, and how far those decisions will be sustainable under appeal.

incident upon the firm. The firm is assumed to treat such penalties as a 'cost of doing business' and to treat their minimization in very much the same way as it would treat the minimization of any other cost.

Criminalization provides another dimension to the EPA's armoury — the penalty for wrongdoing is no longer an entry in the corporate accounts. The Agency, in conjunction with the Department of Justice, can pursue individual employees within firms — those with responsibility for environmental management — with a view to holding them criminally liable for environmental damage. Every year in the USA many dozens of executives are tried and imprisoned for the environmental damages of the firm that employs them. The EPA in the USA puts great emphasis on the availability of this as a weapon. Though the numbers of convictions remain comparatively small they may be disproportionately important — the recognition of individuals that *they themselves* may face prison for the failings of the firm for which they work having a substantial impact. As Russell (1990, p. 264) notes:

> A third line of enforcement effort is a new stress on criminal prosecution. Since penalties for conviction then include time in prison, and since the effort has been accompanied by a strong PR exercise, it appears that the EPA is striving to plant fear in the hearts of executives deciding whether or not to comply with environmental regulations.

The extent to which identifying and attributing blame to particular individuals within organizations is likely to be effective in generating incentives will depend upon a variety of factors, including the extent to which there are likely to exist specific individuals within a firm who have the controls necessary and sufficient to determine environmental performance (these have been investigated by, among others, Tietenberg and Segerson, 1994). In the longer term one might expect a continued trend towards criminalization to encourage corporations to restructure job descriptions to ensure that no individual (say of board level) has 'responsibility' for environmental compliance. While this may serve to avoid the risk to personnel of prosecution, the pursuant muddying of lines of environmental control may not be socially desirable.

Criminalization appears to have lost favour as a 'way ahead' in the UK and elsewhere in the EU in recent years.[16] The role that it could and should play remains, however, one of the most debated.

[16] Much (almost all) of UK environmental regulation is underpinned by criminal law. The difference in style between the USA and UK is in the application of criminal penalties. In the UK very minor offences — which in the USA would be treated as administrative offences — can be criminalized, but there is comparatively little use of major criminal penalties (imprisonment) for bigger offences. What may be needed in the UK is not an increase in criminalization but a more selective approach, focusing on more substantial breaches.

(g) *Privatization of the Enforcement Function*

It is inevitable that private individuals will have an impact on compliance incentives — they may influence Agency policies through political channels, and their responses are likely to underlie the so-called 'market incentives' whereby firms behave well to avoid losing customers, employees, and investors. This said, however, it is usually taken for granted that government — through one or more of its agencies — will have monopoly over regulatory enforcement.[17]

The most striking and potentially far-reaching shift in emphasis in the USA in the 1990s, however, has been the increasing frequency with which individual citizens and citizen groups have intervened in the enforcement process directly. This is a trend which has not been mirrored in the UK or the rest of the EU. Before 1970, the state and federal agencies held exclusive enforcement responsibility in the USA. In 1970, Congress amended the Clean Air Act to allow private parties to pursue non-compliant firms which the EPA fails to pursue. Since then similar provisions have been built into other statutes, including the Clean Water Act and Toxic Substances Control Act (ToSCA). The number of citizen suits has increased dramatically since the early 1980s and now represents a substantial proportion of the total.[18] Citizen involvement in the process in the UK is much more limited — despite persistent pressure from some of those groups for channels to be widened. Individuals and groups can in theory take out a prosecution against polluters in the UK, but will not in general be able to force agencies to reveal data or information beyond what is on public registers. It is more likely that public groups such as non-governmental organizations (NGOs) will seek judicial review.

The desirability of direct private involvement in enforcement is open to question. As Naysnerski and Tietenberg (1992) note: 'While the role of NGOs in environmental policy is growing rapidly, our analytical

---

[17] Note that we are not talking here about situations where individuals sue firms to gain compensation for damage inflicted against them personally — a type of action familiar in tort law — but rather where individuals or private groups move to enforce a piece of regulation more generally.

[18] In the early 1980s '[H]igh rates of non-compliance with the water pollution and other laws generated private enforcement at a level not before seen in American regulatory law' (Yaeger, 1991, p. 320). In the 5 years before 1983 private groups filed only 41 lawsuits under the water law, in 1983 the number was 103, with 87 in the first-quarter of 1984 alone. 'This activity, much of it organized by various national environmental groups, began to rival the federal government's own enforcement action: of the 108 actions in 1983, 62 eventuated in actual citizen lawsuits, compared to the 77 suits filed by the Department of Justice on behalf of the EPA' (Yaeger, 1991, p. 321). For some excellent legal discussion see Fardil (1985).

understanding of the consequences of this emerging role has not kept pace.' They put forward what is probably the most straightforward view of the impact of private involvement: 'Adding the likelihood of private enforcement action to that of public enforcement implies a higher probability that a non-compliant firm will be penalized which . . . should increase the observed degree of compliance with the regulation' (Naysnerski and Tietenberg, 1992, p. 43).

According to such a view public and private enforcement efforts are additive. There are several reasons, however, for thinking such a view may be too simplistic. While it holds in a world in which the public agency operates a random but incomplete enforcement programme, as soon as one allows for the possibility that the EPA may do anything more subtle than this it breaks down. When the agency is exploiting penalty leverage (as in Harrington, 1988) or engages in regulatory dealing (as in Heyes and Rickman, 1998) — both of which will be explained a little later — the decision not to pursue a particular violation is a strategic decision by the EPA and may be compliance-enhancing such that intervention by a private enforcer could be expected, in general, to compromise the overall efficacy of the programme. Similarly — and depending upon the budgetary process by which the agency's budget is set — private enforcement could lead to a cut in funds for the public enforcement effort and so have a deleterious effect overall.

None of which is to say that private enforcement effort is necessarily a bad thing — just that it needs more consideration. The opposition by agencies in some countries to the extension of private enforcement rights should not necessarily be interpreted cynically.[19] In addition, insofar as direct private involvement in the enforcement of environmental regulations is to be privatized, more attention should be paid to how 'efficient' levels and patterns of such activity can be encouraged through fiscal or other means (see Heyes, 1997).

4. Why Do Firms Comply so Much?

While the aim in this paper is not to survey the large body of empirical research which has developed in this field, it is worth noting a particular empirical regularity which has been identified in a variety of contexts by a variety of authors.

[19] Boyer and Meidinger (1985, p. 841) assert that '[t]he agencies resist private enforcement in the belief that the plaintiff groups are intruding on bureaucratic turf'.

Winston Harrington (1988, p. 29) and others have noted—in the context of all of the major enforcement programmes operated by the EPA in the USA—that despite the fact that:

(i)   when the EPA observes violations it often (almost always) chooses not to pursue the violator and

(ii) the expected penalty faced by a violator who is pursued is small compared to the cost of compliance, it is still the case that

(iii) firms comply a significant proportion of the time.

While the exact terms differ by context, the underlying and recurrent pattern is the same: firms appear to over-comply—to comply more fully and/or more frequently than would be suggested by consideration of the private costs and benefits of so doing. The same pattern has been noted outside the USA—see Heyes and Rickman (1998), Hawkins (1983), and a variety of the citations listed.

This so-called Harrington Paradox is perhaps the best known empirical 'result' in this field, and various commentators have provided alternative rationales for it—we list five. The apparent puzzle provides a good context within which to think about most of the important issues in enforcement.

So why might it be that firms would seem to comply too much?

(i) Voluntary compliance

So far we have assumed that firms are cynical profit-maximizers. It is sometimes contended that there is in fact such a thing as a 'green corporation' which has a social conscience and attaches weight to its environmental performance *per se*. The main problem with such a theory is evolutionary—a firm that forgoes profit to pursue other objectives (green or otherwise) is likely to find itself displaced in the market by one that does not. Alternatively, in contexts where there are barriers to entry in the product market, the disciplinary function of the market for corporate control is to ensure that managers who fail to maximize shareholder value will come to be replaced by others who do.[20] Authors such as Arora and Cason (1996) have provided evidence on voluntary compliance (in that case with the EPA's so called 33/50 programme in the USA) but that 'voluntary' behaviour can be explained in term of other benefits to compliance which generally go unmeasured.

---

[20] The evidence is that the emergence of the green or ethical investor in recent years had had little impact on the overall market for corporate control.

(ii) Misjudgement

It may be that polluters overestimate the probability that wrong-doing will be detected or the penalties that such detection would trigger. There is compelling evidence in the public finance literature that many private individuals misjudge the probability that their tax return will be audited — maybe a similar mechanism is at work here. There is, however, no good survey evidence to support such a conjecture. There is anecdotal support for the notion that individual company employees may overestimate the probability of criminal prosecution (a probability which, despite the growing number of highly publicized cases, remains minuscule).

(iii) Unmeasured costs to violation

Numerical analyses of compliance behaviour routinely assume that the cost of being found non-compliant is simply the administrative or litigative penalty which must be paid. There may, however, be additional 'market' penalties which firms face. The profitability of firms may be adversely affected through the responses of customers, investors, and employees to a poor environmental record. Badrinath and Bolster (1996) estimated that 86 per cent of the penalty for environmental prosecution in the USA is reputational (a higher fraction in the case of violations of the Clean Air Act). Grabosky (1994) and others have emphasized the loss in brand image among consumers and the loss of morale among employees that prosecution may imply.[21] While policies to make information about the environmental performance of firms more widely available — so that consumers, investors, and employees can bring pressure to bear on the 'bad' — will probably work in the right direction of making firms more likely to behave socially, they should not be seen as a panacea. Even in a world in which everyone is fully informed about everything, the fundamental externality problem — that when I consume a product the manufacture of which has caused environmental damage, most if not all of that damage is incident upon others — remains.

(iv) 'Penalty leverage'

The basic model of compliance around which this chapter has been built has been static. Harrington (1988) and others have emphasized the

[21] As Friemann (1995, p. 362) notes: 'Taking care of the social and ecological consequences of corporate activities, even if they promise no immediate financial gains, may turn out to be an element of a modern far-sighted management strategy for a variety of reasons.'

repeated nature of the interaction between firm and agency. Once repetition is taken into account, the agency is likely to condition its attitude towards a particular firm on that firm's past performance — much as a criminal court will take account of an individual's previous behaviour in determining a sentence. Harrington shows that in such a model optimal behaviour will exhibit apparent over-compliance at any *given* moment (or in any *given* repetition of the game). The argument is refined in Harford (1991).[22]

(v) 'Regulatory dealing'

Heyes and Rickman's (1998) model of regulatory dealing is also consistent with the Harrington Paradox. The model takes account of the fact that EPAs typically interact with a given firm in more than one context (the firm might have several plants, operate in several different geographical locations, or be subject to several different sets of environmental regulations). In this case, there is scope for the Agency to exploit 'issue-linkage'. In such a world, firms may *appear* to over-comply in a given setting, but in reality are so doing in exchange for the agency 'turning a blind eye' somewhere else (at another plant, or in its enforcement of some other regulation). This sort of story fits well with the case study and anecdotal evidence of people such a Keith Hawkins (in the UK) and Peter Yaeger (in the USA) who have spent time inside regulatory agencies and find that they engage in various sorts of 'horse trading' of this sort.

The explanations, of course, are neither exhaustive nor mutually exclusive. As usual in the real world the relative importance of different effects will depend upon a range of factors and upon context.

5. Conclusions

Regulations are only useful insofar as they are enforced — either fully or partially. Current rates of compliance with many of the most important pieces of environmental legislation in the USA, EU, and elsewhere are so low that the *effective* stringency of regulation is determined as much

---

[22] As well as conditioning monitoring strategies on the past compliance performance of firms, an agency can also condition those strategies on observable characteristics of firms in a non-random way — identifying the characteristics associated with non-compliance across a population and drawing up risk-profiles of offenders. This is similar to the type of approach routinely used by Customs and Excise, for example, in countering VAT fraud. The Environment Agency in the UK has a new Operator and Pollution Risk Assessment (OPRA) model to help it target inspection in this way.

by the intensity of enforcement efforts and expenditures as it is by the stringency of the legislative decree itself.

Enforcement — the implementation phase — is the nitty-gritty of environmental regulation and one on which policy analysts should and do put increasing emphasis. The aim here has been to provide an idea of the richness of issues involved. An important thing to bear in mind in thinking about these things is how different the various types of pollution are. Noise and radioactive emissions throw up, it is obvious, very different control problems and we should not be surprised if the correct response is a non-uniform one — with different enforcement solutions being best in different control situations.

This said, it is useful — with one eye on the current British context — to draw a few general policy conclusions.

- Enforcement costs and limits must be anticipated in both the choice of regulatory instrument and its calibration.
- Optimal targeting of inspection effort will require conditioning on both the characteristics of the source, and the source's compliance history. The form of such conditioning may be highly complex.
- Administrative control over penalties — allowing, in the British case, the Environment Agency to set penalties — is likely to be beneficial. The agency can have regard not just to the case in isolation but to the incentive properties of the penalty structure as a whole, in particular its marginal deterrence properties.
- Selective use of custodial criminal sanctions for violations at the 'upper end' may well have an important incentive role to play in deterring errant firms from treating financial penalties as a 'cost of doing business'.
- Agencies should be wary of private intrusion in the enforcement process. This is not to say that private prosecution of regulatory non-compliance may not have a role to play in some contexts — merely that its inherently uncoordinated nature may interact adversely with the incentives produced by a well-designed public enforcement programme.

The two most intriguing trends in the USA — ones which have been largely resisted in the UK — are towards criminalization of non-compliance, and the move towards the *de facto* 'privatization' of parts of the enforcement function. The extent to which these are precedents that should be followed — and if so in what settings — is up for debate.

Part Two: Policy

6

Political Economy of the Kyoto Protocol

SCOTT BARRETT*

1. Introduction

The Kyoto Protocol, negotiated in December 1997, is a climate change treaty with a difference. Unlike the Framework Convention on Climate Change that preceded it, the Kyoto Protocol incorporates targets and timetables — that is, ceilings on the emissions of greenhouse gases and dates by which these ceilings must be met. And though global emissions will continue to rise, even if the protocol is implemented to the letter, the reduction from a business-as-usual emissions bench-mark may be close to being optimal in the sense of balancing the global marginal costs and benefits of abatement. Assuming full participation and cost-effective implementation, a recent study by the Clinton Administration estimated the marginal cost of meeting the Kyoto targets to range from $14 to $23/ton (Clinton Administration, 1998). Most estimates of the global marginal damage of greenhouse gas emissions are of a similar magnitude (see IPCC, 1996, ch. 6), and so it would seem that the Kyoto Protocol is a near ideal outcome for the world.

But this is only if the assumptions behind the Clinton Administration's estimates are correct: that participation in the agreement will be full and implementation cost-effective. A number of features of the Protocol will promote cost-effective implementation, including provisions for trading in the entitlements to emit greenhouse gases. How-

* Johns Hopkins University.
    This chapter began to form in my mind at the NBER–Yale Global Change Workshop in Snowmass, Colorado, where I was able to learn from, and put my questions to, some of the leading economists working on this issue. I am grateful to all the participants for sharing their ideas, and especially to Charles Kolstad, William Nordhaus, and Robert Stavins for inviting me to participate in the workshop. I am also grateful to Wilfred Beckerman, Dieter Helm, Tim Jenkinson, Chris Riley, Stephen Smith, Robert Stavins, Peter Zapfel, and an anonymous referee for helpful comments on an earlier draft. David Pearce also provided helpful comments at a seminar presentation.

ever, though the details of the flexible mechanisms incorporated in
Kyoto have yet to be worked out, implementation may turn out to be
very costly, not least because participation is unlikely to be full. The
marginal cost of implementing Kyoto could be ten times the estimates
noted above. Moreover, the reduction in emissions effected by Kyoto
could be less than the amount promised because of 'trade leakage'.
Indeed, since leakage will be greater the greater are the between-
country differences in marginal costs, the same forces causing costs to
be higher will cause benefits to be lower. The Kyoto Protocol may turn
out not be such a good deal after all.

Worse, the agreement may not even be sustainable, and not just
because high implementation costs could impel the parties to renegotiate the treaty. For another potential problem stalks Kyoto: compliance
enforcement and free-rider deterrence. The Protocol defers discussion
of enforcement to a future meeting of the parties, but it is sensible to ask:
what would happen if in, say, 10 years' time, one of the parties to the
agreement announces that it will not be able to comply with it? Or
suppose, instead, that a party announces that it will withdraw from the
agreement, because the costs of meeting it are too steep. What will
prevent such a withdrawal? The treaty, at least in its present form,
offers little protection from such deviations. And this is not just a
problem for the future. Countries can reason backwards. If future
deviations cannot be prevented, why should a country invest in
abatement measures today?

Even this may not be the worst of the Protocol's problems. It is
possible, maybe even likely, that the agreement will never enter into
force. In July 1997, the United States Senate voted 95–0 in favour of a
non-binding resolution urging the President of the United States not to
negotiate an agreement that required that only the industrial countries
reduce their greenhouse-gas emissions or that would result in serious
harm to the US economy, where by 'serious harm' the Senate meant, in
the words of Senator Robert Byrd, a co-author of the resolution, 'capital
flight and a loss of jobs in the United States'. This is important because
the Senate must ratify (by a two-thirds majority) any treaty that is to be
binding on the United States, and an effective climate-change treaty is
sure to require US participation. There are many reasons for this, but
perhaps the most obvious is that United States is the world's largest
emitter. Its emissions are about 50 per cent higher than the entire
emissions of the European Union.

The Clinton Administration previously endorsed the principle that
the industrial countries should reduce their emissions first, and could
not easily reverse out of this promise in Kyoto. And nor was Europe

keen on relaxing the so-called Berlin Mandate. So the agreement reached in Kyoto clashed with the Senate's recommendation that developing countries reduce their emissions (whether implementation of the Protocol will be costly to the United States is a question requiring some analysis, and I shall return to it later). Of course, the Senate could have been bluffing, perhaps in the hope that its resolution would give President Clinton an edge in the Kyoto negotiations. Indeed, during the debate on the resolution, Senator Byrd said that the resolution would 'add strength to our US negotiating team'. But just after the negotiations ended in Kyoto, a number of senators asked that the treaty come to the Senate floor for ratification so that they could reject it. President Clinton has since said that he would not send the treaty to the Senate without 'meaningful participation from key developing countries'.

If the United States does not ratify the treaty, it is possible that the agreement will still come into force. To enter into law, and therefore to become binding on the countries that are parties to it (but not other countries), the Protocol must be ratified by at least 55 countries, responsible for at least 55 per cent of the total carbon-dioxide emissions of the so-called 'Annex I' countries (the industrial countries listed in the original Framework Convention) in 1990. As shown in Table 1, the United States accounts for only 36 per cent of Annex I emissions. So, if enough of the countries making up the balance of Annex I emissions ratify the agreement, Kyoto will still enter the canon of climate law.

As of October 1998, 59 countries had signed the Protocol, including the 15 member states of the European Union and nine other Annex I countries (signatories are identified in Table 1 by an asterisk). These signatories make up just over 42 per cent of total Annex I emissions, and so the minimum participation required by the treaty would seem to be within easy reach. But putting a signature on a treaty does not obligate a country to ratify and, as of October 1998, only one country has ratified the Kyoto Protocol (though this in itself signifies nothing as the treaty was only recently negotiated): the small island state, Fiji.

Ratification by the current signatories is not inevitable. If the USA does not ratify the agreement, the other Annex I countries will benefit less from participating; these countries will have to undertake the emission reductions prescribed by the treaty (and shown in column 3 of Table 1) without the benefit of substantial US abatement. It is even possible that non-participation by the USA will *increase* the cost to these countries of keeping within their Kyoto limits, because of the treaty's trading arrangements (explained later in the chapter). It thus seems likely that many Annex I countries will await US ratification before serving the Kyoto Protocol up to their own parliaments. This means

Table 1
Status of the Kyoto Protocol

Annex I countries	CO_2 emissions 1990 (gigagrams)	Share of Annex I 1990 emissions (%)	Kyoto target 2008–12	Projected emissions 2000 (% relative to 1990 or alternative base year)
United States	4,957,022	36.00	93	104
European Union*	3,288,667	24.05	92	103
Austria*	59,200	0.43	92	111
Belgium*	114,410	0.84	92	n.a.
Denmark*	52,025	0.38	92	103
Finland*	53,900	0.39	92	131
France*	366,536	2.68	92	109
Germany*	1,014,155	7.42	92	90
Greece*	82,100	0.60	92	115
Ireland*	30,719	0.22	92	120
Italy*	428,941	3.14	92	113
Luxembourg*	11,343	0.08	92	67
Netherlands*	167,600	1.23	92	92
Portugal*	42,148	0.31	92	129
Spain*	227,322	1.66	92	122
Sweden*	61,256	0.45	92	104
UK*	577,012	4.22	92	102
Australia*	288,965	2.11	108	115
Canada*	462,643	3.38	94	110
Iceland	2,172	0.02	110	105
Japan*	1,155,000	8.45	94	104
New Zealand*	25,476	0.19	100	116
Norway*	35,514	0.26	101	111
Switzerland*	45,070	0.33	92	97
Liechtenstein	208	n.a.	92	118
Monaco	n.a.	n.a.	92	n.a.
Economies in Transition	3,364,259	24.60	103	81
Alternative base year	3,531,476	—	98	77
Bulgaria* 1990	82,990	0.61	107	84
1988	96,878	—	92	72
Czech Republic	165,792	1.21	92	82
Estonia	37,797	0.28	92	54
Hungary 1990	71,673	0.52	110	96
1985–7	83,676	—	94	82
Latvia	22,976	0.17	92	74
Lithuania*	n.a.	n.a.	92	n.a.
Poland* 1990	414,930	3.03	108	96
1988	478,880	—	94	83
Romania 1990	171,103	1.25	107	n.a.
1989	198,479	—	92	n.a.

Table 1 (continued)

Annex I countries	CO$_2$ emissions 1990 (gigagrams)	Share of Annex I 1990 emissions (%)	Kyoto target 2008–12	Projected emissions 2000 (% relative to 1990 or alternative base year)
Russian Federation	2,388,720	17.47	100	83
Ukraine	n.a.	n.a.	100	n.a.
Slovakia	58,278	0.43	92	84
Croatia	n.a.	n.a.	95	n.a.
Slovenia	n.a.	n.a.	92	n.a.
Total 1990	13,675,067	100	95	98
Total base	13,842,284	–	94	97

Notes: Two Annex I countries (Belarus and Turkey) are excluded from the table, as they are not included in Annex B of the Kyoto Protocol. Four other countries (Liechtenstein, Monaco, Croatia, and Slovenia) are included in Annex B but not in Annex I. *Indicates that the country is a signatory to the Kyoto Protocol, as of 23 October 1998. CO$_2$ emissions exclude land-use change and forestry.
Source: All data are from the web page of the Climate Change Secretariat, http://www.unfcc.de.

that, if the USA does not ratify the agreement, then it may not enter into force.[1]

Why should countries negotiate a treaty that could leave them worse off, or that may never even enter into international law? The scenario seems unlikely, but it is entirely in keeping with the history of climate-change policy. As described in section 2, countries have previously announced their intention to keep within self-imposed emission ceilings — and then failed to meet them. Moreover, the Kyoto Protocol is not unique in the annals of international cooperation. The Law of the Sea Convention, negotiated in 1982, did not enter into force until 1994 — and participation by the major maritime powers, including the United States and United Kingdom, had to await negotiation of a side agreement which effectively rewrote key provisions in the original treaty.

Of course, predicting whether Kyoto will endure, or whether it will achieve much if implemented, depends on many details. It depends, especially, on assumptions about how the important concepts in the agreement will be interpreted, about the institutions that will be developed to support it, about the costs of taking action, and about the

---

[1] Just as it is hard to imagine a Gulf War coalition forming without the support of the United States, so it is hard to see how an effective climate-change regime could develop without American backing.

future evolution of the treaty. All these details are uncertain. They are discussed in my analysis of the agreement in section 3.

In the long run, whether or not Kyoto enters into law will not matter very much. If the Protocol fails to become law, countries will attempt to renegotiate the agreement. If Kyoto does enter into law but later collapses for whatever reason, a new agreement can always be negotiated. Even if Kyoto succeeds—if it enters into law and is implemented to the last detail—a string of amendments will need to be negotiated, to say what must be done after 2012. Kyoto is really just the start of a long process, and it must be remembered that climate change is a very long-run problem. What will matter most in the future is whether countries perceive that substantial mitigation is justified, and whether the international system can muster the cooperation needed to sustain this effort. I turn to these fundamental issues in section 4. The final section of the chapter pulls these different analyses together and revisits the theme of this introduction.

2. Getting to Kyoto

(a) *Preliminaries*

The so-called greenhouse gases include not only carbon dioxide (CO_2), but also methane, nitrous oxide, fluorocarbons (including hydro-fluorocarbons and perfluorocarbons), tropospheric ozone (precursors of which include nitrogen oxides, non-methane hydrocarbons, and carbon monoxide), and sulphur hexafluoride.[2] However, CO_2 accounts for the bulk of aggregate warming potential and, mainly for this reason, the policy debate has focused on the extent to which emissions of this gas should be limited. In 1988, a semi-political conference held in Toronto recommended that, as a first step, CO_2 emissions should be reduced 20 per cent from the 1988 level by 2005. This so-called 'Toronto target' was arbitrary, but the idea that countries should commit to meeting a target for emission reduction (as opposed to, say, a carbon tax or a technology standard) has endured. It is perhaps the most important feature of the Kyoto Protocol.

In the same year that this conference was held, the Intergovernmental Panel on Climate Change (IPCC) was formed, at the request of the

---

[2] Other halocarbons, including chlorofluorocarbons (CFCs) and hydro-chlorofluorocarbons (HCFCs), are also potentially important from the policy perspective, but are being controlled by the Montreal Protocol and its associated amendments. Moreover, it is now known that the direct warming effect of these gases is partly offset by a cooling effect caused by the reduction in stratospheric ozone.

UN General Assembly. The IPCC was asked to report on what was known and not known about climate change, on the potential impacts of climate change, and on what could be done to forestall and adapt to climate change. The IPCC's first assessment report, published in 1990, concluded that 'emissions resulting from human activities are substantially increasing the atmospheric concentrations of the greenhouse gases . . . [and] will enhance the greenhouse effect, resulting on average in an additional warming of the Earth's surface' (IPCC, 1990, p. 1). The report calculated that 'the long-lived gases [including CO_2] would require immediate reductions in emissions from human activities of over 60 per cent to stabilize their concentrations at today's levels', and it predicted that, under the 'Business-as-Usual' scenario, global mean temperature would rise by between 0.2 °C and 0.5 °C, and mean global sea level would rise by between 3 and 10 cm, per decade during the next century. Rather ominously, the IPCC noted that 'the complexity of the system means that we cannot rule out surprises'.

(b) Unilateral Pledges

Following publication of the IPCC's 1990 report, a number of OECD countries announced intentions to reduce their CO_2 emissions.[3] Some pledged to meet the Toronto target (Austria, Denmark, Italy, Luxembourg; New Zealand pledged that it would do so by 2000 rather than 2005). Some set a goal of stabilizing their CO_2 emissions at the 1989 level by 2000 (Norway) or at the 1990 level by 2000 (Finland, Switzerland, United Kingdom) or to reduce emissions 3–5 per cent by 2000 (The Netherlands). Germany, helped by unification, set the most ambitious target: to reduce CO_2 emissions 25–30 per cent from the 1987 level by 2005. Australia pledged to reduce its emissions of all greenhouse gases not controlled under the Montreal Protocol (that is, excluding CFCs and HCFCs), while other countries (Canada and the United States among them) set a target of stabilizing the emissions of all greenhouse gases, including those covered by the Montreal Protocol. France and Japan pledged to stabilize their CO_2 emissions at the 1990 level by 2000 but only on a per-capita basis (allowing emissions to increase as population increased). Spain, a relatively poor OECD member, set the goal of limiting its growth in CO_2 emissions to 25 per cent. Finally, some countries merely promised to play a part in achieving a collective target. In October 1990 the European Community (EC) announced its intention to stabilize Community-wide emissions at the 1990 level by 2000, a target to which all its member states were collectively bound. Members

[3] The International Energy Agency (1992) has compiled a comprehensive listing of climate-change policies, and I am drawing here from this report.

of the European Free Trade Association, including Iceland and Sweden, were in turn bound by a separate agreement jointly to meet the EC target.

All this may give the impression that much was being done, but the reality was different. Few countries put into place policies that would contribute to their targets being met, and there seemed little need to do so. For some of these targets were intended merely as goals, while others were conditional on other countries taking similar action (this was true of Britain, for example, under the Thatcher government). Though New Zealand set for itself an ambitious goal of reducing its CO_2 emissions 20 per cent from the 1990 level by 2000, it simultaneously insisted that any policy adopted should have a net benefit for New Zealand. Several countries claimed to be 'committed' to achieving a particular emission ceiling, but none truly was committed. If a country learned later that its interests would be badly served by meeting its target, then there would be nothing to stop it from failing to meet it. Indeed, it would be hard to argue that a country would even be morally bound to meet a target which it had set for itself, especially when other countries were at the same time failing to meet *their* targets.

The EC's climate policy was especially important, partly because of the Community's relatively large share of global emissions and partly because of the way the Community's target was framed. When the target was agreed in 1990, no decision was made as to how it would be met, and as it was a collective target, no country was individually responsible for meeting it. A collective policy for meeting the target was needed. The European Commission proposed meeting the target by means of an energy conservation programme coupled with a fiscal measure, a carbon tax. The tax, which was to be set at a rate equivalent to $3 per barrel of oil, rising over time to $10 per barrel, would probably have been enough to meet the stabilization target (see Barrett, 1992). But in May 1992, shortly before the Rio Earth Summit convened, the Community announced a number of modifications to the original tax proposal.

The first of these was to supplement the carbon tax with an energy tax (the combined tax would be equivalent to the per-barrel tax noted above). Ostensibly, the intention was not just to reduce carbon-dioxide emissions but also to conserve energy. But the real reason was to dilute the advantage that a pure carbon tax would give nuclear energy and countries with high shares of nuclear electricity generation (such as Belgium and France). A second modification was to exempt the main energy-using industries from having to pay the tax. This was to stop these industries from suffering a 'competitive disadvantage', relative to non-EC countries. The final modification was to make implementation of the EC tax conditional on other OECD countries (especially the United States and Japan) adopting the same tax. As the chances of this were nil, this meant that Europe was not prepared to implement the policy needed to achieve its own target.

(c) *To Rio*

The Community's policy was being mapped out just as negotiations on the Framework Convention on Climate Change were coming to a close. Throughout these negotiations, Europe tried to persuade the United States to fix a date for stabilizing its CO_2 emissions. The United States refused, however, and the final text of the Framework Convention, which was signed by over 150 countries at the Rio Earth Summit in June 1992, did not commit any signatories to meeting specific targets and timetables (contrary to reports one often reads in the newspapers). Article 4 says that developed country parties recognize 'that the return by the end of the present decade to earlier levels of anthropogenic emissions of carbon dioxide and other greenhouse gases' would be desirable. It also says that these parties should devise policies 'with the aim of returning individually or jointly to their 1990 levels of these anthropogenic emissions'. But in contrast to the Kyoto Protocol, no country was required by the Framework Convention to meet any particular target by any particular date. Indeed, it was precisely for this reason that this agreement was ratified by so many countries and came into force so quickly (in December 1993).

(d) *After Rio*

The IPCC revised its earlier predictions in 1995, partly to take account of the effect of aerosols on radiative forcing. Aerosols are tiny airborne particles, released when fossil fuels are burned, and result in a local cooling effect (unlike some greenhouse gases, which can persist in the atmosphere for decades, even centuries, aerosols have an atmospheric lifetime of about a week). Once aerosols were included in the climate models, the IPCC predicted more modest change: an increase in global mean temperature of about 0.14–0.28 °C per decade, as compared with an increase of 0.16–0.36 °C per decade when the effects of greenhouse gases alone were considered. Aerosols were also predicted to limit mean sea level rise to about 2–8 cm per decade.

Though inclusion of aerosols lowered slightly the predicted consequence of climate change, it also increased confidence in the estimates of climate models. When aerosols were included, the predicted changes accorded better with the historical record. Partly for this reason, the IPCC (1995, p. 22) was able to warn that, 'the balance of evidence suggests that there is a discernible human influence on global climate'. Still, even today the science of climate change is riddled with uncertainties: about the extent and timing of climate change; about regional variations; about whether small changes in atmospheric concentrations could, beyond some point, trigger a discontinuous change in some important climate feature.

(e) *From Berlin to Kyoto*

At the first Conference of the Parties to the Framework Convention, held in Berlin in 1995, the industrialized parties agreed to negotiate emission limits within specified time frames, such as 2005, 2010, and 2020. These quantitative ceilings were to be included in a new protocol that might be ready for signing by the end of 1997. Importantly, developing countries were not expected to limit their emissions. It was this differential treatment of industrialized and developing nations in the so-called 'Berlin mandate' that the US Senate later objected to and that ultimately came to be embodied in the Kyoto Protocol.

It is as well to recall, however, that at this time most countries had still not devised, let alone implemented, effective policies for meeting the targets they had set unilaterally years before. Some countries, including Norway and Finland, conceded that they did not expect to meet their targets (Grubb, 1995), despite having imposed hefty carbon taxes. The few countries that did expect to meet their targets were only able to do so for reasons of fortuitous circumstance (in Britain, the 'dash for gas'; in Germany, unification), not determined policy. Most importantly, the European Union (EU) signally failed to devise a policy sure of meeting its 'commitment' to stabilize emissions at the 1990 level. In a letter to the chairman of the European Parliament's environment committee, leaked on the eve of the Berlin conference, Jacques Santer, the President of the European Commission, conceded that 'a single tax . . . applicable in all member states [was] no longer conceivable'.[4] At the same time, the Commission had not developed an alternative collective policy for meeting the EU's target. Evidence supplied to the European Commission suggested that at most three of the EU's 15 member states would stabilize their own CO_2 emissions at the 1990 level by 2000.[5] And, yet, when Europe's diplomats headed for Kyoto, they were hoping to tighten up on the earlier targets, to secure an agreement that would reduce emissions (of the three main gases, carbon dioxide, methane, and nitrous oxide) 7.5 per cent by 2005 and 15 per cent by 2010.

[4] *The European*, 17–23 March 1995, p. 1.
[5] *Ibid.*

3. Analysis of the Kyoto Agreement

As noted in the Introduction, the Kyoto Protocol specifies maximum emission levels for the so-called Annex I countries (see Table 1), and dates by which these ceilings (calculated relative to 1990 emission levels) must be met. Just as significant, the emissions of developing countries are entirely unconstrained by the protocol. These twin features fulfil the promise made at the First Conference of the Parties in Berlin in 1995, and in this sense made Kyoto a success. Ultimately, however, whether Kyoto succeeds will depend on how it becomes implemented, and especially on whether implementation can be made cost-effective.

A variety of so-called 'flexible mechanisms' are built into Kyoto, and they have the *potential* of supporting a cost-effective final allocation of climate-change mitigation. It is hard to say, however, to what extent this potential will be realized. The data are sketchy in places and analyses of some features of the agreement have not yet been undertaken. Much will also depend on how the flexible mechanisms take shape and how countries devise their own policies. We can say something about certain bench-mark cases, and problem areas can be pointed out. But that is about as far as our analysis can go. It happens, however, that this is enough to support the warning that introduced this paper.

(a) *Cost Implications of the Emission Limits*

Suppose that the limits negotiated in Kyoto were met exactly, with no potential for arbitrage across countries. That is, suppose that the EU kept its emissions to 92 per cent of its 1990 level, that the USA limited its emissions to 93 per cent of its 1990 level, that China emitted as much as it pleased, and so on. Then the marginal cost of climate-change mitigation would vary from country to country. It would be zero in China, where emissions were unconstrained (and growing rapidly), and high in Europe and the United States. How high? According to one study (Nordhaus and Boyer, 1998), the marginal cost of implementing the individual targets in the protocol could be $125 per ton of carbon by around 2010. Another study (Manne and Richels, 1998) predicts that marginal costs could be $240 per ton of carbon in 2010. This difference in marginal cost ($0 in the developing countries compared to $125 or $240 in the OECD countries) in turn implies that the total cost of achieving any given emission ceiling will be excessive. Shifting just one ton of abatement from the OECD countries to the developing countries would save the world at least $100, perhaps much more. Shifting more abatement would save even more money (though of course the marginal cost saving will fall as more abatement is shifted). Total costs will, of course, be minimized where the marginal cost of abatement is everywhere equal.

As noted earlier, estimates prepared by the Clinton Administration suggest that a cost-effective agreement—that is, an agreement which reduced global emissions by the same amount as required by the Kyoto Protocol, but which did so by distributing the burden of abatement such that marginal costs were everywhere equal—could lower marginal costs to around $14–23 per ton, about one-tenth the level that would be needed to implement the individual emission ceilings in the protocol. This is a huge difference, and one that is reflected also in other studies. For example, Nordhaus and Boyer (1998) estimate the marginal cost of a cost-effective Kyoto Protocol to be $11/ton in 2010. Manne and Richels (1998) obtain a much higher figure—$70/ton in 2010—but one that is still low in comparison with their estimate of marginal costs when the Kyoto Protocol targets are met exactly.

Estimates of reductions in total costs are of a similar relative magnitude. According to the Clinton Administration's analysis, the total cost to the USA of implementing Kyoto could be just $7–12 billion per year, if the agreement is implemented cost-effectively, but perhaps ten times as large otherwise. Manne and Richels (1998) predict that cost-effective implementation of Kyoto would cost the USA around $20 billion or 0.25 per cent of GDP in 2010, but perhaps four times as much if implemented without trading. (Would this cause 'serious harm' to the US economy? Ask the Senate.) Nordhaus and Boyer (1998) estimate that the total cost of implementing Kyoto without trading (in present value terms) would be about seven times the cost-effective level.

But this is to compare extremes. As detailed below, the Kyoto Protocol offers a number of mechanisms intended to lower total implementation costs. As also explained, these mechanisms will not work perfectly, and so will not mimic the cost-effective outcome. The costs of implementing Kyoto are likely to lie somewhere between the bench-marks given above.

Note, however, that we cannot even be sure of this. For example, the estimates of marginal and total costs given above assume that domestic implementation by every nation is cost-effective—that the marginal costs of abatement are everywhere equal *within* each country. This is unlikely to happen. It is certainly not a feature of most environmental policies that have been adopted in the past. The carbon taxes adopted by most Nordic countries, for example, vary by sector, with households having to pay more than industry (partly out of a concern for trade leakage). Until we know the policies that countries will develop to meet their targets—and these have not been spelled out yet—we will not know how costly it will be to meet the Kyoto targets.

(b) *Flexible and Market Mechanisms*

(i) Net emissions targets

The extent of climate change will depend on atmospheric concentrations (though with a lag) of greenhouse gases, and changes in these concentrations depend on the removal of CO_2 from the atmosphere as well as gross emissions. CO_2 removal depends in turn on land use: growing trees absorb carbon from the atmosphere; the standing forest stores carbon (if burned, trees release carbon back into the atmosphere). So if trees are planted and the standing forest is prevented from being burned, concentrations will fall (all else being equal), and these activities should be encouraged just as emissions are discouraged. The emission limits specified in the Kyoto Protocol do this. They allow deductions for 'removals by sinks resulting from direct human-induced land-use change and forestry activities, limited to afforestation, reforestation and deforestation since 1990'. In other words, the Kyoto targets limit *net* emissions.[6]

Will including carbon sinks reduce the costs of meeting the Kyoto limits substantially? The Clinton Administration's (1998, p. 24) analysis suggests that it could. 'Promoting afforestation and reforestation,' the report maintains, 'may reduce atmospheric concentrations of CO_2 at much lower costs than reducing emissions of greenhouse gases resulting from industrial activity.' At the margin, assuming that only abatement of gross emissions is undertaken, this must surely be right. However, Stavins (1998b) finds that the marginal cost of carbon sequestration rises steeply—more steeply than marginal gross abatement costs for the United States. So the aggregate cost savings from carbon sequestration may not be all that large.

Measurement problems are also bound to be rife. The Protocol insists that the changes in net emissions be 'measured as verifiable changes in carbon stocks', but such changes cannot be measured with the same precision as the carbon emissions resulting from fossil fuel consumption. And how is one to interpret whether an action constitutes a 'direct human-induced land-use change'? Would the recent fires in Indonesia count? Settling these matters is a subject of ongoing negotiations.

[6] To be precise, the Protocol allows sinks to play a role in capping emissions. It does not include carbon sinks in the emissions baseline, with one exception. If a country's carbon sinks were a net source of greenhouse-gas emissions in 1990, then its net emissions from sinks must be incorporated into the baseline.

(ii) Comprehensive emissions targets

The Protocol's net emission limits apply to a bundle of greenhouse gases and not just carbon dioxide. The other gases include methane, nitrous oxide, hydrofluorocarbons, perfluorocarbons, and sulphur hexa-fluoride.[7] These are bundled up with carbon dioxide into an aggregate measure, with the weights attached to individual gases reflecting their 'global warming potentials'. Abatement of a ton of nitrous oxide, for example, is equivalent to abatement of around 315 tons of carbon.

This 'comprehensive approach' to climate change mitigation was championed by the Bush Administration, and is to be welcomed. In allowing for trade-offs between different types of gases, the total cost to climate-change mitigation will be lowered.

By how much will this mechanism lower costs? I have not seen any estimates, though in a statement before the US House of Representatives,[8] Janet Yellen of the Council of Economic Advisers noted that 'a strategy of reducing non-CO_2 greenhouse gas emissions by a greater percent than CO_2 emissions could lower emissions permit prices (that is, marginal costs) by as much as 10 per cent'.

(iii) 'Banking'

Kyoto does not require that the emission ceilings shown in Table 1 be met every year; it requires only that they be met by each Annex I party on average over the 5-year period, 2008–12. Moreover, parties are allowed to carry forward additional reductions to a future control period. That is, if a country reduces its emissions by more than required in the first control period (2008–12), it can 'bank' or carry forward the surplus to the next control period. Finally, certified emission reductions, carried out under the Clean Development Mechanism (CDM; see below) from 2000 to 2007 can also be carried forward to the first commitment period, 2008–12. This allows Annex I countries to benefit from taking early action through the CDM.

These provisions could be helpful, but they do not go far enough. In particular, Kyoto does not allow parties to shift emission reductions toward the future—that is, to 'borrow' future emission reductions. Of course, if abatement is shifted forward, the benefits of the abatement

[7] Note that the European Union and Japan sought to limit just three gases. It was the USA that insisted on including all six gases.

[8] Janet Yellen, Statement before the US House of Representatives Committee on Government Reform and Oversight, Subcommittee on National Economic Growth, Natural Resources, and Regulatory Affairs, 19 May 1998, http://www.state.gov/www/policy_remarks/1998/980519_yellen_climate.html

in present value terms will fall. But costs may fall much more. If abatement is rushed (and it will be under the Kyoto timetable), some of the existing capital stock will have to be scrapped before its useful life is up. It would be cheaper if emission reductions could be effected by incremental investments. Manne and Richels (1998) estimate substantial savings to a gradual transition to the Kyoto targets, with marginal costs being reduced by a factor of ten or more in 2010.

(iv) Emissions trading

Perhaps the most important flexible mechanism in the Kyoto agreement is the provision for trading among the Annex I countries. According to the Clinton Administration's (1998) analysis, this provision could lower the marginal cost of implementing Kyoto by 72 per cent, and lower the total cost of implementation by 57 per cent, compared with the benchmark of meeting the national targets unilaterally. Nordhaus and Boyer (1998) obtain a similar result. By their calculations, the present value total cost of implementing Kyoto would be reduced 45 per cent by Annex I trading.

Whether savings like these will ever be realized will depend on how the institutions supporting trading develop. If the trading arrangements allow a market to develop which provides ready price discovery and low transactions costs, then the bulk of these gains will be realized. Otherwise just a fraction, perhaps a small fraction, of these gains will be pocketed.

Europe has thus far been suspicious of the concept, believing it to be a ploy for letting the United States evade its responsibilities. This is a gross misunderstanding of the problem. As noted before, *where* abatement takes place is of no relevance to the climate. Absolutely nothing can be gained by making the United States or any other country pay more than is necessary for abatement. Indeed, it is not even obvious that the USA would gain disproportionately from trading. Calculations by McKibbin *et al.* (1998) show that Europe would gain more from trading than the United States.

(v) 'Hot air' trading

One reason that trading among the Annex I countries would lower marginal and total costs is that the economies in transition are allowed by Article 3 to choose an alternative base year to 1990 (subject to some restrictions). As shown in Table 1, Bulgaria has chosen 1988 as a base year; Hungary, the average of 1985–7; Poland, 1988; and Romania, 1989. The effect is to create a surplus of emission entitlements that may not be exhausted by economic growth in these countries, even by 2010.

Russia must retain its 1990 base year, but it will still have a huge surplus
by the year 2000, if the projections shown in Table 1 prove correct
(unfortunately, projections to 2008–12 are not available).

As long as these emission ceilings do not bite, marginal abatement
costs in the economies in transition will be zero without Annex I
trading. Trading, however, will lower costs for all the Annex I countries
for two reasons: first, by redistributing abatement within the Annex I
group of countries, such that marginal costs are everywhere equal; and
second, by relaxing the total constraint on Annex I emissions.

To see the importance of this second effect, consider the consequences of trading within a US–Russian umbrella. In the year 2000, the
estimates in Table 1 suggest that emissions in the USA could not exceed
0.93 x 4,957,022 = 4,610,030 gigagrams without trading. If the estimates
in the table are to be believed, Russia will easily stay within its limits,
emitting only 0.83 x 2,388,720 = 1,982,638 gigagrams of CO_2 in 2000.
Hence, without trading, total emissions for both countries would not
exceed 4,610,030 + 1,982,638 = 6,592,668 gigagrams. But Russia is
allowed to emit up to 2,388,720 gigagrams of CO_2 in 2000. So total
allowed emissions for both countries under a trading regime are
4,610,030 + 2,388,720 = 6,998,750 gigagrams. Trading thus eases the total
constraint on the two countries by 6,998,750 – 6,592,668 = 406,082
gigagrams in 2000. For reasons that should be obvious, this difference
in aggregate emissions between the trading and no-trading cases is
sometimes referred to as 'hot air'.

As noted at the bottom of Table 1, the Kyoto emission constraints are
expected to bind in the aggregate, even by the year 2000. Annex I
emissions are projected to be 97 per cent of the adjusted base-year
emissions, whereas Kyoto requires that they be 94 per cent of this level.
However, the 'hot air' released by trading does ease the aggregate
emissions constraint for Annex I emissions. Annex I trading lowers
costs partly by lowering total abatement.

Note, however, that though the 'hot air' provision appears to be a
loophole, had it not been created—had the economies in transition been
given tighter emissions constraints—it is likely that the other Annex I
countries would have insisted that their own emission constraints be
relaxed. For in reducing the amount of 'hot air', the costs to the other
Annex I countries of fulfilling *their* commitments would increase. When
seen in the context of the negotiations, a bigger problem with the 'hot
air' provision may be that it gave away something for nothing.

Of course, the economies in transition could be justified in putting
their resources somewhere other than in climate-change mitigation
(many of these countries are poorer than some non-Annex I countries).
But the other Annex I countries have given these economies *more* than

was needed to make their participation incentive compatible. This is not just a matter of redistributing the gains from cooperation. Had less been given away, the incentives for the other Annex I countries to participate in the agreement would have increased, whereas the European economies in transition would still have had an incentive to participate, so long as their incentive compatibility constraints were satisfied.

(vi) Joint implementation

The Kyoto Protocol also allows 'joint implementation' (JI) trades among the Annex I countries. These are bilateral project-based, rather than market-based, trades, in which one country receives 'emission reduction units' for undertaking projects in another country that reduce net emissions.

JI trades must be individually negotiated, and so will entail transactions costs. These costs will likely be high because of the elusive nature of the commodity being traded. JI projects must provide 'a reduction in emissions by sources, or an enhancement of removals by sinks, that is *additional* to any that would otherwise occur' (emphasis added). Calculating this additional reduction will not be easy, because of course one is not able to observe the emissions profile that would have been realized had the trade not taken place. This must instead be inferred. Costly analyses will thus need to be undertaken. Experience with the emissions trading programme in the United States suggests that where transactions costs are high, bilateral trading will be limited.

(vii) Clean development mechanism

The JI concept is extended to include non-Annex I countries through the CDM. This allows Annex I countries to meet their emission ceilings by undertaking projects in developing countries that provide 'additional' and 'certified' emission reductions. The CDM is potentially of huge significance, for it provides the only means within the Kyoto framework of shifting abatement toward the non-Annex I countries.

But the CDM has a number of problems. One is that it is not obvious whether the CDM would be limited to emission reductions or whether it can include sequestration projects. The provisions for JI explicitly allow sequestration projects to be included, but the CDM article is silent on this question.

An even more important difference is that one of the parties to a CDM transaction will not have its emissions capped. Potentially, therefore, the CDM could produce only 'paper' emission reductions. Moreover, as Stavins (1998a) warns, it is likely that the least beneficial CDM projects will be adversely selected by this mechanism. Indeed, the problem is doubly worrying. Not only do developing countries have incentives to offer projects that would have been undertaken anyway, but the Annex I countries have incentives also to select these projects, if they can be acquired at lower cost (this is just another manifestation of the free-rider problem).

It will therefore be a matter of interest not only to the parties engaging in a CDM transaction but also to all other parties whether a transaction really will provide 'reductions in emissions that are additional to any that would occur in the absence of the certified project activity'. And it is for this reason, in contrast to the JI provisions, that the emission reductions resulting from a CDM transaction must be 'certified by operational entities to be designated by the Conference of the Parties'.

Though necessary, certification will be costly, and the countries carrying out CDM trades will have to pay for certification (as noted in the Protocol, 'a share of the proceeds from certified project activities [will be] used to cover administrative expenses'). Moreover, Kyoto insists that a share of the proceeds from CDM trades also be used 'to assist developing country Parties that are particularly vulnerable to the adverse effects of climate change to meet the costs of adaptation'. This sounds like a tax. If CDM transactions are taxed, and if transactions costs are high, the volume of CDM trades will be very low.

There is no way of knowing by how much costs will be reduced by the CDM, not least because the important details have yet to be negotiated. In her statement to the US House of Representatives, however, Janet Yellen offered a guess:

> The CDM cannot realistically be expected to yield all the gains of binding targets for developing countries, but it might shave costs by roughly another 20 to 25 per cent from the reduced costs that result from trading among Annex I countries.

As suggested by this statement, CDM transactions costs could have been reduced considerably had the Kyoto diplomats succeeded in negotiating emission limits for the developing countries. The issue is not whether these countries should pay to participate. Most poor countries would have every incentive to walk away from an agreement that required them to dig into their pockets, and few people would blame them for doing so. But if developing countries had agreed to be bound by targets, then they would be able to trade with the Annex I countries and—subject to appropriate choice of their emission ceilings—be virtually sure of being better off. An earlier draft of the Protocol allowed developing countries to choose, at any time and on a voluntary basis, a level of emissions control that was appropriate to their circumstances, but the provision was subsequently expunged, apparently at the insistence of China and India (see Jacoby *et al.*, 1998). Since inclusion of developing countries in some manner is vital, the matter is sure to be on the agenda of future meetings of the parties.

(viii) 'Supplemental' trading

A further problem is that JI, CDM, and emissions-trading transactions are intended to be 'supplemental' to domestic actions, a constraint reaffirmed by the G8 group of countries meeting in April 1998. According to a *Financial Times* article (6 April 1998) on the G8 summit, the virtue in this constraint is that it will prevent the leading industrial nations (plus Russia) from being able 'to evade painful domestic reductions in greenhouse gas emissions'.

This is a twisted logic. It cannot be good for the environment. If anything, the restriction on trading, in elevating between-country differences in marginal costs, will harm the environment by magnifying the leakage problem. And it cannot be sure to make developing countries any better off either.

Whether this constraint will ever bite, however, is another unknown, for the parties have not defined what 'supplemental' means. If the notion is interpreted as being qualitative, then it will easily be satisfied, for even with unconstrained trading every Annex I country will undertake *some* abatement at home. More serious would be an arbitrary, quantitative limit on trading. Unfortunately, there is some support for such a cap, especially in Europe. The European Parliament adopted a resolution in September 1998 calling for 'an agreement to have a quantitative ceiling on the use of flexibility mechanisms to ensure that the majority of emissions reductions are met domestically'.

(ix) 'Bubbles' and 'umbrellas'

Article 4 of the Protocol allows parties to negotiate a side agreement, in which they pledge to fulfil their Kyoto ceilings jointly. This provision was important in that it made it possible for the European Union to negotiate on behalf of its 15 member states in Kyoto. The emission ceiling shown in Table 1 for the European Union is thus an aggregate ceiling. The European side agreement, establishing emission ceilings for individual member states, was negotiated in September 1998 and resulted in the burden-sharing agreement shown in Table 2.

Under the terms of the Kyoto agreement, Europe is thus treated as a 'bubble' (in the jargon of the US emissions-trading programme). As long as the total target for Europe is achieved, each member state is

Table 2
European Union Burden-sharing Agreement

Member state	National target (%)
Austria	−13
Belgium	−7.5
Denmark	−21
Finland	0
France	0
Germany	−21
Greece	+25
Ireland	+13
Italy	−6.5
Luxembourg	−28
Netherlands	−6
Portugal	+27
Spain	+15
Sweden	+4
United Kingdom	−12.5
Total EU	**−8**

considered also to be in compliance. However, should the total target not be met, each member state is held individually accountable for meeting the targets it accepted in the side agreement.

Note that the concept need not be confined to Europe. A number of countries (Australia, Canada, Japan, New Zealand, Russia, Ukraine, and the United States) have discussed setting up an 'umbrella' group of trading countries under this article, and it is likely that international trading will begin in this way.

(c) *Non-permanent Emission Caps*

Another concern about the emission limits in the Kyoto Protocol is that they are not permanent (as are the limits in the Montreal Protocol and the US sulphur-dioxide trading programme, for example). Emission limits for subsequent control periods will be established by future conferences and codified in future amendments; negotiations of the second round of limits (that is, those that apply beginning in 2013) are required to begin by 2005, but Kyoto has nothing more to say about these limits.

This matters because many actions to reduce emissions involve investments with very long lifetimes. Whether these investments will be worth making will depend on the magnitude of future limits. If one believes that future limits will be very tight, then long-term carbon-saving investments will appear more attractive today. If one believes that future limits will be slack, then costly carbon-saving investments will not pass the required hurdle.

Strategy may also intrude. If a country invested more in abatement than needed just to meet its target in the 2008–12 period, then this may only increase the emission reduction that it would have to meet in the next period. The reason is that, once the costs of the investment have been sunk, the costs to this country of reducing its emissions in the next period will be lower; its bargaining position will therefore have been compromised. Turning this argument around, a country might be able to negotiate an easier target for the next control period if it invested less in reducing its abatement costs in the first control period.

But it is easy to overstate this problem. Suppose Kyoto *had* imposed permanent emission ceilings. Then a different problem would arise: the parties to the protocol would question the credibility of the ceilings, knowing that the limits could always be renegotiated. If the countries believed that the future ceilings were too tight, they would 'under-invest' in abatement. Of course, once they had done so, the costs of meeting the original limits would be higher, and the case for lowering these ceilings would therefore be strengthened. The belief that the initial limits were 'too tight' would be self-fulfilling.

(d) *Arbitrary Emission Limits*

Nordhaus and Boyer (1998, p. 17) question Kyoto's choice of emission limits, noting that they do not relate to 'a particular goal for concentrations, temperature, or damages'. The targets certainly should take account of damages (see especially section V); at the very least they should provide a benefit (measured in terms of the damages avoided by the mitigation) that exceeds the cost of meeting the targets. But they should not take direct account of concentrations or temperature (even though these will be linked to damages).

One reason for this is that it is very hard to say by how much emissions should be limited. For example, though the Framework Convention requires that concentrations be stabilized at 'a level that would prevent dangerous anthropogenic interference with the climate system', no one knows what this level is.

But there is a deeper reason, too. For suppose that such a level could be identified. Then, if parties to the agreement pledged to ensure that this level was not exceeded, every party would have a strong incentive to withdraw from the agreement (or not to accede to it in the first place). The reason is that, if a party withdrew and increased its emissions, the remaining parties would have to reduce their emissions to ensure that the aggregate concentration target continued to be met. In a sense, the withdrawal would be rewarded. Similarly, if a country acceded to the agreement, the burden of meeting the aggregate target would be spread more widely, and, as a consequence, the original signatories would presumably be allowed to reduce their abatement levels — at the expense of the additional party having to increase its abatement. Accession would essentially be punished. An aggregate target thus exacerbates any incentives that may already exist for countries to free ride. That Kyoto does not specify an aggregate target is a virtue.

So, how should the targets reflect damages? Obviously, if the concern were with limiting total damages, then the effect would be the same as just described. However, suppose parties to the agreement were concerned only with maximizing their own collective pay-off (the difference between their total benefit and cost of mitigation). Then the incentives would be better aligned. If a country withdrew from the agreement, the remaining parties would reduce their abatement (since the aggregate marginal damage for the parties to the agreement would fall with the withdrawal); the withdrawal would be punished. If a country acceded, the countries that were already parties to the agreement would increase their abatement (since the aggregate marginal damage for parties would increase); the accession would be rewarded.[9]

(e) *Quantities vs Prices*

Setting quantitative targets may seem to be the obvious remedy, and it has been at the forefront of negotiations ever since the Toronto conference. But it has problems.[10] One problem is that the link between actions and outcomes, as measured in emissions relative to an historical base year, is tenuous. Carbon-dioxide emissions were 7 per cent lower in Britain in 1995 compared with 1990, even though Britain has not adopted a radical policy for reducing emissions. Similarly, emissions in Germany fell 12 per cent between 1990 and 1995. Emissions in Bulgaria, the Czech Republic, Estonia, Hungary, Latvia, and Slovakia fell by even more — by up to 50 per cent over this same period, without any of these countries adopting radical climate change mitigation policies. By contrast, emissions in all the countries that imposed carbon taxes in the early 1990s (Denmark, Finland, The Netherlands, Norway, and Sweden) were 4–15 per cent *higher* in 1995 than in 1990.

---

[9] This is the basic mechanism underlying the self-enforcing agreements studied in Barrett (1994).

[10] Hahn (1998) summarizes a number of alternative prescriptions. See also Nordhaus (1998).

Another problem is uncertainty. There is, of course, great uncertainty about the magnitude of climate-change damages. But there is uncertainty also about the costs of climate-change mitigation, and in a seminal paper Weitzman (1974) showed that the latter kind of uncertainty can have important implications for the choice of policy instrument (emission limit versus carbon tax). If a quantitative limit were fixed, marginal costs would be uncertain. If a tax were fixed, emission reductions would be uncertain. Weitzman showed that the tax is superior if the marginal cost curve is steep relative to the marginal benefit curve. Essentially, the tax ensures that marginal costs and benefits do not differ by much.

Pizer (1998) has calculated that taxes would be much more efficient than quantity limits for climate-change mitigation (in his simulations, the net benefits to using the tax are five times the estimate for a quantity control). A combination of policies can do even better (Roberts and Spence, 1976), though Pizer (1998) finds that a hybrid policy is unlikely to improve much on the pure tax scheme in the case of climate change. The essential point is that, even if the Kyoto targets were met cost-effectively, an alternative policy that leaned more in the direction of controlling marginal costs directly (carbon taxes) would be even better.

(f) Leakage

Because participation in the Kyoto Protocol is not full, there is a potential for 'leakage'. As the Annex I countries reduce their emissions, comparative advantage in the greenhouse-gas-intensive industries will shift towards the non-Annex I countries. This trade effect will be reinforced by the workings of the energy market; as demand for the carbon-intensive fuels in the Annex I countries falls, world prices for these fuels will fall, and consumption in the non-Annex I countries will therefore increase. Consequently, emissions outside the Annex I countries will increase; the environmental benefits of the agreement will be reduced. Potentially, if leakage is strong enough, the agreement would only succeed in redistributing global emissions. The effort to negotiate and implement the agreement would have been wasted.

How significant a problem is 'leakage'? The Clinton Administration (1998, p. 72) maintains that, with cost-effective implementation, the Protocol 'would likely have little impact on competitiveness'. Maybe so. But if implementation is not cost-effective — and as I have already explained it could be far from this mark — then the consequences could be different. Bernstein et al. (1998) find that leakage could be significant: for every 100 tons of carbon abated by the Annex I countries, non-Annex I emissions could rise 5–10 tons (global emissions would thus fall by only 90–5 tons). Manne and Richels (1998) and Nordhaus and Boyer (1998) also predict significant levels of leakage.

These levels may not appear high, but they will certainly be politically visible.[11] Leakage would damage particular industries, and these will surely lobby for protection. The Senate resolution drew attention to the problem, and the proposed EC carbon tax was modified partly to take account of the concerns voiced by the energy-intensive industries about a possible loss in 'competitiveness'. It is no surprise that unilateral carbon taxes within countries vary by sector, with industry – and especially the energy-intensive export industries – always paying the lowest amount. When the EU burden-sharing rule was being negotiated, a number of countries (Austria, Denmark, The Netherlands, Spain, and Finland) wanted to make meeting the national targets conditional on the introduction of EU-wide emissions-control measures. These countries were concerned that, as they reduced emissions, perhaps by imposing steep carbon taxes at home, output in the sectors most highly taxed would shift elsewhere within the Union. The Danish minister said that, though he accepted that Denmark's –21 per cent target was unconditional, Denmark would only be able to achieve –17 per cent without EU-wide measures being adopted.[12]

This links up with a point made in the Introduction: that concerns about leakage provide another reason for wanting to encourage trading. In reducing the between-country difference in marginal costs, trading reduces leakage. Trading therefore lowers costs *and* increases benefits.

4. Compliance Enforcement and Free-Rider Deterrence

Assume the best: that enough countries ratify Kyoto that it comes into force and that the flexible mechanisms in Kyoto allow abatement to be cost-effective. Then we can ask: Will the parties to Kyoto actually comply with the agreement? Will they stay within the limits prescribed by Tables 1 and 2?

It is a remarkable fact that non-compliance with international agreements is extremely rare. And, when it does occur, the reason is usually that the deviant was for some reason unable to comply, rather than that it chose not to comply.

[11] Previous studies have shown that leakage could be more substantial (IPCC, 1996, ch. 11).
[12] 'EU States Agree Kyoto Emissions Limits', *ENDS Environment Daily*, 17 June 1998, http://www.ends.co.uk/subscribers/envdaily/articles/98061701.html

But why do parties comply? One reason is that they are expected to by customary of international law. And it is obvious why custom demands compliance. If states could not be relied upon to act as they said they would act, then what would be the point of entering into agreements?

But does this mean that compliance is not a problem? If it does, then it should not matter that the Kyoto Protocol does not (yet) include any provisions for punishing non-compliance. As Chayes and Chayes (1995, pp. 32–3) note, the authority to impose sanctions 'is rarely granted by treaty, rarely used when granted, and likely to be ineffective when used'. So Kyoto's failure to enforce compliance by sanctions may be an irrelevance.

However, the facts are open to a different interpretation, that:

> both the high rate of compliance and relative absence of enforcement threats are due not so much to the irrelevance of enforcement as to the fact that states are avoiding deep cooperation — and the benefits it holds whenever a prison-ers' dilemma situation exists — because they are unwilling or unable to pay the costs of enforcement. (Downs *et al.*, 1996, p. 387)

This last interpretation may seem cynical and unconvincing. After all, as we have seen, Kyoto does strive to sustain 'deep' cooperation — a treaty that imposes a cost measured as a fraction of GDP can hardly be described as 'shallow'. But, then again, Kyoto has not even entered into force yet, let alone been implemented. So we cannot really choose between these different theories.

Indeed, it would not even be sensible to choose between them because neither quite gets to the heart of the matter. The Chayeses consider the need to enforce compliance as being independent of the need to deter free-riding — something that they dismiss as being of little practical importance. Downs *et al.*, by contrast, conflate the two problems. Compliance enforcement and free-rider deterrence are re-lated problems and should be analysed jointly.

It is important to note that customary law does *not* require that states be parties to a treaty. Sovereignty means that countries are free to choose to participate in a treaty or not as they please (Barrett, 1990). So if free-riding is to be deterred — if participation in a treaty is to be full — then some kind of treaty-based mechanism must provide the right incentive. It must correct for the harmful incentives that otherwise condemn countries to the fate of the famous prisoners' dilemma.

Suppose that an agreement exists, that it consists of a certain number of parties, and that it requires that these parties undertake some action. The required action (climate-change mitigation) is costly to the parties that undertake it, but provides a benefit that is shared by parties and non-parties alike (climate-change mitigation is a public good). So each party will have an incentive to withdraw from the agreement, for in doing so each can gain more from avoiding steep mitigation costs than it loses from its own small slice of greenhouse-gas abatement.

If a party is to be deterred from withdrawing—which it is entitled to do under international law[13]—then it will need to be punished for withdrawing, and punished severely. It will be up to the other parties to the agreement to impose the punishment, but they may be reluctant to do so. The reason is that it is very hard to punish a deviant without also harming oneself. For example, suppose the punishment is that, in the event of one country withdrawing (and therefore cutting its abatement substantially), the other parties reduce their mitigation. Then the countries called upon to impose the punishment will be shooting themselves in the foot, so to speak. The punishment may not be credible.

Let us suppose, however, that a credible punishment can be found to deter some level of free-riding. Then it can be shown that the same punishment can be relied upon to enforce compliance (deter non-compliance); see Barrett (1999a). The reason is intuitive. Suppose a party contemplates 'cheating' on the agreement, perhaps by reducing its emissions by less than required by the agreement. To be deterred from cheating, it must face a punishment, and the punishment must be sufficiently severe that the country is made better off by not cheating. The larger the deviation from compliance, the larger must be the punishment which deters non-compliance. But the larger the required punishment, the larger will be the harm self-inflicted on the countries asked to impose it. If a punishment becomes too large it will cease to be credible and non-compliance will not be deterred.

Recall, however, that I have assumed that there exists a credible punishment that can deter (further) withdrawals from the agreement. The worst harm that a signatory could do by not complying would be for it to choose an emission profile that matched what it would do if it withdrew from the agreement. Hence, if every signatory is deterred from withdrawing, each also is deterred from not complying. The binding constraint on international cooperation is free-rider deterrence, not compliance enforcement. Once free-riding can be deterred, compliance can be enforced free of charge.

The example of the Montreal Protocol is relevant here. This agreement, which is phasing out the use of ozone-depleting chemicals world

---

[13] The Kyoto Protocol allows a party to withdraw 3 years after the Protocol has entered into force for a party, upon giving 1 year's notice.

wide, is among the great successes of international cooperation. It is also often held up to be a model for future agreements. Like Kyoto, the Montreal Protocol did not initially incorporate a mechanism for punishing non-compliance; choice of such a mechanism was to be deferred to a future meeting of the parties. So failure by Kyoto to include a mechanism for enforcement might seem not to matter. However, there is a big difference between the two treaties. The Montreal Protocol *did* offer incentives for countries to participate in the form of a trade sanction between parties and non-parties in the substances controlled by the treaty and in products containing these substances. And this device has succeeded in making participation in the Montreal Protocol virtually full.[14] It has also been invoked to enforce compliance with the agreement.[15] When seen in this light, compliance enforcement is a problem for Kyoto because the agreement does not employ a mechanism to deter free-riding.

Actually, the minimum participation clause may provide some assistance in deterring free-riding. You can think of it this way. Suppose more than 55 countries have ratified the treaty, and Annex I participation falls just a tiny bit short of the 55 per cent minimum required for entry into force. Then, if one more Annex I country ratifies, and so makes the minimum participation clause bind on all parties, it will have a non-marginal effect on the behaviour of others—the other Annex I parties will now have to fulfil their obligations under the treaty. This might just provide the incentive for the marginal ratification, and push the treaty over the minimum participation threshold.[16]

However, this trick is not sure to work—and even if it did succeed, it provides absolutely no incentive for *successive* accessions to the treaty. To see this, notice that the next country to ratify will not alter the behaviour of the existing parties one little bit. So why should it accede? The Kyoto Protocol does not provide any incentives for more than the minimum of participation. This is in sharp contrast to Montreal, which provides ample incentives for full participation.

Let us suppose, however, that Kyoto's minimum participation level is met and that the agreement enters into force. Could full implemen-

[14] A provision was also made for controlling trade in products made using these substances, but this was never implemented.

[15] The biggest challenge to the Montreal Protocol came when Russia declared that it would not be able to comply by 1996. The Implementation Committee threatened to invoke sanctions—and the combination of this threat and the sweetener of financial assistance was enough to compel Russia into preparing a plan for eventual compliance. The carrot of financial assistance was justified, by the way, since the original Montreal Protocol was negotiated by the Soviet Union in 1987, before its collapse. See Barrett (1999*b*).

[16] This is what I call a 'linchpin' equilibrium. See Barrett (1999*a*).

tation then be relied upon? The answer is not obvious. Suppose just one country foresees that it will fail to comply. Then it could withdraw from the agreement, upon giving sufficient notice, and so avoid having to deviate from the custom of compliance. Of course, its withdrawal would be penalized if it brought about the collapse of the agreement, as required by the minimum participation clause. But the other parties may not want the agreement to collapse, even taking as given this country's withdrawal, perhaps because, having previously sunk money into abatement investments, the cost of sticking with the agreement would be low. But if this is true—if a country cannot expect to be punished for deviating, then every party would have an incentive not to try very hard to comply with the agreement.

A more likely scenario is that a number of countries will wait to undertake substantial investments in abatement until others have already done so. The risk is that, with everyone behaving in this way, the policies and investments needed to implement Kyoto will not be made. The Protocol seems to have anticipated this problem, for it requires that every Annex I party demonstrate progress in achieving its target by 2005. But this will not suffice. If enough of these parties have made little progress, then none can be singled out for having acted unusually. Anyway, if no penalties can be applied, a lack of progress by all parties, or a large enough number of parties, would only provide a reason for renegotiating the agreement. To compound these problems, delay in implementing Kyoto will raise the costs of sticking to the Kyoto timetable, and so increase the incentives not to stick to this timetable.

The solution to all these problems may seem obvious: invoke the kind of sanctions used by the Montreal Protocol. However, production of every good has implications for greenhouse-gas emissions. Should *all* trade between parties and non-parties be banned? The threat to do so would almost certainly not be credible. Should trade in a select range of products be banned? That might be credible, but it might also threaten the stability of the multilateral trading arrangements. The answers are not obvious. But perhaps the questions should be asked (I was told that the subject never came up in Kyoto).

5. Summary

If there is one lesson to draw from this analysis it is this: the Kyoto Protocol must produce for its parties a favourable benefit–cost ratio or else it will either never enter into law or it will collapse.

As I noted in the opening paragraph of this paper, the overall reductions in emissions contained within Kyoto probably could provide a benefit–cost ratio for the world in excess of one. However, actually realizing this potential gain will not be easy. The overall level of abatement prescribed by Kyoto would have to be achieved cost-effectively — and this will require that abatement be undertaken in non-Annex I countries. Participation by the non-Annex I countries could potentially be achieved through the Clean Development Mechanism, but this would be sufficient only under the most favourable of assumptions. It seems more likely that emission caps would also need to be negotiated for the developing countries. Let me repeat here that this does *not* imply that the non-Annex I countries would need to pay for this abatement themselves. The reason for broadening participation is not to redistribute costs so much as to lower the total bill. There is an important precedent for this. The Montreal Protocol capped emissions of ozone-depleting substances in developing countries, and these countries did not have to pay to stay within these limits; the 'incremental costs' of their compliance were paid for by the industrialized countries.

Achieving a favourable benefit–cost ratio implies not just that costs must be kept low, but also that benefits must be kept high. As noted earlier, lowering implementation costs will actually raise benefits by lowering leakage. But there is another problem: one way of lowering costs is to approve CDM transactions that may not ultimately yield reductions in net emissions (so-called paper trades). Shaving costs in this way would ultimately ruin the agreement. This is yet another reason why Kyoto should be revised to include emission caps for the developing countries.

If these requirements can be met (and that is a big if), then the US Senate's objections would fall away, and the Kyoto Protocol could then enter into force. The problems of non-compliance and free-riding would at the same time be eased. If the costs of participation were lowered (and the benefits increased), then the incentives to deviate in these ways would be reduced.

However, these incentives to deviate would not be eliminated by cost-effective abatement. Achieving a favourable benefit–cost ratio is only a necessary condition for achieving global cooperation; it is not sufficient (Barrett, 1994, 1999a). And it is not obvious how the required sanctions could be made credible. So Kyoto has two mountains to climb. The first — achieving a favourable benefit–cost ratio — is challenge enough. The second — deterring free-riding and non-compliance — has not yet come into view, but it may prove the harder climb.

Post Script

After this chapter was written, the parties to the Framework Convention met in Buenos Aires (in November 1998). The issues raised in this paper were not resolved at this meeting, but a Plan of Action was agreed, with deadlines for finalizing the Protocol's flexible mechanisms. For the first time, the issue of how compliance should be enforced was raised, though to my knowledge no mechanism for enforcing compliance was proposed. At the meeting, the United States became the 60th country to sign the Kyoto agreement. Another small island state, Antigua and Barbuda, became the second to ratify it. Argentina, which hosted the meeting, announced its intention to adopt an emission limit voluntarily, and Kazakhstan said that it would join the group of Annex I countries and accept, in the words of the press release, a 'legally binding target' (adding more 'hot air'?).

These developments are to be welcomed, but the fundamental problems raised in this paper remain. The press release issued at the start of the Buenos Aires talks concluded by noting that the agreement would not become legally binding until the minimum participation requirements had been met. 'It is hoped,' the statement reads, 'that this will happen in 2001.' It is regrettable that we cannot anticipate with more confidence an event of such importance.

Post Post Script

As of my receipt of the manuscript proof of the current version of this chapter (March 2000), 22 countries have ratified the Kyoto Protocol. Half of these countries are small island states. The others are developing countries. No Annex I country has ratified Kyoto yet.

At the Fifth Conference of the Parties (COP 5) to the Framework Convention on Climate Change, held in November 1999, the European Union called for ratification and entry into force of the Kyoto Protocol by 2002. In March 2000, the British Deputy Prime Minister, John Prescott, urged the European Union to set an example to other Annex I countries by pledging to ratify Kyoto as soon as possible after COP 6, due to be held in November 2000. The aim would be to encourage enough other Annex I countries to ratify that the agreement would enter into force by 2002.

However, the problems identified within this paper remain. Signatories have not agreed how the Kyoto mechanisms will operate — whether trading must be capped, for example, as the EU has so far insisted. Nor have they decided what the consequences of non-compliance will be. The draft UK climate change programme says that these issues 'are due to be resolved at COP 6, clearing the way for ratification and entry into force'. It is certainly possible for signatories to resolve their differences over issues such as supplemental trading. Given time, other details can also be worked out. Compliance enforcement, however, will be much harder to remedy.

There is also the problem of US ratification. The COP 6 negotiations will begin only days after the US presidential election. Will the new president—whether Bush or Gore—be prepared to negotiate seriously in these meetings? And if he is not, will he risk taking the agreement negotiated there to the Senate for ratification? Will the new Senate be more inclined to ratify?

There are still mountains for Kyoto to climb—and doubts about whether it will survive the journey.

7

Bartering Biodiversity: What are the Options?

DAVID MACDONALD*

1. Introduction

Environmentalism, which is the ideal of prevention of further deterioration in the natural environment and repair of damage already done, is a topic in which everybody is a stakeholder. This realization has, rightly, elevated the perception of environmental issues from the province of eccentric enthusiasts to mainstream political and business agendas.

Within this arena, a pivotal professional discipline is conservation biology — a highly interdisciplinary field which blends principles gleaned from ecology, geophysics, and economics, among others. Much of conservation biology is concerned with understanding processes — most of them dauntingly complicated — that underlie the functioning of nature or, more technically, of ecosystems. These processes link the geophysical world, through patterns in resource availability, to the activities of individual organisms which lead to the emergent properties of populations and communities. It is these properties which underpin the ecosystem goods services on which humanity depends — the provision of oxygen, water, nutrients, a stable climate, and so forth. A first, albeit controversial, attempt to value these goods services estimated their annual worth to humanity at US\$33 trillion (Costanza et al., 1997). Understanding such processes provides the basis for predicting the likely consequences of change. During recent human

* Wildlife Conservation Research Unit, Department of Zoology, University of Oxford.

I am deeply grateful for the hard work and stimulating discussions that Clive Hambler and Mike Packer have contributed to this paper, and for the help of Fiona Donaldson and Robin Smale. This paper was written within the Jerwood Business and Biodiversity Initiative at the Wildlife Conservation Research Unit (WildCRU). I am also grateful for additional comments made on an earlier draft by Tom Tew and Frank Vorhies, and to Dieter Helm for his editorial forbearance.

history, from an environmental point of view, many changes have been for the worse — humanity has single-handedly precipitated an extinction crisis that rivals those previously triggered by colliding meteorites or rampaging ice ages. The consequences of these extinctions for the stable functioning of ecosystems are ominously uncertain.

A useful yardstick whereby to evaluate the state of nature is biodiversity — the variety of life — most easily measured as the diversity of species within an ecosystem. If natural processes are anthropogenically perturbed, biodiversity is likely to change, and it is odds on the change will be for the worse. This is because the functioning of the global environment depends on processes within ecosystems — cycling of nutrients, minerals, and water — which are founded on that biodiversity. Nobody can yet be very precise about how much biodiversity (or other measures of naturalness) can be jettisoned before reaping calamitous consequences, but it would be imprudent to push our luck. This is one pragmatic reason why biodiversity is on hard-nosed political and business agendas — others range from bio-prospecting through eco-tourism to public relations — and add to its monumental aesthetic value and the welter of moral reasons for fostering nature. Biodiversity cannot be dismissed as the preoccupation of a clique of unworldly enthusiasts with a tendency to wear open-toed sandals; it is also a commodity with immense monetary value to humanity at large. A first attempt to estimate the cost of conserving biodiversity across 15 per cent of the global land area (which might be enough to sustain ecosystem services) is US$22.6 billion annually (James *et al.*, 1999). This sum is small in comparison to the estimated US$1 trillion currently spent annually on environmentally harmful, or 'perverse' subsidies (those used to promote over-exploitative agricultural production, energy use, road transportation, water consumption, and commercial fishing, by keeping resource prices below market values) (Myers, 1998).

Conservation biology is a science and, as such, strives for objectivity in its interpretations; but as an applied science it also aspires to inform political processes. My purpose here is to explore one such interface between science and policy, namely the question of whether biodiversity can properly be bartered as a commodity in environmental regulation. In practice, does some form of exchange, more or less directly, provide a mechanism whereby money from business can contribute towards that $22.6 billion that must be found to conserve biodiversity?

Of course, there is one starting point for all environmental issues: human population, with an ecological focus on its size relative to limiting resources, and a political focus on the inequitable and unsustainable consumption of these resources. Pundits differ in their projections, but a fair sense of the problem is provided by the Food and

Agricultural Organization's (FAO) estimate that the world can support *under* 6 billion people if all suitable land (*including* wetland and forest) is used sustainably. As of 1999, world population exceeded 6 billion, having doubled since 1950. Even though the rate of population growth is falling, global population is predicted to reach at least 8 billion. The relevance is that consumption by these people will erode biodiversity.

In the meantime, decision-makers struggle to decide how environmental damage is to be regulated and how conservation is to be paid for. One family of ideas involves swapping or offset. The nub of this is that a business or nation intent upon causing (unavoidable) environmental damage will be permitted to do so only if it compensates this environmental 'bad' by implementing a corresponding environmental 'good'. Since even the most bullish regulator must acknowledge that some environmental damage is unavoidable, the idea of exacting some compensatory action from the polluter is superficially appealing. However, on closer inspection, it raises a morass of issues. Among these is the issue of how to ensure that the swapping mechanism does not become a loophole through which polluters can sidestep the maximum possible constraints upon the damage they cause. Furthermore, how are different environmental 'goods' and 'bads' to be valued to ensure an equitable exchange of, say, biodiversity gain per unit of toxin emitted?

(a) *Precedents and Parallels*

The problems of valuation involved in bartering biodiversity are scarcely unfamiliar; lessons can be learnt from various parallels of swaps both within and between nations. For example, there is already trade in national debts, such as debt–equity swaps (Bowe and Dean, 1993). Here, an external creditor (a rich country) can redeem a debt (owed by a poor country), usually at a discounted rate, in exchange for ownership rights to equity in the debtor country. Ownership of equity is more risky than maintaining the capital debt and interest payments. This is true even when the equity traded is a purely commercial commodity that could be sold on: a trade that seems unlikely to benefit the debtor except insofar as interest payments on the debt are cancelled. However, the swap might involve enhancement of something which benefits the debtor and wider humanity, such as fostering education or nature. For example, Harvard University entered into a debt-for-education swap with Ecuador: Harvard took over some of Ecuador's debt on the condition that saved interest repayments were used for educating Ecuadorians at Harvard and facilitating Harvard researchers in Ecuador. The distinction between this debt-for-education swap and no-strings aid is that the donor can dictate how the money is spent. In this case, one analysis indicates that Harvard's investment was commercially as well as educationally profitable: the scheme attracted good publicity and the Ecuadorian students spent their grants in the USA (Van der Meulen Rodgers, 1993).

Directly analogous debt-for-nature swaps involve the transfer of 'conservation land' in developing countries to an organization (usually an international non-governmental organization (NGO)) in exchange for payment of part of the national debt. Such swaps have taken place in Poland, the Philippines, Bolivia, and Costa Rica. So far the valuations of the land and opportunity costs have been somewhat *ad hoc* (Barbier *et al.*, 1994). Approximately US$200m has been spent on debt-for-nature swaps worldwide, and proposed legislation in the USA would provide a budget of US$400m to protect tropical forests through a debt-for-nature scheme. Doubtless, there is room for debate as to whether such swaps are adequate compensation for the transfer of development rights. However, this debate is not substantially different to the valuation of land for conventional purchase.

The complexity of these trading issues is increased when one environmental 'bad' is to be traded against another, neither easily measured in monetary terms. This is the main focus of this chapter: for example, how much 'unavoidable' pollution (say, of carbon) might be offset against how much land conservation? That this is a relevant question is illustrated by the fact that such swaps have been made: in 1988 Applied Energy Services Inc. of Arlington, Virginia, paid US$2m to enable 40,000 small-holders in Guatemala to plant 50m pine and eucalyptus trees as a means of making acceptable the building of a coal-fired power plant in Connecticut (Michaelowa, 1998). While tree planting sounds superficially as if it might be an environmental bonus, it is noteworthy that forest monocultures are associated with reduced soil fertility and ground-water, erosion, compaction, fire risk, and loss of biodiversity. As such they are seen by some as alien to the interests of local peoples (*vide* Montevideo Declaration, 1998).

2. Options for Biodiversity Conservation

In general, practices that damage the environment in ways that threaten the sustainability of ecological–economic systems, need to be 'balanced' by efforts to protect the environment. There are two basic approaches to environmental protection: avoidance of damage and compensation for damage. The offsetting of carbon-dioxide (CO_2) emissions through carbon sequestration and conservation management in forest ecosystems are mitigatory activities — and are the examples I explore as a case study later in this chapter. The avoidance of environmental damage is a direct response to the increasingly accepted need (Schlapfer, 1999) to maintain ecosystem function and resilience, so that economic opportunities for future generations are maintained (Barbier *et al.*, 1994). One mechanism whereby damage may be avoided is commercializing nature in order to conserve it. There is potential to develop business that is commercially viable and beneficial for biodiversity, potential examples being ecotourism, organic farming, sustainable forestry, and fisheries. The prospect of nature paying its own way is a great hope of many conservationists and doubtless it has potential as a mechanism for curtailing environmental damage (meriting a paper in itself). None the less, the value of marketable nature will never be sufficient to forestall many environmentally damaging activities, so the need remains to consider compensation for damage. However seductive, the lure of swapping one's way out of trouble should not obscure the fundamental environmentalist dictum that prevention is better than cure, especially when there is no guarantee that the 'cure' will work. There are circumstances, however, when compensation for damage may be the only way to 'balance' losses. These circumstances should be tightly defined. For example, the European Union's Habitats Directive states that damage to a site is 'acceptable' when there are no alternatives and, in UK legislation, where there are 'imperative reasons of overriding public importance'. Only governments (or courts) can define such imperative reasons. Under these circumstances a site can be damaged provided compensation is provided. Compensation is likely to involve designation of another site for protection or restoration.

The principle of compensation might be used, for example, when considering the restoration of degraded ecosystems to offset the consequences of environmental damage to intact ecosystems. In the case of compensating for loss of biodiversity, this pragmatic perspective does not allow that extinction is acceptable (it is, after all, irreversible) but does accept that change is inevitable and proposes that compensation is possible for, say, local changes in biodiversity. As such, the approach presents opportunities for innovation as well as lower-cost improvements in environmental performance.

(a) *'Like-for-like' Compensation*

This form of compensation is sometimes called mitigation (a term popularized by 'mitigation banking' of wetlands in the USA) and acknowledges the legitimacy of development needs that inflict specific environmental damage. In passing, this raises an issue of terminology.

I use mitigation to mean alleviate or reduce severity of an action *directly*. That is, a power company building a generating plant on an environmentally valuable site might take action to mitigate its impact on that site. Additionally, it might seek to swap or compensate for the unavoidable damage by protecting or restoring comparable habitat elsewhere. Of course, this distinction between mitigation and compensation is somewhat scale-dependent (compensation for the loss of one site by the creation of another on the other side of the world might be said to mitigate the global loss of biodiversity); it may none the less avoid some confusion. Thus, American 'mitigation banking' might better be termed 'compensation banking', where the compensatory response is either to identify another threatened location that has an equal or greater area of the type of habitat to be destroyed, which can be bought and set aside under long-term protection, or to identify an area of degraded habitat which can be bought, restored, and set aside. Clearly, net environmental gain from such transactions necessitates that the area to be protected or restored must otherwise have been at genuine risk. Calculating the details of the swap involves consideration not just of the area of land involved, but of its geometry within a functioning ecosystem. It is also noteworthy that the process of restoration involves uncertainties and takes time, and so compensation ratios often involve doubling or more the area to be gained from the swap.

(b) 'Like-for-unlike' Compensation

'Like-for-unlike' swapping involves allowing the exchange of an environmental 'bad' (such as pollution) for an environmental 'good' (such as habitat protection). The exchange might involve different forms of natural capital (sacrificing a coastal marsh for an inland forest, for example), or swapping between natural capital and manufactured capital. The latter exchange of ecosystem goods or services for manufactured goods or human services is, generally unhappily, illustrated by logging companies in tropical countries that offer social infrastructure (health, education, and amenity facilities) in partial exchange for timber. From a conservationist standpoint, and because the values of different aspects of nature often appear incommensurable, it is important to ask how very different kinds of environmental 'goods' and 'bads' can be valued, and whether the agreed compensation really can 'make up' for the negative effects of environmental damage and loss of biodiversity. Obviously it is difficult to value nature (e.g. Brown and Shogren, 1998), and to calculate environmental damage and opportunity costs (Brown *et al.*, 1996).

The acceptability of these two broad approaches to compensation for environmental damage is influenced by views on sustainability, which may be arranged on a continuum notionally referred to as varying from weak to strong sustainability.

(c) *Sustainability*

The concept of sustainability is increasingly influential in the debate about how to tackle environmental problems, particularly biodiversity loss. Sustainability is the condition in which patterns of resource utilization and conservation provide economic, social, and environmental benefits (the 'triple bottom line') in the long term.

Two broad viewpoints of sustainability are relevant to a consideration of compensation mechanisms. The 'weak sustainability' viewpoint accepts that effects of the depletion of biodiversity (natural capital) on economic wellbeing can be offset by reinvestment in human-made capital. The 'strong sustainability' viewpoint emphasizes limits to substitution between natural and human-made capital, on the grounds that natural capital has irreplaceable features (such as ecosystem services) which cannot be compensated for by manufactured capital. This view assumes that the maintenance of future economic opportunities demands that levels of biodiversity are maintained, with the obvious corollary that contemporary biodiversity has very high value. In that the strong sustainability stance highlights limits (critical natural capital) to substitutability, this viewpoint is unlikely to favour 'like-for-like' swaps, and even less likely to favour 'like-for-unlike' swaps.

(d) *The Value of Biodiversity*

Biodiversity comprises a resource base that provides food, modern and traditional medicine, genetic resources (e.g. for crop improvement), building and industrial materials, and recreational, educational, research, and tourism opportunities. Biodiversity thus has direct use value, and so is marketable. Biodiversity also provides non-market goods and ecosystem services — that is, it has passive use value. Directly marketable biodiversity is dependent on non-market biodiversity, for instance, species with a direct value may require non-marketable prey. Indeed, ecosystem services support the production of marketable commodities and include atmospheric, hydrological, and climatic regulation, nutrient recycling, soil formation and maintenance, pest control, photosynthesis, pollination, and resilience of ecosystems to natural or human-made perturbations. Of course, biodiversity also has intrinsic worth, irrespective of utilitarian values, and this intrinsic worth often has an aesthetic, cultural, spiritual, or ethical aspect.

Any system of swapping clearly necessitates attributing a value to the commodities involved. The logic and practice of valuing biodiversity is a major challenge in conservation biology. Where degradation of ecosystems diminishes the productivity of marketable biodiversity or other limited resources (such as clean water) there are opportunities to market passive use (non-market) goods and services. An example might be investment in the protection of watershed forests that are responsible for cleaning rainwater as it moves through the catchment rather than in more expensive water filtering technology (Parlange, 1999). Otherwise, determining the market equivalents of *non-market use* biodiversity relies on indirect valuation, such as willingness-to-pay or travel-cost methods. Valuing biodiversity involves long-term accounting, since protection of biodiversity is an intergenerational matter (Hambler, 1995*b*).

(e) *Metric of Conversion*

There are cases where it is apparently relatively easy to trade consumption quotas (as for New Zealand fisheries), pollution permits (as for sulphur dioxide in the USA), or units of wetland habitat (as in wetland 'mitigation banking'). The units of consumption are clear (such as tonnes of catch or pollutant, or hectares of habitat). However, the interdisciplinarity that characterizes the science of conservation biology means that incommensurable units are a frequent stumbling block in this field. This dilemma is particularly evident in the case of biodiversity swaps, and worsened when conversions to a common monetary currency involve existence values. Existence value is that which an individual attaches to a site, good, or service that is not visited, consumed, or used by that individual. Well-known examples are the existence values attached to the preservation of Antarctica and whales by individuals who do not come into contact with either nor derive any services from them. In calculating the metric of swapping, the precautionary principle should bias in favour of biodiversity

Techniques for measuring non-use and use values exist—such as willingness to pay compensation or accept compensation—and employ statistical and survey methods to calibrate models of consumer choice. Where valuation measurement techniques are not appropriate, either because of poor public understanding of the issues or because the preferences cannot be gathered, a fall-back position is the so-called 'Delphi technique' which relies upon the consensus of a jury of experts. This, however, is increasingly unlikely to satisfy stakeholders where the environmental impacts are complex and are weighted against social and economic development benefits. It also rests on the demonstrable impartiality of the experts.

3. A Case Study: Climate Change and Carbon Offset

In general, thinking about biodiversity swaps is in its infancy. However, one arena in which swapping has been more thoroughly discussed is carbon offset as a mechanism for ameliorating climate change caused by greenhouse gases. I explore this as a case study of the complexities raised by swapping.

The Intergovernmental Panel on Climate Change (IPCC) estimates that humanity produces some 7 billion (thousand million) tonnes of CO_2 pollution per year, of which 5.4 billion tonnes are from fossil-fuel use and 1.6 billion tonnes from forest combustion, mainly in the developing world (Houghton *et al.*, 1992, 1996). The cost of damage due to this pollution has been estimated at US$50–100 per tonne of carbon (Houghton, 1997) or US$27 per tonne of CO_2 (see also Fankhauser, 1997). These greenhouse-gas emissions provide an example of an environmental 'bad' which is largely unavoidable for the foreseeable future, and which therefore has prompted thoughts on various mitigatory and compensatory mechanisms.

Given the option, the emphasis should always be on reducing emissions rather than cleaning them up. This is not only because of the damage done by emissions before they are cleaned up, but because cleaning up itself requires energy, resources, and funds. However, reducing CO_2 emissions radically would require substantial changes to society, including reduced affluence in some regions and decreased rates of population growth. Therefore, insofar as disposal of pollutants is a more realistic option at present, how can CO_2 be cleaned up? Various speculative possibilities include storage in gas-fields or saline aquifers, membrane separation, and use as feedstock in polymers and in bioprotein through farming algae (US DoE, 1998). However, one of the most publicized options, first proposed by Freeman Dyson (1976), is carbon offset forestry: creating plantations (so called forest sinks) to soak up the excess CO_2 from the atmosphere.

This is not the place for a major review of climate change, but before evaluating the carbon sink option, and asking whether it holds lessons for the wider topic of biodiversity swaps, some background is necessary.

(a) *Climate Change – Basics and Background*

Climate change is a natural phenomenon that has taken place over millennia. What is new is that today the greatest contribution to climate change is human-made (e.g. Tett *et al.*, 1999), at a time when people are single-handedly responsible for increasing contemporary extinctions to greater than 1,000-fold the background rate (Lawton and May, 1995;

Myers, 1996). The loss of biodiversity risks calamitous effects on ecosystem production and services, human health, and business (Stone *et al.*, 1997), and raises the academically exacting question of how much biodiversity we can afford to lose.

People are responsible for climate change insofar as human activities release a surplus of greenhouse gases into the atmosphere: CO_2 is produced when fossil fuels are used to generate energy and when forests are cut down and burned. Rising levels of all greenhouse gases directly contribute to climate change. To understand why, one must think back to the carbon cycle. There are estimated to be about 700 billion tonnes of CO_2 in the Earth's atmosphere, and each year about one tenth of this is 'fixed' into the carbon-based molecules of living tissue by photosynthesis. Eventually, when plants, or those that eat them, die and rot, carbon is released back to the atmosphere as CO_2. For many millions of years carbon has cycled between living organisms, the atmosphere, and the oceans in what has been a relatively stable cycle, which has resulted in the atmosphere comprising about 260 parts per million (ppm) of CO_2. Carbon dioxide has the interesting quality of letting short-wave radiation, of the sort emitted by the sun, pass through on its way to Earth, but of absorbing the longer-wave, infra-red radiation that bounces back from Earth. Without this heat-trapping blanket of CO_2, the average temperature of Earth would be about –20 °C rather than +15 °C. This is called the greenhouse effect, and without it life would be improbable on Earth. The problem is that contemporary human activity, such as the burning of fossil fuels, releases more CO_2 than can be fixed by the world's stock of photosynthetic plants and algae, with the net effect that CO_2 concentration of the atmosphere now tops 350 ppm and is rising. The greenhouse effect is thereby enhanced, with the potential to throw the Earth's climate into turmoil.

By 2100 global warming of 1–3.5 °C and sea level rise of 15–95 cm are likely. The complexity of these processes challenges comprehension, but the current focus is on the risk of sudden, chaotic climate change, with impacts likely to reverberate into all walks of life (McMichael, 1995; Hulme, 1996; Birdlife International/WWF, 1997; Gryj, 1998; Martens, 1998). The ramifications are legion: changes in water re-sources, affecting people, agriculture, and the environment, could become political flashpoints, as could shifting patterns of human disease (Rogers and Packer, 1993). Some agricultural regions will be threatened by climate change, while others may benefit (e.g. Myneni *et al.*, 1997). The composition, geographic distribution, and stability of ecosystems is already changing (e.g. Hersteinsson and Macdonald, 1992; McCleery and Perrins, 1998) and one startling estimate foresees the loss of two-thirds of all contemporary species by 2100.

Better late than never, the last decade has seen concern about climate change mature from an academic eccentricity to a major driver of political thinking. At the May 1998 G8 summit, the leaders of the world's eight most powerful industrial countries called climate change 'the greatest environmental threat to our future prosperity'. Meanwhile the Kyoto Protocol commits countries to promoting sustainable management of biomass and forests (Article 4.1(d)) as part of tackling climate change. The enormity of this injunction is paralleled by that from the Convention on Biodiversity, agreed at the UN Conference on Environment and Development (the 'Earth Summit') in Rio de Janiero in 1992, which commits governments to encouraging or requiring business involvement in maintenance or restoration of biodiversity. Businesses will soon be expected to reduce greenhouse-gas emissions (and I predict that it will not be long before they are also required to identify and reduce their impacts on biodiversity). I have summarized (Macdonald, 1999) some turns on the road to this legislative milestone which led the Buenos Aires summit (Conference of the Parties (COP)-4, 1998) to require the refinement of three flexibility mechanisms (emissions trading, clean development mechanisms, and joint implementation) by COP-6 in 2000. This requirement focuses attention on the concept of nations (or corporations) trading in pollution as a means of tackling climate change and the swapping of environmental 'bads' for 'goods'. It also raises preoccupying issues not just in science and macroeconomics, but also in morality and rights (Corner House, 1999).

(b) *Options for Tackling Climate Change*

The case for curtailing emissions of CO_2 is compelling, and the most effective method must be direct restriction. However, three classes of indirect ways (or swaps) to offset the pollution problem are being investigated: carbon sequestration and storage management (expansion of carbon sinks and stores in forest ecosystems, such as through afforestation, reforestation, and agroforestry); carbon conservation management (conservation of existing carbon stores in forests through protection, controlled deforestation, and reduced degradation); and carbon-substitution management (increasing transfer of forest carbon into products such as biofuels and construction materials that replace fossil-fuel-based energy and products).

(i) Offsetting carbon pollution through sequestration

Sequestration of carbon is a means of offsetting the continued production of CO_2. This mechanism is controversial, not least because it diminishes the incentive and responsibility to improve performance on direct reduction of emissions. Nevertheless, having committed itself at Rio, Kyoto, and Buenos Aires to reducing its net emissions, the UK plans to achieve this partly by planting trees intended to act as sinks for CO_2 (DoE, 1994b). Some believe that this approach might provide spin-off benefits for wildlife (Barker et al., 1996; Brown et al., 1996; CST, undated), while others are sceptical even of the potential to sequester carbon (for example Adger et al., 1997b).

The view that afforestation might be a beneficial form of habitat enhancement, for instance for some vulnerable species such as UK mammals, bears closer analysis. The cost of planting forestry to sequester carbon in Britain has been estimated at very roughly £10 per tonne of carbon (£3 per tonne CO_2) (Adger and Brown, 1994; Adger et al., 1997a). If a small fraction of the 150m tonnes of carbon Britain releases each year were disposed of in forestry at this price, then millions of pounds might be available for afforestation. This possibility raises two linked questions: would this forest creation significantly (a) enhance conservation and (b) diminish atmospheric carbon levels? If the answer to both questions were 'yes', then diminishing anthropogenic climate change and enhancing habitat creation might share a common mechanism, and, in a qualitative sense, two environmental 'goods' might be swapped for one 'bad'.

These questions have been widely reviewed (e.g. Houghton et al., 1993; Adger et al., 1994; Adger and Brown, 1994; DoE, 1994b; Barker et al., 1996; Adger et al., 1997a,b; Houghton, 1997; and references within these reviews). There are already agreements between carbon-emitters and forestry companies, for example between the Dutch Electricity Generating Board and forestry projects in the Netherlands, Africa, Asia, Latin America, and Central Europe (Brown et al., 1996; Stone et al., 1997), and between Formula-One racers who have paid £38,000 per year to plant 30,000 trees in Mexico to offset the emissions from their cars. Applied Energy Services Inc. (Virginia) are sequestering 15.5–58 MtC in a US$14m 'sustainable agroforestry' project (Brown et al., 1996). The Carbon Storage Trust, Future Forests, and SGS Forestry, among others, offer or accredit schemes whereby pollution is offset by soaking up CO_2 in forests planted (or protected — see below). But will these swaps either reduce greenhouse gases or enhance biodiversity, and what are their implications for the citizens of the developing countries in which large-scale plantings are most likely to be sited?

(ii) Is forest-planting a realistic option for carbon offset?

Opinions as to whether a significant part of the global CO_2 problem can be offset vary dramatically. Cogent arguments for pessimism are deployed by Adger et al. (1994), Adger and Brown (1994), Brown et al.

(1996), and various authors in Adger *et al.* (1997a). Indeed, compared to the atmospheric increase in CO_2 from fossil-fuel combustion, the sequestration capacity for CO_2 by massive plantations seems to be only modest (Bouwman, 1990).

Trees are a sink for carbon only so long as they keep growing: once mature (which may take decades, or even over a century; Adger and Brown, 1994) they become, instead, a carbon store, and when they die, a source. The bio-physics of the carbon cycle are very complicated. For example, losses of carbon from the soil pool resulting from planting activities on heathland, rough grassland, or wetland may counteract gains from forestry for 10 or more years after planting (Adger *et al.*, 1994; Gatto and Merlo, 1997). Indeed, despite afforestation between 1947 and 1980, UK forestry was not a net CO_2 sink because soil carbon was released as land was prepared for planting (Adger *et al.*, 1994; Adger and Brown, 1994; Gatto and Merlo, 1997).

Is agroforestry more promising from a British perspective? It is government policy to double the UK's forest cover during the next century, through schemes such as Community Forests. However, we have already seen that the wide-scale planting between 1947 and 1980 in the UK was not a net sink. Worse yet, soaking up all Britain's emissions would require planting more than the country's total land area of 24.3 million hectares (Mha) (Cannell and Cape, 1991).

Afforestation inevitably competes with other land uses, or potential uses. In the USA, Adams and Alig (1995) and Ciesla (1997) envisage that much offset planting would occur on agricultural land, as in Germany (Böswald, 1997), while the UK government (DoE, 1994b, p. 72) foresees tree-planting on land set aside from agriculture (the future of which is already uncertain). If productive land were used, it would be at the expense of potential food production in a hungry world, whereas if marginal land were used it could compete with grazing, sporting, and amenity uses, and arguably with conservation. Using any sort of productive land raises the sinister spectre that the displaced uses might shift to previous wilderness sites. Much of the land deemed available by Houghton *et al.* (1996) is in fact available only if increases in agricultural productivity on other lands allow these marginal lands to be removed from production (Ciesla, 1997). In short, any major change in land-use to accommodate agroforestry for carbon offset is likely to have complicated ramifications for both food production and conservation, not to mention the land tenure and rights of local people.

These issues are highlighted by the sales package for Mazda's Demio car. In Britain this is sold with one year of 'carbon-free' driving. The car comes with a certificate from Future Forests which promises to plant five trees to absorb the CO_2 generated by the car that year. Buying the

car obviously involves the driver directly in the environmental consequences of mining, oil refining, and CO_2 pollution, but the Mazda deal
also ensures that trees will be planted which may possibly suck up
sufficient carbon to compensate for the driving. Mazda works with
Community Forests in the UK, but the deal might be less appealing if
the plantations were in some corner of the Third World where they
(and by implication, the driver) might displace biodiversity or even
people.

Despite these causes for pessimism, others believe that a tree-
planting programme is feasible and that land is available for it on the
scale required (Houghton, 1997, p. 179). Böswald (1997) concludes that
in Germany up to 5 per cent of the country's annual CO_2 emissions could
be sequestered by large scale afforestation of agricultural land where
'forests and forestry might serve to reduce carbon emissions. It would
be an economic, ecological and political failure to neglect these extraordinary possibilities'. Indeed, even if the contribution is small compared
to other measures, the Department of the Environment's document,
'Climate Change: The UK Programme' (DoE, 1994b), concludes (p. 72):
'The creation of new woodlands and forests could in the future make
a significant contribution towards the UK's efforts to help limit increases in atmospheric concentrations of CO_2.'

(iii) How much carbon offset might be achieved by forestry?

In the most productive tropics carbon sequestration rates of over 20 tC/
ha/yr (tonnes carbon per hectare per year) can be achieved (with
extremes of 70 claimed on some land; Brown *et al.*, 1996). Thus
industrial plantations in the tropics harvested every 8 years over 100
years can yield 3,500 cubic metres of wood — seven times the yield from
a natural forest established at the same time. By improving management, with rotations of 5–15 years for hardwoods and 12–20 years for
conifers, Adger and Brown (1994) foresee potential tropical sequestration rates of 9 tC/ha/yr.

In the UK, rates of carbon sequestration of 5 tC/ha/yr could be
achieved in intensive poplar plantations, 3.7 tC/ha/yr in conifer plantations, and less than 2 tC/ha/yr would be more typical of a broadleaf
woodland. There is a trade-off between the rate of carbon uptake and
storage, such that coniferous species accumulate carbon at a faster rate
than do broad-leaved species, whereas at equilibrium they store less
carbon (68 tC/ha for Sitkas spruce, compared to 140 tC/ha for mixed
oakwood in Britain) (Adger and Brown, 1994). Alternative calculations
considering the soil, litter, and forest products give exotic un-thinned
Picea sictchensis plantations sequestration rates of up to 5 tC/ha/yr, and

equilibrium storage of 254 tC/ha, compared to oak plantations (1.85 tC/ha/yr and 154 tC/ha, respectively) (Crabtree, 1997). One million hectares of poplar woodland (among the most carbon-hungry trees), covering 4 per cent of the island, could sequester 3 per cent of Britain's annual emissions while they continued to grow (Cannell and Cape, 1991; Adger and Brown, 1994; Cannell and Dewar, 1995).

Extrapolating from these sequestration rates is clearly uncertain, but Winjum *et al.* (1992) estimate a theoretical global upper limit to forestry mitigation options at 180 GtC of the 500 GtC predicted to be emitted by human activities globally by 2050. However, Brown *et al.* (1996) argue that, in practice, the maximum is 60–87 GtC by 2050, at a total cost of US$247–302 billion, on 700 Mha of land. On Brown's calculation the cost is thus at least US$2–8/tC (excluding transaction costs such as land purchase). About 80 per cent of the carbon sequestration potential is in the tropics (putting aside the question of whether those living in the tropics might favour their countries being turned into vast plantations). This practical maximum offset represents 12–15 per cent of projected carbon emissions from fossil fuel by 2050. It is based on a combined programme of agroforestry, reafforestation, and better management and protection of forests (see below); it therefore embraces an optimistic blend of both prevention and cure.

A final caveat regarding the debated figures on carbon sequestration is that they may grossly overestimate the rate of uptake by ignoring the complex interactions between oceanic and terrestrial sinks. Plantation uptake mitigates emissions tonne for tonne, but because uptake by plantations slows oceanic uptake in the very long term, plantations need to take up 6 tonnes for every 1 tonne reduction in atmospheric content (Price, 1997). Furthermore, as air temperatures slowly rise in response to increased CO_2, the ratio of plant photosynthesis (absorbing CO_2) to respiration (emitting CO_2) will shift towards net production of CO_2.

Would the benefits to conservation be great? Sadly, the ideal forest for carbon sequestration is far from that which is ideal for wildlife: the best sequestration rates are achieved by fast-growing, generally exotic species, with low parasite/herbivore burdens, growing on good, fertile, well-watered land (see Brown *et al.*, 1996). Therefore, while it would be foolish to dismiss the potential, and not least the public appeal, of the idea of carbon-offset afforestation, this mechanism seems unlikely to contribute significantly either to carbon offset in the UK or directly to provide a habitat enhancement for conservation (Crabtree, 1997, p. 194; Price, 1997, p. 87). Indeed, if semi-natural or mature forest is cleared or peatbogs are drained to make way for new planting the consequences are likely to be counterproductive for both atmospheric carbon and biodiversity.

(iv) Offsetting carbon pollution through habitat protection

Deforestation leads to CO_2 emissions through burning and through soil disturbance. Forest loss is now mainly a southern-hemisphere phenomenon. The FAO (1993) estimated that 15.4 Mha were deforested annually between 1980 and 1990, with a further 5.9 Mha/yr harvested and degraded (and so exposed to subsequent deforestation). The main threats to forests are slash-and-burn agriculture driven by population pressure (up to 79 per cent of deforestation between 1973 and 1988 (Harrison, 1993), and over 60 per cent of current deforestation), with much smaller contributions from pasture and logging. A square kilometre of tropical forest when burnt releases some 7,000–17,000 tonnes of CO_2 (Houghton, 1997).

In the context of carbon sinks we asked whether agroforestry would reduce the surplus of atmospheric carbon and/or benefit biodiversity. The same questions can be asked of forest protection, with the logical distinction that protecting forests cannot reduce atmospheric carbon, but merely reduce its rate of increase. None the less, the nub of the issue is whether a pound of spending on forest sinks contributes more or less benefit (measured in both carbon and biodiversity) than a pound spent on forest stores.

Bekkering (1992) estimates that expected carbon concentrations in the atmosphere would be reduced by 12 per cent if deforestation were halted. In reality, however, deforestation cannot be halted, although Trexler and Haugen (1994) estimate that 20 per cent of the predicted deforestation by 2050 may be avoidable. Protection of the high carbon density of a natural forest is very cost-effective in slowing the trend of increasing atmospheric concentrations of CO_2 (Brown et al., 1996; Houghton, 1997). As Brown et al. (1996) point out, new protected forest areas should therefore include those that contain large carbon pools, such as forests growing on peat soils at high and low latitudes, and high-biomass old-growth forests.

Protecting forests has the obvious advantage that the ameliorating effect on carbon release is instantaneous. However, policing protection is technically difficult and bedevilled by fears of vandalism. There are potential loopholes (Adger et al., 1997b): protection of one area may merely displace the clearing to another, and individuals, organizations, or governments might falsely declare an intent to burn forest, solely to obtain payment not to burn. In practice, however, these fears may be overwhelmed by the reality that in many countries—from Madagascar to the Ivory Coast—all the forest seems doomed (Harrison, 1993).

SGS Forestry, among others, is already certifying carbon offset based partly on preservation, for example in Costa Rica (Tickell, 1998). In Belize, various American utilities have bought 6,000 ha of forest that was apparently otherwise destined to be felled for mechanized agriculture. The forest is to be logged sustainably, apparently averting the release of the annual equivalent of the exhaust emissions of hundreds of thousands of cars.

Does forest protection contribute to conservation? Certainly. For example, 65 per cent of 1,111 threatened birds are forest species (Birdlife International/WWF, 1997). The proportion of biodiversity protected is much higher than the proportion of CO_2 offset, and so, when protecting primary forest, more is done to prevent extinction than to offset the greenhouse effect. In comparing the consequences for biodiversity of sequestration by tree planting as distinct from storage in forests, it is crucial to bear in mind that plantations are profoundly different to forests. The proposal by Wise Use (1999) to clear-cut old forest growth and replace it with plantations is thus catastrophic in biodiversity terms.

From a conservationist standpoint, any measure which can protect forests (or other wilderness) has an appeal, even if buying off one environmental loss (scheduled forest destruction) in exchange for tolerating another (permitting pollution) may seem shoddily like extortion ('I promise not to rob that bank if you let me rob this one'). Of course, the moral and practical legitimacy of such an exchange hinges on the genuineness of unavoidabilities: if polluting is genuinely unavoidable, then it seems appropriate at least to compensate for the damage, and if forest was genuinely scheduled for destruction, then a guarantee of protection is a gain. However, a moment's reflection reveals the morass of practical uncertainty in this chain of logic.

A possibility between the sink and store options is to foster the regeneration of partly degraded forest. In the USA, Barker *et al.* (1996) estimate that regenerating hardwood wetland on 4 Mha of marginal cropland and 2 Mha of bottomland in the Conservation and Wetlands Reserve Programs would sequester 850 MtC over the next 50 years, while bringing biodiversity benefits of wetland restoration. Of course, this compromise sequesters less carbon than intensive plantations, and conserves biodiversity to a lesser extent than forest protection (insofar as specialist species may already have been lost during the degradation phase through logging or fuelwood use) (e.g. Thiollay, 1992; Hambler and Speight, 1995a,b).

(v) Carbon substitution

From their extensive review, Brown *et al*. (1996) conclude that

> The most effective long-term (>50 years) ways in which to use forests to mitigate the increase in atmospheric CO_2 are to substitute fuelwood for fossil fuels and for energy-expensive materials. However, over the next 50 years or so, substantial opportunities exist to conserve and increase the C store in living trees and wood products (High Confidence).

Substitution has a higher capacity for carbon offset than storage, since the same land is repeatedly used for intensively harvesting fuelwood or products. However, its usefulness for biodiversity conservation will depend crucially on the management regime, and the most productive plantations will be undesirable as biodiversity reserves.

(c) *Is Carbon Offset a Good Mechanism for Biodiversity Conservation?*

This case study has revealed enormous uncertainties in the arguments for carbon offset, (as distinct from trading) (see Brown *et al*., 1996; Ciesla, 1997). Paramount among these difficulties are: land availability; economic methods for valuing land fully, including opportunity costs and non-market benefits; transaction costs; protection opportunities and costs; demographic trends; efficiency of production and conversion into wood products; lifetimes of wood products; climate change and its impact on productivity; local productivity; and impact on local populations and land use. The number of confounding variables involved is mind-boggling. For example, the rather small benefit (3 per cent of emissions) of planting a million hectares of poplar in the UK could produce additional benefits through substitution if the trees were used as biofuel. However, the instant appeal of this thought is dampened by considering the environmental costs of planting, harvesting, transporting, and using this product (e.g. Adger and Brown, 1994).

There are many standpoints from which to evaluate the proposal to offset carbon emissions through planting and protection of forests. My focus is on its merits as a mechanism to conserve nature, conveniently referred to as biodiversity and most easily measured as species diversity. On an evolutionary timescale, rates of biodiversity loss over the past decade have, like rates of climate change, been unusually high and are increasing. Major threats to biodiversity are habitat loss, habitat fragmentation, and climate change (followed by the impact of alien species transported out of context by people; Macdonald and Thom, forthcoming). Insofar as loss of biodiversity through extinction is irreversible, there is an argument that alleviating anthropogenic impacts on biodiversity is at least as important as mitigating those on

climate. Furthermore, biodiversity, structured into complex and dynamic ecosystems, provides humans with goods and ecological services
beyond human invention. Those brokering a biodiversity deal must
consider for how long is it reasonable to demand the security of habitats
that have been credited in the swap. The interests of sustainability
necessitate that the answer must be 'for a very long time'.

In this context, and considering the tangle of uncertainties—technical, legal, and economic—bedevilling tree planting to sequester carbon,
it would appear at best poor and at worst perverse, as a method for
biodiversity conservation (and a dubious one to reduce carbon pollution). Planting forests of conservation value is worthwhile in itself, and
may usefully become part of the metric of bartering biodiversity gain
for pollution damage, but sequestration of carbon is a relatively
dubious element of that metric. Similarly, safeguarding forests from
destruction is a huge priority for conservation. Added to a list of
compelling motives for forest conservation—protecting biodiversity,
ecosystem services, and tribal rights—preventing further leakage of
carbon is a measurable but minor bonus.

The wildest optimists estimate that carbon sequestration and storage can at most offset about 15 per cent of a single environmental
problem, at a cost of over US$250 billion globally (an approach which
brings with it the risk of diverting pressure from the fundamental need
to reduce CO_2 release, and also risks reducing awareness of environmental guilt and intergenerational inequity). Such immense sums could
have a huge impact on biodiversity, habitat, and wilderness conservation and are of the same order of magnitude to that estimated by the
Rio Conference to support a global programme of sustainable development (some US$500 billion) (see also James *et al.*, 1999).

In conclusion, this case study of carbon offset reveals a morass of
ecological, geophysical, economic, and legal difficulties that lead me to
judge that planting sequestration forests is an unpromising and probably counterproductive option for biodiversity conservation (others
judge it unhelpful to community development, e.g. Corner House,
1999). Furthermore, carbon offset to prevent or reduce future pollution
is relatively low on the list of good reasons to protect forests. None the
less, anything that promotes primary forest conservation is a good
thing, and some conservation reafforestation (especially of corridors,
with an eye to the landscape scale of processes) is also highly desirable.
If carbon swaps can provide a mechanism for realizing these environmental benefits, then the pragmatist might turn a blind eye to the fact
that the logic is not overly compelling. Be that as it may, and even if
carbon offset raises more problems than it is likely to solve, does it teach
us anything about the practicality of biodiversity swaps in general?

4. Discussion: Bartering Biodiversity

An obvious lesson to be drawn from the discussion of carbon offset is that the whole notion of swapping is much more complicated than its beguiling initial appeal would suggest. None the less, the inevitability of many environmental 'bads' and the increasing need to find mechanisms to pay for environmental protection and repair mean that nervousness at the complexity of the transaction is no reason to rule it out. Furthermore, while carbon offset swaps are particularly complex because they often occur between countries, and largely across the north–south divide, swaps within countries may be much easier to broker.

Can we, from this tangle of considerations, devise a scheme that captures the fundamentals of good practice for companies, institutions, or individuals which have an impact on biodiversity?

(a) *The Biodiversity Impacts Compensation System (BICS)*

The ultimate goal of impact management is to cause no damage to the environment. This lofty goal is already the explicit aim of, for example, BP Amoco. However, since some commercial activities clearly involve unavoidable environmental impacts, even net environmental neutrality necessarily involves compensatory investment in environmental improvement. An iterative process of improvement is suggested by the obvious fact that current impacts of business on biodiversity can be categorized as either irreducible (consequences of essential business activities whose impact can be neither avoided nor mitigated) or reducible (by current best practice). First, the mitigation of reducible impacts should be mandatory, and as know-how and technology improve, continual reassessment should result in the transfer of formerly irreducible impacts into the reducible category. Clearly, the judgement on reducibility will involve cost–benefit analysis, but in principle the value attached to biodiversity in such analyses should be high and precautionary.

A second dichotomy concerns the location of the biodiversity impact: some will be direct and local, such as habitat loss or water contamination, and others will be indirect and global, such as CO_2 emissions. This distinction has practical relevance to the target of compensation: communities are likely to demand that local damage is compensated for locally. The priority for compensation for such local impacts may more often, but not inevitably, be like-for-like. However, where impacts are indirect, greater opportunities arise for implementing forms of biodiversity conservation with the highest priority. I have suggested elsewhere (Macdonald *et al.*, 2000) that companies causing unavoidable environmental damage could make compensatory payments into an Environmental Pool, which could then fund biodiversity conservation worldwide. This system, the Biodiversity Impacts Compensation Scheme (BICS), schematized in Figure 1, would hinge on (*a*) calculation of the compensatory levy imposed on companies, (*b*) the prioritization of conservation activities to which payments were made, and (*c*) development of robust performance indicators, which could monitor both the company's (hopefully diminishing) impact on biodiversity and the (hopefully enhanced) biodiversity conservation achieved by compensatory projects. The BICS will require a staged process, similar to the Conservation Quartet (Macdonald *et al.*, 2000), embracing the linked stages of research, community involvement, education, and implementation.

Let us take these three prerequisites of the BICS in reverse order.

(i) Biodiversity performance indicators

The development of biodiversity performance indicators is no less challenging than the tasks faced by those producing performance league tables of everything from schools to health authorities. Like any other indicators, they must be a good proxy for the performance target, easy to measure and collate, and simple to interpret. Biodiversity performance indicators must also be comprehensible to the public. Companies which implement robust biodiversity performance indicators may reap diverse rewards, ranging from enhanced brand value, reflecting consumer goodwill, to employee satisfaction. Such indicators will increasingly be subject to close scrutiny and companies which adopt toothless or cosmetic measures are more likely to reap ridicule. Currently, there is minimal evidence of industry standards concerning biodiversity impact reporting, or corporate performance measurement. A useful step towards the development of biodiversity performance indicators might be adoption of the Logical Framework (logframe) analysis widely used by NGOs to force project planners to evaluate potential projects, and produce indicators of their success, before their implementation.

The conservation community is itself wrestling with the development of performance indicators. For example, under Local Agenda 21 (the international action plan *signed* by 179 countries at the 1992 Earth Summit) each local authority in every country should produce a sustainable development plan. The evaluation of these plans will rest on indicators. Thus, in the UK, the Improvement Development Agency is developing a core menu of local indicators to be linked to the 14

Figure 1
Biodiversity Impacts Compensation Scheme

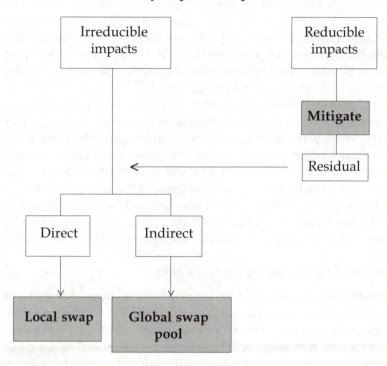

Headline Indicators of the UK's sustainable development strategy (in response to the Convention on Biological Diversity). The headline wildlife indicator of this strategy is 'population of wild birds', based on monitoring the performance of 139 breeding birds in Britain. Species useful as indicators should demonstrate certain qualities, such as being noticeable, recognizable, likely to respond to change, widespread, be capable of quantification without undue effort, be indicative of processes (e.g. eutrophication), demonstrate wider landscape patterns, and detect subtle changes of habitats (this list emerged from the consideration of the Wye Valley Area of Outstanding Natural Beauty Joint Advisory Committee, 1999). Indicators may also be measured above the species level. Indeed, the most important things to be protected are the processes that underlie ecosystem function and embodied in natural communities of plants and animals. Proxies for communities may be habitats and measures of their deterioration or loss (including size, configuration, and dispersion).

(ii) Prioritization of conservation activities

Conservationists are painfully familiar with ranking priorities. The selection of projects may be aided by quasi-quantitative classifications of rarity and endangerment (e.g. Mace–Lande (1991) criteria), but ultimately the deciding factor is often the collective judgement of expert committees. Similar expert opinion would doubtless be essential to the disbursement of funds by the Environmental Pool. This would involve difficult judgements about the relative importance of ecosystems or species, perhaps focusing on levels of endemicity, sensitive, marginal or rare ecosystems, pristine sites, and ecosystems providing the most environmental services. Attempts to quantify the prioritization process include the efforts of WWF-US, IUCN and several others to produce criteria to advise the timber industry on areas of the world that should be closed to forestry . Similarly, WWF International has been publishing a global 'Living Planet' index since 1997, and is working with the IUCN to develop the Red List as a regional indicator of biodiversity health.

(iii) A currency for evaluating compensation

Undoubtedly, the most difficult issue of all is how the costs of biodiversity damage are to be computed. For the BICS to be operable, there must be a common currency for cost–benefit analysis. Pearce (this volume) explains that gains and losses can be calculated in terms of increments or decrements to human wellbeing (measured as willingness to pay for a gain, or avert a loss, or accept compensation), but this task is complicated by the incommensurables (items — including much of Nature — for which there is no market, and whose dimensions may appear more moral than financial). In fact, the difficulty here is not the misplaced moral indignation that Nature (specifically, biodiversity) is beyond or above monetary value, but rather the practical matter of how to persuade markets to accept that the environment has extremely high monetary value (even if much of this is non-use value).

Value is usually calculated through the service or utility of an object. Biodiversity, as embodied in the existence of functioning ecosystems, clearly has such value in, for example, climate regulation, water and nutrient cycling, resource provision, and even recreation. These are the so-called ecosystem services that authors such as Costanza et al. (1997) and James et al. (1999) use to value the totality of biodiversity. But what of a given element of biodiversity — the last Lesser Spotted Obscurity (LSO)? Loosely, the economist's price on its head would be the lowest in a range of possibilities running from its value to the consumer to the willingness of that consumer to accept compensation for its loss, or pay for its translocation or replacement cost. Being irreplaceable, the last

LSO may be infinitely valuable, and the consumer may attach enormous non-use value to its existence. However, if the consumer ranks it as worthless, then it will be so. The likelihood of the consumer taking this miserly view of the LSO may be diminished if he perceives it to have scarcity value or if he fears the risk that loss of the species will cause unpredictable unravelling of ecosystem function with direct cost to himself. The latter possibility may give the LSO option value (the potential saving that flexibility can provide), but if the cost is likely to be felt far in the future (perhaps by future generations) it may be discounted (costs diminished in proportion to the time likely to pass before they are imposed). Yet the observable fact is that some people do attach substantial value to creatures they will never see (far less use) themselves — *vide* the donors to projects conserving giant pandas or Siberian tigers. Indeed, companies, too, acknowledge these existence values: in 1999 ICI donated £60,000 to conserve in the UK the pearl-bordered fritillary — a butterfly that seems vanishingly unlikely to have significant bearing on ecosystem services (although the precautionary principle prevents too glib a dismissal of its significance). Of course, in this particular instance the sponsor may have reaped some sixfold that value in advertising revenue. The point here, however, is not about the undoubted profile-building benefits to companies volunteering to sponsor conservation (but pity the species whose fate depends on finding a second champion when the first one tires of it). Rather, the point is how are we to put a value on compensation for biodiversity that is threatened but has no market price?

There are two families of approach to this. First, expressed preference techniques include contingent ranking (people choose between baskets of options, thereby establishing their relative preferences for particular ecosystem services relative to goods that have an easily measured market price) and contingent valuation (people state a monetary value that they would be willing to pay for an improvement in service, or would be willing to accept for a degradation in service). Second, indirect preference techniques include avertive expenditure (how much people would pay to reduce the magnitude of an impact), travel cost (the value of the service provided is assumed to be at least the cost in time and money spent in travelling to reach it), or hedonic pricing (which uses statistical methods to estimate the relationship between the market price and the attributes of the service). In the latter case, the impact of access to Areas of Outstanding Natural Beauty on the value of a house can be estimated through a statistical analysis of the variation in house prices with proximity to parks.

The nature of these valuations is clearly subjective. Furthermore, it is axiomatic that estimates of willingness to accept compensation are

generally much greater than willingness to pay. Hanley and Milne
(1996) note that while 99 per cent of people questioned thought wildlife
had the right to exist, only 49 per cent were at ease with this right
translating into a cost in money or jobs. (On the other hand, and
astonishingly, 19 per cent continued to express a willingness to pay as
much as 25 per cent of their income.) If the fate of biodiversity is to hinge
on expressed or indirect preference techniques, then one thing is clear:
education is essential. Willingness to pay will be directly driven by
understanding and appreciation that can only be fostered by education.
Insofar as education is never complete, these valuations will be under-
estimates and dynamic, and a nerve-wrackingly labile—not to say
whimsical—basis for globally important decisions. Indeed, the lack of
understanding of ecosystems worldwide is so profound that even
specialists (as used in the Delphi technique) struggle to prioritize, far
less to monetize the value of their components, so to pass this responsibility to an uninformed public is ludicrous. Therefore, while indirect
valuation techniques reveal intriguing and important aspects of public
perception, I am sceptical that they can provide a sensible solution to
valuing Nature.

Species diversity, or measures of habitat, provide measurable proxies for biodiversity. Money provides a measure for economic models.
In a world where the drivers of policy and action are economic, an
important step in conserving biodiversity is to hasten its incorporation
as a valuable asset into economists' models. For this to happen, its value
must be translated into a currency that economists can use, for example
in cost–benefit analysis. The strongest candidate currency appears to be
money, and one of the greatest challenges to conservation biology's
inter-disciplinarity is to devise a sensible method of monetizing biodiversity's value.

(b) *Business and the Environmental Pool*

Increasingly, business is involved in the environment and environmental politics (e.g. Macdonald *et al.*, 2000), and this involvement includes
biodiversity (Rhodes, 1998). The BICS offers a framework for regulating the relationship between business and biodiversity. It seems likely
that, whether voluntarily or through the instruments of regulation or
taxation, industry will increasingly be required not merely to declare
and limit, but also to repair its impact on the environment. Already,
there is a clear first-mover advantage to corporations associating
themselves with successful biodiversity projects, especially those aimed
at sustainability. At least some of the steps in the BICS process could be
mandatory in the foreseeable future. The crux of this system is compen-

sation, so it is sensible to ask what mechanism would transfer money from industry to environmental enhancement. Obviously, the mechanism should not provide a soft option for developers and polluters. For example, it is ominous that in 1994 the US Department of Energy was suggesting that 'Tree planting will allow US energy policy to go on with business as usual out to 2012' (Pearce, 1994). This is a deluded and environmentally dangerous interpretation. It has recently been shown that the assumed large US carbon sink does not exist (Field and Fung, 1999; Houghton *et al.*, 1999) with the fundamental conclusion that forests are not going to solve the problem of carbon emissions (Adler, 1999). The BICS diagram (Figure 1) makes it clear that mitigation to minimize reducible impacts should be a mandatory first step.

Similarly, there is a need to guard against perverse consequences: for example, trading in carbon credits should not generate an industry that is profitable to traders but unhelpful to the environment. In this context, it has been suggested that the World Bank is benefiting from supporting new fossil-fuel developments and from cleaning up after them (Wysham, 1998). Indeed, the World Bank estimates that carbon trading could amount to US$150 billion by 2020, whereas the Electric Power Research Institute envisages CO_2 emissions permits totalling a value of £13 trillion by 2050 (Holder, 1999).

Where biodiversity impacts are direct, and locally felt, compensation will generally have to benefit the same community. However, the BICS system proposes an Environmental Pool to disperse funds compensating for indirect impacts. How might such an Environmental Pool function?

Businesses whose activities, despite the tightest feasible regulation, cause unavoidable environmental (biodiversity) damage might be required, or given the opportunity to, fund an 'Environmental Pool'. This could facilitate like-for-unlike swaps. The contributions to the pool would be an honest signal of a business's commitment to the environment. Indeed, willingness to pay for environmental action could translate into business advantage through customer loyalty, or increased market share. Businesses and products chosen by the customer would then be influenced by two factors: the environmental record of the business and the environmental contributions to the fund (as a percentage of profit). Indeed, taking a leaf out of the books of the Carbon Storage Trust, which offers carbon offsets at £20 per tonne (Tickell, 1998), perhaps there is scope for a Biodiversity Trust which sells 'Biosphere Futures' to fund the Environmental Pool.

In the example of carbon pollution, compensation for damage could involve payment to the Pool in direct relation to tonnes of carbon emitted. This might involve agreement on the value of the economic damage done per unit of CO_2 (estimated at US\$50–100/tC, Houghton, 1997), the market value of carbon offsets per unit CO_2, or the cost of the cheapest method to offset CO_2, tropical forest protection (estimated at US\$0.4–15/tC, Brown *et al.*, 1996). If the estimated 154m tonnes of carbon emitted per year from Britain were linked to payment at US\$0.4–15 per tonne, somewhere between US\$62m and US\$2.3 billion would be available for the 'Environmental Pool' each year!

Climate change offers an interesting case study of how the 'Environmental Pool' might operate. Customers and companies wishing specifically to help reduce the impact of climate change could opt to earmark spending for ecosystems, habitats, and species which are most threatened by climate change. These include coral reefs, coastal habitats, islands, mountain systems, and fragmented ecosystems, including forests. Many of these are under intense immediate pressure independent of climate change, and are being lost for lack of funds.

To earmark funds, those paying into the 'Environmental Pool' could choose which of a portfolio of projects interested them most. It might be necessary for the value of projects to be weighted by an expert committee to balance any tendency for companies to earmark charismatic projects at the risk of under-funding more important ones. Projects might be ranked according to diverse criteria. Those contributing to both climate change *and* biodiversity might be attractively priced—forests and peatlands are particularly important to carbon balance. Customers might be given a choice as to whether a premium on fuel or other products was dedicated to making a *very* little contribution to ameliorating CO_2 pollution, or a larger contribution towards a more achievable environmental target. Those with a responsibility for approving and valuing projects for the 'Environment Pool' would face the dilemmas already familiar to conservation professionals—for example, how are the rights of tribal peoples to be accommodated alongside those of wildlife conservation? In some instances UNESCO's Man and the Biosphere reserves might offer a good model for integration.

(c) *Precedents for Biodiversity Swaps*

Compensation, the necessary corollary of irreducible damage within the BICS, has been explored in the USA. There, the Habitat Conservation Planning (HCP) system, developed from clauses in the US Endangered Species Act, provides a theoretical safety valve to allow some 'take' of land of a listed species in exchange for purchase and/or protection of similar land elsewhere in the region—and in theory an overall improvement of the prospects of the species. Resources are made available for conservation of the species that would not have been available in the absence of an economically powerful developer. The HCP process is thus a formal means of 'balancing' an accepted negative impact on some protected species by activities to compensate the loss and improve the species's overall chances of survival. HCPs are increasingly used to resolve conflicts in the USA between species protection and development interests (Beatley, 1994). Indeed, there are, as at February 1999, some 240 approved plans and 200 more being developed.

However several such plans have failed to benefit the species in question (Beatley, 1994), and the process has been likened to planning gain (Hambler, 1995a) with the associated adverse connotations. A difficulty is that few HCPs have existed for more than a few decades, and thus insufficient time has elapsed to take serious measurements of the security they have brought to species or habitats. It is alleged that developers commonly neglect responsibilities associated with agreed protection in perpetuity, and critics assert that conservation decisions in HCPs are generally based on inadequate scientific data (Reichhardt, 1999) and are inflexible in the light of changing knowledge (Reichhardt, 1998). Fears are mounting that, in practice, high budget wetland compensation projects founded on ecosystem restoration or creation in the USA are failing to achieve their HCP targets (Zedler and Callaway, 1999). If so, the swaps have not been fair.

Hitherto much of the work (and even more of the publicity) associated with conservation has concentrated on single-species pres-ervation, whereas conservation of habitats is the most effective way of protecting biodiversity (Noss et al., 1997). This requires a focus on the dynamic nature of the environment and the need to conserve ecological processes which are the fundamental 'machinery' of ecosystem func-tioning (Southwood, 1995). Shifting the focus, if not the hype, from species to ecosystems acknowledges the latter's complexity, non-linearity, and consequent unpredictability. That same unpredictability poses problems for brokering swaps which involve restoring a de-graded habitat: predicting the trajectory and outcome of restoration is difficult (Meffe et al., 1997), and more so the more dissimilar the habitat to be restored is from the target habitat (Zedler and Callaway, 1999). Swaps involving protection rather than restoration may, in this respect, be a safer bet and the metric of exchange should, as a precaution, allow a considerable margin of error.

(d) *Costs*

It is interesting to ask how much conservation projects might cost. In 1994, the UK government made provision for creating an additional 60,000 ha of woodland at a cost of £90m (this is an area equivalent to a forest of 20 x 30 km, or 6,000 km of woodland corridor 100m wide). Allowing natural regeneration along a 100 m wide corridor through Grade 2 arable land might cost £40,000 per kilometre for land purchase. Locally, four projects from Oxfordshire illustrate the costs of smaller restoration projects: at Pinkhill Meadow a plan to create a mosaic of wetland habitats, including permanent and temporary water, gravel islands, mudflats, reedbeds, wet grassland, and scrub, costs £112,000 for only 2 ha. The cost to restore an ancient water meadow system, Sherbourne Water Meadows, and thus improve the ecological value of the floodplain, is £120,000 for 57 ha. To restore 2.5 km of the River Cole channel from a straightened and deepened profile into a meandering, shallow profile and to re-establish natural integration of the river with its floodplain costs £140,000 for 25 ha. The Royal Society for Protection of Birds has recently raised £600,000 towards restoration of 103 ha of Otmoor, of which £500,000 is from the Heritage Lottery Fund. Indeed, the HLF has donated £25m to conservation land purchases by the Wildlife Trusts in the UK. The costs of all these projects are high in the context of current conservation spending, but they are trifling in the context of the costs of carbon emissions alone, not to mention the wide array of other sources of environmental damage for which society might decide the polluter should pay. This is made graphically clear when comparing the costs of conserving the world's biodiversity with the costs estimated for offsetting global carbon pollution. James *et al.* (1999) estimate the costs of a comprehensive global conservation programme to be about US$320 billion per year, consisting of US$27.5 billion for the conservation of an ecologically representative global network of protected areas and US$290 billion for biodiversity conservation in the farming sector. This compares favourably with the (wildly variable) estimates of cost for a practicable programme of carbon offset. James *et al.* (1999) remind us that environmentally 'perverse' subsidies total from US$950 billion to US$1,450 billion per year!

So, is bartering biodiversity a topic worthy of exploration? While this preliminary review discloses that the topic is amply supplied with banana skins on which the unwary might skid, when cautiously approached biodiversity swaps may offer a useful, indeed a massive, opportunity for conservation. Further, insofar as some biodiversity impacts are irreducible, a BICS-like scheme is the only possibility for compensating that loss. As companies become more aware of consumer, expert, and hence governmental, pressure to measure and to mitigate and compensate their environmental impact, contributing to something akin to the proposed 'Environmental Pool' may become socially *de rigeur*. I suspect it will also become legally mandatory. It is essential, therefore, to produce more sophisticated mechanisms for valuing biodiversity. The only prospect for these values being high enough to safeguard biodiversity lies in mass environmental education. BICS, or any other framework for environmental protection will only be as good as the performance indicators through which it is monitored. The refinement of transparent, quantitative and painfully sharp-toothed biodiversity performance indicators is a priority. No company has yet achieved these in its environmental reporting. A strategy of improving environmental performance through (*a*) rigorous mitigation of reducible impacts and (*b*) compensatory swapping mechanisms to offset the indirect, irreducible environmental bads (such as carbon emissions) must be credible to critical environmentalists. It may also become compulsory, as biodiversity is increasingly protected in policy and legislation.

Part Three: Sectors

8

Environmental and Public Finance Aspects of the Taxation of Energy

STEPHEN SMITH*

1. Introduction

'Ecotax reform' has become a catchphrase with considerable political resonance in many European countries. A number of European governments have established Ecotax Commissions, or other study projects, to assess the potential for major environmentally inspired tax reform, and practical instances of environmental taxes have multiplied dramatically (OECD, 1995). In the UK, the arguments for ecotax reform — in various guises — have been adopted right across the political spectrum: both Conservative and Labour Chancellors of the Exchequer have taken tax policy measures which they justified by using some of the arguments used by the supporters of ecotax reform, and the Liberal Democrats have adopted a more fundamental ecotax programme as party policy.

Part of the impetus for ecotax reform comes from the recognition of the limitations of environmental policies pursued solely through conventional regulatory instruments. Increasingly, there is a recognition that some environmental problems cannot be tackled purely as technical issues, to be resolved straightforwardly through regulations requiring the use of appropriate abatement technologies. To make any serious impact on some of the major environmental problems now facing policy-makers — acid rain, global warming, traffic congestion — environmental policies will need to achieve extensive and far-reaching changes to existing patterns of production and consumption. Achieving the necessary changes will inevitably entail substantial economic costs. The search for instruments capable of minimizing the costs, and capable of achieving behavioural changes across all sectors, has led policy-

* University College London.

The author acknowledges support from the ESRC research centre at the Institute for Fiscal Studies under grant no. M544285001.

makers in the last decade to pay much closer attention to the potential for incentive-based environmental regulation, through taxes, charges, tradable permits, and other 'economic instruments'.

Further pressures for ecotax reform have come from tax-policy-makers and Ministries of Finance, who have quickly recognized the revenue-raising potential of ecotaxes. Some countries that have been concerned about the impact—either economic or political—of high taxes on labour income, have considered ecotax reforms in which the revenue raised from new environmental tax measures would permit reductions in income tax rates. Sweden, for example, actually implemented such a reform package in 1991, in which revenues from new environmental taxes on energy were used to finance cuts in labour income taxes. The political attractions of 'packaging' environmental taxes and tax reform in this way are, perhaps, obvious. The environmental gains, too, are relatively clear-cut, but the fiscal benefits of this type of tax substitution are much more contentious.

An important ingredient in the discussion of ecotax reform is the scale of the tax changes that would be involved, and the notion that the introduction of new environmental taxes might significantly alter the constraints and opportunities in tax policy-making. In practice, however, many environmentally motivated tax measures that might be contemplated do not have the potential to raise significant tax revenues. The tax bases involved are insufficiently large to yield revenues that significantly alter the overall tax structure. Taxes on certain types of battery, for example, or on plastic carrier bags, or on household purchases of garden fertilizers and pesticides, have all been employed in some European countries. In each case, they may have appreciable merit as an instrument of environmental policy, but their revenues are negligible in the context of the overall public finances. Even the substantial tax introduced by the UK on the use of landfill sites for dumping waste, which currently yields about £400m per annum, contributes little more than 0.1 per cent of total revenues. In addition, of course, some environmental taxes may achieve highly elastic polluter responses, eroding the revenue yield. Thus, for example, the tax differential introduced between leaded and unleaded petrol in many European countries has been followed by quite rapid fuel substitution, as consumers have shifted to the lower-taxed fuel.

In practice, significant scope for major tax reform financed by the revenues derived from ecotaxes is only likely to arise in the case of two potential environmental tax bases—taxes on road transport and on energy. Congestion charges on private motoring could, for example, be a major source of tax revenues, if levied at a rate reflecting the congestion externality imposed by each individual motorist on other road users. For example, Newbery (1990) estimated that the congestion cost per vehicle-kilometre averaged some 3.4 pence across the UK. If this was fully reflected in a congestion charge, it would imply revenues of some £18 billion annually at current values, some 6 per cent of total fiscal receipts (or about one-quarter of the revenues from income tax). On the other hand, if congestion externalities are separately taxed, other taxes on motoring may be higher than can be justified in terms of the remaining motoring externalities, and so the overall revenue gain from moving to an efficient structure of externality taxes and changes on motoring would be substantially lower.

The taxation of energy, to reflect the environmental externalities involved in energy use, is the other area with potential to raise major tax revenues. Energy taxes, in the form of a carbon tax, were the main ingredient in Sweden's ecotax reform, and the European Commission's proposal for a carbon-energy tax in the early 1990s would have likewise generated appreciable revenues—between 1 and 3 per cent of total fiscal receipts in member states. In 1994, the UK government ended VAT zero-rating on domestic energy as one of a package of revenue-raising measures. The initial proposal to tax energy at the standard VAT rate of 17.5 per cent would have raised some £3 billion of revenues annually, some 1 per cent of total fiscal receipts, but subsequent modifications have reduced the tax rate to 5 per cent, and annual revenues to around one-third of the original projection.

The Labour government elected in 1997 began giving serious consideration to the possibility of taxing industrial energy use. A Task Force, chaired by Lord Marshall, reported in late 1998 on the scope for using economic instruments to reduce energy use and emissions of greenhouse gases by the industrial and commercial sectors. Its report argued that a 'mixed approach' would be needed, combining existing forms of regulation with economic instruments, to provide clear signals for longer-term emissions reductions (Marshall Report, 1998).

The 1999 Budget announced that a tax on industrial and commercial energy use, the 'Climate Change Levy', would be introduced, starting in April 2001. Subsequent statements, and the 2000 Budget, filled out the details of this measure. The Levy will take the form of a tax per unit of energy used by industry, at initial rates of 0.15 pence per kWh for coal and natural gas, 0.43 pence for electricity, and 0.07 pence for liquid petroleum gas. There will be exemptions from the tax for energy generated in CHP (combined heat and power) plants, and for renewable energy sources, such as wind and solar power. There will be partial exemptions, too, in the form of a rate of tax at one-fifth of the standard rate, for energy-intensive sectors which conclude negotiated agreements to reduce energy use. Revenues raised from the tax will partly be

used to finance corporate tax incentives for energy efficiency investments; the remaining revenue will be returned to business through a
reduction of 0.3 percentage points in the rate of employers' National
Insurance (NI) contributions. Overall, therefore, the package of measures is revenue-neutral, raising no net revenues, but its incentive effect
is forecast to reduce UK greenhouse-gas emissions by some 2m tonnes
of carbon per annum.

The evolution of this tax has shown the political difficulties of
immediate introduction of large-scale environmental taxes on energy.
The political legacy of the previous government's attempt to impose
standard-rate VAT on domestic energy has been that the Climate
Change Levy excludes the domestic sector. This obviously forgoes the
possibility of equal energy-saving incentives in the domestic and
business sectors, but, less obviously, has led to some messy compromises in the design of the tax, requiring it to be imposed nearer the point
at which energy is sold to final users, so that the domestic sector can be
exempted. Fear of the impact that a tax on carbon content might have
on the coal industry has led the government to choose energy content,
rather than carbon content, as the base for the tax, thus forgoing the
possibility that carbon emissions could be reduced through fuel-
switching incentives. Concern about the impact of the tax on the
competitiveness of energy-intensive sectors has led to arrangements
that will exempt these sectors from the levy, in return for negotiated
agreements with these sectors to achieve equivalent improvements in
energy efficiency. This again complicates the design of the levy, reduces
further the proportion of the economy experiencing the incentive
effects of the tax, and relies on the questionable — and untestable —
assertion that the negotiated agreements will achieve energy savings at
least as great as those that the Levy would achieve.

Initially, the Climate Change Levy is set to raise only about £1 billion
in revenues, and this allows only a small, 0.3-percentage-point reduction in employer's NI contributions. There is, in principle, scope for
considerably higher tax rates and revenues to be justified by appeal to
the environmental consequences of energy use. However, concerns
about the impact on industrial competitiveness — whether well-founded
or not — seem likely to constrain the tax rate that individual countries,
acting without international coordination, would feel able to implement. Despite this major constraint, it is likely that in the longer run, as
more stringent reductions in energy-related emissions are needed, and
progress is made in international agreements, an increasing role may
need to be played by energy prices in restraining energy demand
growth. Higher energy tax rates, and an increasing revenue contribu-

tion from this source, are likely to be a feature of taxation and environmental policies in many industrialized countries in coming years.

This chapter considers a number of aspects of the taxation of energy for environmental reasons, and, following this introduction, is in three main parts. Section 2 reviews briefly the arguments for using taxes in environmental policy. These arguments form the backdrop to any discussion of energy-related environmental taxes, and neglecting the basic principles they embody could lead to inefficiently designed instruments, or excessive long-run cost. Section 3 discusses potential applications of environmental taxes in the energy sector—their purpose, their design, and their revenue contribution. Section 4 considers the value of the revenue contribution from environmental taxes on energy. Where would ecotax reform fit into the current pattern of British tax policy, and how far would it alter the constraints and problems which the tax system currently faces? In what sense—if at all—would an ecotax reform provide a 'double dividend', in the form of a less distortionary fiscal system, as well as a cleaner environment?

2. The Case for Environmental Taxes

There is now an extensive literature on the potential for taxes to contribute to more efficient and more effective environmental policy (e.g. Smith, 1992; OECD, 1993a, 1996; Bovenberg and Cnossen, 1995; O'Riordan 1997). In comparison with 'conventional' regulatory policies based on technology or emissions standards, ecotaxes may be able to reduce the costs of achieving a given standard of environmental protection (or, alternatively, can achieve a greater environmental impact for a given economic cost). However, environmental taxes are far from being a panacea for all environmental problems. Consideration of their advantages and disadvantages, as compared with other instruments, suggests that there is a group of environmental problems for which taxes, of various sorts, may be the best instrument available. There are other environmental problems which would be better tackled by other approaches, including other 'economic instruments', such as tradable permits, or various forms of command-and-control regulation.

(a) *Advantages of Ecotaxes*

From the perspective of environmental policy, environmental taxes have attractions for a number of reasons.

(i) 'Static' efficiency gains through reallocation of abatement

Where the costs of pollution abatement vary across firms or individuals, environmental taxes have the potential to minimize costs, for one of two possible reasons. Where other policy instruments cannot fully differentiate between polluters with different marginal costs of abatement, taxes can achieve a given level of abatement at lower total abatement cost. On the other hand, where other policy instruments take account of differences in polluter abatement costs, taxes can sidestep the need for the regulatory authority to acquire detailed information on individual sources' abatement costs, and can thus lower costs of regulation from the side of the public sector.

(ii) 'Static' efficiency gains through performance incentives

Taxes levied on emissions provide an incentive for care and attention in the operation of mandated technologies. In many cases, use of a given abatement technology does not guarantee a precise emissions level; instead, much depends on how the technology is used. Providing businesses with an incentive to cut emissions can be translated into providing individuals within the business with similar incentives, and some individuals may be in a position to take actions which greatly affect the emissions performance of a given technology. The discussion in section 3 of the Swedish nitrogen-oxides (NOx) charge shows that a substantial part of the gains from using an economic instrument came from this, perhaps unexpected, source.

(iii) Innovation incentive

Regulatory policies, stipulating that polluters must use particular technologies, or maintain emissions below a specified limit, do not provide polluters with any encouragement to make reductions in pollution beyond what the regulations require. Indeed, where regulations are negotiated on a case-by-case basis, polluters may fear that any willingness to go beyond what is strictly required by the regulations will simply lead to the regulator assigning the firm a tougher limit in future. Environmental taxes, on the other hand, provide a continuing incentive for polluters to seek ways to reduce emissions, even below the current cost-effective level. This incentive arises because of the tax payments which are made on each unit of residual emissions, which create an incentive to develop new technologies, permitting further abatement at a marginal cost below the tax rate.

(iv) Robustness to negotiated erosion ('regulatory capture')

An important consideration in choosing between different strategies for environmental regulation is the extent to which efficient implementation of the policy requires firm-by-firm negotiation of individual abatement or technology requirements. As noted above, command-and-control regulatory policies could be operated in a way which requires different amounts of pollution abatement from different firms, in order to achieve a more cost-effective pattern of abatement than under a uniform abatement rule. However, the regulator is dependent on the regulated firms for information about their abatement costs, and to obtain this information is liable to be drawn into dialogue and negotiation with the regulated firms. The regulated firms, in turn, then control a key element in the process by which regulatory policies are set, and may be able to extract a price from the regulator for their cooperation, in the form of less stringent abatement targets, or other changes which work to their advantage.

One key difference between regulatory policies which set differentiated firm-by-firm targets and the use of environmental taxes is that environmental taxes achieve a cost-effective distribution of abatement, taking account of the abatement costs of individual firms, while taking a robust, non-negotiated form. All firms face the same pollution tax rate. There is no need for the regulator to consider the circumstances of individual firms, and there is thus little scope for individual polluters to attempt to negotiate more favourable terms with the regulator. The risk that this process of negotiation would erode the environmental effectiveness of the policy is thus substantially reduced.

(v) Cost-limiting properties

As compared with policy instruments which operate by defining a quantitative limit on pollution, environmental taxes have the attraction that they insulate polluters from the risk that regulatory requirements might involve excessive abatement costs. The tax rate per unit of emissions places an upper limit on the unit abatement cost which will be incurred. If abatement turns out to be more costly per unit than the tax per unit, firms will simply pollute and pay the tax, rather than paying for costly abatement. By contrast, regulatory policies which set a quantitative limit on emissions may risk requiring that abatement measures are undertaken which are far more costly than the resulting environmental benefits.

(b) *The Limitations of Ecotaxes*

Likewise, and again from the perspective of environmental policy, ecotaxes have a number of identifiable drawbacks and limitations, which will in some cases be sufficiently important to rule out their use in particular applications.

(i) Uncertain environmental impact

The level of pollution abatement achieved by an ecotax depends on individual polluters' responses to the abatement incentive that the tax creates. It is not possible to guarantee that an environmental tax will achieve a particular environmental impact; polluters' behavioural responses may be less, or more, than expected. In cases where the precise achievement of an environmental target is a high priority, this may be an important drawback of ecotaxes. For example, some pollution problems may exhibit threshold effects, where environmental damage per unit of emissions rises sharply beyond a certain level of emissions. On the other hand, many pollution problems do not involve an abrupt boundary between acceptable and damaging emissions, and precise achievement of an emissions target may be relatively unimportant. In these circumstances, ecotaxes may be more attractive.

It will be noted that this uncertain environmental effect is the counterpart of the cost-limiting property of ecotaxes noted above. Quantitative instruments such as direct regulation (or tradable permits) guarantee a particular impact on pollution, but at uncertain abatement cost, while ecotaxes guarantee an upper bound on marginal abatement costs, but have an uncertain pollution outcome. Which matters more will depend on the environmental problem under consideration, and on whether society would prefer to take risks on environmental quality or on the costs of environmental policy.

(ii) Compatibility with firm decision-making structures

Except in very small firms, it will be efficient for many business decisions to be decentralized. Specialized units or divisions of the firm may be given responsibility for making many decisions requiring specialized expertise or detailed information, subject only to general instructions or guidelines from the centre. This represents an efficient division of labour, but carries with it the implication that not all aspects of the firm's operations will necessarily be taken into account in making a particular decision. The internal organization of the firm needs to be designed so that related decisions are grouped together, while unrelated business decisions are separated.

For environmental taxes to lead to efficient polluter responses, it is necessary for firms to draw together information relating both to technology choice and to tax payments. Firms considering whether to undertake more pollution abatement need to balance the gains, at the margin, in reduced tax payments, against the marginal costs of abatement. This requires a type of interaction that may not otherwise be a high priority in the internal organization of the firm, and may require significant changes to the decision-making structure of the firm, so that tax and pollution-control technology decisions are taken together. Restructuring the firm so that such interactions can take place may be costly, and may well not be worth doing if the tax at stake is small. Firms may not, therefore, respond at all to 'small' environmental taxes, and conventional regulatory measures may be more effective, and—taking decision-making costs into account—more cost-effective, too.

(iii) Lack of experience

In the past, the lack of experience with environmental taxes may have been a significant obstacle to their adoption in any particular practical context. A novel policy instrument is only likely to be employed in preference to one which is familiar where the conventional instrument has clear, and widely recognized, defects. Increasingly, the objection that environmental taxes are untried and untested is untrue. Many studies, such as those of the OECD, document the extensive international experience with ecotaxes which is now available, and there is increasing evidence evaluating their effectiveness.

(iv) Administration and enforcement costs

Both environmental taxes and conventional command-and-control regulation require mechanisms for administration and enforcement. The relative costs of these arrangements should be taken into account in choosing between the different instruments available, and it is difficult to generalize.

However, excise taxes on inputs may be an inexpensive way of regulating polluting processes which use these inputs. Unlike other forms of environmental regulation, there is no need for direct contact between the regulator and polluters, and the number of polluting sources does not, therefore, affect the costs of administration and enforcement. The incentive is transmitted through the excise tax levied on the production or sale of the input. If there is only a small number of producers, this will be comparatively cheap to operate. The excise duties levied on mineral oils are a case in point; there is a small number of petrol companies, and their activities are tightly controlled and well documented.

(v) Geographical differences

If pollution damage varies depending on the source of the emissions, policy based on a uniform pollution tax applying to different sources will be liable to result in inefficiency, and source-by-source regulation may be able to achieve a more efficient outcome. In principle, of course, an environmental tax need not be constrained to applying the same tax rate to all sources, and could thus achieve the efficient outcome through appropriately differentiated tax rates. However, once the tax rate has to be set individually for each source, the tax may become more exposed to lobbying influence from the regulated firms. Also, some possible forms of environmental tax may be constrained to set uniform tax rates, even where damage is known to differ between locations. Thus, for example, ecotaxes based on the taxation of pollution-related inputs to a polluting production process may be unable to differentiate between sources, because of the difficulty (or the costs) of preventing resale of inputs taxed at a low rate to polluters with more-damaging emissions.

(c) *The Balance of Costs and Benefits*

The implications of the above are that environmental taxes are likely to be particularly valuable where wide-ranging changes in behaviour are needed across a large number of production and consumption activities. The costs of direct regulation in these cases will be large, and in some cases prohibitive. In addition, where the activities to be regulated are highly diverse, it is likely that considerable gains could be made from allowing the required changes in environmentally damaging activities to be achieved in the most cost-effective manner.

Private-sector energy use cannot realistically be regulated through source-by-source regulation. There are too many energy users – both businesses and individuals – and their opportunities for abatement are too diverse. The available options boil down to indirect techniques – either those that operate by restricting or widening the range of available technologies (e.g. regulations requiring standards of energy efficiency from appliances, or subsidies to promote the introduction of low-energy technologies), or incentive mechanisms such as energy taxes. In the long term, given the scale of changes that would be needed in household and business energy consumption to maintain or reduce global energy-related greenhouse-gas emissions (despite rapid industrialization outside the OECD area), it is almost inconceivable that an effective climate-change policy could be pursued without significant use of energy pricing measures, such as carbon or energy taxes.

On the other hand, the analysis above suggests plenty of areas of environmental policy where advocacy of ecotaxes would be misguided. There is little to be gained from over-sophistication in the tax structure, through the introduction of finely graded tax differentials to reflect the environmental characteristics of commodities with little environmental significance. Complex tax structures are liable to be costly to operate, and the tax 'boundaries' between products subject to higher and lower rates of tax are always open to costly and socially wasteful litigation, and consequent erosion. Moreover, insufficiently large tax incentives may achieve little change in behaviour. As argued above, it may not be worthwhile for firms to take account of tax incentives in making environmental technology decisions if the tax incentives are too small to justify the costs of changing established decision-making structures. It is perhaps an over-generalization to suggest that environmental taxes should be large, or not be imposed at all. However, the costs of complexity and the risk that minor environmental taxes will simply be ignored should both caution against too much environmental fine-tuning of the fiscal system.

(d) Decision-making Obstacles

In the decision-making process, factors other than objective costs and benefits may well play a major role in the choice between environmental policy instruments. Different actors in the process may have divergent interests, and these may affect the policy finally chosen.

For example, it is often suggested that ecotax policies may encounter opposition from some of the 'stakeholders' in the existing regulatory process who would be liable to lose some of the control and influence that they exert within the current regime. This is, in effect, the counterpart of the 'regulatory capture' argument above. Negotiated firm-by-firm regulation gives significant influence to the regulatory agency and firms, and this would be simply bypassed with a policy based on a uniform ecotax.

A second possible influence on instrument choice is that some participants in the decision-making process may perceive costs and benefits which differ from the overall costs and benefits to society.

From the perspective of firms, ecotaxes impose costs in terms of tax payments that may outweigh the efficiency savings achieved through a more efficient pattern of pollution abatement. These tax payments are not, of course, costs to the economy as a whole, but simply transfer payments, having as a counterpart the revenue flow to government.

Nevertheless, taking firms as a group, and assuming that the revenues are not channelled back exclusively to the tax-paying firms, environmental taxes result in substantial burdens. Only if the efficiency gains from a more efficient distribution of abatement across polluters are very large would it be possible for environmental taxes to result in net gains to polluters as a group. This implies polluters will not select environmental taxes if given the choice, and policy-making mechanisms that accord a significant or dominant voice to polluting firms in the choice of policy instrument are unlikely to result in tax-based policies being adopted.

In addition to these possible influences on the decision whether or not to employ ecotaxes, both objective considerations and political pressures may influence the scale of environmental taxes that can be introduced. As discussed by Rajah and Smith (1993), there may be a number of restraints on the rates of environmental tax that can in practice be applied, that may lead policy-makers to combine environmental taxes, set below the first-best level, with other, 'second-best', policy instruments (such as, for example, abatement subsidies or quantitative regulation). The first-best rate of an environmental tax may, for example, present an excessive incentive for evasion, and may consequently involve excessive costs of administration and enforcement; setting a lower rate for the tax may keep the level of evasion, and the costs of enforcement, within more acceptable bounds. Another possibility is that the first-best environmental tax rate may have undesirable consequences for distributional objectives; if it is impracticable to offset this impact fully through adjustments elsewhere in the fiscal system, it may then be preferable to levy a lower environmental tax, and to supplement it with other measures (such as subsidies to increase the elasticity of behavioural responses). Third, the tax rate that can be set may be constrained by the perception of adverse effects on the international competitiveness of industry. The adverse impact of energy taxes on energy-intensive industry (although balanced by corresponding gains elsewhere) attracts enormous policy attention; the European Commission's proposed carbon/energy tax attempted to 'buy off' these objections through sectoral exemptions, and the Swedish carbon tax was drastically revised under pressure from energy-intensive industry. It is noteworthy, too, that the 1998 Marshall Committee report pays great attention to these effects, and that they figure prominently in its conclusions and recommendations. Whether justified or not, concerns about competitiveness are likely to place severe restraints on the ability of governments to set energy taxes at the first-best level, and other instruments will need to be employed in parallel.

3. Environmental Taxes in the Energy Sector

Environmental taxes could be employed in the energy sector, either as taxes on emissions, or in the form of excises or other sales taxes on energy consumption. Taxing emissions potentially links incentives most accurately to the underlying environmental problems, though it will generally require emissions measurement and firm-by-firm administration, which may be costly. Energy excises depend for their environmental effectiveness on an assumed linkage between energy inputs and environmental impact; only if this linkage is relatively tight will the taxation of energy use be a good proxy for the taxation of emissions. On the other hand, energy excises may be relatively cheap to administer, and can build on the existing system for administering mineral oils excises.

   Generally, because of the importance of end-of-pipe technologies in abatement of sulphur emissions and the significance of combustion conditions in determining NOx emissions from industrial processes, environmental taxes to control acid rain would have to take the form of direct emissions taxes. Section 3(a) below reviews the operation of one such system, the NOx charge applied to large industrial plants and power generators in Sweden, to highlight some of the issues involved. Taxes to control greenhouse-gas emissions may, by contrast, be more efficiently implemented as energy excises. In particular, emissions of the most significant greenhouse gas, carbon dioxide, are directly related to the carbon content of input fuels to the combustion process, and commercially viable end-of-pipe abatement opportunities are negligible.

   Substantial excise taxes are already levied on motor fuels, and rather lower rates of excise duty apply to certain other mineral oil products. These existing excises were created for purely fiscal reasons, but they offer scope for changes in the rates or structure of the excise to reflect current environmental concerns. Changes to the overall level of mineral oil excises will affect the incentives for fuel choice as between those fuels subject to the excise duties and those which are currently untaxed. In addition, the relative tax rates applied to different taxed fuels may be altered to differentiate between those that are more and less environmentally damaging. A number of measures of this sort have already been taken in the UK. In particular, there has, since 1987, been a tax differential between leaded and unleaded petrol, designed to reduce levels of airborne lead in the environment, and to encourage the take-up of catalytic converters. More recently, attention has focused on the environmental implications of the duty differential between petrol and diesel fuels, and on the fiscal treatment of new vehicle fuels such as liquefied petroleum gas (LPG). There are further possibilities for differentiation: Sweden, for example, has introduced a sulphur tax on mineral oils, designed to encourage substitution to lower-sulphur fuels.

More dramatically, the large duty differential that currently exists between mineral oils used as motor fuels and those used for other purposes cannot be justified in terms of differences in environmental impact. Instead, it has the effect of concentrating incentives for carbon emissions reduction excessively on the transport sector, while providing negligible incentive for more efficient energy use and reduced carbon emissions from industrial processes.

Beyond these possibilities for differentiation within the structure of existing excises, there are possibilities for extending the scope of excise duties to tax energy sources hitherto outside the duty regime. In particular, an extension of energy excises to natural gas and coal, perhaps accompanied by a tax structure which reflected the relative carbon content of each fuel, would broaden the range of activities facing incentives for better energy use and reduced carbon-dioxide emissions, and would encourage fuel substitutions in the direction of lower-carbon fuels. Extension of existing energy excises to fuels currently untaxed would require additional administration and enforcement activities, but since relatively few energy suppliers are involved, these additional costs of administration will probably be quite limited. Section 3(b) reviews the issues that would arise in extending the scope of excise duties to embrace fuels which are currently untaxed, so as to create a coherent tax structure, with tax rates systematically related to their greenhouse-gas potential.

(a) *Direct Emissions Charging: NOx Emissions Charge in Sweden*

The nitrogen oxides charge in Sweden, introduced in 1992, is levied on measured NOx emissions by a relatively small group of large industrial plants and power stations. This system provides an example of an environmental tax levied on the basis of direct measurement of emissions, rather than input or output proxies for emissions. The need for direct measurement arises in this case because there is no stable relationship between input characteristics or activity levels and the amount of NOx emitted. NOx emissions are greatly affected by the precise operating conditions in the combustion process, which govern the extent to which NOx is produced through interactions between atmospheric nitrogen and oxygen. Use of a tax based on direct emissions measurement is thus able to target the incentive more precisely than a tax based on an emissions proxy.

The costs of emissions measurement per source are high, and have had a significant influence on the way the system has been designed. The annual costs of measurement, including the costs of inspecting and checking the equipment, are estimated at around 300,000 kronor (some £30,000) per plant (SMENR, 1994). In order to limit total measurement costs, the NOx charge was confined to a relatively small group of large sources, for whom measurement costs were likely to be low, relative to the potential abatement cost saving. Initially the charge applied to a total of some 185 plants, having an output of at least 50 GWh/year, which accounted overall for around 40 per cent of total NOx emissions from Sweden's energy sector. The qualifying threshold has subsequently been lowered to 25 GWh/year.

The tax rate is set at SKr40 per equivalent kilogram of nitrogen dioxide. It is calculated on the basis of measured emissions, or using 'presumptive' emissions levels of 250 mg/MJ for boilers and 600 mg/MJ for gas turbines. Plant operators are able to choose to pay the charge on the basis of presumptive emissions levels instead of installing measuring equipment, although in general the presumptive emissions levels are substantially higher than actual emissions, so measurement will generally be preferable. The presumptive levels also apply where the measuring equipment is faulty (Lövgren, 1993).

To avoid distorting the pattern of competition between the large sources which are subject to the NOx charge and their smaller competitors (and possibly introducing incentives for inefficient substitution towards uncharged smaller boilers), the system is operated so that almost all of the charge revenues are returned to the participating sources, in proportion to their final energy output. Thus sources with high emissions relative to their energy output are net payers to the scheme, while sources with low emissions relative to energy output are net recipients. Despite this revenue-neutrality, there is some evidence of tax-induced distortions in activity close to the qualifying output threshold for the system; a significant 'cluster' of plants appear to be maintaining emissions levels just below the level at which they would have to participate in the scheme (SMENR, 1994).

During autumn 1993, after the system had been in operation for some 20 months, a commission examined its operation. A reduction in aggregate NOx emissions of some 8,700 tonnes had been achieved, about 55 per cent of initial emissions (SMENR, 1994). A wide range of different techniques had been employed to reduce emissions, at a range of marginal costs per tonne of NOx abatement from SKr4,000 to SKr 52,000; the average cost of abatement was about SKr10,000/tonne. In addition, it was found that changes in operating procedures for a given plant could have a substantial impact on the level of NOx emitted, without any change in the technologies employed. Decisions made by individual employees responsible for the operation of the plant thus had a major influence over its emissions level. In order to encourage emissions-conscious behaviour by these employees (and hence savings in tax payments), some plants had introduced wage bonuses relating to the emissions reductions which the plant achieved.

(b) *Environmental Excise Taxes on Carbon or Energy*

A 'first-best' tax structure for an excise tax to reduce carbon-dioxide emissions would tax fuels in proportion to their carbon content. Different fossil fuels would be therefore be taxed at different rates per unit of energy. Fuels with a higher carbon content per unit of energy (such as coal, for example) would bear a higher tax burden than fuels with a lower carbon content per unit of energy (such as natural gas). Such a tax structure, combined with tax rates set at the first-best level, would encourage efficient responses, of two sorts. By raising the price of energy relative to other industrial inputs, and relative to other household spending, the carbon tax would act to discourage energy use in general. In addition, by raising the price of fuels differentially, in proportion to their carbon content, the tax would encourage substitution away from high-carbon energy sources towards lower-carbon fuels. Both the reduction in overall energy use and the substitution towards lower-carbon fuels would have the effect of reducing carbon-dioxide emissions.

However, if the overall level of energy taxation is, for some reason, constrained below the first-best level, it may no longer be appropriate to tax fuels in proportion to their carbon content. The direction in which the relative taxation of fuels should then depart from the 'carbon yardstick' will reflect the nature of the constraints. Constraints on the aggregate burden of energy taxes, for example, will imply that the tax structure should be designed to maximize the environmental impact from the relatively low environmental taxes that are feasible. This would require the tax structure to be shifted in the direction of taxing relatively more heavily those fuels where consumption responses are price-elastic, and taxing less heavily those fuels in more inelastic demand.

In the European countries (Sweden, Norway, Finland, the Netherlands, and Denmark) which have actually introduced carbon taxes, these have taken the form of extended systems of fuel excises. Rates of tax are defined separately for each fuel, in terms of fuel quantities, and relative tax levels on different fuels are set so as to equate the implicit rate of tax per unit of carbon across fuels. This requirement is not, however, always observed; in Denmark and Norway, for example, some fuels are not subject to the carbon tax. Also, the level of tax can vary across types of energy user; in Sweden and the Netherlands, for example, much lower rates of tax apply to industrial energy users than to energy use by private households. However, the basic principle has been to extend fuel excises to cover all relevant fossil fuels, and to structure the relative tax rates on these fuels (for the carbon tax component of the excise) according to the relative carbon content.

Likewise, the carbon/energy tax proposed in 1991 by the European Commission would most probably have been implemented by adding to the rates of existing fuel excises, and extending the scope of fuel excises to cover fuels previously untaxed. This proposal was, in fact, not for a pure carbon tax, but for a two-part tax, reflecting both the carbon and energy content of fuel. Fossil fuels such as gas, coal, and oil would have borne a tax comprising two components, one related to their carbon content, the other related to their energy content. Non-renewable forms of energy other than fossil fuels (mainly nuclear power) would have been subject to the energy-related part of the tax, but not the carbon component. The tax rates per tonne of carbon and per joule of energy would have been set so that on a barrel of oil the carbon and energy components would have been weighted 50:50.

As Pearson and Smith (1991) discuss, the logic behind introduction of the energy component to the proposed EC tax was unclear and poorly justified. It would have reduced the strength of the incentive to switch from high-carbon to low-carbon fuels compared with a tax of the same overall scale levied purely on carbon content. One possible explanation for including the energy element in the tax base was to avoid giving undue preference to nuclear power, or to avoid giving an undue competitive advantage to those member states (France, especially) which already generate a substantial proportion of their electricity from nuclear sources.

An alternative to implementing a carbon tax as an extension of existing excises would be to levy a 'primary' carbon tax, which would take the form of a new excise levied on primary fuels (e.g. crude oil, coal, and gas) where they are mined, extracted, or imported. Pearson and Smith (1991) discuss the merits of this approach compared with the extended excise approach, under which carbon tax would be levied on final fuel products (such as coke, anthracite, four-star petrol) sold to industrial users or households. Although there are advantages and disadvantages associated with each form of carbon tax, the 'primary' carbon tax has two significant attractions. The first is that it would involve fewer taxable individuals than a 'final' tax, and no need for fiscal supervision of the energy chain beyond the first point; administrative costs would be expected to be low, and there would be scope for tight supervision to prevent evasion. The second is that it would be better able to tax the full contribution of individual fuels to carbon-dioxide emissions, taking account of emissions during fuel processing as well as their carbon content when finally sold. A carbon tax in the form of excises on refined fuels has to make assumptions about carbon-dioxide emissions during processing; these can vary greatly between different refining technologies, and using 'average' values for these processing emissions can be a poor approximation.

It will be noted that levying a 'primary' carbon tax at an earlier stage in the production chain would not necessarily imply that it would have different economic or environmental effects from an equivalent excise-type carbon tax, levied on refined fuel products. The incidence, for example, of the carbon tax on fuel consumers could be largely invariant to the stage at which tax is formally incident; some part of the burden of a primary carbon tax would be passed on in the prices of fuel products according to their carbon content, so that the prices of fuels purchased by industry and consumers would be much the same as if an equivalent excise-type carbon tax had been levied.

Similar issues arise in the choice of arrangements for the taxation of electricity under a carbon tax. Electricity can be taxed either by taxing the fuels used in electricity generation, or by exempting fuels used in electricity generation from the carbon tax and taxing sales of electricity at a rate reflecting average fuel inputs. Generally, it will be more efficient to take the former route; taxing electricity at a rate reflecting average carbon emissions during generation provides no incentive for generators to use low-carbon fuels for generation. However, in considering how the European carbon tax might operate, the Commission was strongly tempted by the second approach. One reason for this is that if electricity is traded between member states, the excise approach makes it easier to attribute tax revenues to the country of final sale. Another possible reason might again be to avoid giving any fiscal advantage to electricity generated from nuclear power.

4. Public Finance Aspects of Energy Taxes

How much of a difference could environmental taxes on energy make to UK fiscal policy? Table 1 shows that currently the UK raises about 40 per cent of total revenues from two taxes levied on individual incomes (income tax and the quasi-tax NI contributions), 30 per cent from consumption taxes (VAT and excises), and 15 per cent of revenues from

Table 1
UK Fiscal Revenues, 1997–8

	£ billion	Percentage of total revenues
Income tax	76.7	25.9
Corporation tax	30.5	10.3
Other Inland Revenue taxes	10.2	3.4
VAT	51.0	17.2
Excise duties: petrol	19.1	6.5
tobacco	8.3	2.8
alcohol	5.7	1.9
Other Customs and Excise	5.7	1.9
Business rates	14.7	5.0
Council tax	11.1	3.7
National insurance (NI) contributions	50.5	17.1
Vehicle excise duties	4.6	1.6
Other miscellaneous taxes	8.1	2.7
Total taxes and NI contributions	296.1	100.0

Source: HM Treasury (1998, Table B9 General government receipts, estimate 1997–8).

two business taxes (corporation tax and business rates). Total tax revenues are roughly £300 billion. Would it be possible to raise sufficient revenues from environmentally-motivated energy taxes to permit radical change in this pattern of UK tax revenues — and what, if any, would be the fiscal (as opposed to environmental) benefits from such an 'ecotax reform'?

(a) *Some Orders of Magnitude*

Table 2 presents some very unsophisticated estimates of the potential revenue yield from an environmental tax on energy, to illustrate the broad orders of magnitude involved, assuming that the tax was imposed at two different possible rates on today's pattern of energy use. The calculations assume, throughout, that there is no behavioural response to the imposition of the tax, and thus will tend to overstate the revenues that would in practice be obtained. However, presenting the results in this way makes it relatively straightforward to assess the revenue implications of different assumptions about the scale of behavioural responses in energy consumption.

Revenues are calculated with two alternative tax rates. The first is a carbon tax of £60 per tonne of carbon, which is roughly equivalent to the

Table 2
UK Energy Use and Potential Energy Tax Revenues: Orders of Magnitude

Carbon tax on all energy used	
UK energy consumption (million tonnes of oil equivalent)	227 mtoe
Carbon content of UK energy consumption	160m tonnes C
Carbon tax per tonne of carbon:	
(i) EC proposal ($10 per barrel of oil) = $88 per tonne of carbon	
Current sterling equivalent	£59
(ii) Burniaux *et al.* (1991) = $308 per tonne of carbon	
Current sterling equivalent	£206
Carbon tax revenues (assuming unchanged energy consumption):	
(i) Carbon tax of £60/tonne C	£9.6 billion
Revenues as percentage of total fiscal receipts	3.2%
(ii) Carbon tax of £200/tonne C	£32 billion
Revenues as percentage of total fiscal receipts	10.8%
Carbon tax on business energy use only	
(i) Carbon tax of £60/tonne C	£4.4 billion
Revenues as percentage of total fiscal receipts	1.5%
(ii) Carbon tax of £200/tonne C	£14.7 billion
Revenues as percentage of total fiscal receipts	5.0%

carbon tax of $10 per barrel of oil proposed by the European Commission in 1991. The second is a carbon tax of £200 per tonne of carbon, roughly equivalent to the carbon tax which Burniaux *et al.* (1991) estimate would be required in the OECD area in order to keep aggregate global emissions of carbon dioxide at 1990 levels over the period until the year 2020. Two different assumptions are made about the base of the tax. The first case applies the carbon tax to all energy consumption, including energy used in industry, for transport, and by the household sector. The second case restricts the base of the carbon tax to industrial and commercial energy use alone (some 46 per cent of total energy use). It is assumed in both scenarios that no adjustments are made to other energy taxes (such as those already imposed on motor fuels), and that no sectors of industry are exempted from the tax (except for industrial processes which use energy for non-fuel purposes).

The revenues obtained from the tax would range from some £4 billion, for the lower of the two tax rates, applied to industrial energy alone, to some £30 billion, if the higher rate of tax were to be levied on all energy consumption. As a percentage of total existing fiscal receipts, the revenues would range from about 1.5 per cent of existing revenues, to some 11 per cent of revenues. Placed in relation to existing taxes, the first case would permit a reduction of some two percentage points in the basic rate of income tax, a relatively minor tax adjustment (especially if it is borne in mind that the energy tax revenues could be eroded by behavioural responses, and by any tax exemptions given to particular sectors). The second case, however, would permit a drastic reshaping of the tax system. Revenues of some £30 billion would, for example, imply that rates of income tax could be almost halved, or corporation tax abolished, while even substantial erosion of these revenues through elastic behavioural responses by energy consumers would still probably leave enough revenue to permit the abolition of business rates.

(b) *Revenue Sustainability*

The revenues that would be raised from environmental taxes on particular raw materials or products associated with pollution will be a function of the responsiveness of demand and supply to price. The more effective the tax is in restraining production and use of the taxed good, the lower will be the revenue derived from the tax. In some sense, therefore, revenue issues arise in inverse proportion to the environmental effectiveness of an environmental tax; the tax is paid and revenues obtained only where the good continues to be produced and consumed.

The effects on revenues of an environmental tax are likely to change over time. Since, in general, supply and demand responses to the imposition of an environmental tax are likely to be rather greater in the long run (when taxpayers' patterns of production and consumption can be freely adjusted), than in the short run (when taxpayers' production and consumption decisions may be constrained by existing capital equipment), there may be circumstances where the revenues to be obtained from the environmental tax could decline over time. Where long-run supply and demand responses to the environmental tax are large, reflecting the existence of close substitutes which are less heavily taxed, the opportunities and problems posed by the tax revenues and the burden of additional tax payments will be short-lived.

In practice, forecasting the long-run revenue effect of environmental taxes is unlikely to be a precise matter. Not only are there likely to be important uncertainties regarding the size and timing of the effects of the tax on production or consumption of the good in question, but also demands and hence revenues will be a function of the overall economic climate and level of economic activity. Economic growth may increase demands for the polluting good, partly (or fully) offsetting the effects of the environmental tax. Where the price elasticity of demand for the taxed good is low, and the income elasticity is high, the increases in demand due to growth are likely to be large relative to the reductions in demand due to the environmental tax. Thus, one concern in considering the use of tax on energy to control environmental problems associated with energy use is that the price elasticity of energy demand is so low, that a steeply rising energy tax would be needed merely to keep energy demand constant in the face of rising incomes.

(c) A 'Double Dividend'?

From the perspective of fiscal policy, what are the gains from using ecotaxes? Do they have the potential to reduce the overall costs involved in raising fiscal revenues? Some commentators (e.g. Oates, 1991; Pearce, 1991) have drawn attention to a potential 'double dividend' from environmental taxes—the possibility that, in addition to their merits as instruments of environmental policy, they have a second benefit in that the revenue raised from the environmental taxes allows other taxes, with possible distortionary effects on labour supply, investment, or consumption, to be reduced. There are a number of strands to this argument.

(i) 'Distortion-correcting taxes are better'

Empirical studies of the marginal distortionary costs (the marginal excess burden) of existing taxes show that these costs can be appreciable. For example, Ballard et al. (1985) estimate the marginal excess burden of public revenues in the USA at 20–30 cents for each extra dollar of tax revenue. These costs reflect the fact that most taxes (apart from lump-sum taxes) lead to behavioural adjustments which reduce individual welfare, over and above the value of the actual tax payment by the private sector. Raising the rate of conventional taxes will typically increase these distortionary costs. However, the behavioural adjustments that arise from environmental taxes include some which are positively desirable, reflecting changes in private-sector activities that reduce emissions. In these circumstances, making use of environmental taxes to raise revenues would appear distinctly preferable to relying on conventional taxes, which generate undesirable distortions in activity. Surely it must be better to raise revenues from taxes that correct distortions, rather than create them?

Starting from a position in which the system of taxes has been designed to minimize excess burden, without any concern for the environmental implications of the tax structure, there would, indeed, usually be gains from shifting the balance of revenue-raising towards greater reliance on environmental taxes. In this sense, the tax system will be more efficient if ecotaxes are used, than if they are neglected. However, there are two key observations.

First, the particular meaning of 'excess burden' in this argument should be noted. Environmental taxes on energy can be said to have negative excess burden (at least over some range) if we include within the definition of the excess burden the environmental benefits from the induced behavioural changes. Ecotaxes, on this argument, may have negative excess burden, but to say that they have this desirable property *in addition to* their environmental benefits involves double counting.

Second, although there will almost certainly be gains from some shift to distortion-correcting taxes, this will be true only up to a certain point. The purely fiscal component of the excess burden, in the form of such things as the reductions in energy consumption and expenditures on energy-saving technologies, will have costs that rise more than proportionately with the rate of tax. Raising the tax rate on energy will initially confer benefits, in the sense that the environmental gains offset the costs of these behavioural adjustments, but as the energy tax rate is further increased, the costs of these behavioural changes will rise more than proportionately, eventually overtaking the additional environmental benefits. As Oates (1991) observes, economic efficiency in raising public revenues requires that the marginal deadweight burden from each revenue source be equal; in other words, that there should not be scope to raise the same revenues at lower deadweight cost by changing the pattern of public revenues. This will imply shifting the pattern of revenue-raising towards ecotaxes, up until the point where the marginal excess burden of each ecotax has risen to equal the marginal excess burden from other taxes.

The above form of the argument that introducing ecotaxes will lead to more efficient fiscal policy does not establish clear and separate 'environmental' and 'fiscal' dividends from the use of ecotaxes. The environmental benefits form part of the claim that revenues can be raised at lower cost through ecotaxes; there are not two separate 'dividends'.

(ii) 'Using ecotax revenue to reduce other tax rates reduces excess burdens'

A second strand in the 'double dividend' literature concerns the significance, or value, of the revenues raised from environmental taxes. What, if any, are the benefits from choosing an environmental policy instrument which raises revenues, in preference to one which has similar environmental effects but raises no revenues? If we employ a

revenue-raising environmental policy instrument, such as an environmental tax or auctioned tradable permits, do the revenues collected as
a 'by-product' of its environmental effects give us a more efficient fiscal
policy, compared with the use of an equivalent non-revenue-raising
instrument?

The closest comparison that can be made between a revenue-raising
environmental policy instrument and one that is otherwise identical but
raises no revenues, is that between auctioned and 'grandfathered'
tradable permits. Auctioned tradable permits trading at a price x per
unit of emissions would provide the same incentive for pollution
abatement, and raise the same revenues, as an emissions tax set at the
same rate x per unit. The comparison between auctioned and grandfathered tradable permits thus provides a way of thinking through the
consequences of two equivalent instruments, differing only in the fact
that one raises revenues.

Under a 'grandfathered' scheme, permits are distributed free of
charge, according to some system of distribution. Polluting firms may,
for example, be allocated permits in proportion to their emissions levels
in some past period. The free allocation of permits on the basis of
historic emissions levels has a clear opportunity cost to the government.
Revenues could have been raised by auctioning the permits, since they
are of value to the firms that receive them, and, instead, the government
is making a transfer to the firms, of a value equal to the number of
permits allocated, times the price at which they subsequently trade.
Aside from the possibility that the number of firms in the industry
might be affected if permits are auctioned rather than distributed free,
it would be expected that the market price at which permits trade
would be identical under the two regimes, and the level and pattern of
pollution abatement would be identical. The only difference between
the two regimes is, then, that one raises revenues, while the other
forgoes the opportunity to raise revenues. The latter case may be seen
as equivalent to the case where permits are auctioned, and the revenues
raised then transferred back to firms through lump-sum transfers.[1]

Looking at the above comparison between auctioned and grandfathered tradable permits, the environmental effects are held constant,
and the only difference is that revenues are obtained under the former,
but not under the latter. Any fiscal policy benefit from the revenues

[1] In a one-off, unanticipated, permit allocation, the transfers are lump-sum in the
sense that they cannot be influenced by any current decision of the firms. In a repeated,
or anticipated, allocation, firms may realize that their current decisions could influence
future permit allocations, and grandfathering could be distortionary rather than
equivalent to a lump-sum transfer.

raised can be clearly distinguished from the environmental benefits from the instrument, which are identical across the two cases.

The revenues raised from the revenue-raising instrument do clearly have a benefit in that they reduce the need to raise revenues from other taxes, and reduce the need to incur the distortionary costs involved in raising revenues through these taxes.

In his discussion of the double-dividend debate, Goulder (1995) refers to this case as that of a 'weak' double dividend. Cost savings are made by using ecotax revenues to reduce distortionary taxes, rather than returning tax revenues to taxpayers through lump-sum payments. He points out that the existence of a double dividend, in this sense of the term, is uncontroversial, because 'the idea that swapping a distortionary tax for a lump sum tax has a positive welfare cost is part of the usual definition of *distortionary*'.

The claim of a double dividend in this form is undramatic, but not without policy significance. In making a choice between policy instruments, it implies that—other things being equal—a substantial premium should be placed on selecting revenue-raising instruments, and on then using the revenues raised to reduce the rates of existing distortionary taxes. There are significant costs if the potential revenues from environmental taxes are dissipated or forgone.

Two examples can be drawn from the recent discussion of the possible use of economic instruments to reduce business use of energy in the Marshall Report (1998). First, the Marshall Report pays considerable attention to the idea that the tax revenues derived from energy taxes levied on industry should be returned to firms, rather than used in other ways. The economic arguments which would support this recommendation are considerably less clear-cut than Marshall appears to think. In the long run, it is not at all obvious that reducing taxes on firms would enhance UK firms' competitiveness by more than if taxes on individuals were reduced. However, if we accept Marshall's recommendation that the revenues should be returned to industry, the implication of the analysis above is that it matters how this is done. Efficiency gains will be made if this is done by reducing the marginal rates of other taxes, and arrangements for revenue return which have a more lump-sum character (as with the return of revenues from the Swedish NOx charge described earlier) will forgo these fiscal gains.

Second, the Marshall Report discusses the relative merits of grandfathered and auctioned tradable permits. The report rightly observes some significant difficulties with grandfathered permits. The basis for allocation may well be controversial, and allocation on the basis of historic emissions would tend to disadvantage firms which had already reduced emissions in the past, and give greatest benefit to the least dynamic firms. Also, grandfathering may discourage competition, because new entrants to an industry (which have to buy permits) do not compete on equal terms with existing firms (which receive an allocation of free permits). However, the report omits to mention probably the most serious disadvantage of grandfathering, which is that it simply forgoes the chance of raising revenues. If the estimates of marginal excess burden from Ballard *et al.* (1985) are taken, the cost of grand-fathering, in terms of the forgone fiscal gains from recycling the revenues through cuts in the marginal rates of distortionary taxes, is of the order of 20–50 per cent of the forgone revenues.

A corollary of the double-dividend argument in this form is that the optimal level of pollution abatement will not be independent of the environmental policy instrument used (Lee and Misiolek, 1986). Where increasing the rate of the environmental tax increases tax revenue, instruments such as regulation or grandfathered tradable permits which forgo revenue will have a higher total marginal abatement cost (taking into account the marginal deadweight burden of raising public revenues as well as the conventional marginal abatement costs) than environmental tax instruments, which can use the extra revenue raised to reduce the distortionary costs of other taxes. In this case, an efficient policy will set a higher level of pollution abatement if the tax instrument is used than if an environmental policy instrument is employed which does not raise revenues.

(iii) 'Switching to ecotaxes reduces excess burdens'

There has recently been a spate of theoretical papers which have modelled the conditions under which a double dividend would arise, in a more demanding sense of the term, defined by Goulder (1995) as a 'strong' double dividend. He defines this as the claim that a tax switch which increases taxes on energy and reduces existing non-environmental taxes would have negative 'gross costs'. In gross costs he includes all the welfare costs of all behavioural changes from the tax switch, but *excluding* the environmental benefits. This is an extremely demanding criterion, and will be seen to be a substantially different claim from that being made at the start of this section. A shift towards environmental taxes would have a double dividend only if there were environmental gains (the first dividend), and if the total deadweight costs of revenue raising (including abatement costs in the form of behavioural substitutions to higher energy prices, but excluding the environmental benefits) are negative. The double-dividend argument in this 'strong' sense becomes a 'no regrets' argument; even if the changes in energy use turn out to have no environmental benefit, achieving them has been costless because the overall fiscal costs of the tax change are negative.

One obvious group of circumstances in which the gross costs of a particular tax switch might be negative are those where existing fiscal policy has not been optimized with respect to purely fiscal considerations. Where existing fiscal policy has failed to set the pattern of tax rates so that the marginal excess burden of each tax instrument is equalized, the aggregate deadweight costs of revenues are not minimized (as noted above). It may be possible to reduce the total excess burden of raising public revenues (and, in other words, to make a tax switch with negative gross costs) by introducing an energy tax and using the revenues to reduce a tax which at the initial pattern of tax rates has above-average marginal excess burden. (Goulder refers to such a case as an 'intermediate form' double dividend.) Although perhaps of interest in the context of practical policy, where inefficiency in the pattern of revenue-raising may well exist and where the introduction of an environmental tax on energy might offer a politically palatable route to a shift to a more efficient pattern of taxation, this case introduces little of theoretical interest.

The more demanding requirement for a 'strong' double dividend, that the gross costs of a tax switch will be negative even where the existing pattern of tax rates is set optimally with respect to fiscal considerations, and equalizes marginal deadweight burdens across all taxes, can be satisfied only in a set of somewhat special circumstances. A series of papers by Bovenberg and co-authors has identified the limited range of possible cases where a double dividend of this form could exist (e.g. Bovenberg and de Mooij, 1994; Bovenberg and Goulder, 1994; Bovenberg and van der Ploeg, 1994; see also Parry, 1995).

Bovenberg and de Mooij (1994) argue that the distortionary cost of taxation needs to be considered in a general equilibrium context, in which the effects of taxes on both goods and factor supplies and demands are taken into account. Taxes on goods, for example, will tend to distort not only the pattern of spending on goods, but will also distort labour supply. Since a uniform tax on all goods is formally equivalent in a one-period model to a uniform tax on labour income (since both affect the quantity of goods which can be purchased with the income earned from an additional hour's labour), a shift in the pattern of taxation from income tax to a uniform tax on goods would leave the deadweight burden unchanged (i.e. would have zero 'gross cost' in Goulder's terminology). A shift to a non-uniform tax on goods, in the form of a tax on one good, energy, alone, would, in addition, have a distortionary effect on the pattern of spending (if any environmental benefits are disregarded), and would therefore have a higher deadweight burden than the uniform tax on labour; such a tax switch would have a positive gross cost.

Bovenberg and de Mooij observe that the size of this gross cost will depend on the extent of pre-existing distortionary taxation. The additional distortions to labour supply and other markets from the environmental tax will be greater, the greater the initial degree of distortion in the economy; where an economy is initially highly distorted, the double-dividend argument will then be weaker than where the initial marginal excess burden of taxation was small.

Only a limited range of circumstances is identified in which the strong form of the double-dividend argument holds. Bovenberg and de Mooij (1994) find that it can hold if the uncompensated wage elasticity of labour supply is negative: Goulder (1995) notes that this condition is generally rejected in empirical studies of the labour market. Shah and Larsen (1992) point out that pre-existing, inefficient, subsidies can generate a strong double dividend, if the tax switch helps to counteract the inefficiency arising from these subsidies. A strong-form double dividend is also possible in the model of Bovenberg and van der Ploeg (1994), where involuntary unemployment can arise owing to a fixed real wage, and where part of the burden of the energy tax can be borne by a fixed factor other than labour. Since the tax borne by the fixed factor has little distortionary cost, the gross cost of the tax switch can be negative. This model, they observe, may be appropriate to the case of small open economies.

Pearson and Smith (1991) observe that there is a close link between the impact of an environmental tax on the excess burden of taxation, and the distributional impact of the environmental tax. Where policy-making operates on the basis of a trade-off in taxation between efficiency and equity objectives, it would generally be possible to reduce the excess burden of taxation by relaxing the distributional constraint. If the distributional objectives are weakened, it will be possible to increase the lump-sum, non-distortionary, element within the tax structure, and this will reduce the excess burden of raising a given revenue. An environmental tax which is sharply regressive would tend to increase the lump-sum, non-distortionary component of the tax system, and this will, in turn, tend to reduce the overall welfare costs of raising revenue. This provides a way in which, in practice, environmental taxes could reduce the distortionary costs of the tax system. However, they would, in part, do so only to the extent that the distributional incidence of the tax system is permitted to become more regressive; if the original distributional incidence is restored, this source of efficiency gains would be eliminated.

5. Conclusions

Environmental taxes may have an increasingly important role to play in environmental policy, especially in achieving the extensive changes in the energy use of firms and individuals that will be required if global greenhouse-gas emissions are to be held constant, or, still more, reduced. Energy-pricing measures, in the form of energy taxes, would provide a common incentive signal to a wide variety of energy users with different abatement costs and opportunities. This will promote cost-effective responses, reducing the cost of achieving any given level of emissions abatement. In addition, the use of taxes instead of regulation can spread the burden of adjustment efficiently across all energy users, rather than simply concentrating on those most amenable to direct regulation.

Few ecotaxes have the potential to raise revenues sufficient to alter the constraints and opportunities in fiscal policy. Environmental taxes on energy and congestion charges on motor transport are the two areas where ecotaxes could make a major contribution to tax revenues. In both cases the available tax base is broad, demand is inelastic (so revenues will not be greatly eroded by behavioural responses), and high rates of tax may well be warranted by the environmental externalities resulting from energy use and vehicle congestion.

The UK Climate Change Levy on business energy use announced in the 1999 Budget represents a relatively modest step towards harnessing the power of tax incentives to the achievement of the UK's Climate Change policy commitments. The Levy takes the form of a tax based on the energy content of fuels, and various political constraints (especially the aim of avoiding adverse effects on the coal industry) have meant that it has not been differentiated to reflect the carbon content — and hence, global warming potential — of different fuels. The tax rates are relatively low (0.15 pence per kilowatt hour on gas and coal), and energy-intensive sectors that have concluded negotiated agreements to improve energy efficiency will pay only one-fifth of the standard rate. Overall revenues will amount to about £1 billion, of which part will be used to pay for corporate tax incentives for energy efficiency, and the remainder will finance an 0.3-percentage-point reduction in employer's NI contributions.

In the longer run, environmental taxes on energy have considerably greater revenue-raising potential. To illustrate the broad orders of magnitude involved, a carbon tax levied on all energy uses (including domestic-sector energy consumption) at a rate of £200 per tonne (almost ten times higher than the 0.15 pence per kWh standard rate of the Climate Change Levy) could raise revenues equivalent to about 11 per cent of total UK tax receipts, allowing income tax to be halved, or corporation tax abolished. Even a rather lower carbon tax of £60 per tonne (broadly equivalent to the carbon/energy tax proposed by the European Commission in 1991) levied on business energy use alone could still raise revenues of more than £4 billion, equivalent to about 1.5 per cent of total tax receipts, which would permit a reduction of about 2 percentage points in the basic rate of income tax.

Revenues on this scale clearly present opportunities for significant change in the UK fiscal system. The revenues raised from environmental taxes have an enhanced value in the sense that—as with all taxes— the welfare costs of transferring resources to the public sector are high. Estimates of the distortionary costs of taxation in the USA suggest that the marginal welfare costs of existing tax revenues could be of the order of 20–50 cents for each dollar raised (Ballard et al., 1985). If the tax system of the UK has similar costs, then the revenues raised as a by-product of pursuing environmental policy through taxation have a social value some 20–50 per cent higher than the nominal tax receipts. The benefit from these revenues will be maximized if they are used to permit reductions in the marginal rates of existing taxes, and will be dissipated if the revenues are returned to taxpayers as a lump sum, or in equivalent ways. A lump-sum return of the revenues would forgo the opportunity to reduce tax rates, and thus avoid the opportunity to save on the distortionary costs of other taxes. However, it may be unavoidable in some circumstances.

Thus, for example, offsetting the regressive distributional effects of taxes on household energy may require at least some of the revenue to be returned to households in 'lump sum' form. Pearson and Smith (1991) note that this will generally mean that maximizing the 'double dividend' gains from environmental taxes requires tax revenues to be used in the opposite way to that required to maintain the original distributional incidence of the fiscal system.

Lump-sum revenue return may also be needed where environmental taxes are levied on the emissions of some subset of polluters only. The Swedish NOx charge, for example, is restricted to large firms only, because the high costs of measurement rule out its application to smaller firms. To avoid distorting the conditions of competition between large and small firms, the NOx tax revenues are returned to the participating firms in lump-sum payments unrelated to emissions levels.

A third case where potential fiscal revenues from an environmental policy instrument are dissipated, in such a way as to forgo the economic gains that could be achieved by using the revenues to reduce other taxes, is where a non-revenue-raising instrument is chosen in preference to an equivalent, revenue-raising, instrument. A case in point is the possible use of grandfathered tradable permits as an alternative to energy taxation. Auctioned tradable permits and ecotaxes are closely similar, in both their environmental and revenue effects. By contrast, grandfathered tradable permits forgo the opportunity to raise revenues, and hence forgo the possibility of reductions in fiscal distortionary costs, by granting the permits, uncharged, to existing polluters. The implication of this is that grandfathered tradable permits are a substantially more costly way of achieving a given outcome than ecotaxes set at an equivalent level. They may appear politically attractive as a way of avoiding tax burdens on industry, but, at the same time, have a higher resource cost, equivalent (if the figures of Ballard *et al.* are used) to some 20–50 per cent of the tax revenues that could be raised.

Achieving reductions in greenhouse-gas emissions through the use of environmental taxes may confer future environmental benefits, but it is highly unlikely to confer fiscal gains in the sense of reducing the excess burden of taxation below current levels. Ecotaxes are likely to involve distortionary costs at least as high as those involved in raising equivalent revenues through existing taxes. If the question is posed whether we would choose to use energy taxes, in preference to existing taxes on labour or other bases, in the absence of any environmental benefits, then the answer is almost certainly that we would not. Energy taxes would be likely to involve just as much distortion of the labour market as income taxes, and at the same time distort the commodity market. Only if there are expected to be environmental gains can the use of environmental taxes be justified, and the case for ecotax reform must be made primarily on the basis of the environmental gains that would result.

The fiscal aspects of ecotax reform are important, since inappropriate use of the revenues, or their unnecessary dissipation, can greatly add to the costs of environmental policy. But an appeal to the fiscal consequences of ecotax reform cannot justify measures that do not pay their way in purely environmental benefits.

9

Water Pollution, Abstraction, and Economic Instruments

SIMON COWAN*

1. Introduction

Since environmental issues returned to prominence in the 1980s it has become common for governments to emphasize that cost–benefit analysis should play a role in the design of pollution standards and that economic instruments, such as taxes and tradable permits, should be used to achieve these standards. Such sentiments were expressed in the Rio Declaration on Climate Change and, at the European Union (EU) level, when the European Community Fifth Environmental Action Programme was adopted. Progress, however, has been slow. In the UK the role of economic instruments was discussed in the 1990 White Paper on the environment, *This Common Inheritance* (DoE, 1990*a*), but it was not until 1996 that the first instrument, the tax on disposal of waste to landfill sites, was implemented. Similarly, the 1995 Environment Act establishing the Environment Agency (EA) was the first piece of legislation to have a clause referring to the need to consider costs and benefits when setting objectives.

At the time of privatization in 1989 the water supply industry in England and Wales embarked on a large programme of spending on environmental and quality improvements. Much of the spending was to ensure that European Directives on bathing beach quality and drinking water quality were met. At the same time the institutional structure of environmental and economic regulation was changed. The environmental regulatory functions of the ten regional water authorities were transferred to the National Rivers Authority, which later became part of the Environment Agency. The Environment Agency also has responsibility for licensing suppliers' abstraction of untreated water from surface and underground sources, so it controls the key raw material

* Worcester College, University of Oxford.

and will influence the development of direct product-market competition. Control of the prices and investment programmes of the companies was taken away from direct control by the Department of the Environment (DoE) and given to a new economic regulator, the Office of Water Services (Ofwat).

The tightening of standards and the consequent need for higher spending on pollution abatement has led to an increased policy focus on the cost-effectiveness of environmental expenditure. Regulation of water pollution remains of the command-and-control type, but the UK government has explored the use of economic instruments. A discussion document, *Economic Instruments for Water Pollution*, was published in November 1997 by the Department of the Environment, Transport and the Regions (DETR, 1997*a*) and another document on water abstraction (DETR, 1998*g*) followed in May 1998. Following the consultation, however, the government decided in 1999 not to pursue the option of national water pollution charges for point source discharges. But the option of using a more market-oriented approach to abstraction licensing is being considered.

In this chapter I discuss the role for economic instruments in water pollution and abstraction. Economic instruments of pollution control, such as effluent charges and tradable permits, offer the potential for savings in abatement costs, for cost-effective increases in environmental quality, and for new revenue streams for the government. The incentive issues involved in economic instruments are, however, quite subtle, so they should be designed with care. One important difficulty in applying economic instruments in the water context is that the location of pollution sources is critical, so any system of economic instruments would need to be adaptable to local conditions. Marketization of the abstraction regime can similarly be expected to increase productive efficiency and to generate potential new sources of public revenue.

Section 2 describes briefly the water supply process and the externalities associated with abstraction and discharges of effluent. In section 3 I discuss current UK policies on abstraction and pollution, experience in other countries, and how environmental regulation interacts with economic regulation. Section 4 covers the role of economic instruments in the water context. Conclusions are in section 5.

2. Water Pollution and Abstraction

Public water supply involves taking ('abstracting') untreated water from underground sources, known as aquifers, and surface sources, such as reservoirs, lakes, and rivers. Water is also abstracted directly by industries such as steel and electricity generation. Raw water destined for public supply is treated and distributed via networks of pipes to customers. Customers use very little water for drinking or cooking — the major uses are for washing and flushing lavatories. Most used water is returned to the sewerage system as waste water, which is then cleaned to varying degrees before being returned as effluent to watercourses.

There are three main reasons for close regulation of the water industry and these are reflected in the institutional structure of regulation. First, there are natural monopoly conditions in the provision of the networks that distribute water and collect sewage. Second, most consumers cannot easily assess the quality of water, and even if they could they cannot interpret the consequences for their health. In other words there is an asymmetry of information, which would typically lead to sub-optimal quality provision in the absence of regulation.

The third reason for regulation is the existence of important externalities. Abstraction from an aquifer or a surface source will reduce the amount that can be abstracted by other parties and can cause structural damage.[1] Effluent from sewage treatment plants, if unregulated, usually pollutes the watercourses to which it is discharged. The polluting effect of effluent depends on the amount of dissolved oxygen present in the receiving water, the concentration of bacteria in the effluent, volume (since higher volume increases flow, which other things equal is good for quality), the temperature of the discharge, and on whether poisons such as heavy metals are present. Rivers and other watercourses are able to clean themselves if effluents that reach them are not too dirty or voluminous, though poisonous substances such as heavy metals will always remain. Various parties suffer from water pollution. Abstractors of water further downstream will find that purification costs are higher. Those using rivers or estuaries for leisure activities, such as fishing and swimming, will also be affected.

Water pollution is mostly a local or regional issue in the UK. It becomes of international concern when there is pollution of the sea or of rivers such as the Rhine or the Danube which constitute or cross national boundaries. The local nature of the problem means that economic instruments must be tailor-made for local circumstances. Taxes on effluents would need to vary across rivers depending on how

---

[1] Noll *et al.* (1998) note that Mexico City is sinking as the water abstracted from the aquifer is not naturally replaced by rainfall. Parts of the city centre have fallen by 2 metres in the last decade, causing severe problems for buildings. In London the water table is rising as industrial abstraction of water has declined.

polluted each river is in the first place. Tradable-permit schemes are likely to require trading to be restricted to one river, river basin, lake, or estuary—abatement in one watercourse is not a perfect substitute for abatement in another. Even along one river different degrees of regulation might be appropriate. Discharging effluent upstream might cause little damage if it is weak, increases river flow and there are few abstractors or leisure users of the river downstream of the river. In another place along the river an equivalent discharge might be considerably more damaging.

Some pollutants, such as pesticides and nitrates from agricultural activity, enter aquifers in a diffused way so the causes of the pollution cannot be traced back to individual sources. When sources cannot be identified explicitly such pollution is sometimes known as 'non-point source pollution'.

3. Current Policies

It is currently a criminal offence in the UK to pollute watercourses. Sewage treatment works and industrial sources of effluent can obtain 'consents' and 'authorizations' from the Environment Agency which allow controlled discharges of pollutants into rivers, estuaries, and the sea without threat of prosecution.[2] The conditions under which such discharges can be made might cover aspects such as time, place, volume, temperature, and composition. Consents are set to achieve standards for maximum concentrations of specified substances. These standards are either informal objectives of the EA or statutory requirements under European Community legislation. European legislation also in some circumstances requires particular technologies to be installed. The general principle of 'no deterioration' from current quality is applied by the EA. Rivers in England and Wales are placed into six classes, and over 25 per cent of river length has improved by a class or more between 1990 and 1996 (DETR, 1997a, p. 11) in terms of both chemical and biological quality. Out of 40,000 kilometres of river length monitored by the EA, only just over 25 per cent are in the highest class and 10 per cent were still in the lowest class in 1996.

Discharge consents are fixed by the EA on the basis of the consequences for water quality, and the costs of abatement play no role in the determination. Authorizations, however, which apply to effluents from particular industrial processes known as 'prescribed processes',

---

[2] In Scotland and Northern Ireland separate agencies perform a similar role to the Environment Agency in England and Wales.

are designed to reflect costs as well as benefits so that emissions limits reflect 'best available techniques not entailing excess cost'.

Charges for discharge consents have been imposed since 1991. Charges are the same throughout the country, relate to maximum allowed discharges rather than actual discharges, and are designed in the long run to recover the administrative costs the EA incurs for running the consent system. Smith (1995, p. 32) notes that 'the structure of the tariff is intended to reflect the costs that each discharger imposes in terms of monitoring and compliance work, rather than the pollution damage of the effluent. Thus the tariff rises with the size of the discharge, but less than proportionately with volume, since monitoring costs do not rise proportionately.' While the current charges are not designed to provide incentives for abatement, they could be adapted, i.e. increased, to promote incentives.

The abstraction licensing system is relatively straightforward. The EA issues licences to abstract. The current allocation of abstraction licences largely reflects the historic granting of licences on a grand-fathered basis, though recently the EA has allocated new licences on their merits and has limited the length of the licences. Just over 48,000 licences are in place, of which all but the most recently allocated ones operate indefinitely. Total water abstracted has fallen by 16 per cent over the last 25 years because of industrial decline, though abstraction for public water supply has increased by 20 per cent. Public water supply now accounts for half of total abstraction. The EA levies charges for abstraction, but, as in the case of consent charges, these are meant to recover the EA's costs of administering the abstraction licensing scheme. In effect they are lump-sum taxes since they are based on the maximum allowed volume of abstraction rather than the actual amount abstracted. They thus provide no marginal incentives to reduce the amount of abstraction.

France, Germany, and the Netherlands have well-established taxes on direct discharges to watercourses.[3] In all these cases the taxes are in addition to existing direct regulations. In France large dischargers (defined as those that discharge pollution loads in excess of 200 'inhabitant equivalents') are charged on the basis of loads estimated by the regional water agency, although either side may ask for charges to be based on direct measurement rather than estimates. The charges are designed to provide revenue for investment in sewage treatment and other water pollution control measures.

[3] See Commission of the European Communities (1995) and OECD (1994) Table 3.8.

In Germany the water pollution charges are administered by the *Länder*, which use the revenue to cover administrative costs and for waste water treatment. Charges are uniform across the country, and have risen significantly in real terms since their introduction in 1981 (Smith, 1995, Table 4.2). The charge can be reduced if the source demonstrates compliance with a new standard before the latter becomes binding. It appears that the charges have had significant incentive effects (though it is difficult to disentangle the effects of the charges from that of the associated direct regulations). In particular, there was a large increase in abatement investment in the run-up to the introduction of the charges.

In the Netherlands the charges are set to finance sewage treatment costs. Households and small firms pay flat-rate charges, firms that have an intermediate pollution load can choose whether to pay on the basis of predicted or actual loads, while large sources pay according the quantity and concentration of actual emissions. Charges have risen over time, and they differ between regions. There is some evidence of an incentive effect for large sources that are metered, although again it is difficult to disentangle the effect of direct regulation from the effect of the effluent charges.

The United States has generally favoured permit schemes over taxes. Examples are the schemes for the Fox River in Wisconsin and the Dillon reservoir (Hahn, 1989). Because of the need to restrict trading to the particular watercourse, markets for permits have always been very thin, and the schemes have not been successful.

For non-point source pollution, tradable-permit schemes would be difficult to implement on a local basis because enforcement would be hard. But a tax on the purchase of pesticides and nitrates can be used, and indeed many countries have such charges. See OECD (1995b, pp. 36–7) for a description of the main schemes. Inevitably, such tax is a rather blunt instrument. Nitrates, for example, which are used in fertilizers, are harmful if they leak into a watercourse and cause eutrophication, but otherwise they are not. It would be impossible to tax nitrates only in areas which are nitrate-sensitive.

The Director-General of Water Services (DGWS), who heads Ofwat, has the statutory duty to ensure that regulated water companies can finance their functions and can earn a reasonable return on their capital. This has important implications for the way economic and environmental regulation interact. When price limits have been reviewed, which has been at 5-year intervals, the regulator has asked companies to provide detailed estimates of the costs that they will incur in meeting their environmental targets. The targets themselves are partly the outcome of discussions between the DGWS and the environmental and quality regulators. The DGWS judges whether the estimated costs are reasonable and allows those costs to be passed through into prices for the next 5 years. Under the system of price-cap regulation the price limits are not meant to be reviewed during the 5-year period between formal reviews, though in practice, especially in the early years of the regime, there has been some regulatory intervention.

The use of economic instruments for both pollution control and abstraction licensing has consequences for economic regulation. An instrument such as a tax will usually increase the overall cost to the industry of pollution control because, as well as paying the abatement costs, the industry will have to pay a tax on residual effluents. The government benefits from a new source of revenue, but water consumers will find that prices are higher because of the tax payments. If the government and the economic regulator do not want prices to final customers to rise, but must also ensure that the firms can finance their functions, some non-distorting way should be found to recycle any revenues earned from pollution taxes or their equivalent. This issue is explored further in the next section.

Whether revenues are recycled or not, a mechanism to determine how the costs of achieving environmental objectives are passed through must be found. At present Ofwat monitors costs and outcomes closely. Firms which consistently under-spend or under-perform relative to their stated targets find themselves penalized. But the point of economic instruments is that they decentralize decisions and allow the sources themselves to choose their spending. If the introduction of economic instruments promotes cost minimization by the sources, but the economic regulator then steps in to lower prices, there is less incentive to minimize costs in response to the introduction of the instruments.

4. Economic Instruments

(a) *Economic Instruments for Water Pollution*

The textbook solution to the problem of environmental externalities is to levy a Pigouvian tax on pollution equal to marginal social cost at the optimal level of pollution. Applying such a tax requires knowledge of what the optimal level of pollution is and how damaging extra emissions are at that point. Some work has been done for the EA on the use of contingent-valuation methods to estimate the benefits of local improvement of environmental quality, but it is too early to claim that optimal pollution levels can be calculated. But even if it is not possible to identify optimal levels of pollution, there is a powerful argument in favour of the use of economic instruments, which is that they ensure that abatement of pollution is done at the lowest cost without the need for the regulator to know what those costs are.

A condition for least-cost abatement is that the marginal costs of abatement of different sources are equal. Abatement will proceed until the marginal cost of abating equals the marginal benefit. Under a tax system the marginal benefit is the tax on each unit of pollution, which is the same for each source. Under a permit system the marginal benefit of abatement is the price of a permit — a net purchaser of permits saves on buying the permit and a net seller has an extra permit to sell — which again is the same for all sources. So marginal abatement costs will be equal as long as sources choose abatement to minimize their own total costs.

An economic instrument only provides a cost saving, for a given total pollution level, if marginal abatement cost functions differ. The more similar these functions are, the smaller the static gains from an economic instrument. In the water context the case for economic instruments should not be overplayed. Similar sources, such as sewage treatment works operated by one company that discharge into one river, might have similar abatement cost functions, although industrial plants that discharge might be expected to have different costs because they use different processes. Another important assumption which was implicit in the above analysis was that the regulator does not care which source causes pollution. In the water context, however, pollution is mostly of local concern. A river which has little amenity value and from which little water is abstracted downstream might be able to bear the burden of more polluting discharges than another river.

With economic instruments the residual pollution generates revenue for the government. (Under a permit system this holds as long as the permits are auctioned competitively.) If there are no other distortions in the tax system the optimal policy is to give the revenue back to households in lump-sum fashion.[4] In practice there are distortionary taxes and the revenues from environmental taxes can be used to reduce such distortions. One practical example of this is the UK government's use of the revenue generated by the tax on disposal of waste to landfill sites to reduce employers' social security contributions. Although

---

[4] A point that is often overlooked is that there is no efficiency case for recycling the revenue from a pollution tax to those who are harmed by the pollution. Victims who are fully compensated for suffering pollution will not undertake sufficient defensive activities that alleviate the effects of the pollution — see Baumol and Oates, (1988, ch. 4) and Cropper and Oates (1992).

recycling of tax revenue back to the industry itself plays no role in the efficiency argument for economic instruments, I argued above that such recycling would be necessary to avoid price increases for final water customers. We have already seen that the effluent charging schemes in continental Europe generate revenues that are recycled.

One way to recycle tax revenue to the industry would be to give to each source the tax rate multiplied by that source's existing maximum level of effluent under the consent. Since the tax revenue is returned as a lump sum, there is no distortion of the marginal incentives to abate. Moreover, the introduction of a tax system of this type would benefit, or at least not harm, all sources of pollution, and so might be relatively easy to implement. Sources which decide not to alter their effluent levels from the maximum level allowed under the consent would have their tax payments returned exactly and their abatement costs would be the same as under the consent, so total costs would not rise. Sources which want to change their effluent levels will benefit from the introduction of such a policy.

An alternative way to recycle revenue would require a balanced budget for the government or its agency. A simple scheme would return to each source the average tax payment made by all the *other* sources. Thus for source i the rebate is $t\Sigma_{j \neq i} x_j/(n-1)$ where t is the tax per unit of pollution, x_j is the pollution of source j, and n is the total number of sources. Since the rebate is independent of source i's choice of effluent level, there is no distortion of incentives. Total tax payments are equal to total rebates under such a scheme.

How should policy-makers choose between tax and permit systems? The systems are only identical when there is full information. It is true that the total amount of abatement will be efficiently done, but the amount of abatement is uncertain under a tax. Under a permit system, however, the total quantity of pollution can be fixed. A permit system provides certainty about the overall level of pollution, combined with uncertainty about the costs of achieving the required abatement, while a tax system makes pollution levels sensitive to abatement costs. Under a tax, if abatement costs are very high then the pollution target is relaxed, while if costs are low then more abatement is undertaken. Weitzman (1974) provides the classic analysis of taxes versus permits when there is uncertainty about the position of the aggregate marginal abatement cost curve. He shows that taxes are preferred when the marginal benefit of abatement is flatter than the marginal abatement cost, while permits are preferred if the marginal benefit is relatively steep. Although such information is likely to be difficult to find, there is an *a priori* expectation in the case of water pollution that quantitative targets are preferred because of the uncertainty of outcome under a taxation system. If the tax is set too low, there is little incentive to abate and the watercourse might become overpolluted, possibly causing permanent damage.

In addition to the above theoretical concerns, a number of practical issues arise in the choice between taxes and permits. Tax rates should vary with local conditions, but this requires that the regulator has sufficient local information. More importantly, if regulators at a local or regional level have the power to set tax rates then there is the danger of regulatory capture. This provides an argument for national tax rates, but this in turn might mean that the incentive for abatement will be too strong for some watercourses and too weak for others. Permits offer more flexibility than taxes. If permits are auctioned competitively then the revenue effects are the same as with a tax system. But if permits are given for free, perhaps on a grandfathered basis, then the regulator avoids the problem that the sources will be made worse off with the economic instrument. Allocating the same number of permits to each source as its current consent makes all sources better off. A source can always choose not to alter its behaviour, and it is no worse-off with a permit scheme than with the consent. If it does alter its abatement it must be strictly better off.

I have argued that in a straight choice between permits and taxes in the water context the former are likely to be preferable because of the greater certainty about the outcome for pollution. But a permit system might operate inefficiently if trading has to be restricted to localities because markets will be thin and sources might try to buy up permits to deter entry. Permits might, though, work for large estuaries, such as the Thames estuary, where there are many sources, and it might work at a national level as a way of meeting national or EU targets for reducing the inputs of certain substances to the sea.

Pollution and abstraction are closely related. More abstraction will reduce flow and thus increase the polluting effect of any given discharge, while increasing the volume of effluent will enable more water to be abstracted downstream. If economic instruments are to be introduced they will need to take account of such interactions. To some extent the externalities between abstraction and discharges are internalized automatically when there is joint ownership of water supply and sewerage along a river basin, but without joint ownership inefficiencies remain, and much abstraction and discharging is not associated with public water supply.

DETR (1997a) and Helm (1993b) make the important point that it is possible to combine taxes and the consent system, and in countries where effluent charges have been introduced they have always been added to existing quantitative regulations. In general such a combined policy is attractive—it ensures that the environment is at least as well protected as under a pure consent scheme, while sources that are efficient at abatement are encouraged to reduce pollution further. As with all tax schemes, resources are taken out of the industry concerned—in fact all sources are worse off unless the tax revenues are recycled in a non-distorting way. Such a combined policy is attractive as it allows economic incentives to be introduced without harming environmental quality, and it will generate revenue.

The design of a combined tax-and-consent scheme needs very careful consideration, as DETR (1997a) notes. As with all forms of regulation, inefficiencies can be created if the regulator is unable to commit to the announced scheme and the source sinks capital in order to reduce pollution. DETR (1997a, p. 22) argues that tightening the consent over time in a joint scheme might act as a disincentive to abatement. In fact, a natural version of such a scheme, which sets the consent equal to the previous period's pollution level while the tax is constant, does *not* generate incentive problems. Faced with a given tax and having already chosen its sunk capital, the source chooses the pollution level that equals the consent.

DETR (1997a) notes several complications about the practical design of economic instruments for water pollution. Effluent contains many different substances, and schemes should ideally take account of their chemical interaction. Only about one-tenth of households are metered for water supply, so most customers do not receive any marginal signals about the use of water and about the disposal of waste water to sewers. Industrial wastes, known as trade effluent, that go into the sewerage system are, however, priced according to strength and volume because it is feasible to meter such large customers. Here the question is how to reflect any pollution charges in the charges for discharges to sewers. For direct discharges to watercourses it is not clear how much metering of discharges is efficient. The theoretical discussion assumes continuous metering, but this might be prohibitively expensive.

The UK government has announced that it will not be introducing a national water pollution charge scheme (DETR, 1999f). The complexity of such a scheme outweighed any theoretical efficiency advantages. It argued that the extra costs imposed, including additional monitoring costs of £200m per annum, would not justify the benefits, and that targeting the charge would be too difficult.

(b) *Economic Instruments for Abstraction*

While the government does not want to change the structure of the current regulation scheme for water pollution it is actively seeking reform of the regime for water abstraction, though at the time of writing final decisions have not been made. The current charging scheme, as discussed in the previous section, does not provide marginal incentives for the efficient abstraction use of water. Charges are based on the recovery of the EA's administrative costs, are lump sum in form, and do not take account of scarcity of raw water or of the environmental damage caused by abstraction. Efficiency requires proper prices for water abstraction which take account of the value of raw water in alternative uses, the fact that some sources are exhaustible, the common pool problem where several abstractors are taking from the same source, and the interaction of abstraction with water pollution.

DETR (1999e) envisages that an incentive-based charge would be in addition to the existing regulatory regime, and in the interim several changes to the current charging schemes are proposed. The EA must currently compensate an abstractor whose licence is removed (though this is likely to change since it conflicts with the Polluter Pays Principle). The EA's costs thus include an allowance for such compensation, and the government will allow charges to reflect this. Effectively, a national fund will be built up to cover any compensation required. The EA will also be able to charge more when a drought order is in place. Metering of abstraction volumes is also likely to be required.

The government is also seeking to increase the flexibility of the system by making abstraction licences time-limited, with the average duration of a licence being 15 years. Six years' notice will be given if the EA intends not to renew a licence. Increased flexibility and tradability will help to promote the government's objective of introducing more product market competition into the water industry, especially via common-carriage arrangements. Where abstractions are shown to be the cause of damage to Special Areas of Conservation, Special Protection Areas, or other sites of Special Scientific Interest, the EA will seek 'voluntary action' by abstractors. This voluntary action will be backed by the threat of direct regulation banning excessive abstraction in the event of non-agreement.

5. Conclusion

The use of economic instruments in the water sector offers several potential benefits. Abatement costs can be lowered, or environmental quality enhanced, at lower cost than would otherwise be the case. Continuing incentives to reduce discharges are provided. Nevertheless the case for such instruments in the water context, where pollution is generally a local problem and there are complex interactions between pollutants, the weather, and water flows, is not overwhelming. The government has consequently decided on grounds of complexity and monitoring costs not to proceed with national water pollution charges. There remains the prospect of more use of economic instruments for abstraction, and the design and implementation of such schemes will require careful analysis. The government should not lose the opportunity to introduce more sensible economic principles into the design of the water abstraction regime than those currently operating.

10

Agri-environmental Policy: A UK Perspective

IAN HODGE*

1. Agricultural Change and Environmental Concern

The changes that have taken place in agriculture and their consequences for the rural environment over the past 50 years are well-known (Bowers and Cheshire, 1983; Skinner *et al.*, 1997). The substitution of machinery for labour, the increasing specialization of farms on a smaller range of enterprises, often involving a shift from mixed farming systems to predominantly arable or livestock, the reliance on artificial fertilizers and pesticides, the increasing scale of operation, and the intensification of land use, especially at the extensive margin, have all had consequences for the environment. Hedgerows have been re-moved as they have lost their function in the management of livestock and interfere with the operation of modern machinery. Ponds and wetlands have been drained and rough pastures have been 'improved'. Even the increased effectiveness of modern methods in excluding pest species has the effect of removing the food supply for a range of birds and other wildlife. Agricultural change has not been the only source of change in the rural environment; impacts have arisen through urban and transport developments, flood protection on rivers, or Dutch elm disease. But given the extent to which agricultural land uses predomi-nate, the consequences of agricultural change for the rural environment have been pervasive.

These changes have arisen from three interrelated factors: develop-ments in the technology available to farmers, financial incentives created through the economic environment, and, perhaps less widely recognized, changing institutions that have supported the incentives for individual farmers to concentrate their efforts on the expansion of food production. The context for these changes has been set through the operation of agricultural policy, the framework for which was estab-

* Department of Land Economy, University of Cambridge.

lished in the post-war period and subsequently continued through the Common Agricultural Policy (CAP) of the European Union (EU). Policy has maintained farm output prices above those generally available on world markets by restricting imports and providing subsidies for exports. These relatively high and secure prices have raised both profitability and confidence, stimulating higher levels of investment in agriculture and accelerating technological change. This has thus acted as a major stimulus to environmental damage through changes to the landscape, loss of habitats, and the introduction of chemicals.

In the light of the wider changes, this policy has been unsustainable. Production levels have increased, raising the costs faced by consumers and governments in maintaining agricultural support and thereby stimulating efforts to control the burden on taxpayers. The causal linkages with the environmental impacts have become better understood, eroding popular support for the CAP. Concerns about domestic food availability have eased as the world contemplates alternative challenges to its security. Internationally, food-exporting countries have exerted pressures to limit levels of agricultural protection. At the same time, the anticipated enlargement of the European Union to include the central and eastern European countries raises difficult questions about the sorts of agricultural policy that can be funded in the longer term.

These factors have altered priorities, but agricultural interests, assisted by the complexities of decision-making across the differing contexts and motives of the member countries of the EU, have successfully resisted fundamental reforms of the CAP. Nevertheless, incremental changes in policy have been made. Restrictions have been placed on production levels through the use of output quotas and set-aside. Environmental schemes were introduced to give targeted support for local environments threatened by agricultural change. The most significant changes to date were introduced in 1992 with a reduction in the levels of support for market prices, in return for which farmers received direct compensation payments.

The 1992 policy reforms were accompanied by a package of measures designed to encourage environmentally favourable farming practices throughout the EU, under Regulation 2078/92. These are commonly referred to as the 'agri-environmental' measures and the term has subsequently come to be used to refer more generally to many elements of rural environmental policy that were in effect prior to the 1992 reforms and even policies which have had no direct linkage with agricultural policy at all.

A second major stimulus for the development of policy towards the rural environment has been through the introduction of EU environment policy. This has had most immediate impact on farming through legislation relating to water quality and in particular requiring member states to take actions to control the concentrations of nitrates in water. Other significant pieces of European legislation have related to the protection of birds and the conservation of natural habitats, although these have, as yet, had fewer implications for agricultural practices.

In this context, the European Union has adopted a number of principles of environmental law that should guide the application of environmental policy (see, for example, Kramer, 1995). These include:

- *preventive action should be preferred to remedial measures*
  This is of importance in that it indicates that action should be taken at an early stage (Kramer, 1995). Examples of actions already taken of this sort include requirements for environmental impact assessment, to take measures to prevent major accidents, and measures to restrict the transport of waste. Thus, where agriculture represents a source of environmental change the implication is that policy should target agriculture rather than seek environmental remediation.

- *environmental damage should be rectified at source*
  If environmental impacts are caused, they should be tackled as early as possible to avoid any spread throughout the environment. This has been interpreted as implying that the Community should adopt emission standards rather than environmental quality objectives, although it may not be possible to judge the significance of the emission in isolation from its wider environmental context.

- *the 'polluter pays principle'*
  This principle was widely promoted by the OECD in the 1970s and indicates that the agent causing the pollution should bear the cost of pollution control, and thus that the costs of environmental damage and clean-up should not be met from taxes. This raises questions about the definition of pollution and polluters to which we return below.

- *the precautionary principle*
  The Maastricht Treaty added the 'precautionary principle' to the list. The principle is open to broad interpretation as no definition is given in the Treaty. This is generally taken to mean that measures should be taken even before a causal link has been established between pollution and environmental harm (Ball

and Bell, 1994). This implies a requirement for action despite the uncertainty surrounding many of the consequences of agricultural changes.

Both the European Union and the UK government have subscribed to the principle of sustainable development. The recent UK strategy (DETR, 1999*a*) emphasizes four objectives: social progress which recognizes the need of everyone; effective protection of the environment; prudent use of natural resources; and maintenance of high and stable levels of economic growth and employment. The strategy identifies a number of headline indicators and it is the government's aim for all of these to move in the right direction over time. Policies will be adjusted where the trend is unacceptable. Bird numbers are regarded as a good indicator of the health of the wider environment and are taken as an indicator of the overall status of biodiversity. Data show that populations of farmland and woodland birds are in long-term decline and action is pledged to reverse this.

2. The Determination of Property: Polluter Pays or Provider Gets?

Many of the significant environmental consequences of agriculture may be crudely divided between impacts which involve the introduction of chemicals into the environment where they may not be wanted, and consequences arising from the alteration of landscape and habitat. The former is a classic example of pollution with the clear implication that the conventional environmental policy mechanisms may be called for. In this context we would generally apply the 'polluter pays principle' (PPP), although in practice, despite the rhetoric, this has not always been applied to agriculture (Baldock, 1992; Tobey and Smets, 1996).

The second category of environmental impact is less easy to characterize. The general assumption is that landowners do hold the rights to alter flora and fauna on their land and that, as a consequence, they should be given positive incentives to produce the patterns of landscape and habitat that are socially desired. This is most clearly demonstrated in the application of the 'voluntary principle' in agri-environmental policy. We thus refer to the provision of 'countryside goods' representing a variety of land uses, including attractive landscapes, wildlife habitats, and public access, that benefit the public. These goods commonly have public-good characteristics and are generally produced jointly with agricultural output. Policy takes the approach of creating positive incentives for the provision of countryside goods, following a 'provider gets principle' (PGP) parallel to the PPP. Thus the provider of a public good should receive payment for the provision of that good.

This is also sometimes discussed in association with a 'beneficiary pays principle' that argues that the beneficiaries from the provision of public goods should be expected to pay for them. However, the PGP may be seen as a means of promoting efficient resource use, in that it establishes incentives for resource managers to provide public goods where the benefits exceed the costs. In contrast, the beneficiary pays principle is essentially an equity principle making a judgement that those who enjoy public goods should be expected to pay, in preference to payment being made through taxation. However, in practice the information requirements and resulting transactions costs often preclude the implementation of the BPP (Blöchliger, 1994; Hanley et al., 1998).

In the next section of this chapter we examine the problems associated with the CAP and the potential gains from liberalization. Following this, we turn to the control of pollution from agricultural sources and then to policy mechanisms adopted in the provision of countryside goods. It is not possible to provide a comprehensive discussion of agrienvironmental policy. Thus in respect of pollution, we focus on the control of nitrates and pesticides arising from arable production systems. With regard to the management of landscape and habitat, we outline the approaches taken towards the management of land in Sites of Special Scientific Interest (SSSIs), Environmentally Sensitive Areas (ESAs), and the Countryside Stewardship Scheme.

3. Reducing the Disincentives

Support for agriculture under the CAP increases the pressures on the environment leading to damage to the landscape, a loss of biodiversity, and environmental pollution. But it has other impacts, too. Agricultural support involves both costs to the exchequer and higher food prices for consumers. The consumer cost represents a major element of the total cost. Estimates based on the position in 1996 suggest that liberalization of the CAP could benefit consumers by about £4 billion, equivalent to 7 per cent of the average food bill (MAFF, 1999). This tends to have a relatively greater impact on those on lower incomes, who spend a higher proportion of their incomes on food. At the same time, despite the cost, it is not obvious to what extent the CAP benefits low-income farmers. Increased returns to farming become capitalized into higher agricultural land prices. Thus new entrants into farming will have to pay a higher price, such that the return on their investment may be no higher than if there had been no agricultural support in the first place. The rents paid by tenant farmers will also tend to be raised in line with increased profitability, benefiting the landlord rather than the farmer. Those firms selling products to agriculture which have some market power may be able to raise their prices and hence their profits. Finally the increased returns in agriculture will tend to draw resources away from other sectors in the economy where they may have generated a higher rate of return.

We can thus see the attractions of liberalizing the CAP. Lower levels of agricultural support will reduce the incentives for more intensive production and relieve some of the pressure on the environment. But not only can the incentives for environmental damage be reduced, there can also be benefits arising from a reduction in the other distortionary effects. And there may even be less impact on the levels of incomes received by low-income farmers than would be expected. There is then potential for a 'double dividend' to be gained from agricultural reform.

Some advantages will already have been gained from the CAP reforms introduced in 1992 and somewhat extended under the Agenda 2000 reforms agreed in 1999. These have shifted a significant element of support away from the maintenance of output prices above levels of the world market, towards direct payments to farmers as 'compensation' for these reductions in market support. This will reduce the incentives to use higher levels of inputs, because an increased proportion of agricultural support received is independent of the intensity of production — i.e. it does not increase the return to input use at the margin. But to the extent that the payments remain associated with agricultural production, then many of the distortionary effects remain. Land prices, rents, and input prices are likely to remain higher than they would be in the absence of support. Clearly, a more comprehensive liberalization of the CAP is called for.

However, the position is complex in that liberalization can itself lead to environmental damage. In some circumstances environmental quality and agricultural output can be complementary, joint products. Particularly within long-settled areas such as Europe, valued landscapes are the products of particular agricultural systems. They thus depend upon particular forms of management that may be lost with reduced levels of support for agriculture (Hodge, 2000). Land may be abandoned or insufficiently managed. This is more often the case in the more extensive agricultural systems in upland and mountain areas. The 'double dividend' is then most likely to be gained in the more intensively farmed arable areas.

Thus, a comprehensive liberalization of the CAP will not of itself be sufficient to deliver the standard of rural environmental quality that is demanded. Policies towards the rural environment need to be related to specific outputs. In some circumstances it may be possible to link policy mechanisms directly to the environmental outputs demanded, such as a payment per kilometre for the maintenance of stone walls in the uplands; sometimes, and probably more often, the environmental outputs may not be readily quantified and more general support will be provided for certain types of agricultural system. But it will be important to identify a clear relationship between the systems supported and the intended environmental objectives. The continuing negotiations over international trade will act as an incentive in this respect. Increasingly, countries will be required to demonstrate that their agricultural policies are operated for legitimate reasons rather than simply giving their farmers extra incomes and an unfair competitive advantage. It is thus important to develop clear criteria against which policy mechanisms may be assessed to test whether they can demonstrate clear objectives and rationale (Ervin, 1999).

4. The Regulation of Pollution

Risks of pollution from agriculture take many forms and may arise through a variety of pathways. Agricultural production takes place across a wide area, leading to 'non-point' pollution — diffuse sources of environmental contaminants which enter the environment at many points and are transported through the environment through different pathways. In arable production systems the main concerns are associated with the use of chemical fertilizers, especially nitrates (see, for example, Romstad et al., 1997), and pesticides. The basic characteristics of the two examples are outlined in Table 1.

High nitrate concentrations can lead to the presence of nitrates in drinking water where there are concerns for its possible impacts on human health. In surface waters high nutrient levels can cause eutrophication where excessive nutrient levels lead to algal bloom and subsequently to anaerobic conditions in the water, killing fish and other species. They can also have undesirable effects on sensitive natural habitats. The processes involved in nitrate leaching are complex. While losses of nitrates from agricultural systems are generally associated with intensive production, it is apparent that there is a very large pool of nitrogen held within the soil compared with the amounts that are being applied in the form of fertilizer or being lost by leaching. Thus relatively small percentage changes in the size of the stock of soil organic matter can have relatively large impacts on the level of nitrate leaching. In consequence, some agricultural processes, such as plough-

Table 1
Nitrate and Pesticide Pollution Problems in Agriculture

	Nitrates	Pesticides
Sources in agriculture	Fertilizers and animal manures	Very broad range of active chemicals
Environmental pathways	Complex reactions within the soil. Main losses through surface and groundwater leaching but also atmospheric losses.	Numerous pathways
Current regulations	Control over production processes within targeted areas to achieve a defined standard based on nitrate concentrations in water, using voluntary agreements and compulsory measures.	Pesticide approval and registration. Regulations on application, storage, and disposals. Codes of practice on application methods.

ing up permanent pasture, can cause very large fluxes of nutrients, and losses can be associated with weather conditions and movements of soil.

Pesticides include an enormous range of different chemicals (it is suggested by DETR (1997a) that about 450 different active ingredients are approved for use in the UK) each with potential impacts on the environment. Given the objective of pesticides to destroy pests, we should not be surprised if we find that they have impacts on non-target species, too. But perhaps of more significance is the lack of information. There is considerable uncertainty about the consequences of agricultural chemicals in the environment. The principles of environmental law indicated above suggest that risks should be avoided even when causal relationships have not been confirmed and the prevention should be at source. This implies controls over the agricultural sector rather than treatment after chemicals have been released, although it does not resolve the question of how much regulation should be applied.

(a) *The Current Regulatory Regimes*

Controls over nitrate pollution were stimulated by European directives on water quality establishing a limit of 50 mg nitrate per litre, first dealing with nitrates in drinking water and subsequently more generally with nitrates in water. This led to the introduction of a voluntary scheme targeted at farmers in designated Nitrate Sensitive Areas

(NSAs). There are 32 NSAs in England covering a total of 37,000 ha (Hawke and Kovaleva, 1998). Within these areas farmers are offered payments in return for accepting limits on the use of fertilizer, below economic recommendations, for winter wheat and oilseed rape, and limits on the applications of manure. Maintenance of green cover, which can take up nitrates which would otherwise be leached from the soil, is also required where land would otherwise be bare through the winter. Additional payments are available to farmers who convert arable land to low-intensity grassland. Subsequently further areas have been designated as Nitrate Vulnerable Zones (NVZs). Since 1998 mandatory measures control both the timing and rate of applications of both inorganic nitrogen and organic manures. There are closed periods for the application of nitrogen to land over the autumn and winter, and farm-based limits on total application rates per hectare. These rules are assumed by the Ministry of Agriculture to represent 'good agricultural practice' and so no compensation is provided to farmers in NVZs (Hawke and Kovaleva, 1998). Farmers are provided with free advice.

On the face of it, NSAs are an unusual way of addressing a pollution problem. We do not generally subsidize polluters in order to encourage them to reduce their pollution. Various reasons may explain why this approach has been adopted in this case: that the NSAs are experimental, although this is harder to sustain given the period over which NSAs have now operated; that farmers who follow 'good agricultural practice' should not be penalized because we subsequently discover that they happen to farm in places where nitrate pollution is a problem; or that there could be legal difficulties in forcing farmers to bear the costs of control, given the difficulty of demonstrating a clear relationship between farmers' actions and nitrate leaching; or perhaps it is attributable to the political influence of the farm lobby.

The use of pesticides in agriculture is already highly regulated. Products must be individually approved and registered prior to their sale. Training is required for people applying chemicals, and regulations govern their storage application and disposal. The government has issued Codes of Practice for the safe use of pesticides on farms, relating to the suitable methods and conditions of application. Although a failure to follow these does not constitute an offence, the provisions of the Code are admissible in evidence in criminal proceedings.

(b) *Extending Cost Effective Controls*

Despite the controls over the uses of pesticides and nitrogen in agriculture, concerns remain over their environmental impacts. Nitrates continue to affect the aquatic environment and to be found in drinking water. Pesticides can be detected in foods and drinking water in excess of defined environmental quality standards. While there may not be clear evidence as to any immediate adverse effects, there is uncertainty as to their possible long-term impacts on human health and the environment.

The non-point nature of agricultural pollution presents particular challenges to the development of effective policy mechanisms. Measurement and monitoring of pollution emissions and subsequent movements through the environment are very costly and generally limited to experimental contexts. Thus policy operates without being able to establish a clear relationship between individual farmer actions and the presence of chemicals in the environment.

The full internalization of external costs into agricultural systems would generate incentives for least-cost measures for the reduction of the environmental impacts. Conceptually this would arise where the marginal costs of control were equal to the marginal damage costs across the various environmental impacts. However, it will be apparent that this would be impossible to define empirically in practice. But policy mechanisms should establish incentives for users to favour softer chemicals over harder ones, to seek out biological or mechanical methods where these could complement or replace chemical ones and which would particularly discourage chemical use in certain localities, such as near sources of drinking water supplies or sensitive habitats. It would favour the use of higher levels of information over higher levels of pesticide and would stimulate the search for agricultural technologies with lower environmental impacts. Present forms of regulation do little to create these incentives and a general reduction in the levels of input use in agriculture would be unlikely to represent a cost-effective solution.

The approach towards nitrates is also very prescriptive in determining how farmers should change their systems so as to reduce leaching and in requiring similar responses by all farmers. In practice it is likely that the least-cost responses will vary from farm to farm and there is no incentive for individual farmers to seek out least-cost solutions for their own specific circumstances. We may therefore expect that an incentive policy approach may be able to achieve the desired standard at a lower cost.

Arguments are commonly made in environmental economics (e.g. Hanley et al., 1997) that incentive mechanisms have the potential to achieve reductions in risk of environmental damage at a lower cost than the types of regulations that are currently in place. Firms would have an incentive to select least-cost methods of reducing environmental impacts and greater adjustments would be made by firms with lower marginal costs of pollution reduction. There would also be an incentive to develop and apply new technological solutions to environmental problems and there would be a continuing incentive to reduce pollution levels as costs of control fell.

Policy, whether it be by command and control or by incentive mechanism, must be targeted on some defined and measurable variable. This may in principle be at various points in the chain of relationships leading up to any final human impacts. The possible targets are illustrated in Figure 1. Generally, policies should be targeted on indicators correlated as closely as possible to the impacts on human welfare. The ideal, and the focus of attention in much of the theoretical economics analysis, would be the environmental damage cost, but given the problems that have been described, the data are simply not available for this approach. It is not possible simply to establish a private liability regime owing to the impossibility of an impact being proven to be attributable to a specific individual. Further, in the presence of significant transactions costs it may be less costly to link the policy to an input to a production process rather than to the emissions from it (Vatn, 1998). Given this, there is a need for indicators that represent the environmental consequences of particular actions (Falconer and Hodge,

Figure 1
Potential Environmental Policy Targets

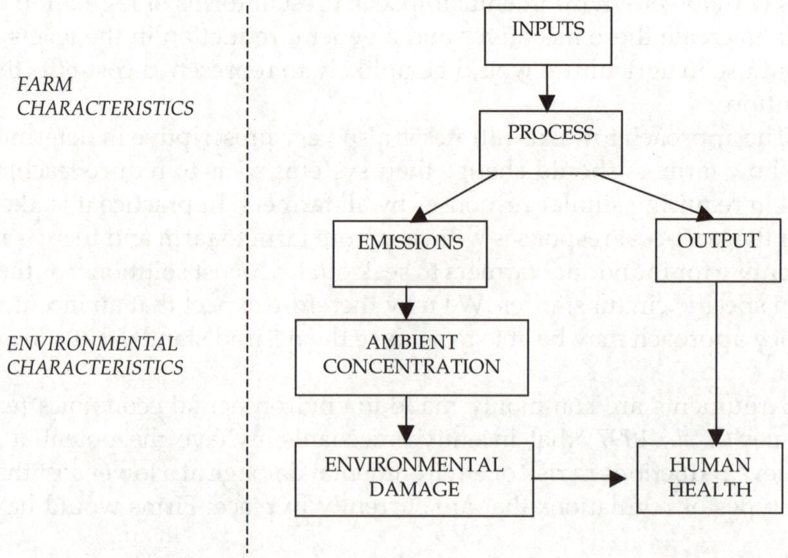

1999). The major options for incentive policies are through some form of taxation or permit scheme.

(c) *Taxation*

The most commonly proposed approach is to introduce some sort of charge for the use of inputs associated with agricultural pollution. On nitrates in inorganic fertilizer, this would increase the marginal cost of fertilizer applications, encouraging lower use and hence, presumably, assuming a correlation between fertilizer use and nitrate emissions, lower levels of nitrate leaching. It has also been argued that a tax of this type would lead to a more efficient use of organic nitrogen (Vermersch *et al.*, 1993). Several studies of fertilizer taxes (e.g. England, 1986; Dubgaard, 1989) have suggested that producers' responses to a tax would be relatively inelastic, indicating that high rates of tax would be necessary in order to achieve significant reductions in fertilizer usage. Thus a tax would lead to significant reduction in farm income levels. If this was to be regarded as inequitable to farmers, then some mechanism would need to be found to compensate them for income reductions which did not obscure the incentives created by the fertilizer tax. However, this would be unlikely to achieve perfect compensation and some redistribution of income among farmers would have to be accepted. The more closely the compensation correlates with the cost of the tax, the more it is likely to reduce the incentive effect of the tax.

Even so a number of problems remain. Perhaps most significantly the relationship between the volume of fertilizer applications and the levels of environmental damage is complex. Much depends upon such factors as the exact location of the application, the season, the current conditions of plant growth, the rainfall and temperature conditions, the soil characteristics and moisture content, the presence of other nitrate sources, and so on. An input tax would do little to encourage farmers to take these factors into account, beyond increasing somewhat further the incentive to avoid waste from an agricultural production perspective. The proximity of sensitive environments, either boreholes for water abstraction or vulnerable habitats, is an important influence on damage costs. But it would not be feasible to seek to introduce a spatially differentiated tax. There may also be perverse incentives. Legumes that fix their own nitrogen do not require the application of nitrates. In consequence, a tax on fertilizers would make them relatively more profitable and the area grown would increase. But they can be a source of nitrate leaching. Thus, the tax on fertilizers would have to be set at a higher level if water quality standards are to be achieved through the regulation of fertilizer applications alone.

An alternative might be to apply a tax on farm-level nitrogen surpluses. Budgets would have to be kept at a farm level, recording both nitrogen brought on to the farm as well as nitrogen removed with products sold. Any difference may then be regarded as a surplus that increases the risk of nitrogen loss to the environment. Several European countries are linking their nitrogen policies to this measure and it has some advantages, although clearly it would have significantly higher transactions costs owing to the need for recording and the complexities of enforcement.

Taxes on pesticides have also been proposed, but face similar difficulties. More challenging in this context is the decision as to what aspect of pesticides should be taxed. Should it relate to the volume purchased, price paid, weight of active ingredient, or perhaps number of treatments? Each would have different implications for the pattern of pesticide use. The consequences of a tax are uncertain; studies have suggested that a simple tax by value could actually increase the level of environmental hazard associated with pesticide use as cheaper more hazardous chemicals are substituted for more expensive environmentally sensitive ones (Falconer, 1997).

The government has signalled its intention to explore the scope for the use of the tax system to deliver environmental objectives (HM Treasury, 1997). It will aim to shift the burden of tax from 'goods', such as labour, to 'bads', such as environmental pollution. The possibility of a tax on pesticides is under active consideration and has recently been evaluated (DETR, 1999g).[1] This report proposes a tax levied per kilogram of active ingredient. Pesticides would be grouped into bands according to the level of hazard associated with their use. A tax would complement existing regulatory instruments, providing a dynamic incentive to minimize pesticide use and to develop alternative approaches towards pest control. By being banded, users gain information on the relative level of hazard associated with different chemicals and face greater incentives to minimize the use of more hazardous chemicals. At present the presumption tends to be that, provided that chemicals are used according to the manufacturers' instructions, they are all similarly 'safe'. A tax would add to government revenue, permitting a reduction in other, more distortionary taxes. There would of course be costs, primarily in terms of lost farm incomes. It is estimated that a 30 per cent tax could lead to an overall loss of some 3 per cent of farm income in the short term, but this would impact differentially on different types of agriculture. In the longer term,

[1] The government announced in February 2000 that it did not plan to go ahead with a pesticides tax.

losses would be reduced as farmers made adjustments to their businesses. However, to the extent that this represents an internalization of an external cost, the tax may be seen as a correction rather than a distortion to economic incentives.

(d) Permit Systems

Permit systems offer an alternative to taxes. These can be more readily applied within defined regions. An initial requirement would be to define the maximum allowable environmental load within a catchment, expressed in terms of input use or some environmental indicator. Permits equivalent to the total allowable emission would be allocated to landholders, who would then have to ensure that they held sufficient permits to cover the particular land uses on their holdings. Assuming that the allowable load was less than the current load, some adjustment of land uses would be required. Thus some landholders would have to acquire permits so as to be able to maintain their land use pattern and others would sell permits and shift to other forms of land use. Under certain assumptions, this approach can achieve a target level of pollution emission at minimum cost (Montgomery, 1972), although in practice the assumptions cannot be met fully.

Research by Moxey and White (1994) has provided an indication of the potential advantages of incorporating a spatial dimension to nitrogen control policies, and this approach allows spatial variability in environmental risks to be taken into account as environmental standards can be set for individual catchments. Even within catchments, zones can be defined where particular restrictions apply. Various policy formulations are possible, with permits linked to input uses, surpluses, or land uses. For instance, it could be possible to link permits to predicted leaching levels associated with particular land uses (Pan and Hodge, 1994). Similar arguments apply to pesticides, although the relevant spatial unit within which to establish permit markets is less obvious, given the more complex pattern of pesticide movements and impacts within the environment.

5. The Provision of Countryside Goods

In the UK there has been a particular concern with the implications of agricultural change for landscape and wildlife and policies have been introduced in order to promote the provision of countryside goods (see e.g. Dabbert et al., 1998). These have public-good characteristics and so there are typically incomplete markets for their provision.

The basic position is illustrated in Figure 2 (following Fraser and Russell, 1997), describing the provision of countryside goods over an area of agricultural land. MEB represents the declining marginal external benefit from an increasing level of provision and MPC the marginal private cost to the landholder. The MPC originates at a positive level of countryside-good provision because at low levels of production the agricultural and environmental outputs are complementary. This suggests that an optimal provision of countryside goods will arise at A1. MPC^1 is included to represent the marginal private cost of supplying countryside goods in the absence of agricultural policy support. Thus, in the absence of price support a higher level of countryside goods would be provided at a lower marginal cost at A2.

Figure 2
The Optimal Provision of Countryside Goods

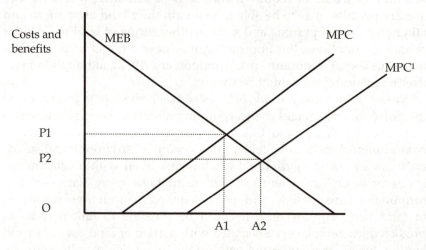

Countryside goods

In some instances, given the effects of CAP support, there can be net savings to the exchequer from the introduction of environmental policy, even without including a benefit for the value of countryside goods provided, i.e. the reduction in the costs of agricultural policy exceeds the payments made under the environmental policy.

A number of problems have to be dealt with in creating the appropriate incentives for the provision of countryside goods.

- There are problems of measurement. While we may appreciate an attractive landscape or enjoy an environment rich in wildlife, it is difficult if not impossible to measure the outputs of such goods. An attractive landscape depends upon the presence of a range of elements, perhaps trees and hedgerows, hills, pastures, or water bodies. It depends, too, upon the way in which these elements are arranged. But it is unlikely to be purely visual. Landscape appreciation often depends upon cultural associations, knowledge of the area, and, perhaps, nostalgia. Even wildlife is not simply a matter of abundance. There may be a concern to ensure the survival of rare species or we may value the presence of certain species as indicators of environmental quality or as symbols of a landscape type.

- There is uncertainty in the production processes. While the production of conventional agricultural products is susceptible to variability owing to climate or pests, there is often uncertainty as to the best means whereby some countryside goods may be supplied at all. Thus, for instance, if the objective is to enhance the numbers of birds within a local area, habitat can be provided, but the birds may not arrive. The production cycle may be long in requiring the establishment of particular habitat. Ecological research on the re-establishment of habitats is developing expertise on these issues, but knowledge remains limited.

- The scale of provision may exceed the area typically under the control of individual landholders. Attractive landscapes require a particular style across a broad region. Habitats may need to be provided at a sufficient scale to maintain a wildlife population. This indicates a need for coordination among local landholders to achieve a desired objective.

Under these circumstances the range of options available may be limited and provision tends to be made through the implementation of voluntary environmental contracts established between a landholder and a government agency under which the landholder agrees to follow a particular set of practices and not to undertake others. In return, the agency makes a payment, generally on an annual basis. Agreements accept that the farmer will continue in occupation of the land and assume that any specialist knowledge can be provided to farmers, either within or in association with the particular contracts on offer. The underlying premise to these contracts is that farmers hold the property rights to alter the environment and thus should be given positive incentives to change their practices—the provider gets principle applies.

The implementation of a more active policy for the management of the countryside to protect the environment dates from the early 1980s.

The first widespread application of this general approach was in the development of management agreements in SSSIs, promoted through legislation passed in 1981 (Keith *et al.*, 1998), and with ESAs, established in British law in 1986 (e.g. Whitby, 1994). More recent has been the introduction of the Countryside Stewardship Scheme. Similar approaches have been adopted in respect of NSAs, the Habitats Scheme, and the Countryside Access Scheme, and there are broadly equivalent schemes in Scotland and Wales. These types of policies have subsequently been promoted across the European Union in measures accompanying the 1992 reform of the CAP (Whitby, 1996).

There are three major approaches in use within England. Their general characteristics are summarized in Table 2. While there are some differences in detail, the approaches in Scotland and Wales are similar. While these elements of agricultural policy have received substantial publicity, they remain a relatively small proportion of total policy expenditure. Expenditure on agri-environment and other measures associated with the environment in 1997/8 represented less than 4 per cent of total UK public expenditure under the CAP. The evaluations that have been undertaken of these schemes have been reviewed by Hanley *et al.* (1999).

SSSIs are notified under the 1981 Wildlife and Countryside Act[2] in respect of their fauna, flora, or geological or physiographical features. Landholders are informed of a list of potentially damaging operations (PDOs) and if they wish to undertake any of these, they are required to notify the government's nature conservation agency. If the agency wishes to prevent these operations in order to protect the conservation value of the site, it will then enter into negotiation with the landholder. This may lead to a management agreement under which the landholder will agree not to undertake the PDOs and in return can receive financial compensation based on the value of the income forgone. The agreements are essentially voluntary and after a specified period the landholder can legally go ahead with the operation in the event that an agreement has not been reached. In principle, as an ultimate sanction, powers of compulsory purchase may be available to the nature conservation agency in certain circumstances to prevent this, although the use of these powers has been extremely rare. SSSIs cover 7 per cent of the total area of England, representing just less that 1m ha.

---

[2] A bill introduced in 2000 significantly changes the position by giving owners and occupiers a duty not to carry out operations likely to damage an SSSI unless permission has been granted by the Nature Conservancy Council (English Nature).

Table 2
General Characteristics of Major Schemes for the Provision of Countryside Goods

	Management agreements in SSSIs	Environmentally Sensitive Areas	Countryside Stewardship
Objectives	Conservation of specifically identified sites of significant habitat and species.	Conservation of landscape and characteristic habitat arising from 'traditional farming systems' within designated regions.	Conservation and promotion of landscape and habitat within selected locations.
Property rights	'Voluntary' management agreements within legal framework. Payments based on opportunity costs.	Voluntary participation, applicants accepted if able to meet conditions.	Voluntary participation. Applications accepted if offer good value for money.
Transactions costs	Detailed site assessment prior to notification. Individually negotiated agreements.	General designation of region. Participation on basis of standard contract and conditions.	Individually evaluated applications. Standardized contractual arrangements.

Provision for ESAs arises through European regulations implemented in the UK through the 1986 Agriculture Act. They are designated with the aim of pursuing environmental objectives in areas of high environmental value, through the encouragement of appropriate agricultural practices. In selecting suitable areas for designation, they must be of national environmental significance and conservation must depend on adopting, maintaining, or extending particular farming practices. Either changes to farming practices must pose a threat to the environment, or the adoption of particular practices must be capable of resulting in significant environmental improvements, and each area must represent a discrete and coherent unit of environmental interest (NAO, 1997).

Within the designated areas, farmers and agricultural land managers are able to enter 10-year management agreements with the Ministry of Agriculture, Fisheries, and Food (MAFF) (with an option of termination after 5 years). A farmer receives annual payments on each hectare of land entered into the scheme. All ESAs have one or more tiers, each tier prescribing a specific set of agricultural practices to be followed. Details of the practices will reflect the specific objectives of individual ESAs. Payment rates are based on income forgone, although they also take into account any incentive that may be required to encourage the agreement holder to change his management approach. Typical payments range from £20–50 per ha for the management of upland grassland, £100–200 for lowland grassland, and £240–310 for reversion from lowland arable to grassland. The highest payment is £415 per ha for raising water levels to create wet grassland in the Somerset Levels and Moors. ESAs designated in England cover about 1m ha, of which 46 per cent was entered into agreements in 1996.

The Countryside Stewardship scheme was first introduced as a pilot by the Countryside Commission, but was taken over by the MAFF in 1996. Similarly to the ESAs, it offers payments to farmers and other land managers to enhance and conserve landscapes, their wildlife, and history, and to help people to enjoy them. The major difference lies in the fact that there are no designated areas, so that agreements are in principle available throughout England outside of the ESAs. The scheme is directed at the conservation of specific landscapes, and targets are set annually to reflect current priorities and the progress made in previous years. Countryside Stewardship agreements usually run for 10 years and each is drawn up individually with the landholder to address particular management objectives and local circumstances. In 1996, about 100,000 ha were entered into the Countryside Steward-ship scheme in England.

(a) *Property Rights*

These alternative arrangements imply a somewhat different treatment of property rights with respect to the owners of land within SSSIs and ESAs. In both cases, landowners are presumed to hold rights to develop their land for agricultural use so that a claim for compensation arises if this right is restricted. However, Whitby and Saunders (1996) point out that within SSSIs limits are imposed on holders' rights to undertake potentially damaging operations without first obtaining permission from the conservation agency. A failure to observe this procedure can result in the imposition of a fine on the landowner. The appropriateness of landowners holding a right to damage SSSIs has recently been questioned and the legislation is currently under review (DETR, 1998*h*).[3] In the case of ESAs, no such requirement is made, landholders simply are given the option of voluntarily exchanging the right to develop the agricultural potential of their land or the right not to

---

[3] As noted above (n. 2), a bill revising the leglislation has been introduced.

maintain hedges, walls, or buildings, on a temporary basis for an annual payment.

(b) *Designing Optimal Contracts: Transactions Costs and Information*

Two aspects of these arrangements are worthy of attention: the transactions costs and information problems. These problems are addressed in rather different ways in the three types of policy outlined above. The costs of operating environment schemes includes both the payments made to landholders as an incentive for them to participate in the scheme, typically reflecting the opportunity cost of lost production, and the costs to the agency in administering the scheme. These transactions costs are often not separately recorded but can represent a significant component of the total costs of the scheme (Falconer and Whitby, 1999). The information available to the parties to the environmental contracts is important in determining the likely outcomes. Generally information is asymmetric; the landholder knows more about the operations on his land than the government agency. This has two implications: the agency cannot identify the costs facing landholders in supplying countryside goods, raising the problem of *adverse selection*, and the agency cannot easily observe the behaviour of the landholder in order to monitor what actions are taken, raising the problem of *moral hazard*.

In the case of SSSIs, sites are individually assessed and notified, management agreements are tailored to the specific circumstances and the compensation payment is negotiated on a site-by-site basis. Each individual site is notified in respect of some particular conservation value, with the objective of protecting the best examples of representative habitats. This intensive process implies relatively high transactions costs. In negotiating payment levels, the landholder has superior information to the agency on the costs of protecting the site and may be able to exploit this in securing payments in excess of his or her true costs. The holder may threaten to make changes which would actually not be carried out in practice or to claim higher returns from the changes than could actually be realized. The agency is in a relatively weak position to resist, in that it has identified this individual site as being of particular value and is under pressure to ensure its protection; generally simply abandoning the negotiations is not an option. Enforcement may be difficult given the scattered nature of the sites and the varied nature of the individual agreements. Economic analysis thus predicts agreement favourable to the landholder (Moxey *et al.*, 1999).

In practice, while there have also been some extremely large and well-publicized payments, things do not appear to work out quite in the way predicted. Many owners of SSSIs do not have management agreements and some payments are nominal. Management agreements have been negotiated over only about 13 per cent of the total area of SSSIs. Agreements are often reached which promote positive actions by the landholder to promote the conservation values of the site with relatively modest payment levels.

The explanation for this is unclear, but it suggests that landholders are not operating in quite the rather narrow, self-interested way typically assumed in economic theory. They may personally value the conservation values that have been identified on their land or else feel some moral duty to look after them in the interests of society without seeking to extract the maximum payment from the conservation agency.

Within ESAs, agreements are available to all farmers within areas which are designated on the basis of broad landscape and habitat objectives. Participants have to opt for one of a limited number of standard agreements. While a high participation rate is clearly desired, there is no special pressure to ensure that any particular site is brought into an agreement. There is thus considerably less individual negotiation and no scope to offer high payments to owners who may otherwise be reluctant to participate. Thus the individual bargaining power of potential participants is limited and the levels of transactions costs may be expected to be lower. On the other hand, the approach is likely to deliver excess payment levels to most landholders. A standard price has to be set in order to attract a sufficient number of participants into the scheme. This is represented by P1 in Figure 2 and is paid to all participants. This then represents the costs faced by the marginal participant. All other participants may be assumed to have lower costs and thus to receive a level of payment in excess of their costs. This excess transfer payment is represented by the area above MPC below price P1.

Enforcement is more straightforward, provided that the conditions required in the scheme are observable to the agency. The holdings are located within a defined region and the contracts have standard conditions. These conditions will be familiar to all landholders within the region such that there may be an element of self-policing among local landholders.

Two ways may be suggested in order to reduce this level of transfer payment. One is to divide the designated area into smaller units within which landholders are relatively homogeneous and thus face similar costs. The price paid for entry into the scheme could then be varied between these smaller units (Smith and Colman, 1997). The second is to admit landholders to the scheme on a competitive basis whereby they would have to tender for participation. Given effective competition, the agency would be able to reduce the levels of transfer payments and thus reduce the exchequer costs of the scheme (Latacz-Lohmann and Van der Hamsvoort, 1997).

The Countryside Stewardship scheme falls some way in between the approaches to the SSSIs and ESAs. The agency specifies in general terms objectives for the scheme for particular regions based on local consultations. Landholders are then invited to apply to provide these countryside goods. While payments are made at standard rates, the applications will specify the outputs that are planned to be provided. These applications are assessed by the agency in terms of the anticipated benefits against the costs in terms of payments that will be made. The agency has discretion whether or not to accept applications and will select those which are judged to represent the best value for money. It is thus possible to take account of the value of countryside goods within a particular location, for instance schemes offering to provide public access are judged against the anticipated level of demand for access to this particular site. But the competitive process does not cover the rates of payment paid to landholders.

(c) Developing Policy

Agri-environmental policies are at a relatively early stage in their development. The idea of attempting to use public policy measures to enhance the landscape is a novel one and there is much to learn about the best methods. There is scope for the further development of policy mechanisms in a variety of ways. Generally there is a need to view agri-environmental policy within a wider institutional framework, to take account of other participants and a broader range of resource allocation mechanisms (Hodge, 1998). But the existing schemes may be developed in a number of ways.

(d) Optimizing Transactions Costs

As we have noted, policy mechanisms to promote specific practices on particular farms inevitably involve relatively high transactions costs. These costs tend to be disregarded in policy discussion and, where considered, it is generally assumed that they should simply be minimized. But they should be viewed in a positive light. In principle we should seek to optimize administrative effort. We may assume generally that there are decreasing returns to administrative effort in terms of identifying the relative values of alternative countryside goods, targeting policies towards particular regions and landholders, negotiating specific agreements with individual landholders, and so on. The more valuable the environmental benefits, then the greater will be the optimal level of investment in administrative effort. The outputs from the three approaches discussed here are rather different, so that we may expect to observe different levels of administrative cost. It may be that the European rules that only reimburse national governments in respect of a proportion of the transfers made to farmers create an incentive to increase their scale at the expense of an optimal degree of administration. It may thus be appropriate to reimburse a proportion of the total costs of the scheme.

However, the concern remains that there is little incentive to minimize costs within the public sector, so that we cannot be sure that administrative expenditures are justified in terms of their contribution towards the public good. One way of approaching this might be to introduce some element of competition into the administration of the schemes. Thus it may be possible to put the administration of such schemes for a period of time out to tender. A range of organizations might have the potential to administer them, both government organizations and private conservation bodies or private firms.

(e) *Securing Property Rights*

Characteristic landscapes and conservation values are generally only created over significant periods of time. Thus relatively long-term agreements are necessary so as to permit the development of new environmental assets. However, once the term of the contract has expired, there can be no guarantee that the conservation assets will continue to be maintained. Even if government continues to offer a contract, higher agricultural prices or new market opportunities may persuade farmers to return to more intensive forms of agricultural production at the expense of any conservation benefits that have been achieved. This also raises questions about the ownership of the environmental assets generated through environmental contracts. The public may feel that it has a proprietary interest in them to the extent that the assets have been created through the contribution of public funds and so it should have a right to prevent damage to this part of the environment in the future.

The implication is that consideration should be given to the acquisition of long-term rights over environmental assets. This might take the form either of outright landownership or else the acquisition of a covenant over the land. In some instances, landowners are themselves keen to ensure the protection of the land in perpetuity and are thus willing to forgo agricultural development rights at a low cost. These rights might be acquired by government agencies, although public preference might be for them to be acquired and managed by Conservation, Amenity and Recreation Trusts (Dwyer and Hodge, 1996).

(f) *Promoting Entrepreneurship*

There are no incentives for producers themselves to seek out new opportunities for environmental improvement or new methods of reducing costs. Standardized contracts agreed between individual landholders and a government agency are unlikely to have the flexibility to be able to take these opportunities into account. But more generally there is no incentive to act entrepreneurially, to introduce original ideas, or to be willing to take risks for the provision of countryside goods.

The Countryside Stewardship Scheme represents an improvement on the ESAs in this respect. It encourages a more imaginative approach to conservation opportunities and is open to a wider range of landowners, beyond farmers. One quarter of those applying to enter the Countryside Stewardship Scheme between 1991 and 1996 were non-farmers (Countryside Commission, 1998). However, this might be further encouraged by increased use of competitive mechanisms and a higher level of participation of Conservation, Amenity and Recreation Trusts who have incentives to develop new approaches and techniques and thus can investigate and demonstrate the potential opportunities and techniques to a wider range of landowners.

6. Conclusions

Concerns for the impacts of agricultural practices on the quality of the rural environment are relatively recent. Twenty years ago, it was widely assumed that a profitable agricultural sector represented the most effective means of protecting the rural environment. It is now recognized that given changes in the ways in which it is practised, agriculture represents a serious threat to environmental quality across a large proportion of the land area. Evidence of the continuing decline in the numbers of wild birds is taken by the government as an indicator of a more general decline in the quality of the rural environment. The government has accepted the objective of reversing this trend. But this will depend both on more fundamental changes being made to the CAP and to the further development of targeted policies to protect and promote the conservation of the rural environment. It is not yet clear that the policies are in place to achieve the intended reversal.

The development of agri-environmental policy presents a significant challenge owing to the diffuse nature of the activities influencing environmental quality and the intangible nature of many of the impacts involved. When agricultural policy was primarily directed towards increasing supplies of domestically produced food, the policy approach was relatively straightforward. Increased output prices stimulated increased production, even if some of the other consequences were unexpected and unwanted. We as yet have relatively little experience with the development of agri-environmental policy and have much to learn about the ways in which social objectives can be identified and incentives put in place for cost-effective pollution control and for the provision of countryside goods.

11

Transport and the Environment

CHRIS NASH*

1. Introduction

Transport was one of the first sectors in which the importance of externalities was recognized with respect to traffic congestion, and the proposed solution in the form of a Pigouvian tax formulated. More recently, more attention has shifted to environmental effects as externalities. Here, there are a wide variety of effects, as listed in Table 1. Transport is a very significant source of most of these pollutants. For instance, in Great Britain over a million people are exposed to road noise in excess of 70 A-weighted decibels (dB(A)), and around 15m to in excess of 60 dB(A) (Mauch and Rothengatter, 1995). Transport accounts for 55 per cent of nitrogen oxides, 72 per cent of carbon monoxide, 41 per cent of volatile organic compounds, and 26 per cent of particulates (Department of the Environment, Transport and the Regions (DETR), 1998*l*); in each case it is the dominant mode, road transport, that is responsible for virtually all the emissions.

The impact of these externalities varies from purely local, in the form of land take, property destruction, noise, and local air pollution, to regional, in the case of acid rain and its impact on wildlife, forests, and buildings, and to global in the case of greenhouse gases. It is true that the use of catalytic converters — now compulsory for all new cars within the European Union — is leading to a decline in most transport-related air pollution. However, the situation regarding greenhouse gases continues to worsen. In 1996, transport accounted for 26 per cent of carbon-dioxide emissions, and these emissions were projected to increase by at least a third by 2020 (DETR, 1998*l*).

While land take, property destruction, and the extraction of building materials may be seen as not being external costs, since they are generally the subject of market transactions, the transactions in question are frequently not entered into voluntarily as market transactions,

* Institute for Transport Studies, University of Leeds.

Table 1
Principal Environmental Effects of Transport Systems

Resource	Effects
Land	Land take, property destruction, extraction of building materials Visual intrusion, waste disposal
Air	Local pollutants (CO, HC, NO_x, lead, particulates) Acid rain (NO_x, SO_x) Global warming (CO_2)
Water	Pollution by run-off; oil extraction and transportation
Other	Noise and vibration

Source: Adapted from OECD (1988)

but rather as a result of compulsory purchase orders, and they frequently have an effect on third parties through changing the amenity level of the environment in which they live and work, or, indeed, through more drastic implications, such as the elimination of jobs. Thus there may well be externalities associated with these effects. In all other cases, the effect concerned is quite clearly an externality.

It is worth commenting also that these effects may have a variety of impacts. For instance, local air pollution may be a direct disamenity (i.e. perceived as unpleasant), and it may have indirect effects (e.g. damage to property or damage to health). In the latter case the indirect effect may be perceived without the recipient knowing the cause of it, a matter of some importance when it comes to valuation procedures.

Thus it is clear that the transport sector is the producer of many environmental effects which are the cause of serious concern. In the next section, we offer a brief history of recent British transport policy and the role of environmental considerations in it. We then consider alternative policies which may be adopted to deal with the problem, and examine critically the approach to date in Great Britain. We follow this with a discussion of attempts to place money values on environmental costs of transport before considering the uses to which such values may be put in pricing and investment decisions. We then seek to draw some conclusions.

2. Transport Policy in the UK

Button and Gillingwater (1986) characterize the period from the Second World War until the mid-1970s as the *age of administrative planning*, in which the transport sector in most countries was largely controlled by the state. Even so, this was the period of most rapid growth of road traffic in Britain, which saw the development of the motorway network and of the 'predict and provide' approach to road building. The period from the mid-1970s on is called by them the *age of contestability* in which the idea that transport markets could and should be contestable (that is, open to competition from new entrants) took hold. In pursuit of this, extensive deregulation and privatization of the transport sector took place in Britain and in many other countries throughout the world. The transport sector was transformed from one dominated by the state to one where many functions are undertaken by private companies in markets which, if still often subject to a degree of regulation, are much freer than before. In Britain, transport planning fell from fashion, and the government sought to make the sector much more market-oriented, privatizing air, bus, and rail sectors and even starting with the process of privatizing roads through the 'shadow tolling' approach, whereby the government paid private developers for building or upgrading roads in terms of a payment per unit of traffic using them. If the market dictated a rapid expansion of roads and road traffic, and a decline in public transport, then this is what would happen.

However, some writers, notably Goodwin (1991), identified the emergence of what he calls the 'new transport realism' in the late 1980s This is the realization that environmental and budgetary constraints make it impossible to provide for the rate of growth of road traffic that then existed, making a new set of interventions inevitable. The transport Green Paper of the last government (Department of Transport (DoT), 1996) is seen as representing a significant step towards a more interventionist policy, and of course the White Paper of the Labour government (DETR, 1998a) moves further in that direction.

A major part of the problem of transport is its very rapid growth. In the passenger sector, the total amount of travel has more than trebled since the early 1950s. This has been partly due to an increase in the number of motorized trips (with a corresponding reduction in walking and cycling), and partly due to a substantial increase in mean trip length. Also notable is the reduction in bus and coach travel over this period. Rail has managed to maintain its volume in absolute terms, but of course now has a greatly reduced market share.

In the freight sector, there has also been a big rise in traffic, again due to a large extent to increases in average length of haul. Reasons for this include the decline of bulk commodities and their replacement by high-value goods which are distributed over a much wider area, and changes in production and distribution systems emphasizing concentration, specialization, and trading over much wider areas. Again road has

Table 2
Road Traffic Growth
(Index 1988 = 100)

1958	25
1968	50
1978	68
1988	100
1989 forecasts for 2025	
Low	183
High	242
1997 central forecast for 2026	180

Sources: DoT (1989); DETR (1997c).

become dominant, but this time rail has declined sharply in absolute as well as relative terms. The rapid growth of water transport is mainly associated with North Sea oil.

The result of these trends has, of course, been a rapid growth in road traffic, which has quadrupled since 1958 (Table 2). In 1989, the DoT issued its National Road Traffic Forecasts (DoT, 1989), which predicted in rough terms a further doubling of road traffic by the year 2025. These forecasts have since been revised downwards partly on the assumption that worsening congestion will restrain traffic growth (DETR, 1997c). The 1989 forecasts played a substantial part in the emergence of the 'new transport realism', which will be discussed below.

For many years, roads policy had been described as 'predict and provide' — i.e. predict what the demand will be and provide the appropriate capacity. There is a sound economic argument for following such a policy as part of the 'market' approach to transport, provided that pricing policy is appropriate and takes full account of all the costs of road use, including environmental effects. However, the roads programme came under vehement attack from environmental concerns. At the technical level, the Department's cost–benefit analysis programme came under assault from a range of criticisms, including the failure to take adequate account of environmental factors (while these were listed in a framework of effects of schemes, they were not valued in the cost–benefit analysis undertaken), the failure to take a strategic view of investment options (what were appraised were mainly small individual stretches of new or improved roads), and the failure to allow for the traffic-generating capacity of new roads. The problem was brought home in a particularly influential report from the Royal Commission on Environmental Pollution (RCEP, 1994), and a follow-up report in 1997 (RCEP, 1997). A further significant factor was the conclusion of the Standing Advisory Committee on Trunk Road Assessment (SACTRA, 1994) that, on balance, the evidence suggested that building new roads does generate additional road traffic, as had long been alleged by environmentalists, although not allowed for in the DETR appraisal methodology.

An important part of the 'new realism' is an appreciation of environmental constraints, but it is also argued that in purely practical and fiscal terms it would simply not be possible to cope with forecast traffic growth by increasing road space. Congestion would worsen so seriously that alternative policies would have to be sought.

The reaction of the then government to the new transport realism was to launch a 'national transport debate' focused on three questions:

- is the present balance right between promotion of economic growth, protection of the environment, and support for personal choice?
- if the balance needs to be shifted (for example, towards greater environmental protection or towards enhancing competitiveness by reducing road congestion), what measures need to be taken and how will they achieve their stated objectives?
- are we prepared to accept the wider consequences (for the environment, for personal choice, for industrial competitiveness, jobs, and the economy as a whole) of any such measures?

This culminated in the publication in the spring of 1996 of a transport Green Paper (DoT, 1996), which accepted that there was a need to pay increased attention to the environmental impact of transport policy and to reduce dependence on the car. Ways of achieving this would include market-oriented measures, such as action to reflect better social costs in the prices of transport modes, and planning-oriented measures such as a presumption against planning permission for further out-of-town retailing (already implemented by the Department of the Environment) and switching the emphasis in investment from roads to public transport. It was also accepted that quality improvements were needed in bus services, and that if these could not be secured by voluntary 'quality partnerships' between local authorities and bus operators, then legislation might be needed to introduce an element of force.

Not surprisingly, Labour Party transport policy sought a much greater return to a planned approach (Labour Party, 1996). According to that document, it too wished to reduce the need to travel and to divert investment resources from roads to public transport. It would consult on how best to regulate the bus industry in order to achieve better services, and would abolish the franchising of rail passenger services, bringing passenger operations back into the public sector as existing franchises expired. Subsidies would be paid direct to Railtrack in order that investment could be increased and track-access charges reduced. It would also seek to reacquire ownership of Railtrack 'in the light of available resources'. Perhaps most remarkably, the Labour document commits itself to the Royal Commission target of increasing the rail share of freight tonne kilometres from 6.5 per cent to 20 per cent by 2010.

Following its election in May 1997, the first step taken by the Labour government was to issue a consultation document (DETR, 1997d). This saw the aim of transport policy as:
- promoting environmental objectives;
- promoting economic development across all parts of the country;
- promoting greater efficiency in the use of scarce resources;
- meeting the needs of rural areas;
- reducing social exclusion and taking account of the basic accessibility needs of all sectors of the community;
- ensuring a high standard of safety;
- promoting greater awareness of the issues.

In July 1998, the long awaited White Paper appeared. Its key features are as follows.
(i) An emphasis on integration: between and within modes; and between policy areas — transport, environment, land use, health, education.
(ii) A central role for local transport plans.
(iii) New regulatory arrangements for public transport, including a strategic rail authority and the promotion of bus quality partnerships or quality contracts.
(iv) A new appraisal framework to be applied to government funding of all modes of transport.
(v) Powers for local authorities to introduce road pricing or a tax on non-residential parking and to retain (most of) the revenue to finance other transport measures.

A series of daughter documents has since provided more detailed proposals for urban road pricing and parking taxes (DETR, 1998i), trunk roads (DETR, 1998j) the rail sector (DETR, 1998k), buses (DETR, 1999h) and for sustainable distribution (DETR, 1999i). Clearly, the extent to which the government sees itself as reversing the trend to deregulation and privatization has diminished since the election; taking the rail industry back into public ownership seems to have disappeared as an option, and there is more emphasis on voluntary quality partnerships as a way forward for the bus industry, with legally enforceable quality contracts seen as very much the exception. Nevertheless, taken as a whole, the set of documents still proposes quite radical change, with a major cut in spending on roads, legal powers for local authorities to introduce road pricing and a pledge that they can retain the revenues for at least ten years, and—as well as other measures to improve public transport—the likelihood that the revenues from road pricing will enable local authorities to undertake many of the transport projects they have planned but never been able to afford.

Thus environmental issues have risen much higher on the agenda in the transport policy debate, although many critics doubt the adequacy of the proposed policies to deal with the problem, and also the determination of the government to see them through. In the next section, we offer a critical review of the various policies that have been proposed to cope with the environmental effects of the transport sector.

3. Policy Options

Transport policy instruments are frequently divided into the following categories (Institution of Highways and Transportation (IHT), 1995):
- infrastructure measures;
- management measures;
- information measures;
- pricing;
- land-use.

Their impacts on the environment also follow a variety of pathways. Infrastructure measures may be aimed at reducing congestion, and thus pollution, by provision of more road space, or at encouraging use of alternative modes of transport. Management measures may aim to influence the technology in use, for instance by imposing tighter emission standards, or at controlling the way in which the technology is used, for instance traffic management measures, or improved public transport integration. Information ranges from attempts to encourage more economical driving styles though route guidance to the promotion of public transport. Pricing includes both the closer alignment of charges to the true costs of alternative modes of transport (whether by means of road pricing, or public transport subsidies) and measures to encourage the use of cleaner vehicles or fuels. Land-use planning may be aimed at segregating pollution from homes and jobs, at reducing the demand for travel, or at promoting the use of public transport, walking, or cycling.

Broadly these impacts may be characterized as:
- encouraging less-polluting vehicles;
- changing where and when vehicles are driven;

- mode switching;
- reducing demand for travel.

The potential for each of these strategies is considered in turn.

(a) *Encouraging Less-polluting Vehicles*

The requirement that all new cars be fitted with catalytic converters is still working its way through the fleet, with generally beneficial effects on air quality, and further tightening up of emissions standards is foreseen. Progress on diesel engine emissions is less rapid, and it is small particulate matter from diesel engines which is now believed to pose one of the greatest threats to health; nevertheless, more advanced designs and the use of particulate traps are becoming more common. The result is that the problem of air pollution from road transport is being contained despite traffic growth, and the situation should continue to improve within the foreseeable future.

The more radical solution is often seen as being to encourage alternatively fuelled vehicles. Battery technology and the problem of emissions at the point of generation continue to make electric vehicles attractive only for limited applications; liquid petroleum gas, compressed natural gas, and, ultimately, hydrogen are seen as more promising fuels for wider application. However, there are proposals under consideration for much tighter emissions standards for internal combustion engines, including diesel engines. Regulations at European Union (EU) level are the principal way of carrying this issue forward.

None of these measures would in itself address what many see as the crucial environmental sustainability issue—that of greenhouse-gas emissions. Indeed, some of them make the problem worse. Continued traffic growth will inevitably raise greenhouse-gas emissions unless non-carbon-based energy sources can be used and/or energy efficiency increased. It is believed that there remains considerable scope for improved energy efficiency (Wootton and Poulton, 1993), but in recent years improvements in this field have been offset by the trend to larger, heavier, and more powerful vehicles. The government intends to continue to raise fuel taxes in real terms, and—despite popular opinion—research indicates that these do have a significant effect both on road traffic levels and in the longer term on the energy efficiency of vehicles (Schipper *et al.*, 1993), while voluntary agreements at EU level with the car industry to reduce average fuel consumption may also play a part.

Even if all the above-mentioned problems of emissions could be successfully tackled by means of technological solutions, problems of congestion, visual intrusion, safety, and the general unpleasantness of heavily trafficked areas would remain.

(b) *Changing Where and When Vehicles are Used*

Obviously changing where and when vehicles are used is most relevant to relieving congestion, but it will also influence local environmental impacts and have some effect on greenhouse-gas emissions, in that energy efficiency is reduced by congestion. Relevant policy instruments include road pricing and traffic-management measures; general measures to raise the cost of motoring are not helpful in this context because their effect is indiscriminate. While road pricing remains expensive to implement, it appears to be particularly effective at influencing the timing and routing of trips, and studies suggest considerable net benefits, at least in large congested cities such as London (MVA, 1995). A number of cities outside London (including Bristol and Edinburgh) are also showing considerable interest, and the government is planning to proceed with technical trials. One remaining concern is that if this policy is successful it may be so at the expense of diverting activities from cities to green-field sites, which may threaten the social sustainability of cities and have damaging second-round effects on the environment by encouraging other journeys by car.

(c) *Mode Switching*

The idea that the environmental problems caused by transport may be solved simply by improving public transport and rail freight services is an attractive fallacy. Certainly, improved public transport has a role to play, particularly for commuting in cities, and there is potential for increasing the use of rail for freight (NERA *et al.*, 1997). But the evidence is that, by themselves, even major investments in public transport only have a rather marginal effect (Chartered Institute of Transport, 1996). What they may do is to increase the acceptability of other measures designed to restrain the growth of road traffic, and to help prevent undesirable side effects such as decentralization. Mode switching is more likely to come about when public-transport improvements are combined with measures to restrain car use, such as road pricing or parking controls, and there is evidence that park-and-ride facilities are particularly effective in this context. But park-and-ride also encourages some trips to switch from using public transport throughout, and its overall effectiveness remains the subject of controversy (Parkhurst, 1994).

(d) *Reducing Demand for Transport*

The enormous growth in road traffic is almost equally due to increases in the number of motorized trips, and to increases in trip length. These increases are clearly bound up with changes in life styles and patterns of land use which are not easy to halt, let alone reverse. Nevertheless, the fact remains that a large proportion of car travel takes the form of journeys which would be very difficult to serve by other modes of transport and, without modifying travel patterns and patterns of land use, the part played by increased walking, cycling, and public transport to the relief of environmental problems will be limited. We have already commented on the effect that both general measures to raise the cost of motoring and road pricing may have on this. But better integration of the need to reduce demand for transport with land-use planning, as proposed by the government, is also clearly a factor. Improved telecommunications, leading to teleshopping and teleworking from home, are also often cited as factors likely to reduce the demand for transport. Again, however, the effectiveness of all these developments has been subject to doubt.

Thus there is a wide range of policy instruments available to influence the environmental impact of the transport sector. The government has proposed a package which includes land-use planning, improved public transport, and increased taxes on private transport, both by means of continued increases in fuel taxation and by permitting road pricing on urban and perhaps some inter-urban roads. However, most of the restraint measures, such as road pricing, will be left up to local authorities to implement, and they may be reluctant to do so, especially if neighbouring authorities do not, as these may attract economic activity away from them. No effective way of reducing inter-urban traffic is proposed, and overall excessive emphasis appears to be placed on the potential role of public transport. However, it is very difficult to assess the economic efficiency of these measures without a quantification of the environmental costs the measures are intended to relieve. It is to estimates of these costs that we turn in the next section.

4. Estimates of the Environmental Costs of Transport in Great Britain

Enormous efforts have been put into quantifying and placing money values on environmental effects in recent years. The main alternative approaches to valuation are divided into direct and indirect methods. Direct methods rely on surveys which essentially ask people how much they would be prepared to pay for environmental improvements, or what compensation they would require to put up with losses (the contingent-valuation approach). An alternative way of examining people's willingness to pay for environmental improvements is by examining their choices in real or hypothetical circumstances in which they trade off environmental quality against cost. The most common case in which this occurs is in the housing market, and relative house prices are frequently used as a way of valuing environmental goods. However, all the above approaches rely on obtaining willingness-to-pay type values for the environmental effect itself, and it may be argued that this is only appropriate where the individuals concerned perceive the effect and understand its consequences, as in the case of the disamenity effects of noise or visual intrusion (Nash, 1997). Where the consequences are indirect, in terms of health or damage, for instance to buildings and crops, it is argued that an alternative approach, usually known as the dose-response approach, should be used. This traces through the consequences and then seeks to value those, either simply using market values, or using one of the above approaches if market values do not exist or are thought inappropriate. For instance, a major EU-funded project (EXTERNE) has undertaken this process for air pollution, and developed it into what they call the 'impact pathway approach' (CAPRI, 1999). It is now widely accepted that where the resulting effects are in terms of increased probability of mortality or morbidity, this should be valued on the basis of studies of what people are willing to pay to reduce risk, rather than the loss of output method which used to be used. However, debate still continues over whether the life expectancy of the victim should be allowed for in this calculation. Many of those killed by air pollution are already ill and have a short life expectancy, but should the 'value of a statistical life lost' be scaled down to allow for the life years lost?

Table 3 shows four recent estimates of the accident and environmental costs of road transport in the UK. One point that may be made is that all are large, with the smallest still far exceeding the cost of providing and maintaining the road system. Thus when considering appropriate charges for the use of the road system, to ignore external costs, even leaving aside congestion, is to ignore a large part of the costs.

One of the biggest problems facing work in this area is the fact that different studies tend to come up with totally different results for the external costs of transport. It will be seen that Mauch and Rothengatter's estimates for 1991 are substantially higher than those of Pearce *et al.*, with the biggest difference being in the category of air pollution/climate change.

A detailed examination of the differences makes it clear that there are differences not just of detailed methods but also of principle in the way the costs are assessed. In the case of climate change, for example, Pearce *et al.* rely on studies which have attempted to predict the cost of climate change over centuries and thus work out the marginal external

Table 3
UK External Costs of Transport
(units: £ billion)

	Pearce et al. (1993)	Mauch and Rothengatter (1995)	RCEP (1994)	Maddison et al. (1996)
Year	1991	1991	1994/5	1993
Accidents	4.7–7.5	13.3	5.4	2.9–9.4
Noise	0.6	3.4		2.6–3.1
Air pollution and climate change	2.8	10.3	4.6–12.9	19.8
Total	8.1–10.9	27.0	10.0–18.3	25.3–39.3

cost of the emissions which cause it. Most such studies only examine the effect on GDP, and typically they use results for the USA to generalize to the world as a whole. Generally these costs are found to be relatively small when discounted (even at low rates of discount) and expressed per unit of emissions. According to their methodology, it is only worth incurring a very small increase in costs or loss of benefit from reduced travel to offset the effects of climate change. In other words, according to the results of Pearce et al., climate change should be a fairly minor consideration in transport policy.

Mauch and Rothengatter adopt a totally different approach. They do not attempt to cost climate change. Rather they take the view that, in the light of the uncertainties involved, the precautionary principle should rule and targets for the reduction of greenhouse gases should be achieved. They select the fairly stringent target of a reduction in greenhouse-gas emissions for western Europe of 50 per cent by the year 2040, this target being met 50 per cent by an equiproportionate reduction and 50 per cent by a move towards an equal emissions allowance per capita. In this case, the costs of additional transport emissions of greenhouse gases, in terms of the need to offset these by reductions in greenhouse-gas emissions elsewhere in the economy, are very much greater than the direct damage cost estimates used by Pearce et al. In other words, Mauch and Rothengatter are using an approach which rests on politically determined standards rather than a direct attempt to assess the damage caused by global warming. The same issue arises regarding valuation of a number of other pollutants.

The Royal Commission study reinforces the uncertainty by quoting a wide range of figures, while that of Maddison et al. (essentially the same team as Pearce et al.) appears to have reached a consensus with

Rothengatter and Mauch at the upper end of the range. However, the consensus is more apparent than real; the main reason why Maddison *et al.* have greatly increased their figures is new evidence on the health effects of small particulate matter from (mainly) diesel engines; this evidence was not available at the time of the earlier studies.

Thus, while there may be problems resulting from different studies giving different results which derive from inadequacies in valuation methodology, many of the differences in this case derive from a far more fundamental source. The basic issue is whether it is appropriate to seek to value directly effects which may be poorly understood and remote in time, or to derive values which result from an environmental policy which put forward standards in the form of constraints within which conventional economic analysis may proceed. The notion of sustainability as most commonly defined (i.e. seeking to meet the needs of the current generation without compromising the ability of future generations to meet their needs) might be taken, in the face of uncertainty, as lending support to the second view.

It should be noted, however, that attempts to value the total external cost of transport are not necessarily very helpful when it comes to pricing and investment decisions. What is needed is the *marginal* cost in specific circumstances. The costs of noise and local air pollution vary greatly with location and time of day, and the relationship between emissions and social cost is not necessarily linear (for instance, it is generally stated that changes in noise of less than 3 dB(A) are imperceptible; changes in some pollutants below a safe threshold may involve no cost). Table 3 also makes no attempt to value many site-specific costs, such as property destruction and visual intrusion.

Table 4 reproduces the range of estimates of the external accident and environmental costs of different modes of transport for case studies undertaken in a number of EU-funded projects. Again, it may be seen that the range of estimates is large. In part this reflects the differences in the circumstances between the case studies, and in different vehicle types, but it is hard to believe that this is the sole cause of the variation. Nevertheless, it does seem safe to conclude that the expected results — that external costs of road transport are much higher in urban areas than on inter-urban roads, and that except at low load factors external costs are less for rail transport than road — hold. On the higher values of air pollution, diesel buses do not come out of the comparison well, however, because of the importance of particulates in the calculation; only at occupancies well above the current average in Britain do they appear to have lower environmental and accident costs than the private car.

Table 4
Range of Illustrative Values from Recent Research,[a] 1995
(ECU/1,000 vehicle or train km)

Mode	Accidents	Air pollution	Noise	Climate change[b]	Total without congestion
Cars					
urban	56.0–204.0	7.3–83.8[c]		2.3–5.4	65.6–293.2[h]
inter-urban	8.0–25.0	7.8–109.0[d]	3.3–13.5	2.0–10.1	29.1–157.6
Trucks					
urban		23.9–912.6[e]		6.0–24.2	29.9–936.8[i]
inter-urban	50.0–60.0	20.0–343.5[f]	71.2–277.7	22.1–68.4	163.3–749.6
Bus: diesel	814–870.0	152–1,575	210	7.9–8.7	1,183.9–2,663.7
Tram/					
underground	8.0	19.2		33.1	60.3[h]
Rail					
passenger	13.0–36.0	36.8–500.6[g]	50.6–455.6	14.6–460.5	115–1,452.7
goods	13.0–36.0	91.0–723.1[g]	848–3,152.0	48–1,744	1,000–5,655.1
Air passenger	7.0–35.0	804.0	250	710	1,771–1,799

Notes: [a] Ranges are built by selecting the lowest and the highest of values of all case studies reviewed; [b] illustrative restricted range: 66–170 ECU/tC; [c] range consists of petrol cars with three-way catalytic convertor (TWC): 7.3–12.2; petrol cars without TWC: 33.0–37.5, diesel cars: 49.1–83.8; [d] values differ for the three main technologies and also for different European routes; [e] range consists of light goods vehicle (LGV): 23.9–133.8 and heavy goods vehicle (HGV): 219.3–912.6; [f] range consists of LGV: 20.0 and HGV: 53.9–343.5; [g] depending heavily on location and fuel mix (the lowest result is estimated for a Swiss route); [h] without noise; [i] without accidents and noise.
Source: CAPRI (1999).

The most recent attempt to recommend values for the DoT to use in practice (Tinch, 1995) was relatively pessimistic. He only felt able to recommend values for noise and local air pollution. Figures for global warming he felt were not robust, and other effects generally had inadequate evidence (Table 5).

5. Relevance of Values for Practical Policy Decisions

In practice, there are two main ways in which valuations of externalities might be used. These are in transport pricing policy and in cost–benefit

Table 5
Suggested Values of Environment for Use in Transport Appraisals (£)

	Low	Best estimate	High
Noise (per dB(A) per person p.a.)	5.50	7.75	10.00
Health effects of local air pollution (PM_{10}) per gm^{-3} per person per annum (urban)	5.75	11.50	17.25
Global warming		Estimates not robust	
Land take, visual amenity		Site-specific	
Other effects		Inadequate evidence	

Source: Tinch (1995).

analysis of transport investments or other transport projects (such as regulatory measures).

In an ideal world, vehicles would be charged in accordance with the externalities they created. This would require a pricing structure in which a price per kilometre was charged which varied with:

(a) the characteristics of the vehicle, which determine the noise, emissions, delay to other vehicles, and accident risk involved. Strictly, these obviously depend not just on the characteristics of the vehicle when new, but also on its condition and the way it is driven; accurate measurement would therefore require continuous monitoring of every vehicle on the road;

(b) the characteristics of the road it is being driven on, including physical features (width, gradient, curvature) of the road itself and the surrounding land use (housing, countryside, etc.). These again influence both the congestion effects and the environmental impact;

(c) the time at which it is being driven (which is important in terms of the degree to which noise is a nuisance) and the traffic conditions on the road at that time.

Such a pricing structure, in which the price per kilometre is adjusted in accordance with continuous monitoring of the location and condition of the vehicle and the road conditions in which it is being driven is currently still in the world of science fiction, although the road pricing proposals recently considered in Cambridge, in which the charge would depend on traffic speeds, would, if implemented, represent a significant move towards fulfilling it for a particular city. Even if it were technically feasible, one would still need to consider whether it was worth the cost of implementation, and whether people would actually adjust more effectively to a simpler more understandable tariff than one where one would not know the price one was going to be charged for a journey at the time of setting out on it.

What most countries have at the moment is a very different structure consisting of a fuel tax, which may vary with the type of fuel (diesel, leaded/unleaded petrol) and an annual fee which varies with the type of vehicle. Additional tolls may be charged on motorways (where one might expect that typically external costs would be less than on other types of road). This structure of charges offers some possibility for influencing both the type of vehicle people buy and the extent to which it is used, but can only charge for external costs on the average in each case. The case remains then for using a variety of other means to influence the way in which vehicles are used in specific circumstances. These means might include pricing measures (e.g. electronic road pricing in particular areas, kilometre-based taxes using metering of specific types of heavy goods vehicles) and physical measures (bans on particular types of vehicles, parking controls, traffic management). There is no prospect in the foreseeable future of being able to handle transport externalities solely through pricing measures, even if that were clearly seen as the most efficient approach. Nevertheless, having information on the value attached to the externality in question is an essential element in the appraisal of any measure to overcome the problem of transport externalities.

If the application of money values of externalities in pricing is not straightforward, what about the position regarding project appraisal? The position in Britain is that environmental effects of road building are not explicitly valued in money terms. For many years they have been considered along with those items (construction and maintenance costs, operating cost savings, time savings, and accidents) that are valued in money terms in a table of impacts based on that originally recommended by the report of the Advisory Committee on Trunk Road assessment back in 1978, and still often referred to, after the Chairman of that committee, as the 'Leitch framework' (Leitch, 1978). Some idea of the range of effects taken into account in this approach is given in Table 6. This permitted the full consideration of local environmental impacts (regional and global effects are not considered) of a particular road scheme when the individual decision is taken. But because the formal cost–benefit analysis was undertaken excluding valuation of environmental impacts, it did not contribute to more strategic decisions about road investment. Benefit–cost ratios for individual schemes were quite misleading as a guide to the extent to which resources should be diverted from elsewhere in the economy into building roads, partly because of the omission of environmental costs but also because they were assessed as the rate of return on short stretches of new road and

Table 6
Costs and Benefits of Road Schemes:
The Leitch Framework

Incidence group	Nature of effect	No. of financial measures	No. of other measures
Road-users	Accidents	1	3
	Comfort/convenience	6	
	Operating costs	5	
	Amenity		2
Non-road-users directly affected	Demolition disamenity (houses, shops, offices, factories, schools, churches, public open space)		37
	Land take, severance, disamenity to farmers		7
Those concerned	Landscape, scientific, historical value, land-use, other transport operators		9 (+ verbal description)
Financing authority	Costs and benefits in money terms	7	
TOTAL		19	59

Source: Leitch, 1978.

on the assumption that traffic growth is going to be allowed to continue at a substantial rate—i.e. they fail to look strategically at alternative policies for corridors or areas as a whole.

Given the above discussion of the difficulties of environmental valuation, would the introduction of money values for environmental effects in investment appraisal be beneficial? (This issue was discussed by the Standing Advisory Committee on Trunk Road Appraisal (SACTRA, 1992).) In favour of such a move would be the fact that it would permit a more accurate assessment of the overall rate of return on road building to be assessed, that it would ensure that regional and global environmental externalities were taken into account as well as local, and that it would promote clarity and consistency at the level of decisions on individual schemes. Against it are the arguments that environmental valuation remains very uncertain, that as we have seen above there is no consensus even about the basic principles on which it should be based, and that it is usually incomplete. At the project appraisal level, valuation of local environmental effects is particularly problematic, in that it is dealing with the value to be placed on particular assets such as parks, buildings, and the aesthetic amenity of the townscape or landscape.

In 1998, the government announced both the development of a series of corridor studies, designed to look at multi-modal options for corridors as a whole, and the introduction of a new appraisal frame-work, linked more specifically to the objectives in the White Paper, and listed above (DETR, 1998*m*). A specific list of indicators related to each objective is defined, and where other quantification is impossible, the impacts are rated on a seven-point scale, which ranges from large beneficial effect through moderate, small, or neutral to large harmful effect. The list of indicators used has also been improved, and specifi-cally the effect on greenhouse-gas emissions has been added. (This follows acceptance by DETR that new road building may generate additional road traffic and thus contribute to the problem of global warming.) However, aggregation of all these measures remains a matter of judgement; there is still no formal weighting of the various indicators to produce an overall summary measure of the value of the scheme. If values for factors which are, in principle, readily measured, such as noise and air pollution, are to be used in pricing decisions — and arguably here there is no choice — then there seems no good reason not to use them in project appraisal as well. What is of more doubt is whether it makes sense to introduce values of unique local features into project appraisal. But it must always be remembered that if this is not done, then any benefit–cost ratios quoted are incomplete and mislead-ing.

6. Conclusion

We have seen that the treatment of environmental effects of transport projects in transport policy has undertaken radical change over the past decade. From a position where the appropriate policy was seen as one of forecasting transport demand and building new facilities accord-ingly, we have moved to a situation where a complex range of measures is seen as being necessary to take adequate account of environmental effects as part of an integrated transport policy.

A common view of transport externalities is that they are a relatively simple case of market failure, to be resolved by valuing them in money terms and charging a tax which will lead decision-takers to place appropriate weight on them when making transport decisions. In reality the position is much more complex than this. First, we have found that there is no consensus on the principles that should be used in environmental valuation, and in particular on when it is appropriate to use willingness-to-pay-type measures and when opportunity cost derived from environmental standards. Second, we have found that, even if there is agreement in principle, existing methods of valuation are not adequate reliably to value all the relevant externalities. Third, we have found that it is not possible actually to devise pricing structures which fully reflect the way in which external costs vary across vehicles, times, and places.

Nevertheless, significant progress on quantifying and valuing environmental costs of transport has been made. At the end of the day, a political judgement has to be made on how much it is worth paying to reduce their costs, but at least that judgement can now be better informed. Through the reforms it is proposing, including powers to introduce urban road pricing, corridor studies, and the new appraisal framework, the government is providing the instruments to take these costs into account more adequately in pricing and investment decisions. Whether it will actually do so remains to be seen.

12

The UK Landfill Tax

INGER BRISSON AND JANE POWELL*

1. Introduction

The landfill tax was introduced into the fiscal framework of the United Kingdom on 1 October 1996, and immediately acquired landmark status. This rank can be explained by two reasons; first, the tax was designed to reflect the actual environmental cost of landfilling waste, and so it became the first true environmental tax in the UK. Second, in a further digression from previous practice, the Treasury agreed to the hypothecation of a portion of the revenue from the tax, to facilitate the search for alternative methods of waste disposal.

This chapter reviews the background to the introduction of the landfill tax, and discusses the final version of the tax. It continues by assessing the efficacy of the tax, and endeavours to ascertain whether further improvements are warranted, or whether the measure needs to be complemented by other regulatory or economic instruments.

2. The Background of the Landfill Tax

The predominant historical method for the disposal of solid waste in the UK has been landfilling.[1] The extractive industries have continually created a large number of potential sites, which appeared to offer an effective, and inexpensive, solution to the disposal of waste. This is in marked contrast to the approach adopted in other western countries, which has either involved the development of their waste incineration capacity, feeding the generated heat and power into their district

---

* Respectively, IERM, University of Edinburgh, and CSERGE, University of East Anglia.
[1] The term solid waste in this context includes household as well as industrial and hazardous waste.

Table 1
Waste Management 1985–98 in the UK, Denmark, Germany, and the Netherlands (%)

	UK		Germany		Netherlands			Denmark	
	'90	'97	'90	'93	'85	'90	'96	'85	'96
Landfill	85	63	68	55	42	31	16	39	20
Incineration	4	2	3	4	7	8	11	26	19
Recycling	7	31	21	25	51	61	74	35	60

Sources: DoE (1990*b*); DETR (1999*j*); European Environment Agency (1998); National Reference Centres (1998*a,b*).

heating systems and national grids, or their respective recycling industries. Both these options have enjoyed only limited take-up in the UK.

However, when the Thatcher government introduced the 1990 Environmental Protection Act (DoE, 1990*a*) it appeared this was about to change. This act sought, among a number of other objectives, to minimize waste disposal, through the promotion of recycling and the introduction of higher standards for the disposal of waste. Integrated Pollution Control (IPC) was to assist in attaining this objective, and a target was set, specifying the recycling of 25 per cent of household waste by the year 2000 (50 per cent of the estimated potentially recyclable content of household waste).

Table 1 provides a comparative illustration of the respective proportions of total household waste in the UK, the Netherlands, Denmark, and Germany, that were landfilled, incinerated, and recycled over the period 1985–97.

This policy was given added, albeit nominal, impetus, by the broad commitment of local authorities to Local Agenda 21.[2] In the context of sustainable waste management, Local Agenda 21 requires local authorities to decrease their dependence on the landfilling of waste, and employ a hierarchical approach in their waste-management practices, to attain this objective. This hierarchy ranks the options in the following order of preference: the minimization of waste generation, reuse,

[2] Local Agenda 21 is a term that originates from the international Earth Summit in Rio in 1992. Over 150 nations, including the UK, endorsed the Agenda 21 document, which set out how developed and developing countries can work together towards sustainable development. A high proportion of the actions in Agenda 21 requires the active involvement of local authorities. Chapter 28 called on local authorities to initiate Local Agenda 21 processes which would develop partnerships for sustainable development at a local level.

Box 1
The Waste Hierarchy

1. Reduction   Reducing the production of waste to the minimum consistent with economic sustainability.

2. Reuse   Putting objects back into use, e.g. reusing glass bottles.

3. Recovery   (i) Recycling – putting materials back into use, e.g. reusing the glass from bottles.
               (ii) Composting – processing organic waste to produce a soil conditioner or growing medium.
               (iii) Energy – burning waste and recovering the energy.

4. Disposal   Incineration or landfill without energy recovery; the emphasis being on ensuring that disposal is environmentally sound.

---

recycling, recovery of energy, and, finally, disposal to sanitary landfills representing the 'last resort' (see Box 1). Thus, Local Agenda 21 requires local authorities to adopt the waste hierarchy as their lodestar for waste management.

A further policy amendment emerged in 1992, when a recycling credit scheme was introduced. This scheme requires waste-disposal authorities to pass on any savings in landfill costs, which are realized through recycling, to the collection authorities (Turner and Brisson, 1995). This measure is intended to improve the sustainability of waste management through the broader application of the principles of the waste hierarchy. The underlying rationale is that by decreasing the costs of recycling relative to landfill the financial viability of the former will be strengthened.

It is also likely that the negotiations about a new EU Landfill Directive influenced UK government thinking and policy, at the time the landfill tax was under consideration. This Directive came into force on 16 July 1999.[3] In its final form, it imposes significant curbs on the amount of organic waste that can be landfilled.

3. The Origins of the Landfill Tax

In the UK, as in many other countries, the traditional approach to environmental problems was through regulatory measures, the so-called 'command-and-control' measures. These approaches have a number of advantages. They offer a way of hiding the true cost of

---

[3] Council Directive 1999/31/EC.

environmental protection, and thus avoid political discussion about the distributional impacts of new taxes and charges. Second, they are often more acceptable to the labour-force, as they increase costs, rather than impose a requirement to reduce subsidies, and hence endanger employment. Finally, a number of environmental pressure groups, and the public at large, often prefer a regulatory framework because they believe this offers a better guarantee of environmental protection (OECD, 1993).

However, the regulatory approach has been challenged in academic circles for a number of years, and there is now increasing emphasis on the potential contribution of market-based, or economic instruments, in the attainment of policy targets (see, for example, Pearce and Turner, 1990; Gale and Barg, 1995; Smith, 1995). This is not to say that the limitations of these are not also recognized (Bohm and Russell, 1985; Baumol and Oates, 1988). The rationale of the market-based approach is that an economic instrument, by focusing on the price rather than quantities, can attain, at least, the same level of environmental protection as a regulatory measure, but in a more efficient manner.

Waste management was seen as an area of environmental protection that appeared suitable for the introduction of radical new measures, and, as such, was deemed a suitable test bed for an economic instrument. A first step along the road to the design of an appropriate instrument was the commissioning of research into landfill pricing and the use of economic instruments.

One conclusion of this research was that economic instruments, specifically collection or disposal charges, represented an efficient way of internalizing the externalities of waste disposal, and would, therefore, be expected to reduce the amount of waste going to landfill (Environmental Resources Limited, 1992). A further justification for the introduction of a landfill tax was that, as it would, presumably, reflect the wider environmental costs of landfill, it would indirectly encourage recycling and waste minimization, and equalize UK landfill costs with those of other EU countries.

It was envisaged that such a tax, together with tighter planning controls, would increase landfill costs, and together with a predicted decrease in the costs of incineration, cause a partial shift from landfill to incineration. However, even a landfill tax as high as £20 per tonne of waste was expected to have only negligible effects on recycling, which was expected to reach only 12 per cent, by the year 2000 (Coopers & Lybrand, 1993). Despite these rather pessimistic conclusions, and the express target of increasing recycling, it was decided to press ahead and further examine the option of a landfill tax.

Further research involved the estimation of the externalities of landfill and incineration, within the context of a landfill tax (CSERGE *et al.*, 1993). The calculations were based on the respective contributions of landfill and incineration of waste to the emission of global and regional air pollutants. The results suggested an external cost of approximately £1–2 per tonne of waste in the case of landfills where energy was recovered from landfill gas, and approximately £4 per tonne of waste for landfills without energy recovery. Waste incineration was estimated to result in an external benefit of £2–4 per tonne of waste, owing to avoided, or reduced, emissions of global and regional air pollutants in this case. These results suggested an 'externality differential' between landfill and incineration in the order of £6–8 per tonne of waste, which in turn suggested that an appropriate level for the landfill tax, would be £6–8 per tonne of waste for landfills without energy recovery.

However, this study was constrained both by scope and by the available technical information, and so consideration was restricted to a subset of total potential externalities. The respective contribution of the various disposal methods to water pollution, toxic air pollution from incineration such as dioxins, or the disamenity effects[4] associated with the waste-disposal facilities, were not considered.[5]

4. The Introduction of the Landfill Tax

The proposal to introduce a new tax on waste disposed to landfill was announced in the Budget of November 1994. The tax was to take effect from 1996, and was to be collected by HM Customs and Excise. The detailed proposals were unveiled in March 1995, when a consultation paper was released and comments sought from interested parties.

---

[4] Disamenity effects in this context are the loss in quality of life due to the presence of waste-treatment facilities, e.g. effects caused by unpleasant odours and visual intrusion.

[5] Subsequently a cost–benefit analysis was undertaken for the European Union (Coopers & Lybrand *et al.*, 1996), which examined recycling and composting in addition to landfill and incineration. While there were some differences in the estimated externalities associated with landfill and incineration compared with the earlier UK study, they were in the same ballpark. However, frustration over the omission of externalities associated with water and soil contamination has led the European Commission to commission new research to be carried out in 2000, to identify the available information relating to these media and to recommend further research on these externalities.

The stated objectives of the landfill tax were:

* to ensure that landfill waste disposal is properly priced, which will promote greater efficiency in the waste management market and in the economy as a whole; and
* to apply the polluter pays principle and promote a more sustainable approach to waste management in which we produce less waste, and reuse or recover value from more waste. (HM Customs and Excise, 1995a)

The overall aim of the tax was to increase the proportion of waste managed by the techniques at the top of the hierarchy of waste management options (see Box 1). The tax was also seen as a way of demonstrating the government's commitment to the use of economic instruments as a means of achieving environmental objectives (HM Customs and Excise, 1995). It represented a first move by the government to transfer taxation away from labour and profits and towards pollution and resource use.

The latter aim has since gained additional importance in the light of the need to reduce landfill to fulfil the obligations, which have arisen under the recent EU Directive on landfill. This Directive (Council Directive 1999/31/EC), which will have to be transposed on to the British statute book by 16 July 2001 at the latest, will impose a number of additional legally binding targets.

* Policy-makers will be required to reduce the amount of biodegradable municipal waste going to landfill in three successive stages, over a 15–19-year period. The stages will include: 75 per cent of 1995 biodegradable municipal waste arisings after 5 years, 50 per cent after 8 years, and, eventually, 35 per cent.
* A ban will be introduced on the landfill of certain hazardous waste, liquid wastes, and tyres.
* Separate landfills will be required for hazardous, non-hazardous and inert waste, effectively ending the current practice in the UK of co-disposing of particular hazardous wastes with non-hazardous waste.
* Waste to be landfilled, with certain exceptions, will require prior treatment, to reduce the hazard to human health or the environment, and to reduce the quantity of the waste.

The initial proposal outlined in the government's consultation paper was for an *ad valorem* landfill tax, of 30–50 per cent on the disposal price paid. An *ad valorem* tax was recommended on the basis that it would provide a straightforward proxy for the environmental impacts of landfill disposal. The line of argument was that, by charging in proportion to the costs of landfill disposal, it would result in a higher tax for more 'difficult' wastes, which were more expensive to dispose of, and a lower tax for inert waste, which is cheaper to dispose of. Also, the tax would be higher where land was scarcest and the impact on communities was greatest.

The compliance costs of an *ad valorem* tax were also considered to be lower than for a weight-based tax, and evasion easier to detect (HM Customs and Excise, 1995). Based on an estimate of 100m tonnes of waste disposed to landfill in England and Wales each year, at a cost of £10/tonne, an *ad valorem* tax rate of 50 per cent would raise £500m. If a 30 per cent tax rate were set, this would raise £300m per year.

The tax was not intended to impose additional costs on business. Therefore, the government proposed to use the revenue to offset the impact of the new tax by making reductions in employers' National Insurance contributions (HM Customs and Excise, 1995). The landfill tax would pay for an 0.2 per cent cut in National Insurance contributions (ENDS, 1995). There would also be the potential for landfill operators to obtain tax rebates by making payments to proposed Environmental Trusts.

Some of the responses to the consultation document were against a tax on landfill *per se*. They saw no technological, financial, or moral justification as to why landfill was 'bad', and therefore argued that singling landfill out for taxation was unfair. The majority of the responses, however, were slightly more considered, expressing support for a landfill tax, in principle, but declaring misgivings about an *ad valorem* tax. It was perceived that the initial intention of internalizing externalities arising from landfill disposal, had been abandoned in favour of a revenue-raising exercise (ENDS, 1995), and that an *ad valorem* tax would increase the existing price differential between sites. This would penalize those expensive sites with higher environmental standards, and contribute both to an increase in environmental pollution and the transport of wastes over long distances (ACBE, 1995; CIC, 1995). These latter concerns were explicitly acknowledged as valid by HM Customs and Excise (Romanski, 1995).

The transportation of waste to cheaper sites would directly contradict government policy to raise landfill standards and promote regional self-sufficiency in waste disposal (UK Waste, 1995), and reduce revenues to the Treasury. Furthermore, if hazardous wastes were attracted to cheaper co-disposal sites,[6] their operators would require more household waste for its attenuating properties, and might be prepared to reduce prices charged for household waste (ENDS, 1995).

---

[6] Co-disposal sites are landfill sites where hazardous waste is co-disposed with non-hazardous waste.

A number of responses suggested that a weight-based landfill tax would be preferable, arguing that this would result in lower price differentials, that the revenue would be more predictable, and that, with calibrated weigh-bridges, there would be less scope for fraud and evasion (UK Waste, 1995).

5. The Final Form of the Landfill Tax

The consultation process contributed significantly to the final form of the landfill tax. The *ad valorem* tax was abandoned in favour of a weight-based tax, which was set at two levels, reflecting the estimated externalities associated with landfill (CSERGE *et al.*, 1993). Inert waste, such as construction waste, which does not release greenhouse gases, was to be taxed at £2 per tonne of waste. Active waste, on the other hand, which includes all other types of solid waste, such as putrescible waste, was to be taxed at a higher level of £7 per tonne, reflecting the higher potential environmental impacts in the form of greenhouse-gas releases and potential for leaching. The tax was introduced on 1 October 1996, and it represented, as mentioned earlier, the first true environmental tax in the UK.

On 1 April 1999, two and a half years after the tax first came into force, the rate for active waste was increased to £10 per tonne. Furthermore, the 1999 Budget contained an announcement of the proposed introduction of a tax escalator, which will result in the tax on active waste increasing by £1 every year until 2004/05, at which point it will have reached £15 per tonne.

The introduction of the landfill tax was sweetened by a *de facto* digression from the orthodox Treasury principle of no hypothecation of tax revenues. However, as the Treasury was not willing explicitly to acknowledge the precedent of hypothecation, a degree of sophistry was required. This involved the establishment of the so-called Environmental Bodies Credit Scheme, which has private-sector status. Under this scheme, any landfill operator can choose to pay up to 20 per cent of its landfill tax dues, as voluntary contributions to an approved Environmental Body of its choice. The landfill operator will receive a 90 per cent tax credit on the contribution.

Since the money flows from the operator to the charity, and is then allowed as a tax credit by the Treasury, rather than from the operator to the Treasury to the charity, technically, the flow of money is an allowable donation, rather than a tax. Therefore the tax revenues are not, *de jure*, hypothecated. The argument was summarized succinctly by Michael Meacher, the Minister of Environment, in evidence to the Select

Committee on Environment, Transport and Regional Affairs (SCETRA, hereafter referred to as the Select Committee): 'These are monies which are dispensed by landfill operators. It is not direct public expenditure' (SCETRA, 1999). The aims of the scheme were to help reduce reliance on landfill and to compensate those living in the vicinity of landfill sites by 'environmental improvements'.

6. The Operation of the Landfill Tax

The landfill tax raised £361m in 1997/8, and the recent increase from £7 to £10 per tonne of active waste is expected to raise another £100m per year. The accelerator is expected to add a further £45m per year for each future £1 increase (HM Customs and Excise, 1999). This suggests that by 2005, the tax will have raised approximately £4.3 billion.

In the spring of 1998, the Select Committee began an investigation into sustainable waste management (SCETRA, 1998). During the course of the investigation, the committee considered the issue of the landfill tax. It had received a number of comments about the deleterious effect of the tax, most notably in respect of: (i) a perceived increase in fly-tipping; (ii) the diversion of commercial waste to exempted sites such as golf courses; and (iii) its impact on local authorities.

A first general problem that was noted by the Select Committee related to the lack of available data on waste, both before and after the introduction of the tax. Thus, it stated: 'The continuing lack of information in Government about waste is extraordinary: . . . The production of accurate statistics on waste arising, the composition of waste at the point of arising and on the demographic structure of households (which affects that composition) must be a Government priority' (SCETRA, 1998).

Thus, in its deliberations, the Select Committee relied primarily on evidence by waste managers, industry, and local authorities. It decided to examine the issues, broadly delineated into five areas:
  (a) the level of the tax;
  (b) fly-tipping;
  (c) the tax on inert waste;
  (d) the effect on local authorities; and
  (e) the Environmental Bodies Credit Scheme.

(a) *The Level of the Tax*

The tax of £7 per tonne of active waste, which was first introduced in 1996, was not found to have had any discernible effect on the amount of waste being landfilled. Thus, the proposed increases in the landfill tax, and the prospective introduction of the accelerator, in the 1999 Budget, were intended to send 'a tough signal to waste managers to look for more environmentally friendly alternatives to landfill', according to Patricia Hewitt, the Economic Secretary to the Treasury.[7]

Hewitt also argued against raising the landfill tax to much higher levels, saying, 'We do not have the kind of evidence which would allow us to say that £15 is the optimal level, or £30 or £40 or any other figure. In the absence of that kind of really good data we think it would be very foolish to pluck a very high figure out of the air' (SCETRA, 1999).

By contrast, the opinion of waste managers was that an increase to £10 per tonne and, ultimately, to £15 per tonne of waste, was too weak a signal to industry, who would, it was predicted, continue to see landfill as the most cost-effective way to dispose of its waste. The waste managers also predicted that the landfill tax will only have a negligible effect on encouraging investment in sustainable waste treatment technologies, suggesting that a level of £25–40 per tonne would be necessary before the tax had a discernible effect on the amount of waste being landfilled. This confirms the conclusion drawn by Coopers & Lybrand 6 years previously, that even at £20 per tonne, a landfill tax would only have negligible effects on recycling (Coopers & Lybrand, 1993). This view is also supported by the recycling rates that have been achieved after the introduction of the landfill tax. Thus, in England and Wales only 8 per cent of household waste was recycled or composted in 1998/9 (ENDS, 1999), while Scotland recycled less than 7 per cent of household waste in 1998/9 (ENDS, 2000).

The Select Committee concluded that the landfill tax, even after the proposed increases, had been introduced merely as a revenue-raising measure. This conclusion is supported by the figures contained in the Treasury Red Book, which illustrates the expected revenue in each year of the tax. The fact that the increase in revenue from the escalator is a flat £45m *per annum*, suggests that the Treasury does not expect the tax increase to engender any behavioural changes, together with an associated reduction in the tax revenue.

The Select Committee concluded that if

the tax is to achieve its objective of reducing the amount of waste sent to landfill, it must be set at a level which changes the economics of waste management so that less environmentally damaging options such as recycling, composting and energy-from-waste plants are no more expensive than landfill. To do this the tax on active waste would need to rise from its present level of £10 per tonne to a level of around £30 per tonne. We recommend that

[7] Giving oral evidence to the environment subcommittee (SCETRA, 1999).

the tax rise to £20 per tonne over the next five years and that the Government set out its proposals for additional increases in the following years. (SCETRA, 1999)

(b) *Fly-tipping*

One of the concerns raised during the initial consultation period was that the introduction of a tax of this form, would increase the potential for fly-tipping. These concerns appear to have been groundless, as since the introduction of the tax, neither the Environment Agency nor the Scottish Environment Protection Agency has found any concrete evidence of an increase in fly-tipping.

However, the Select Committee did report anecdotal evidence of increased fly-tipping. There were submissions from industry, regulators, local authorities, and the Department of the Environment, Transport and the Regions (DETR), noting the problem and suggesting that the practice is likely to increase in line with the tax escalator. Further evidence was provided by a survey of farmers, by the National Farmers Union, which found that almost two-thirds of respondents believed that fly-tipping had increased since the introduction of the tax. In addition about 60 per cent of local authorities have detected an increase in the problem (SCETRA, 1999).

The Select Committee suggested one reason why increased fly-tipping might have followed the introduction of the landfill tax, namely, that efficient enforcement had not been put in place, and that the courts were not fully informed about environmental offences. In the light of this, it made two recommendations. First, it recommended that 'the Government should review the penalties imposed by the courts for environmental crimes and ensure that magistrates receive training which indicates the seriousness of such crimes and the need for appropriate sanctions'.

Second, it recommended that the

> revenues from the landfill tax over and above those channelled through the Credit Scheme should be used both to mitigate some of the undesirable effects of the tax, notably the increase in fly tipping ... and to help achieve the aims of the tax by being redirected into measures to encourage recycling and waste minimisation. (SCETRA, 1999).

(c) *The Tax on Inert Waste*

The landfill tax for inert waste, despite being set at the lower rate of £2 per tonne of waste, appears to have had a significant impact. One estimate suggests that, in the first year after the introduction of the tax, 20–30m tonnes of inert waste were diverted from licensed landfill sites.[8] This is in line with experience in Denmark, where the introduction of a landfill tax in 1987 has gradually been escalated. The current level of DKK335 (EUR45) per tonne, has resulted in a significant increase in the recycling of construction and demolition waste. Thus, in 1985, 2 years prior to the introduction of the Danish landfill tax, the proportion of this type of inert waste being recycled was 12 per cent, but by 1993 this had risen to 82 per cent (Miljøstyrelsen, 1995).

The DETR and Customs and Excise view the development in the amount of inert waste being diverted from landfill positively, and perceive it to reflect the effectiveness of the tax. However, the waste-management industry, planning authorities, and the regulatory authorities have a different view. They believe it is simply a case of waste being diverted to unregulated sites, such as golf courses, which are exempt from waste management licensing. Concern has been expressed that these sites do not have the facilities to assess this material scientifically, and thus there is a danger that some active, or even hazardous, material, such as asbestos, might be finding its way into unlicensed sites.

A second impact of the tax on inert waste has arisen from waste soils and hardcore, previously used for engineering works at the landfill to meet the necessary pollution controls, now being taxed at the inert-waste rate. In many cases, this has led to it being more cost-effective to purchase primary materials for the engineering work, than to use the waste soils. Thus, this unintended aspect of the landfill tax appears to have destroyed a very common-sense regime of utilizing inert waste soils that had previously existed, and imposed an additional environmental burden in the form of unnecessary extraction of primary materials. In this light, the Select Committee recommends that inert materials used for engineering purposes, including daily cover at licensed landfill sites, are exempt from the tax (SCETRA, 1999).

(d) *Effect on Local Authorities*

While the rate of the landfill tax does not appear to be set high enough to have an impact on waste disposal choice, it does, however, impose a significant additional financial burden on local authorities who are responsible for the disposal of household waste in the UK. Approximately 27m tonnes of municipal waste is generated each year in the UK, of which 85 per cent is disposed of to landfill (DETR, 1999k). Thus, at the current rate, the tax burden on local authorities is about £229.5m.

---

[8] Mr Jones from Biffa Waste Services in oral evidence to the environment sub-committee (SCETRA, 1999).

However, since the introduction of the tax, household waste managed by local authorities has increased by 5.5 per cent, owing to a
diversion of waste from commercial and industrial sources into the
household waste stream. Also, any fly-tipped waste becomes the
responsibility of the local authority, upon which they would be required to pay the landfill tax on disposal.

These influences, together with the current pressure on many local
authority budgets, have engendered a rather perverse concomitant to
the landfill tax in some local authorities. Thus, a number of local
authorities are diverting money from improving recycling facilities, in
order to be able to pay the tax. It is believed that this effect will be even
more pronounced, as the planned escalation of the tax comes into force.

While private-sector waste-managers may be able to act according
to the incentive provided by the landfill tax, thus reducing the amount
of waste to be landfilled, local waste authorities do not have this option,
as they do not control the amount of waste produced. On the contrary,
they are legally obliged to collect and dispose of any household waste
and must not relate what they charge via the council tax to the amount
of waste arising from an individual household.

While local authorities would, not surprisingly, like to see a number
of changes, ranging from the exemption of household waste and fly-
tipped waste from the tax, to direct charging of householders for waste
collected, the Select Committee considers most of them to be impractical. The Committee opposes charging individual households for the
disposal of waste by quantity, as they consider it ineffective and likely
to produce unwanted side effects, such as the dumping of waste in
neighbours' dustbins. As an alternative, the Select Committee recommends that local authorities ensure that recycling schemes are more
effective through education and introduction of segregation at source.
However, the Committee, having acknowledged the increased pressure on local authority budgets, does not offer any suggestions as to
how this might be financed.

(e) The Environmental Bodies Credit Scheme

When the landfill tax was introduced, landfill operators who make
voluntary contributions to Environmental Bodies were allowed tax
credits of 90 per cent of their contributions, up to a maximum of 20 per
cent of their tax due.

The aims of the scheme are to help reduce reliance on landfill and to
compensate those living in the vicinity of landfill sites by 'environmental improvements'. There are six approved objectives, namely:

A   reclamation of land, the use of which was prevented because of
     its previous use;
B   reduction of pollution or the effects of pollution on such land;
C   research and development, education, and the collection and
     dissemination of information for the purpose of encouraging
     more sustainable waste-management practices;
D   where it is for the protection of the environment, provision or
     maintenance of a public park or other amenity, provided that it
     is within the vicinity of a landfill site;
E   where it is for the protection of the environment, the restora-
     tion, repair, or maintenance of a building or other structure
     which is for religious worship, or of historical or architectural
     interest, provided that it is within the vicinity of a landfill site
     and open to the public;
F   the provision of administrative or other similar services to other
     Environmental Bodies.

The 1999 Budget statement emphasized the intent to extend C above
to include recycling.

A wide variety of organizations can enrol as Environmental Bodies,
provided they are non-profit distributing and that the qualifying
contributions are spent on the approved objectives. An Environmental
Body must not be controlled, either directly or indirectly, by a local
authority or landfill operator.

Table 2 below shows the distribution of funds between the six
objectives. The majority of the funding is being used for the provision
of public amenity or restoration of buildings, or, to express it in the main
aims of the scheme, 'to compensate for the disamenity effects of landfill
sites'.

The Select Committee (SCETRA, 1999) has expressed concern that a
disproportionate amount of funding is going into the 'information'
categories within the objectives. While the Committee believes that
education is important, it is concerned that some of this might fall in the
publicity category and that contributors are seeking a 'public relations
payback'. The Committee recommends this should be monitored and
must not be excessive. Table 2 also highlights that very little funding is
going towards clean-up of contaminated land.

One of the main aims of the scheme is to reduce reliance on landfill.
Much of the evidence submitted to the Select Committee suggested that
a greater proportion of funds should go to activities which promote
alternatives to landfill, in particular recycling. While the government
supports this view, it argues that the scheme cannot retain its private-
sector status if a public authority dictates the distribution of funds
between the six objectives. However, in its report the Select Committee

Table 2
Division of Expenditure between Objectives

Objective category	Pre-approvals (£m)	Actual spend (£m)	% Funding to each category
A	26	3	6.8
B	1	0.2	0.5
C	137	14.2	32.2
D	339	24.2	54.9
E	88	2	4.5
F	1	0.5	1.1
Total	592	44.1	

Source: SCETRA (1999).

recommends that annual indicative guidelines for distribution to each objective are set by the DETR and monitored by ENTRUST[9] and HM Customs and Excise.

The Treasury argues against the hypothecation of tax revenues on efficiency grounds. When all tax revenues go into the general pool of funds, it argues, the most efficient allocation of resources can be ensured, so that those policies and projects offering the greatest social benefits are those selected for funding. Therefore, having *de facto* accepted hypothecation of 20 per cent of the revenues from the landfill tax to reduce reliance on landfill and to create environmental improvements for those living near landfills, makes it imperative that the funds are allocated to obtain the maximum environmental benefit. However, according to the Select Committee there is little evidence to suggest that this is the case, because there is simply no system for evaluating the environmental benefits of the scheme.

While ENTRUST processes applications for authorization as Environmental Bodies and for individual projects, ENTRUST does not have the powers to evaluate projects on a cost–benefit basis and there is no adequate monitoring of the implementation of schemes nor of their quality. It is the recommendation of the Select Committee that ENTRUST should be given the powers to evaluate schemes using a cost–benefit analysis (SCETRA, 1999).

In addition, the Select Committee in its report expresses concern about a number of potential ways the scheme is open to abuse. First, landfill operators have total discretion with respect to which Environ-

[9] ENTRUST: Environmental Trust Scheme Regulatory Body Limited, a private company limited by guarantee, and appointed by HM Customs and Excise as the Regulator of the Environmental Bodies Credit Scheme.

mental Bodies and which projects will receive their contributions. This means that even if guidelines were issued for the division of funds between the objectives, these would be unlikely to have any effect. Essentially, the landfill operators decide which projects to fund, and thus there is nothing to stop them from only funding projects which they perceive to have some indirect benefit to themselves.

This is related to the second concern, namely that it appears that the operation of the Environmental Bodies is dominated by the waste industry, and the money raised thus far may have gone into projects benefiting public relations rather than the environment (SCETRA, 1998).

Third, the Select Committee also expresses concern that local authorities and landfill operators may wield excessive influence on Environmental Bodies, and that, in some cases, local authorities and landfill operators are in fact represented on the board of Environmental Bodies (SCETRA, 1999). This appears to happen in spite of the clause that landfill operators and local authorities must not control Environmental Bodies. A particular case was reported where an Environmental Body wrote to landfill operators and advised them that if they placed their landfill tax credits with their set-up environmental trust then they (the landfill operators) would gain preferential contractor status. The UK Landfill Tax Credit Scheme User Group pointed out that there was a danger that if local authorities are allowed to control Environmental Bodies they could use this as leverage in planning approvals.[10]

Finally, the Select Committee also expresses concern about the proliferation of third-party contributions to make up the 10 per cent shortfall from landfill operators. The Environmental Bodies scheme gives landfill operators only 90 per cent tax credits for their donations. But some landfill operators refuse to support projects unless third-party donations making up the 10 per cent shortfall can be found. The problem in this, as seen by the Select Committee (SCETRA, 1999), is that these third parties are not registered and regulated by ENTRUST, and only a voluntary code of practice ensures that they do not benefit directly from the projects being funded.

The Select Committee concludes that there is evidence that improvements are being made to the environment but there is insufficient information on the quality of these improvements. There is also inadequate information as to whether the Credit Scheme is reducing reliance on landfill. Therefore, it is not possible to state with any confidence that the Scheme's objectives are being met.

[10] Mr Hardy from the UK Landfill Tax Credit Scheme User Group in oral evidence to the environment subcommittee (SCETRA, 1999).

According to the latest available information for 1997/8, only about 15 per cent of the total 20 per cent potential tax credits are being utilized under the Credit Scheme. The Select Committee recommends that HM Custom and Excise and ENTRUST investigate the possibility of putting arrangements in place which could use under-utilized tax credits.

The Select Committee makes a further recommendation that the tax revenue going to the Treasury should be kept constant, despite any increases in the tax rate. This recommendation is based on the statement by the government, that the landfill tax is a tool intended to reduce the reliance on landfill and is not, primarily, a fiscal instrument. The Committee would like to see the remainder made available to the Environmental Bodies Credit Scheme. If the landfill tax fails to reduce landfill, the percentage of the tax going to the Credit Scheme through tax credits accordingly should rise above 20 per cent.

7. Has the Landfill Tax Failed and What are the Alternatives?

It has been suggested that the landfill tax has failed to meet its two objectives. These are to promote the 'polluter pays principle', by increasing the price of landfill in order better to reflect its environmental costs, while promoting a more sustainable approach to waste management, in which less waste is produced and more is recovered or recycled.

The first criticism is the most easily dismissed. When the landfill tax was first introduced, its level was based on estimates of those externalities that could be valued in a reliable manner, which were associated with landfilling. While the estimates are, of course, open to criticism, no one has seriously asserted that the landfill tax fails to make a serious attempt to internalize the externalities associated with the landfilling of waste.[11]

From a welfare economics perspective, the landfill tax may not represent the 'first best' tax, which produces the optimal level of waste arisings from the point of view of society. But the structure and philosophy of the tax is theoretically sound. The issue can be expressed as one of adjustment, rather than radical reconstruction. So, while the initial level of the landfill tax was based on the best available estimates of the externalities associated with landfill,[12] it will undoubtedly be

---

[11] These estimates, however, did not include environmental damages from leachate nor disamenity effects associated with landfilling.

[12] In fact, it was based on the differential between the estimated externalities associated with landfill and those associated with incineration of waste.

possible to refine the chosen tax rate in future. Improvements in the reliability of valuation techniques, and in the knowledge of the physical impacts of landfilling of waste, will strengthen the estimates of those external effects currently included, and enhance the opportunity of including external effects omitted from the earlier studies.

The second criticism appears to be the more substantive, and centres primarily on the failure of the tax to achieve desired reductions in the amount of waste going to landfill, and corresponding increases in the amounts being recovered or recycled. This raises three main issues. First, are the targets appropriate? Second, has the landfill tax had the 'optimal conditions' to achieve its objectives? And finally, is it the most appropriate instrument to attain the objectives?

The question of the appropriateness of the targets reflects the concern that the targets themselves, the desired reductions, are flawed objectives. This is due to the fact that they are not based on any assessment of the actual environmental externalities associated with the landfilling of waste, but appear to have been set as a result of political discussion. The recent EU Landfill Directive maps out the required reduction in the amount of organic waste than can be landfilled in future years, but the path appears to have been based entirely on the perceived political undesirability of landfilling. This is a judgement that reflects the dogma inherent in the waste hierarchy, rather than any rigorous assessment of the costs and benefits of the landfilling of waste.

The second issue, that the landfill tax has not been given optimal conditions under which to work, essentially revolves around the issue of household charges for waste. The introduction of a charging system by local authorities to provide an incentive to households to reduce waste, is prohibited in the UK. The Select Committee (SCETRA, 1999) advises against introducing unit pricing for household waste services, arguing that the charge would be too insignificant to have any effect, and, somewhat contradicting this claim, that an unwanted side effect would be that people would dump waste in neighbours' dustbins. However, a number of schemes that charge households for the waste that they generate have been introduced around the world, and it is instructive to review this experience briefly.

This type of scheme in the USA appears to have resulted in significant reductions (12–65 per cent in tonnage terms) in the amount of waste going to landfill, coupled with increases in recycling (Blume, 1991; Miranda *et al.*, 1994; Fullerton and Kinnaman, 1995). Indeed, the schemes appear to have achieved greatest success when combined with an aggressive drive for recycling. And although there were some increases in fly-tipping and home incineration to start with, these problems appear to have tapered off after an initial period (Fullerton and Kinnaman, 1995).

Denmark also introduced a tax on both landfill and on incineration in 1987. Since then it has gradually been raised from its initial level of DKK40 (EUR5) per tonne for waste, whether being landfilled or incinerated. Thus, waste going to landfill now attracts a tax of DKK335 (EUR45) per tonne, while waste being incinerated in combined-heat-and-power plants is taxed at DKK210 (EUR28) per tonne, to reflect the lower environmental burden when heat and power is recovered. In the 10 years since the introduction of the landfill tax, Denmark achieved a 26 per cent reduction in the quantity of waste incinerated and landfilled, and attained an overall recycling rate of 61 per cent.

Interestingly, the improvement was even more pronounced in those municipalities which chose to introduce weight-based fees for waste services. These communities saw residual waste fall to about 100 kg per capita per year, compared to 200–50 kg per capita in municipalities that have established recycling facilities but do not have weight-based fees (Andersen, 1998).

However, it is important to point out that these behavioural changes have been engendered by a tax imposed at a rate of DKK335 (EUR45) per tonne of waste, together with weight-based waste fees, which is considerably above the British level. This would seem to suggest that the Select Committee might be right in its conclusion that unit-pricing for waste services in a UK context would not induce changes in household behaviour because the economic incentive would be too small.

The final issue is a reflection of the argument that it is not the landfill tax that has failed, but the policy-makers, who have not adopted an instrument appropriate for the objective. Clearly, if the political system sets quantitative targets for the amount of waste that can be landfilled, a tax is not the best way of achieving such targets. Instead, an instrument should be chosen which controls quantity rather than price. If there is a desire to achieve the quantitative target at least cost, instruments such as tradable targets should be considered. And, indeed, this is one of the options the DETR is seeking views on in its consultation document relating to the new Landfill Directive (DETR, 1999k).

If this is adopted, the DETR has proposed two approaches for issuing permits. The first version allocates the permits to landfill site operators, stipulating how much biodegradable municipal waste each site can receive. However, in this version, the DETR seems ambivalent about allowing the trading of permits, and seems in the first instance mostly concerned about limiting the amount of biodegradable waste a landfill site can accept. While this system would put pressure on the local authority to find alternatives to landfilling, it does not appear to have as its goal to secure the permitted level of landfilling at least cost. This could be achieved, however, if the permits were made tradable, allowing those landfill operators with the lowest costs to purchase additional permits, while those operators with higher costs would be better off selling their permits.

The second approach proposes to allocate the permits to local authorities, stipulating how much biodegradable waste each municipality would be allowed to landfill, with the intention of focusing their attention on the alternatives to landfill. This would encourage local authorities to achieve waste reduction and establish recycling and composting schemes, which are cheaper to run than landfill. If the permits are made tradable, local authorities successful in bringing down the costs of alternatives to landfill can sell superfluous landfill permits to other local authorities, which might not have the same advantages with respect to recycling and composting schemes. Of course, there would indirectly be a pressure on landfill operators to reduce their prices, as they would have to compete with recycling and composting schemes for the waste, but the main focus would be on the alternatives to landfill.

While there are a number of practical and technical issues that will need to be resolved[13] before these schemes can be deemed practicable, these are interesting 'second-best' suggestions which deserve further consideration.

8. Conclusions

The landfill tax is a radical and progressive step forward in pursuit of the objective of sustainable waste management. It is based on an assessment, albeit limited, of the externalities associated with landfilling, and thus represents an initial step to try and ensure that the price of waste services reflects their social cost. It is undoubtedly capable of further refinement, and it could be accompanied by other complementary measures of the type discussed above, to assist in the attainment of policy objectives.

However, much of the discussion surrounding the efficacy of the tax is not a reflection of the tax itself, but the target of the tax. The increasing focus on diverting large quantities of waste from landfill, particularly

---

[13] Such as how to measure the biodegradable content of a load of municipal waste, and how to enforce that no more than the permitted quantities are landfilled.

after the adoption of the new Landfill Directive, only serves to highlight the mismatch between the target and the instrument. However, to the extent that the other stated aim of the landfill tax remains valid, namely to make the polluter pay by internalizing the external effects of landfilling waste, the efficacy of the tax is constrained by antiquated dogma. Until the shibboleth of not charging households in direct proportion to how much waste they produce, is challenged and overcome, no amount of refinement will allow the attainment of the 'first-best' option in welfare-economic, or social, terms.

Bibliography

ACBE (1995), *Response to the Government's Consultation on a Landfill Tax*, Advisory Committee on Business and the Environment, London.

Ackerman, B. A., and Hassler, W. T. (1981), *Clean Coal/Dirty Air: Or How the Clean Air Act Became a Multibillion-dollar Bail-out for High Sulphur Coal Producers and What Should be Done About It*, New Haven, CT, Yale University Press.

Adams, D. M., and Alig, R. J. (1995), 'Assessing the Impacts of Global Climate Change Mitigation Policies with an Inter-temporal Model of the US Forest and Agriculture Sectors', see http://info.metla.fi/iufro95abs/d6pap85.htm

Adger, W. N., and Brown, K. (1994), *Land Use and the Causes of Global Warming*, J. Wiley & Sons.

— Pettenella, D. M., and Whitby, M. (eds) (1997a), *Climate Change Mitigation and European Land Use Policies*, Wallingford, CAB International.

— — — (1997b), 'Land Use in Europe and the Reduction of Greenhouse-gas Emissions', in W. N. Adger, D. Pettenella, and M. Whitby (eds), *Climate Change Mitigation and European Land Use Policies*, Wallingford, CAB International, 1–22.

— Brown, K., Shiel, R. S., and Whitby, M. C. (1994), 'Carbon Dynamics of Land Use in Britain', *Journal of Environmental Management*, **36**, 117–33.

Adler, R. (1999), 'That Sinking Feeling: The US's Carbon Emissions aren't being Soaked up After All', *New Scientist*, 31 July, 13.

AEA Technology (1996a), *Sulphur Dioxide Ambient Air Quality Study*, Report to the Department of the Environment, London.

— (1996b), *Report on the Abatement of Volatile Organic Compounds from Stationary Sources*, report to APARG, Harwell.

— (nd1), *Green Accounting Research Project: UK Case Study*, Harwell, Energy Technology Support Unit.

— (nd2), *A Compliance Cost Assessment of the Proposed Air Quality Regulations for Nitrogen Dioxide and Fine Particles*, report to Department of the Environment, London.

Allison, G., Ball, S., Cheshire, P., Evans, A., and Stabler, M. (1996), *The Value of Conservation? The Economic and Social Value of the Cultural*

Built Heritage, London, Department of National Heritage, English Heritage and Royal Institution of Chartered Surveyors.

Andersen, M. S. (1998), 'Assessing the Effectiveness of Denmark's Waste Tax', *Environment*, **40**(4), 11–15, 38–41.

ApSimon, H., Pearce, D. W., Ozdemiroglu, E. (1997), *Acid Rain in Europe: Counting the Cost*, London, Earthscan.

Arora, S., and Cason, T. N. (1996), 'Why do Firms Volunteer to Exceed Environmental Regulations? Understanding Participation in EPA's 33/50 Program', *Land Economics*, **72**(4), 413–32.

Arrow, K. (1951), *Social Choice and Individual Values*, New York, Wiley.

—   Solow, R., Leamer, E., Portney, P., Radner, R., and Schuman, H. (1992), 'Report of the NOAA Panel on Contingent Valuation', *Federal Registrar*, **58**(10), 4601–14, Washington, DC.

—   Bolin, B., Costanza, R., Dasgupta, P., Folke, C., Holling, C. S., Jansson, B.-O., Levin, S., Mäler, K.-G., Perrings, C., and Pimentel, D. (1995), 'Economic Growth, Carrying Capacity and the Environment', *Science*, **268**, 28 April, 520–1.

Asheim, G. (1994), 'Net National Product as an Indicator of Sustainability', *Scandinavian Journal of Economics*, **96**(2), 257–65.

Atkinson, G., Dubourg, W. R., Hamilton, K., Munasinghe, M., Pearce, D. W., and Young, C. E. F. (1997), *Measuring Sustainable Development: Macroeconomics and Environment*, Cheltenham, Edward Elgar.

Ayres, R. U., and Kneese, A. V. (1969), 'Production, Consumption and Externality', *American Economic Review*, **69**(3), 282–97

Badrinath, S. G., and Bolster, P. (1996), 'The Role of Market Forces in EPA Enforcement', *Journal of Regulatory Economics*, **10**(2), 165–81.

Baldock, D. (1992), 'The Polluter Pays Principle and its Relevance to Agricultural Policies in the EC', *Sociologia Ruralis*, **32**(1) 49–65.

Ball, S., and Bell, S. (1994), *Environmental Law*, 2nd edn, London, Blackstone Press.

Ballard, C., Shoven, J., and Whalley, J. (1985), 'General Equilibrium Computations of the Marginal Welfare Costs of Taxes in the United States', *American Economic Review*, **75**, 128–38.

Barbier, E. B., Burgess, J. C., and Folke, C. (1994), *Paradise Lost?: The Ecological Economics of Biodiversity Loss*, London, Earthscan.

—   Markandya, A., and Pearce, D. W. (1990), 'Environmental Sustainability and Cost–Benefit Analysis', *Environment and Planning A*, **22**, 1259–66.

Barker, J. R., Baumgardner, G. A., Turner, D. P., and Lee, J. J. (1996), 'Dynamics of the Conservation and Wetland Reserve Programmes', *Journal of Soil and Water Conservation*, **51**, 340–6.

Bardach, E., and Kagan, R. A. (1982), *Going by the Book: The Problem of Regulatory Unreasonableness*, Philadelphia, Temple University Press.

Barrett, S. (1990), 'The Problem of Global Environmental Cooperation',
   Oxford Review of Economic Policy, **6**(1), 68–79.
—   (1991), 'The Problem of Global Environmental Protection', in D.
   Helm (ed.), *Economic Policy Towards the Environment*, Oxford,
   Blackwell.
—   (1992), 'Reaching a CO_2 Emission Limitation Agreement for the
   Community: Implications for Equity and Cost-Effectiveness',
   European Economy, Special Edition No. 1, 3–24.
—   (1994), 'Self-Enforcing International Environmental Agreements',
   Oxford Economic Papers, **46**, 878–94.
—   (1998), 'Political Economy of the Kyoto Protocol', *Oxford Review
   of Economic Policy*, **14**(4), 20–39.
—   (1999*a*), 'A Theory of Full International Cooperation', *Journal of
   Theoretical Politics*, **11**(4), 519–41.
—   (1999*b*), 'Montreal vs. Kyoto: International Cooperation and the
   Global Environment', in I. Kaul, I. Grunberg, and M. A. Stern
   (eds), *Global Public Goods: International Cooperation in the 21st
   Century*, New York, Oxford University Press, 192–219.
Barry, B. (1999), 'Sustainability and Intergenerational Justice', in A.
   Dobson (ed.), *Fairness and Futurity*, Oxford, Oxford University
   Press.
Bateman, I., and Langford, I. (1997), 'Non-users Willingness to Pay for
   a National Park: An Application and Critique of the Contingent
   Valuation Method', *Regional Studies*, **31**(6), 571–82.
—   Willis, K. G. (1999), *Valuing Environmental Preferences: Theory and
   Practice of the Contingent Valuation Method in the US, EU, and
   Developing Countries*, Oxford, Oxford University Press.
—   —   Garrod, G. (1994), 'Consistency between Contingent Valua-
   tion Estimates: A Comparison of Two Studies of UK National
   Parks', *Regional Studies*, **28**(5), 457–74.
—   Langford, I., Turner, R. K., Willis, K., and Garrod, G. (1995)
   'Elicitation and Truncation Effects in Contingent Valuation Stud-
   ies', *Ecological Economics*, **12**(2), 161–79
—   Willis, K., Garrod, G., Doktor, P., Langford, I., and Turner, R. K.
   (1992), *Recreation and Environmental Preservation Value of the
   Norfolk Broads: A Contingent Valuation Study*, Report to the Na-
   tional Rivers Authority (now the Environment Agency), Bristol.
Baumol, W. J., and Oates, W. E. (1988), *The Theory of Environmental
   Policy*, 2nd edn, Cambridge, Cambridge University Press.
Beatley, T. (1994), *Habitat Conservation Planning: Endangered Species and
   Urban Growth*, Austin, TX, University of Texas Press.
Becker, G. (1968), 'Crime and Punishment: An Economic Approach',
   Journal of Political Economy, **76**, 169–217.

Becker, G. (1993), 'Nobel Lecture: The Economic Way of Looking at Behaviour', *Journal of Political Economy*, **101**(3), 385–409.

Beckerman, W. (1993), 'Environmental Policy and the Discount Rate: Philosophy and Economics', CSERGE Working Paper GEC 93–12, Centre for Social and Economic Research on the Global Environment (CSERGE), University College London and University of East Anglia.

— (1994), 'Sustainable Development: Is it a Useful Concept?', *Environmental Values*, **3**, 191–209.

— (1995), *Small is Stupid: Blowing the Whistle on the Greens*, London, Duckworth.

— Pasek, J. (1997), 'Plural Values and Environmental Valuation', *Environmental Values*, **6**, 65–86.

Bekkering, T. D. (1992), 'Using Tropical Forests to Fix Atmospheric Carbon: The Potential in Theory and Practice', *Ambio*, **21**, 414–19.

Bernstein, P. M., Montgomery, W. D., and Rutherford, T. F. (1998), 'Trade Impacts of Climate Policies: The MS-MRT Model', paper prepared for the Yale–NBER Workshop on International Trade and Climate Policy, Snowmass, CO, 12 August.

Bigham, A. (1992), ' "Excessive" in BATNEEC', *Integrated Environmental Management*, **7**, 4–7.

Birdlife International/WWF (1997), *Climate Change and Wildlife. A summary of an International Workshop at the National Center for Atmospheric Research*, 19–22 September, Boulder, Colorado.

Blöchliger, H.-J. (1994), 'Main Results of the Study', ch. 5 in *The Contribution of Amenities to Rural Development*, Paris, OECD, 71–86.

Blume, D. R. (1991) *Under What Conditions Should Cities Adopt Volume-based Pricing for Residential Solid Waste Collection?*, Masters' Memo Study, for the Office of Management and Budget Office of Information and Regulatory Affairs, Natural Resources Branch, Duke University, Institute of Policy Sciences and Public Affairs.

Boardman, A., Greenberg, D., Vining, A., Weimar, D. (1996), *Cost–Benefit Analysis: Concepts and Practice*, New Jersey, Prentice-Hall.

Bohm, P., and Russell, C. S. (1985), 'Comparative Analysis of Alternative Policy Instruments', in A. V. Kneese and J. L. Sweeney (eds), *Handbook of Natural Resource and Energy Economics Volume I*, Elsevier Science Publishers, 395–460.

Böswald, K. (1997), 'German Forests in the National Carbon Budget: An Overview and Regional Case Studies', in W. N. Adger, D. Pettenella, and M. Whitby (eds), *Climate Change Mitigation and European Land Use Policies*, Wallingford, CAB International, 227–38.

Boulding, K. (1966), 'The Economics of the Coming Spaceship Earth', in H. Jarrett (ed.), *Environmental Quality in a Growing Economy*, Baltimore, Johns Hopkins University Press.

Bouwman, A. F. (1990), 'Exchange of Greenhouse Gases between Terrestrial Ecosystems and the Atmosphere', in A. F. Bouwman (ed.), *Soils and the Greenhouse Effect*, Chichester, John Wiley, 61–127.

Bovenberg, A. L., and de Mooij, R. A. (1994), 'Environmental Levies and Distortionary Taxation', *American Economic Review*, **84**, 1085–9.

—   Goulder, L. (1994), 'Integrating Environmental and Distortionary Taxes: General Equilibrium Analyses', Working Paper, Stanford University.

—   van der Ploeg, F. (1994), 'Environmental Policy, Public Finance and the Labour Market in a Second-best World', *Journal of Public Economics*, **55**, 349–90.

—   Cnossen, S. (1995), *Public Economics and the Environment in an Imperfect World*, Dordrecht, Kluwer Academic Publishers.

Bowe, M., and Dean, J. W. (1993), 'Debt–Equity Swaps: Investment Incentive Effects and Secondary Market Price', *Oxford Economic Papers*, **45**, 130–45.

Bowers and Cheshire, P. (1983), *Agriculture, the Countryside and Land Use: An Economic Critique*, London, Methuen.

Boyer, B., and Meidinger, E. (1985), 'Privatising Regulatory Enforcement: A Preliminary Assessment of Citizen Suits Under Federal Environmental Laws', *Buffalo Law Review*, **34**(3), 833–940.

Broome, J. (1992), *Counting the Cost of Global Warming*, Cambridge, White Horse Press.

Brouwer, R., and Langford, I. (1997), *The Validity of Transferring Environmental Benefits: Further Empirical Testing*, Working Paper 97–07, CSERGE, University of East Anglia and University College London.

—   — Bateman, I., Crowards, T., and Turner, R. K. (1997), 'A Meta-analysis of Wetland Contingent Valuation Studies', Working Paper 97–20, CSERGE, University of East Anglia and University College London.

Brown, G. M., and Shogren, J. F. (1998), 'Economics of the Endangered Species Act', *Journal of Economic Perspectives*, **12**(3), 3–20.

Brown, S., Cannell, M. G. R., Kauppi, P. E., and Sathaye, J. (1996), 'Management of Forests for Mitigation for Greenhouse Gas Emissions', in R. T. Watson, M. C. Zinyowera, and R. H. Moss (eds), *Climate Change 95 – Impacts, Adaptations and Mitigation of*

Climate Change: Scientific–Technical Analysis, Cambridge, Cambridge University Press, 773–97.

Burniaux, J. M., Martin, J. P., Nicoletti, G., and Martins, J. O. (1991), 'The Costs of Policies to Reduce Global Emissions of CO_2: Initial Simulation Results with GREEN', OECD Economics and Statistics Department Working Papers No. 103, Paris, Organization for Economic Cooperation and Development.

Button, K. J., and Gillingwater, D. (1986), *Future Transport Policy*, London, Croom Helm.

Cabinet Office (1996), *Regulation in the Balance: a Guide to Regulatory Appraisal Incorporating Risk Assessment*, London, Cabinet Office.

Cannell, M. G. R., and Cape, J. N. (1991), 'International Environment Considerations: Acid Rain and the Greenhouse Effect', in Forestry Commission (ed.), *Forestry Expansion: A Case Study of Technical, Economic and Ecological Factors*, Edinburgh, Forestry Commission.

— Dewar, R. C. (1995), 'The Carbon Sink Provided by Plantation Forests and their Products in Britain', *Forestry*, **68**, 35–48.

CAPRI (1999), *Deliverable D3: Valuation of Transport Externalities*, Project coordinator, Institute for Transport Studies, University of Leeds.

Carson, D. (1996), 'Global Warming: Basis for Concern', *RSA Journal*, June.

Carson, R. (1963), *Silent Spring*, London, Hamish Hamilton.

— Mitchell, R., Hanemann, M., Kopp, R., Presser, S., and Ruud, P. (1995), 'Contingent Valuation and Lost Passive Use: Damages from the *Exxon Valdez*', Discussion Paper 95–02, Department of Economics, University of California at San Diego.

Chartered Institute of Transport (1996), *Better Public Transport for Cities*, London.

Chayes, A., and Chayes, A. H. (1995), *The New Sovereignty*, Cambridge, MA, Harvard University Press.

CIC (1995), 'Briefing Papers', response to the Landfill Tax consultation paper, Construction Industry Council, London.

Ciesla, W. M. (1997), 'Forestry Options for Mitigating Predicted Climate Change', in W. N. Adger, D. Pettenella, and M. Whitby (eds), *Climate Change Mitigation and European Land Use Policies*, Wallingford, CAB International, 35–47.

Clinton Administration (1998), 'The Kyoto Protocol and the President's Policies to Address Climate Change: Administration Economic Analysis', White House, Washington, DC, July.

Coburn, T., Beesley, M., Reynolds, D. (1960), *The London–Birmingham Motorway, Traffic and Economics*, Road Research Laboratory Technical Paper 46, London, HMSO.

Cohen, J. E. (1995), *How Many People Can the Earth Support?*, New York, London, W. W. Norton & Co.

Cohen, M. A. (1986), 'The Costs and Benefits of Oil Spill Prevention and Enforcement', *Journal of Environmental Economics and Management*, **13**, 167–88.

Commission of the European Communities (1995), *Waste-Water Charging Schemes in the European Union*, Luxembourg, Office for Official Publications of the European Communities.

Commission on the Third London Airport (The 'Roskill Commission') (1971), *Report*, and *Papers and Proceedings*, 9 vols, London, HMSO.

Common, M., and Perrings, C. (1992), 'Towards An Ecological Economics of Sustainability', *Ecological Economics*, **6**(1), 7–34.

Coopers & Lybrand (1993), *Landfill Costs and Prices: Correcting Possible Market Distortions*, HMSO, London.

—   Centre for Social and Economic Research on the Global Environment (CSERGE), and Economics for the Environment Consultancy (EFTEC) (1996), *Cost–Benefit Analysis of the Different Municipal Waste Management Systems: Objectives and Instruments for the Year 2000*, Report to the European Commission, DGXI, Brussels.

Corner House (1999), *Carbon Offset Forestry and the Privatisation of the Atmosphere. Briefing No. 15*, 1–24, Sturminster Newton, Dorset, The Corner House.

Costanza, R., d'Arge, R., deGroot, R., *et al.* (1997), 'The Value of the World's Ecosystem Services and Natural Capital', *Nature*, **387**, 253–60.

Countryside Commission (1998), *Countryside Stewardship: Monitoring and Evaluation of the Pilot Scheme, 1991–1996*, Research Note 3, Cheltenham, Countryside Commission.

Crabtree, R. (1997), 'Policy Instruments for Environmental Forestry: Carbon Retention in Farm Woodlands', in W. N. Adger, D. Pettenella, and M. Whitby (eds), *Climate Change Mitigation and European Land Use Policies*, Wallingford, CAB International, 187–97.

Cropper, M. L., and Oates, W. E. (1992), 'Environmental Economics: A Survey', *Journal of Economic Literature*, **30**, 675–740.

CSERGE (1992), *The Social Costs of Fuel Cycles*, London, HMSO.

—   Warren Spring Laboratory, and EFTEC (1993), *Externalities from Landfill and Incineration*, London, HMSO.

—   EFTEC, and EEE (1994), *Assessing the Environmental Costs and Benefits of Renewable Energy Technologies in Scotland*, report to the Scottish Office, Edinburgh.

CST (undated), *The Carbon Storage Trust and Climate Care Warranties: A Detailed Analysis*, Oxford, Carbon Storage Trust.

Custance, J., and Hillier, H. (1998), 'Statistical Issues in Developing Indicators of Sustainable Development', *Journal of the Royal Statistical Society A*, **161**.

Dabbert, S., Dubgaard, A., Slangen, L., and Whitby, M. (eds) (1998), *The Economics of Landscape and Wildlife Conservation*, Wallingford, CAB International.

Daly, H. E., and Cobb, J. B., Jr (1989), *For the Common Good*, Boston, MA, Beacon Press.

Dasgupta, A. K., and Pearce, D. W. (1972), *Cost–Benefit Analysis: Theory and Practice*, Basingstoke, Macmillan.

Dasgupta, P. (1993), *An Enquiry into Wellbeing and Destitution*, Oxford, Oxford University Press.

—   (1995), 'The Population Problem: Theory and Evidence', *Journal of Economic Literature*, **33**, 1879–902.

—   Heal, G. (1979), *Economic Theory and Exhaustible Resources*, Cambridge, Cambridge University Press.

DETR (1997*a*), *Economic Instruments for Water Pollution*, London, Department of the Environment, Transport and the Regions.

—   (1997*b*), *Experience with 'Policy Appraisal and the Environment' Initiative*, London, Department of the Environment, Transport and the Regions.

—   (1997*c*), *National Road Traffic Forecasts, Great Britain*, London, Department of Transport.

—   (1997*d*), *Developing an Integrated Transport Policy*, London, Department of the Environment, Transport and the Regions.

—   (1998*a*), *A New Deal for Transport: Better for Everyone*, Cmnd 3950, Department of the Environment, Transport and the Regions.

—   (1998*b*), *Raising the Quality*, Department of the Environment, Transport and the Regions, September.

—   (1998*c*), 'UK Climate Change Programme', consultation paper, Department of the Environment, Transport and the Regions.

—   (1998*d*), *Review of Technical Guidance on Environmental Assessment*, Department of the Environment, Transport and the Regions, November.

—   (1998*e*), *Planning for the Communities of the Future*, Cmnd 3885, The Stationery Office, Department of the Environment, Transport and the Regions, February.

—   (1998*f*), *Policy Appraisal and the Environment: Draft Policy Guidance*, London, Department of the Environment, Transport and the Regions.

—   (1998*g*), *The Review of the Water Abstraction Licensing System in England and Wales*, London, Department of the Environment, Transport and the Regions.

— (1998*h*), *Sites of Scientific Interest: Better Protection and Management*, Consultation Paper, London, Department of the Environment, Transport and the Regions.

— (1998*i*), *Breaking the Logjam. The government's consultation paper on fighting traffic congestion and pollution through road user and workplace parking charges*, London, Department of the Environment, Transport and the Regions.

— (1998*j*), *A New Deal for Trunk Roads in England*, Cm 3950, London, Department of the Environment, Transport and the Regions.

— (1998*k*), *The Government's response to the Environment, Transport and Regional Affairs Committee's Report on the Proposed Strategic Rail Authority and Railway Regulation*, Cm 4024, London, HMSO.

— (1998*l*), *Transport Statistics Great Britain, 1998 edition*, London, Department of the Environment, Transport and the Regions.

— (1998*m*), *Guidance on the New Approach to Appraisal*, London, Department of the Environment, Transport and the Regions.

— (1999*a*), *A Better Quality of Life. A Strategy for Sustainable Development for the UK*, Cm 4345, The Stationery Office, Department of the Environment, Transport and the Regions.

— (1999*b*), *Monitoring Progress*, London, Department of Environment, Transport and the Regions.

— (1999*c*), *Third Consultation Paper on the Implementation of the IPPC Directive*, DETR homepage, London, Department of the Environment, Transport and the Regions, http://www.environment.detr.gov.uk/consult/ippc3/43.htm

— (1999*d*), 'IPPC and Negotiated Energy Efficiency Agreements', Internal Memorandum NA (99)05, May, http://www.etsu.com/ccltexts

— (1999*e*), *Taking Water Responsibly: Government Decisions Following Consultation on Changes to the Water Abstraction Licensing System in England and Wales*, London, Department of the Environment, Transport and the Regions.

— (1999*f*), *Economic Instruments for Water Pollution Discharges: National Water Pollution Charges*, London, Department of the Environment, Transport and the Regions.

— (1999*g*), *Design of a Tax or Charge Scheme for Pesticides*, London, Department of the Environment, Transport and the Regions.

— (1999*h*), *From Workhorse to Thoroughbred. A Better Role for Bus Travel*, London, Department of the Environment, Transport and the Regions.

— (1999*i*), *Sustainable Distribution: A Strategy*, London, Department of the Environment, Transport and the Regions.

DETR (1999*j*), *A Way with Waste , A Draft Waste Strategy for England and Wales.*

— (1999*k*), *Limiting Landfill: A Consultation paper on limiting landfill to meet the EC Landfill Directive's targets for the landfill of biodegradable municipal waste,* http://www.environment.detr.gov.uk/ wastestrategy/landfill/index.htm

— (2000), *Climate Change,* Draft UK Programme.

DETR papers available at http://www.environment.detr.gov.uk/ and http://www.detr.gov.uk/pubs/index.htm.

DoE (1988), *Integrated Pollution Control — Consultation Paper,* London, HMSO.

— (1990*a*), *This Common Inheritance: Britain's Environmental Strategy,* Cm 1200, Department of the Environment, London, HMSO.

— (1990*b*), *Digest of Environmental Protection and Water Statistics,* Department of the Environment, HMSO.

— (1991*a*), *Policy Appraisal and the Environment,* Department of the Environment, London, HMSO.

— (1991*b*), *Improving Environmental Quality: The Government's Proposals for a New, Independent Environment Agency,* Green Paper, London, HMSO.

— (1994*a*), *Options for the Geographical and Managerial Structure of the Proposed Environment Agency,* June.

— (1994*b*), *Climate Change: the UK Programme,* Department of the Environment, London, HMSO.

— (1995), *A Guide to Risk Assessment and Risk Management for Environmental Protection,* Department of the Environment, London, HMSO.

— (1996), *Indicators of Sustainable Development for the United Kingdom,* London, HMSO.

— (1997*a*), *The Wider Costs and Benefits of Environmental Policy: A Discussion Paper,* London, Department of the Environment.

— (1997*b*), *The United Kingdom National Air Quality Strategy,* Department of the Environment, London, The Stationery Office.

— (1998), *Digest of Environmental Statistics 1998,* London, The Stationery Office.

— Welsh Office (1993), *Integrated Pollution Control – a Practical Guide,* London, Department of the Environment.

DoT (1989), *National Road Traffic Forecasts,* London, Department of Transport.

— (1996), *Transport, The Way Forward,* London, Department of Transport, HMSO.

Downs, G. W., Rocke, D. M., and Barsoom, P. N. (1996), 'Is the Good News About Compliance Good News About Cooperation?', *International Organization*, **50**, 379–406.

DTI (1996), *Checking the Cost to Business: A Guide to Compliance Cost Assessment*, London, Department of Trade and Industry.

— (1998), 'Conclusions of the Review of Energy Sources for Power Generation and Government Response to Fourth and Fifth Reports of the Trade and Industry Committee', Cmnd 4071, October.

Dubgaard, A. (1989), 'Input Levies as a Means of Controlling the Intensities of Nitrogenous Fertiliser and Pesticides', in A. Dubgaard and H. Nielsen (eds), *Economic Aspects of Environmental Regulation in Agriculture*, Kiel, Wissenschaftsverlag Vauk Kiel.

Dupuit, A. J. (1844), 'On the Measurement of the Utility of Public Works' (trans. R. Barback), *International Economic Papers*, **2**, 1952.

— (1853), 'On Utility and its Measure—On Public Utility', *Journal des Économistes*, **36**, 1–27.

Dwyer, J., and Hodge, I. (1996), *Countryside in Trust: Land Management by Conservation, Amenity and Recreation Organisations*, Chichester, John Wiley & Sons.

Dyson, F. J. (1976), 'Can We Control Carbon Dioxide in the Atmosphere?', *Energy*, **2**, 287–91.

Eckstein, O. (1958), *Water Resource Development: The Economics of Project Evaluation*, Cambridge, MA, Harvard University Press.

ECOTEC (1997), *Economic Instruments for Pesticide Minimisation*, report to the Department of Environment.

EFTEC (Economics for the Environment Consultancy) (1996), *An Economic Appraisal of the Disposal and Beneficial Use of Dredged Material*, report to Ministry of Agriculture, Fisheries and Food.

— (1998), *Technical Guidance on Environmental Appraisal*, London, Department of the Environment, Transport and the Regions [restricted at time of writing, due for publication shortly].

— CSERGE, CES (1998), *Framework to Assess the Environmental Costs and Benefits for a Range of Total Water Management Options*, report to the Environment Agency, Bristol.

Elliot, R. (1997), *Faking Nature: The Ethics of Environmental Restoration*, Routledge.

Emmott, N. (1999), 'IPPC and Beyond—Developing a Strategic Approach to Industry for European Environmental Policy', *Journal of Environmental Policy and Planning*, **1**, 77–91.

Environment Agency (1996), *An Environmental Strategy for the Millennium and Beyond*.

Environment Agency (1998*a*), *Multi-attribute Techniques for River Water Quality Improvements*, April.

— (1998*b*), *The Price of Water*, May.

ENDS (1980), 'EEC Commission Refuses to Cost Environmental Legislation', *ENDS Report*, **47**, April, 17–18.

— (1995), 'A Not-so-green Landfill Tax', no. 242, March 1995, 15–17, London, Environmental Data Services.

— (1998*a*), 'The Environment Agency's Yawning Accountability Gap', *ENDS Report*, **284**, September, 22–8.

— (1998*b*), 'Water Abstraction Decision Deals Savage Blow to Cost–Benefit Analysis', *ENDS Report*, **278**, March, 16–18.

— (1999), 'UK Aims to Increase Waste Recovery, Recycling', *Environment Daily*, 1 July, London, Environmental Data Services.

— (2000), 'Scottish Domestic Recycling Performance Panned', *Environment Daily*, 17 January, London, Environmental Data Services.

England, R. A. (1986), 'Reducing the Nitrogen Input on Arable Farms', *Journal of Agricultural Economics*, **37**, 13–24.

Environmental Audit Committee (1999), 'The Pre-Budget Report 1999: Pesticides, Aggregates and the Climate Change Levy', Fourth Report, HC 76-1, Session 1999–2000.

Environmental Resources Ltd (1992), *Economic Instruments and Recovery of Resources from Waste*, London, HMSO.

Epple, D., and Visscher, M. (1984), 'Environmental Pollution: Modelling Occurrence, Detection and Deterrence', *Journal of Law and Economics*, **27**, 29–60.

ERM (Environmental Resources Management) (1996), *Costs and Benefits of the Reduction of VOC Emissions*, Report to Department of Trade and Industry.

Ervin, D. (1999), 'Toward GATT-Proofing Environmental Programs for Agriculture', *Journal of World Trade*, **33**(2), 63–82.

European Commission (1999), *Maintenance, Improvement, Extension And Application Of The Externe Accounting Framework*, Directorate-General XII, Brussels, European Commission.

European Environment Agency (1998) *Statistical Compendium for the Second Assessment*, Luxembourg, Office for Official publications of the European Communities.

Falconer, K. E. (1997), *Environmental Policy and the Use of Agricultural Pesticides*, unpublished Ph.D. dissertation, University of Cambridge.

— Hodge, I. (1999), 'Information, Indicators and Incentives: Pesticide Policy Design and Decision-making', in C. Spash and S. McNally (eds) *Evaluating the Impacts of Pollution: Applying Economics to the Environment*, Chichester, John Wiley & Sons.

— Whitby, M. (1999), *Administrative Costs in Agricultural Policies: The Case of the English Environmentally Sensitive Areas*, Research Report, Centre for Rural Economy, Department of Agricultural Economics, University of Newcastle upon Tyne.

Fankhauser, S. (1997), 'The Economic Costs of Climate Change and Implications for Land Use', in W. N. Adger, D. Pettenella, and M. Whitby (eds), *Climate Change Mitigation and European Land Use Policies*, Wallingford, CAB International, 59–70.

FAO (1993), *Forest Resources Assessment 1990. Tropical Countries*, FAO Forestry Paper 112, Rome, Food and Agricultural Organization.

Fardil, A. (1985), 'Citizen Suits Against Polluters — Picking up the Pace', *Harvard Environmental Law Review*, **9**(1), 23–84.

Farmer, M. C., and Randall, A. (1998), 'The Rationality of a Safe Minimum Standard', *Land Economics*, **74**(3), 287–302.

Feinstein, J. S. (1989), 'The Safety Regulation of US Nuclear Power Plants: Violations, Inspections and Abnormal Occurrences', *Journal of Political Economy*, **97**(1), 115–54.

Field, C. B., and Fung, I. Y. (1999), 'The Not-so-big US Carbon Sink', *Science*, **285**, 544–5.

Fisher, J., Pollard, V., Palmer, R., and Smith, F. (1999), 'Guidance on Economic Appraisal in the Environment Agency', *Guidance Note No. 29*, National Centre for Risk Analysis and Options Appraisal.

Forestry Commission (1991), *Forestry Expansion*, Forestry Commission, Edinburgh.

Førsund, F. (1992), 'BAT and BATNEEC: An Analytical Interpretation', mimeo, Department of Economics, University of Oslo.

Foster, C. D., and Beesley, M. (1963), 'Estimating the Social Benefits of Constructing an Underground Railway in London', *Journal of the Royal Statistical Society*, Series A, **126**, Part 1.

Foster, V., and Mourato, S. (1998), 'Are Consumers Rational? Evidence from a Contingent Ranking Experiment', paper presented to 8th Annual Conference of the European Association of Environmental and Resource Economists, Tilburg.

Fraser, I., and Russell, N. (1997), 'The Economics of UK Agri-environmental Policy: Present and Future Developments', *Economic Issues*, **2**(1) 67–84.

Fredman, P. (1994), 'The Existence of Existence Value', *Arbetsrapport 202*, Department of Forest Economics, Swedish University of Agricultural Sciences, Umea.

Freeman, A. M. (1982), *Air and Water Pollution Control: A Benefit–Cost Assessment*, New York, Wiley.

Freeman, A. M. (1990), 'Water Pollution Policy', in P. Portney (ed.), *Public Policies for Environmental Protection*, Washington, DC, Resources for the Future, 97–150.

Friemann, J. (1995), 'Environmental Information Systems and Eco-auditing', in H. Folmer, H. Landis Gabel, and H. Opschoor (eds), *Principles of Environmental and Resource Economics*, Cheltenham, Edward Elgar.

Fullerton, D., and Kinnaman, T. C. (1995), 'Garbage, Recycling, and Illicit Burning or Dumping', *Journal of Environmental Economics and Management*, **29**, 78–91.

FWR (1997), *Assessing the Benefits of Surface Water Quality Improvements*, FR/CL0005, Marlow, Foundation for Water Research.

Gale, R. J. P., and Barg, S. R. (1995), 'The Greening of Budgets: The Choice of Governing Instrument', in R. J. P. Gale, S. R. Barg, and A. Gillies (eds), *Green Budget Reform – An International Casebook of Leading Practices*, Winnipeg, International Institute for Sustainable Development/London, Earthscan Publications, 1–27.

Garrod, G., and Willis, K. (1996), 'Estimating the Benefits of Environmental Enhancement: A Case Study of the River Darent', *Journal of Environmental Planning and Management*, **39**, 189–203.

— — (1998), 'Methodological Issues in Valuing the Benefits of Environmentally Sensitive Areas', *Journal of Rural Studies*, **15**(1), 1–7.

Gatto, P., and Merlo, M. (1997), 'Issues and Implications for Agriculture and Forestry: A Focus on Policy Instruments', in W. N. Adger, D. Pettenella, and M. Whitby (eds), *Climate Change Mitigation and European Land Use Policies*, Wallingford, CAB International, 295–312.

Georgiou, S., Langford, I., Bateman, I., and Turner, R. K. (1998*a*), 'Determinants of Individuals' Willingness to Pay for Perceived Reductions in Environmental Health Risks: A Case Study of Bathing Water Quality', *Environment and Planning*, **30**, 577–94.

— Bateman, I., Langford, I., Day, R., and Turner, R. K. (1998*b*), 'Coastal Bathing Water Health Risks: Assessing the Adequacy of Proposals to Amend the EC Directive', CSERGE, University of East Anglia and University College London, mimeo.

Goldsmith, E. *et al.* (1972), *Blueprint for Survival*, London, Penguin Books.

Goodin, R. E. (1992), *Green Political Theory*, Polity Press.

Goodwin, P. (1991), *Transport: The New Realism* London, Rees-Jeffreys Road Fund.

Goulder, L. H. (1995), 'Environmental Taxation and the Double Dividend: A Reader's Guide', *International Tax and Public Finance*, Vol.
2, 157–83.
—   (2000), 'Environmental Policy-making in a Second-best Setting',
in R. N. Stavins (ed.), *Economics of the Environment: Selected
Readings*, 4th edn, New York, London, W. W. Norton.
Gouldson, A., and Murphy, J. (1998), *Regulatory Realities: The Implementation and Impact of Industrial Environmental Regulation*, London,
Earthscan.
Grabosky, P. N. (1994), 'Green Markets: Environmental Regulation by
the Private Sector', *Law and Policy*, **16**(4), 419–48.
Gray, W. B., and Deily, M. E. (1991), 'Enforcement of Regulation in a
Declining Industry', *Journal of Environmental Economics and Man-
agement*, **21**, 260–24.
—   —   (1996), 'Compliance and Enforcement: Air Pollution Regula-
tion in the US Steel Industry', *Journal of Environmental Economics
and Management*, **31**, 96–111.
Grove-White, R. (1997), 'The Environmental "Valuation" Controversy:
Observation on its Recent History and Significance', in J. Foster
(ed.), *Valuing Nature: Economics, Ethics and the Environment*,
London, Routledge, 21–31.
Grubb, M. (1995), 'The Berlin Climate Conference: Outcome and
Implications', Briefing Paper No. 21, London, Royal Institute of
International Affairs.
Gryj, E. (1998), 'Global Climate Change and Species Interactions', in
P. L. Fiedler and P. M. Kareiva (eds), *Conservation Biology: For the
Coming Decade*, New York, Chapman and Hall, 478–96.
Hahn, R. W. (1989), 'Economic Prescriptions for Environmental Prob-
lems: How the Patient Followed the Doctor's Orders', *Journal of
Economic Perspectives*, **3**(2), 95–114.
—   (1996), 'Regulatory Reform: What do the Government's Num-
bers Tell Us?', in R. Hahn (ed.), *Risks, Costs and Lives Saved: Getting
Better Results from Regulation*, Oxford, Oxford University Press,
208–54.
—   (1998), *The Economics and Politics of Climate Change*, Washington,
DC, American Enterprise Institute for Public Policy Research.
Hambler, C. (1995*a*), 'Book review: Beatley, T., *Habitat Conservation
Planning*, Austin, Texas: University of Texas', *Ibis*, **137**, 122–3.
—   (1995*b*), 'Future Biodiversity?', *Nature*, **374**, 758.
—   Speight, M. R. (1995*a*), 'Biodiversity Conservation in Britain:
Science Replacing Tradition', *British Wildlife*, **6**, 137–47.
—   —   (1995*b*), 'Seeing the Wood for the Trees', *Tree News*, Autumn,
8–11.

Hamilton, K. (1996), 'Pollution and Pollution Abatement in the National Accounts', *Review of Income and Wealth*, **42**, 13–33.

— Atkinson, G. (1996), 'Air Pollution and Green Accounts', *Energy Policy*, **24**, 675–84.

— Lutz, E. (1996), 'Green National Accounts: Policy Uses and Empirical Evidence', Environmental Economics Series Paper No. 39, Washington, DC, World Bank.

— Pearce, D. W., Atkinson, G., Gomez-Lobo, A., and Young, C. E. F. (1994), 'The Policy Implications of Environment and Resource Accounting', CSERGE Working Paper GEC 94–18, Centre for Social and Economic Research on the Global Environment (CSERGE), University College London and University of East Anglia.

Hammond, A., Adriaanse, A., Rodenburg, E., Bryant, D., and Woodward, R. (1995), *Environmental Indicators*, Washington, DC, World Resources Institute.

Hanley, N., and Milne J. (1996), 'Ethical Beliefs and Behaviour in Contingent Valuation', *Discussion Papers in Ecological Economics*, 96/1, Department of Economics, University of Stirling.

— Spash, C. (1993), *Cost–Benefit Analysis and the Environment*, Cheltenham, Edward Elgar.

— Shogren, J., and White, B. (1997), *Environmental Economics in Theory and Practice*, London, Macmillan.

— Spash, C., and Walker, L. (1995), 'Problems in Valuing the Benefits of Biodiversity Protection', *Environmental and Resource Economics*, **5**, 249–72.

— Whitby, M., and Simpson, I. (1999), 'Assessing the Success of Agri-environmental Policy in the UK', *Land Use Policy*, **16**(2), 67–80.

— Kirkpatrick, H., Simpson, I., and Oglethorpe, D. (1998), 'Principles for the Provision of Public Goods from Agriculture: Modelling Moorland Conservation in Scotland', *Land Economics*, **74**(1) 102–13.

Harford, J. D. (1987), 'Self-reporting of Pollution and the Firm's Behaviour Under Imperfectly Enforceable Regulations', *Journal of Environmental Economics and Management*, **14**, 293–303.

— (1991), 'A Reconsideration of Enforcement Leverage when Penalties are Restricted', *Journal of Public Economics*, **45**, 391–5.

Harrington, W. (1988), 'Enforcement Leverage When Penalties are Restricted', *Journal of Public Economics*, **37**(1), 29–53.

Harrison, G. W. (1992), 'Valuing Public Goods with the Contingent Valuation Method: A Critique of Kahneman and Knetsch', *Journal of Environmental Economics and Management*, **22**, 57–70.

Harrison, P. (1993), *The Third Revolution*, London, Penguin.

Harsanyi, J. (1955), 'Cardinal Welfare, Individualistic Ethics, and Interpersonal Comparisons of Utility', *Journal of Political Economy*, **63**(4), 309–21.

Hartwick, J. M. (1977), 'Intergenerational Equity and the Investing of Rents from Exhaustible Resources', *American Economic Review*, **67**, 972–4.

— (1978*a*), 'Substitution Among Exhaustible Resources and Intergenerational Equity', *Review of Economic Studies*, **45**, 347–54.

— (1978*b*), 'Investing Returns from Depleting Renewable Resource Stocks and Intergenerational Equity', *Economics Letters*, **1**, 85–8.

Hartwick, J. M. (1993), 'Notes on Economic Depreciation of Natural Resource Stocks and National Accounting', in A. Franz and C. Stahmer (eds), *Approaches to Environmental Accounting*, Heidelberg, Physica-Verlag.

Hawke, N., and Kovaleva, N. (1998), *Agri-environmental Law and Policy*, London, Cavendish Publishing.

Hawkins, K. (1983), 'Bargain and Bluff: Compliance Strategy and Deterrence in the Enforcement of Environmental Regulations', *Law and Policy Quarterly*, **5**(1), 35–73.

Helm, D. R. (1992), 'Environmental Regulation: The Environment Agency Proposal', *Fiscal Studies*, **13**(2), 66–83.

— (1993*a*), 'Reforming Environmental Regulation in the UK', *Oxford Review of Economic Policy*, **9**(4), 1–12.

— (1993*b*), 'Market Mechanisms and the Water Environment. Are They Practicable?', in A. Gilland (ed.) *Efficiency and Effectiveness in the Modern Water Business*, London, Centre for the Study of Regulated Industries, London, Public Finance Foundation.

— (1994), 'British Utility Regulation: Theory, Practice, and Reform', *Oxford Review of Economic Policy*, **10**(3), 17–39.

— (1998*a*), 'A Radical Change?', *The Utilities Journal*, **1**(November), 35.

— (1998*b*), 'The Assessment: Environmental Policy—Objectives, Instruments, and Institutions', *Oxford Review of Economic Policy*, **14**(4), 1–19.

— Rajah, N. (1994), 'Water Regulation: The Periodic Review', *Fiscal Studies*, **15**, 74–94.

Hennessy, P. (1989), *Whitehall*, London, Secker & Warburg.

Hersteinsson, P., and Macdonald, D. W. (1992), 'Interspecific Competition and the Geographic Distribution of Red and Arctic Foxes', *Oikos*, **64**, 505–15.

Heyes, A. G. (1993), 'A Model of Regulatory Enforcement when Inspectability is Endogenous', *Environmental and Resource Economics*, **4**, 479–94.

— (1996), 'Cutting Pollution Penalties to Protect the Environment', *Journal of Public Economics*, **60**(2), 251–65.

— (1997), 'Environmental Regulation by Private Contest', *Journal of Public Economics*, **61**(2), 407–28.

— Rickman, N. (1998), 'A Theory of Regulatory Dealing—Revisiting the Harrington Paradox', *Journal of Public Economics*, forthcoming.

Hicks, J. R. (1939), 'Foundations of Welfare Economics', *The Economic Journal*, **49**, 696–712.

— (1943), 'The Four Consumer's Surpluses', *Review of Economic Studies*, **11**, 31–41.

— (1946), *Value and Capital*, 2nd edn, Oxford, Clarendon Press.

Highways Agency (1997*a*), *Economic Assessment of Road Schemes: COBA Manual*, Vol. 13 of *Design Manual for Roads and Bridges*, London, HMSO.

— (1997*b*), *Environmental Assessment*, Vol. 11 of *Design Manual for Roads and Bridges*, London, HMSO.

HM Customs and Excise (1995), *Landfill Tax: A Consultation Paper*, London.

— (1999), 'Government Support for Sustainable Waste Management', Press Release C&E, 5, 9 March.

HMIP (1991), *HMIP IPC Manual: Section 4—Determination of Authorisations*, London, Her Majesty's Inspectorate of Pollution.

HMSO (1994), *Sustainable Development: The UK Strategy*, Cmnd 2426.

HM Treasury (1997), 'Environmental Taxation—Statement of Intent', HM Treasury Press Office, 2 July.

— (1998), *New Ambitions for Britain*, Financial Statement and Budget Report 1998, Hc 620, London, The Stationery Office.

Hodge, I. (1998), 'Property Institutions and the Provision of Countryside Goods', in *ROOTS '98; The Proceedings of the RICS Rural Practice Research Conference*, Wilson Centre, Fitzwilliam College, University of Cambridge, Royal Institution of Chartered Surveyors, London, 97–111.

— (2000), 'Agri-environmental Relationships and the Choice of Policy Mechanism', *The World Economy*, **23**(2), 257–73.

— McNally, S. (1998), 'Evaluating Environmentally Sensitive Areas: The Value of Rural Environments and Policy Relevance', *Journal of Rural Studies*, **14**, 357–67.

Holder, V. (1999), 'Salvation or Hot Air', *Financial Times*, 15 April.

Houghton, J. T. (1997), *Global Warming: The Complete Briefing*, 2nd edn, Cambridge, Cambridge University Press.

—   Callander, B. A., and Varney, S. K. (eds) (1992), *Climate Change 1992. The Supplementary Report to the IPCC Scientific Assessment*, Cambridge, Cambridge University Press.

—   Meiro Filho, L. G., Callander, B. A., Harris, N., Kattenberg, A., and Maskell, K. (eds) (1996), *Climate Change 1995: The Science of Climate Change*, Cambridge, Cambridge University Press.

Houghton, R. A., Unruh, J. D., and Lefebvre, P. A. (1993), 'Current Land Cover in the Tropics and its Potential for Sequestering Carbon', *Global Biogeochemical Cycles*, **7**, 305–20.

—   Hackler, J. L., and Lawrence, K. T. (1999), 'The US Carbon Budget: Contributions from Land-use Change', *Science*, **285**, 574–8.

House of Lords (1994–5), Select Committee on the European Communities, Session 1994–1995, lst Report, *Bathing Water*, HL Paper 6–I; and 7th Report, *Bathing Water Quality Revisited*, HL Paper 6–I, London, HMSO.

Howarth, R. B. (1997), 'Defining Sustainability: An Overview', *Land Economics*, **73**(4), 445–7.

Hueting, R., Bosch, P., and de Boer, B. (1992), 'Methodology for the Calculation of Sustainable National Income', Statistical Essays M44, Central Bureau of Statistics, Voorburg.

Hulme, M. (ed.) (1996), *Climate Change and Southern Africa: An Exploration of Some Potential Impacts and Implications in the SADC Region*, Climatic Research Unit, University of East Anglia/WWF International.

IHT (1995), *Guidelines for the Development of Urban Transport Strategies*, London, Institution of Highways and Transportation.

International Energy Agency (1992), *Climate Change Policy Initiatives*, Paris, OECD.

IPCC (1990), *Climate Change: The IPCC Scientific Assessment*.

—   (1995), *IPCC Second Assessment: Climate Change 1995*, WMO and UNEP.

—   (1996), *Climate Change 1995: Economic and Social Dimensions of Climate Change*, Cambridge, Cambridge University Press.

Jacoby, H. D., Prinn, R. G., and Schmalensee, R. (1998), 'Kyoto's Unfinished Business', *Foreign Affairs*, July/August.

James, A. N., Gaston, K. J., and Balmford, A. (1999), 'Balancing the Earth's Accounts', *Nature*, **401**, 323–4.

Johansson, P.-O. (1993), *Cost–Benefit Analysis of Environmental Change*, Cambridge, Cambridge University Press.

Kahneman, D., and Knetsch, J. (1992), 'Valuing Public Goods: The Purchase of Moral Satisfaction', *Journal of Environmental Economics and Management*, **23**, 248–57.

Kaldor, N. (1939), 'Welfare Propositions of Economics and Interpersonal Comparisons of Utility', *The Economic Journal*, **49**, 549–52.

Keith, B., Hamersley, G., Hosking, J., and Du Croz, W. (1998), 'English Nature's Experience with Management Agreements', in I. Hodge (ed.), *Designing Agri-environmental Policy Mechanisms: Theory and Practice*, Vol. 2, Environment Series No. 10, Department of Land Economy, University of Cambridge, 13–29.

Kennedy, P. (1993), *Preparing for the Twenty-first Century*, London, Harper Collins.

Khambu, J. (1989), 'Regulatory Standards, Compliance and Enforcement', *Journal of Regulatory Economics*, **1**(2), 103–14.

Knack, S., and Keefer, P. (1997), 'Does Social Capital Have an Economic Payoff? A Cross Country Investigation', *Quarterly Journal of Economics*, November, 1251–88.

Kopp, R., and Smith, V. K. (1989), 'Benefit Estimation Goes to Court: The Case of Natural Resource Damages', *Journal of Policy Analysis and Management*, **8**(4), 593–612.

Kramer, (1995), *EC Treaty and Environmental Law*, 2nd edn, London, Sweet and Maxwell.

Krutilla, J., and Eckstein, O. (1958), *Multipurpose River Development*, Baltimore, MD, Johns Hopkins University Press.

Labour Party (1996), *Consensus for Change: Labour's Transport Policy for the 21st Century*, London.

Latacz-Lohmann, U., and Van der Hamsvoort, C. (1997), 'Auctioning Conservation Contracts: A Theoretical Analysis and an Application', *American Journal of Agricultural Economics*, **70**, 407–18.

Lawton, J. H., and May, R. M. (eds) (1995), *Extinction Rates*, Oxford, Oxford University Press.

Lee, D. R., and Misiolek, W. S. (1986), 'Substituting Pollution Taxation for General Taxation: Some Implications for Efficiency in Pollution Taxation', *Journal of Environmental Economics and Management*, **13**, 338–47.

Leibenstein, H. (1966), 'Allocative Efficiency v. X-efficiency', *American Economic Review*, **56**, 392–415.

Leitch, G. (1978), *Report of the Advisory Committee on Trunk Road Appraisal*, London, HMSO.

Linder, S. H., and McBride, M. E. (1984), 'Enforcement Costs and Regulatory Reform: The Agency and Firm Response', *Journal of Environmental Economics and Management*, **11**, 327–46.

Little, I., and Mirrlees, J. (1974), *Project Appraisal and Planning for Developing Countries*, London, Heinemann.

Livernois, J., and McKenna, C. (1997), 'Truth or Consequences: Enforcing Pollution Standards', Department of Economics, University of Guelph, Canada, mimeo.

London Economics (1991), *The Potential Role of Market Mechanisms in the Control of Acid Rain*, London, Department of the Environment.

— (1998), *The Environmental Costs and Benefits of the Supply of Aggregates*, report to Department of the Environment, Transport and the Regions.

Lövgren, K. (1993), 'Economic Instruments for the Control of Air Pollution in Sweden', International Conference on Economic Instruments for Air Pollution Control, 18–20 October, IIASA, Austria.

McCleery, R. H., and Perrins, C. M. (1998), '...Temperature and Egg-laying Trends', *Nature*, **391**, 30–1.

Macdonald, D. W. (1999), 'Buenos Aires: Implications for All', *The Utilities Journal*, January, 34–5.

— Thom, M. (forthcoming), 'Alien Carnivores: Unwelcome Experiments in Ecology', in J. Gittleman, R. Wayne, D. W. Macdonald, and S. Funk (eds), *Carnivore Conservation*, Cambridge, Cambridge University Press.

— Mace, G. M., and Rushton, S. (2000), 'British Mammals: Is There a Radical Future?', in A. Entwhistle and N. Dunstone (eds)), *Priorities for the Conservation of Mammalian Diversity: Has the Panda Had Its Day?*, Cambridge, Cambridge University Press

Mace, G. M., and Lande, R. (1991), 'Assessing Extinction Threats: Toward a Re-evaluation of IUCN Threatened Species Categories', *Conservation Biology*, **5**, 148–57.

McKean, R. (1958), *Efficiency in Government Through Systems Analysis*, New York, Wiley.

McKibbin, W. J., Shackleton, R., and Wilcoxen, P. J. (1998), 'What to Expect from an International System of Tradable Permits for Carbon Emissions', mimeo.

McMichael, A. J. (1995), *Planetary Overload: Global Environmental Change and the Health of the Human Species*, Cambridge, Cambridge University Press.

Maddison, D. *et al.* (1996), *The True Costs of Road Transport*, Blueprint 5, London, Earthscan.

MAFF (1999), *Europe's Agriculture. The Case for Change*, London, Ministry of Agriculture, Fisheries and Food.

Magat, W. A., and Viscusi, K. (1990), 'Effectiveness of the EPA's Regulatory Enforcement: The Case of Industrial Effluent Standards', *Journal of Law and Economics*, **33**, 331–60.

Mäler, K.-G. (1991), 'National Accounts and Environmental Resources', *Environmental and Resource Economics*, **1**, 1–15.

Manne, A. S., and Richels, R. G. (1998), 'The Kyoto Protocol: A Cost-Effective Strategy for Meeting Environmental Objectives?', mimeo.

Marglin, S., Sen, A., and Dasgupta, P. (1972), *Guidelines for Project Evaluation*, Vienna, United Nations Industrial Development Organisation.

Margolis, H. (1982), *Selfishness, Altruism and Rationality*, Cambridge, Cambridge University Press

Markandya, A., and Pavan, M. (1999), *Green Accounting: Case Studies from Europe*, Dordrecht, Kluwer Academic Press.

Marshall Report (1998), 'Economic Instruments and the Business Use of Energy', report by Lord Marshall, November, HM Treasury.

Martens, P. (1998), *Health and Climate Change*, London, Earthscan.

Martínez-Alier, J. (1995), 'The Environment as a Luxury Good, or "Too Poor to be Green"?', *Ecological Economics*, **13**, 1–10.

Mauch, S. P., and Rothengatter, W. (1995), *External Effects of Transport*, Paris, Union International des Chemins der Fer.

Meffe, G. K., Carroll, C. R., and contributors (1997), *Principles of Conservation Biology*, 2nd edn, MA, USA, Sinauer Associates Inc.

Michaelowa, A. (1998), 'AIJ Cannot Function without Incentives', in P. Reimer, A. Smith, and K. Thambimuthu (eds), *Greenhouse Gas Mitigation: Technologies for Activities Implemented Jointly*, Amsterdam, World Resources Institute, 403–8. See also http://www.wri.org

Milgrom, P. (1993), 'Is Sympathy an Economic Value? Philosophy, Economics and the Contingent Valuation Method', in J. A. Hausman (ed), *Contingent Valuation: A Critical Assessment*, Amsterdam, North-Holland.

Miljøstyrelsen (The Danish Environmental Protection Agency) (1995), *The Danish Waste Charge Act*, update 24 May, J.no. M 376–0003, JB/ 15, Division for Industrial Waste, The Danish Environmental Protection Agency, Miljøministeriet (The Danish Ministry of the Environment), Copenhagen.

Miranda, M. L., Everett, J. W., Blume, D., and Roy, B. A., Jr (1994), 'Market-based Incentives and Residential Municipal Solid Waste', *Journal of Policy Analysis and Management*, **13**(4).

Mishan, E. J. (1975), *Cost–Benefit Analysis*, London, Allen & Unwin.

Montevideo Declaration (1998), see http://igc.apc.org/wrm

Montgomery, W. D. (1972), 'Markets in Licenses and Efficient Pollution Control Programs', *Journal of Economic Theory*, **5**, 395–418.

Morgenstern, R. (1997), *Economic Analyses at EPA: Assessing Regulatory Impact*, Washington DC, Resources for the Future.

Mourato, S., and Pearce, D. W. (1998), *Environmental Costs and Benefits of the Supply of Aggregates: A Review of the London Economics Report*, report to Department of the Environment, Transport and the Regions.

— Swierzbinski, J. (1998), 'A Framework for Assessing Models of Non-use Value of Preserving Endangered Species', Department of Economics, University College London, mimeo.

Moxey, A., and White, B. (1994), 'Efficient Compliance with Agricultural Nitrate Pollution Standards', *Journal of Agricultural Economics*, **45**(1) 27–37.

— — Ozanne, A. (1999), 'Efficient Contract Design for Agri-environmental Policy', *Journal of Agricultural Economics*, **50**(2) 187–202.

Munasinghe, M., and Cruz, W. (1995), *Economy-Wide Policies and the Environment*, Washington, DC, World Bank.

MVA (1995), *The London Congestion Charging Research Programme: Principal Findings*, The MVA Consultancy, Government Office for London, HMSO.

Myers, N. (1996), 'The Biodiversity Crisis and the Future of Evolution', *The Environmentalist*, **16**, 37–47.

— (1998), 'Lifting the Veil on Perverse Subsidies', *Nature*, **392**, 327–8.

Myneni, R. B., Keeling, C. D., Tucker, C. J., Asrar, G., and Nemani, R. R. (1997), 'Increased Plant Growth in the Northern High Latitudes from 1981 to 1991', *Nature*, **386**, 698–702.

NAO (1997), *Protecting Environmentally Sensitive Areas*, Report by the Comptroller and Auditor General, HC120, Session 1997–98, National Audit Office, London, The Stationery Office.

Nash, C. A. (1997), 'Transport Externalities: Does Monetary Valuation Make Sense?', in G. de Rus and C. Nash (eds), *Recent Developments in Transport Economics*, Aldershot, England, Ashgate.

National Reference Centres (NRCs) (1998*a*), Responses from NRCs to questionnaires from European Topic Centre on waste.

— (1998*b*), Comments to the European Environmental Agency from NRCs on waste to draft figures for the waste chapter.

National Society for Clean Air (NSCA) (1996), *1996 Pollution Handbook*, Brighton, NSCA.

Navrud, S., and Pruckner, G. (1997), 'Environmental Valuation—To Use or not to Use?', *Environmental and Resource Economics*, **10**, 1–26.

Naysnerski, W., and Tietenberg, T. (1992), 'Private Enforcement of Federal Environmental Law', *Land Economics*, **68**(1), 28–48.

NERA (1998), *Economic and Social Value of Leakage Reduction*, for the Foundation for Water Industry Research, London, National Economic Research Associates.

— *et al.* (1997), *The Potential for Rail Freight. A Report to the Office of the Rail Regulator*, London, National Economic Research Associates.

Newbery, D. M. (1990), 'Pricing and Congestion: Economic Principles Relevant to Pricing Roads', *Oxford Review of Economic Policy*, **6**(2), 22–38.

Noll, R., Shirley, M., and Cowan, S. (1998), 'Reforming Urban Water Systems: Evidence from Four Latin American Cities', mimeo.

Nordhaus, W. D. (1995), *How Should We Measure Sustainable Income?*, Economics Department, Yale University, mimeo.

— (1998), 'Is the Kyoto Protocol a Dead Duck? Are There Any Live Ducks Around? Comparison of Alternative Global Tradable Emissions Regimes', mimeo, Department of Economics, Yale University.

— Boyer, J. G. (1998), 'Requiem for Kyoto: An Economic Analysis of the Kyoto Protocol', paper prepared for the Energy Modeling Forum meeting, Snowmass, Colorado, 10–11 August.

Norton, B. G., and Toman, M. A. (1997), 'Sustainability: Economic and Ecological Perspectives', *Land Economics*, **73**(4), 663–8.

Noss, R., O'Connell, M., and Murphy, D. (1997), *The Science of Conservation Planning: Habitat Conservation under the Endangered Species Act*, London, Earthscan.

Nyborg, K. (1996), *The Political Man and Contingent Valuation: Motives Do Count*, Statistics Norway, Discussion Paper 180, Oslo, Statistics Norway.

Oates, W. E. (1991), 'Pollution Charges as a Source of Public Revenues', Working Paper 91–22, University of Maryland, Department of Economics.

OECD (1975), *The Polluter Pays Principle*, Paris, Organization for Economic Cooperation and Development.

— (1988), *Transport and the Environment*, Paris, OECD.

— (1993*a*), *Taxation and the Environment. Complementary Policies*, Paris, Organization for Economic Cooperation and Development.

— (1993*b*), *Economic Instruments for Environmental Management in Developing Countries*, proceedings of a workshop held at OECD Headquarters in Paris on 8 October 1992.

— (1994*a*), *Environmental Indicators*, Paris, Organization for Economic Cooperation and Development.

— (1994b), *Managing the Environment: The Role of Economic Instruments*, Paris, OECD.

— (1995), *Environmental Taxes in OECD Countries*, Paris, Organization for Economic Cooperation and Development.

— (1996), *Implementation Strategies for Environmental Taxes*, Paris, Organization for Economic Cooperation and Development.

ONS (1998), *UK Environmental Accounts 1998*, Office for National Statistics, London, HMSO.

Ofwat (1997), 'Setting Price Limits for Water and Sewerage Services', consultation paper, Birmingham, Office of Water Services.

— (1998), *Prospects for Prices*, Birmingham, Office of Water Services.

O'Riordan, T. (ed.) (1997), *Ecotaxation*, London, Earthscan.

Pan, J. H., and Hodge, I. D. (1994), 'Land Use Permits as an Alternative to Fertiliser and Leaching Taxes for the Control of Nitrate Pollution', *Journal of Agricultural Economics*, **45**(1) 102–12.

Parfit (1984), *Reasons and Persons*, Oxford, Oxford University Press.

Parkhurst, G. P. (1994), 'Park-and-ride: Could it Lead to an increase in Car Traffic?', *Transport Policy*, **2**.

Parlange, M. (1999), 'Eco-nomics' *New Scientist*, 6 February, 42–5.

Parry, I. W. H. (1995), 'Pollution Taxes and Revenue Recycling', Economic Research Service Working Paper, US Department of Agriculture.

Pearce, D. W. (1970), 'The Roskill Commission and the Location of London's Third Airport', *Three Banks Review*, September.

— (1986), *Cost Benefit Analysis*, Basingstoke, Macmillan.

— (1991), 'The Role of Carbon Taxes in Adjusting to Global Warming', *The Economic Journal*, **101**(407), 938–48.

— (1994), 'Assessing the Social Rate of Return from Investment in Temperate Zone Forestry', in R. Layard and S. Glaister (eds), *Cost–Benefit Analysis*, 2nd edn, Cambridge, Cambridge University Press.

— (1998a), *Ecological Economics: Essays in the Theory and Practice of Environmental Economics*, Cheltenham, Edward Elgar.

— (1998b), 'Environmental Appraisal and Environmental Policy in the European Union', *Environmental and Resource Economics*, **11**(3–4), 489–501.

— Atkinson, G. (1998), 'The Concept of Sustainable Development: An Evaluation of its Usefulness Ten Years After Brundtland', *Swiss Journal of Economics*, **134**(3), 251–69.

— Brisson, I. (1993), 'BATNEEC: The Economics of Technology-based Environmental Standards, with a UK Illustration', *Oxford Review of Economic Policy*, **9**(4), 24–40.

Pearce, D. W., and Crowards, T. (1996), 'Assessing the Health Costs of Particulate Air Pollution in the UK', *Energy Policy*, **24**(7), 609–20.

— Turner, R. K. (1990), *Economics of Natural Resources and the Environment*, Hemel Hempstead, Harvester Wheatsheaf.

— Ulph, D. (1999), 'A Social Discount Rate for the United Kingdom', in D. W. Pearce, *Economics and Environment: Essays on Ecological Economics and Sustainable Development*, Cheltenham, Edward Elgar, 268–85.

— Hamilton, K., and Atkinson, G. (1996), 'Measuring Sustainable Development: Progress on Indicators', *Environment and Development Economics*, **1**(1), 85–101.

— Markandya, A., Barbier, E. (1989), *Blueprint for a Green Economy*, London, Earthscan (the 'Pearce Report').

— *et al.* (1993), *Blueprint 3. Measuring Sustainable Development*, Earthscan, London.

Pearson, M., and Smith, S. (1991), 'The European Carbon Tax: An Assessment of the European Commission's Proposals', IFS Report Series, London, Institute for Fiscal Studies.

Perrings, C. (1991), 'Reserved Rationality and the Precautionary Principle', in R. Constanza (ed.), *Ecological Economics*, New York, Columbia University Press.

Pezzey, J. (1989), *Economic Analysis of Sustainable Growth and Sustainable Development*, Environment Department Working Paper No. 15, Washington, DC, World Bank.

Pigou, A. C. (1920), *The Economics of Welfare*, London, Macmillan.

Pizer, W. A. (1998), 'Prices vs. Quantities Revisited: The Case of Climate Change', Resources for the Future Discussion Paper 98–02.

Porter, M. E., and van der Linde, C. (1995), 'Towards a New Conception of the Environment–Competitiveness Relationship', *Journal of Economic Perspectives*, **9**(4), 97–118.

Portney, P. (1990), 'Air Pollution Policy', in P. Portney (ed.), *Public Policies for Environmental Protection*, Washington DC, Resources for the Future, 27–96.

Price, C. (1997), 'Analysis of Time Profiles of Climate Change', in W. N. Adger, D. Pettenella, and M. Whitby (eds), *Climate Change Mitigation and European Land Use Policies*, Wallingford, CAB International, 71–87.

Putnam, R. D. (1993), *Making Democracy Work: Civic Traditions in Modern Italy*, Princeton, NJ, Princeton University Press.

Rajah, N., and Smith, S. (1993), 'Taxes, Tax Expenditures and Environmental Regulation', *Oxford Review of Economic Policy*, **9**(4), 41–65.

Ramchandani, R., and Pearce, D. W. (1991), 'Alternative Approaches to Setting Effluent Quality Standards: Precautionary, Critical Loads and Cost–Benefit Approaches', Report LR3, Medmenham, UK, Water Research Centre, October.

RCEP (1976), *Air Pollution Control: An Integrated Approach*, Fifth Report, Royal Commission on Environmental Pollution, Cmnd 6371, London, HMSO.

—   (1984), *Tackling Pollution – Experience and Prospects*, Tenth Report, Royal Commission on Environmental Pollution, Cmnd 9149. London, HMSO.

—   (1985), *Managing Waste – the Duty of Care*, Eleventh Report, Royal Commission on Environmental Pollution, Cmnd 9675, London, HMSO.

—   (1988), *Best Practicable Environmental Option*, Twelfth Report, Royal Commission on Environmental Pollution, Cm310, London, HMSO.

—   (1994),*Transport and the Environment*, Eighteenth Report, Royal Commission on Environmental Pollution, Cm 2674, London, HMSO.

—   (1996), *Sustainable Use of Soil*, Nineteenth Report, Royal Commission on Environmental Pollution, Cm 3165, London, HMSO.

—   (1997), *Transport and the Environment – Developments since 1994*, Royal Commission on Environmental Pollution, London, HMSO.

Reichhardt, T. (1998), 'Ecologists Seek Flexible Protection Rules', *Nature*, **391**, 829.

—   (1999), ' "Inadequate Science" in US Habitat Plans', *Nature*, **397**, 287.

Rennings, K., and Wiggering, H. (1997), 'Steps Toward Indicators of Sustainable Development: Linking Economic and Ecological Concepts', *Ecological Economics*, **20**, 25–36.

Repetto, R., Magrath, W., Wells, M., Beer, C., and Rossini, F. (1989), *Wasting Assets: Natural Resources in the National Accounts*, Washington, DC, World Resources Institute.

Rhodes, M. (ed.) (1998), *Business and Biodiversity: A UK Business Guide for Understanding and Integrating Nature Conservation and Biodiversity into Environmental Management Systems*, Oxford, Corporate Environmental Responsibility Group, Earthwatch.

Ringleb, A. H., and Wiggins, S. N. (1992), 'Liability and Large-scale, Long-term Hazards', *Journal of Political Economy*, **98**, 574–95.

Roberts, M. J., and Spence, M. (1976), 'Effluent Charges and Licenses Under Uncertainty', *Journal of Environmental Economics and Management*, **5**, 193–208.

Rogers, D. J., and Packer, M. J. (1993), 'Vector-borne Diseases, Models and Climate Change', *Lancet*, **342**, 1282–4.

Romanski, C. (1995), 'HM Customs and Excise', paper given at Coopers & Lybrand Landfill Tax Seminar, London.

Romstad, E., Simonsen, J., and Vatn, A. (eds) (1997), *Controlling Mineral Emissions from Agriculture. Economics, Policies and the Environment*, Wallingford, CAB International.

RPA (Risk and Policy Analysts) (1995), *Risks and Benefits of Agrochemical Reductions*, report to Department of the Environment.

—   (1997), *Private Costs and Benefits of Pesticide Minimisation*, report to Department of the Environment.

—   (1998), *Guidance on Environmental Costs and Benefits*, report to the Environment Agency.

Russell, C. S. (1990), 'Monitoring and Enforcement', in P. Portney (ed.), *Public Policies for Environmental Protection*, Washington, DC, RFF.

SACTRA (1992), *Assessing the Environmental Impact of Road Schemes*, Standing Advisory Committee on Trunk Road Assessment, London, Department of Transport.

—   (1994), *Trunk Roads and the Generation of Traffic*, Standing Advisory Committee on Trunk Road Assessment, London, Department of Transport.

Sagoff, M. (1988), *The Economy of the Earth*, Cambridge, Cambridge University Press.

SCETRA (1998), *Sustainable Waste Management* (HC 484), Sixth Report.

—   (1999), *The Operation of the Landfill Tax*, Thirteenth Report.

Schipper, L., Steiner, R., Figueroa, M. J., and Dolan, K. (1993), *Fuel Prices and Economy: Factors Affecting Land Travel*, Transport Policy.

Schlapfer, F. (1999), 'Expert Estimates about Effects of Biodiversity on Ecosystem Processes and Services', *Oikos*, **84**, 346–52.

Segerson, K. (1988), 'Uncertainty and Incentives for Nonpoint Pollution Control', *Journal of Environmental Economics and Management*, **15**, 87–98.

Sen, A. (1977), 'Rational Fools: A Critique of the Behavioural Foundations of Economic Theory', *Philosophy and Public Affairs*, **6**, 317–44.

Shaffer, S. (1990), 'Regulatory Compliance with Nonlinear Penalties', *Journal of Regulatory Economics*, **2**, 99–103.

Shah, A., and Larsen, B. (1992), 'Carbon Taxes, the Greenhouse Effect and Developing Countries', World Bank Policy Research Working Paper Series, No 957, Washington, DC, The World Bank.

Shavell, S. (1986), 'The Judgement Proof Problem', *International Review of Law and Economics*, **6**(1), 45–58.

—   (1992), 'A Note on Marginal Deterrence', *International Review of Law and Economics*, **12**, 133–49.

Skinner, J. A., Lewis, K. A., Bardon, K. S., Tucker, P., Catt, J. A., and Chambers, B. J. (1997), 'An Overview of the Environmental

Impact of Agriculture in the UK', *Journal of Environmental Management*, **50**(2), 111–28.

SMENR (1994), *The Swedish Experience. Taxes and Charges in Environmental Policy*, Stockholm, Ministry of the Environment and Natural Resources.

Smith, S. (1992), 'Taxation and the Environment: A Survey', *Fiscal Studies*, **13**.

— (1995) *Green Taxes and Charges: Policy and Practice in Britain and Germany*, London, Institute for Fiscal Studies.

Smith, V. H., and Colman, D. (1997), *An Economic Analysis of Fixed Payments, Differentiated Fixed Payments and Management Agreements as Mechanisms for Conservation of the Environment*, School of Economic Studies Discussion Paper 9713, University of Manchester.

Smith, V. K. (1984), *Environmental Policy Under Reagan's Executive Order: The Role of Benefit–Cost Analysis*, Chapel Hill, NC, University of North Carolina Press.

Solow, R. M. (1974), 'Intergenerational Equity and Exhaustible Resources', *Review of Economic Studies*, Symposium, 29–45.

— (1993), 'Sustainability: An Economist's Perspective', Washington, DC, Resources for the Future.

— (1986), 'On the Intergenerational Allocation of Exhaustible Resources', *Scandinavian Journal of Economics*, **88**, 141–9.

Southwood, T. R. E. (1995), 'Ecological Processes and Sustainability', *International Journal of Sustainable Development and World Ecology*, **2**, 229–39.

Squire, L., and van der Tak, H. (1975), *Economic Analysis of Projects*, Baltimore, MD, Johns Hopkins University Press.

Stavins, R. N. (1998a), 'What Can We Learn from the Grand Policy Experiment? Lessons from SO_2 Allowance Trading', *Journal of Economic Perspectives*, **12**, 69–88.

— (1998b), 'The Costs of Carbon Sequestration: A Revealed-Preference Approach', *American Economic Review*, forthcoming.

— (2000), 'Experience with Market-Based Environmental Policy Instruments', in K.-G. Maler and J. Vincent (eds), *The Handbook of Environmental Economics*, Amsterdam, North-Holland/Elsevier Science, forthcoming.

Stevens, T., Echeverria, J., Glass, R., Hager, T., and More, T. (1991), 'Measuring the Existence Value of Wildlife: What Do CVM Estimates Really Show?', *Land Economics*, November, **67**(4), 390–400.

Stone, D., Ringwood, K., and Vorhies, F. (1997), *Business and Biodiversity: A Guide for the Private Sector*, IUCN (World Conservation Union)/WBCSD (World Business Council for Sustainable Development).

Strock, J. M. (1990), 'Protecting the Environment: EPA After 20 Years', *Trial*, August, 22–7.

Swanson, T. (1997), *Global Action for Biodiversity*, London, Earthscan.

Tett, S. F. B., Stott, P. A., Allen, M. R., Ingram, W. J., and Mitchell, J. F. B. (1999), 'Causes of Twentieth-century Temperature Change near the Earth's Surface', *Nature*, **399**, 569–72.

Thiollay, J. M. (1992), 'Influence of Selective Logging on Bird Species Diversity in a Ghanaian Rain Forest', *Conservation Biology*, **6**, 47–63.

Tickell, O. (1998), 'Planting a New Forest to Cough Up for Stepping on the Gas', *Observer*, 28 June.

Tietenberg, T (1991), 'Economic Instruments for Environmental Regulation', in D. R. Helm (ed.), *Economic Policy Towards the Environment*, Oxford, Blackwell, 86–110.

Tinch, R. (1996), *The Valuation of Environmental Externalities*, report to Department of Transport, London (the 'Tinch Report').

— Segerson, K. (1994), 'The Structure of Penalties in Environmental Enforcement: An Economic Analysis', *Journal of Environmental Economics and Management*, **23**(2), 179–200.

— (1995), *The Valuation of Environmental Externalities*, Full Report, Department of Transport, London.

Tobey, J., and Smets, H. (1996), 'The Polluter Pays Principle in the Context of Agriculture and the Environment', *The World Economy*, **19**(1) 63–87.

Toman, M. A. (1998), 'Sustainable Decision-making: The State of the Art from an Economics Perspective', RFF Discussion Paper 98–39, Washington, DC, Resources for the Future.

Trexler, M. C., and Haugen, C. (1994), *Keeping it Green: Evaluating Tropical Forestry Strategies to Mitigate Global Warming*, Washington, DC, World Resources Institute.

Turner, R. K., and Brisson, I. (1995), 'A Possible Landfill Levy in the UK: Economic Incentives for Reducing Waste to Landfill', in R. J. P. Gale, S. R. Barg, and A. Gillies (eds), *Green Budget Reform – An International Casebook of Leading Practices*, Winnipeg, International Institute for Sustainable Development/London, Earthscan Publications, 267–80.

— Bateman, I., and Brooke, J. (1992), 'Valuing the Benefits of Coastal Defence: Case Study of the Aldburgh Sea Defence Scheme', in A. Coker and C. Richards (eds), *Valuing the Environment: Economic Approaches to Environmental Valuation*, London, Belhaven Press, 77–100.

UKCIP (1998), 'Climate Change Scenarios for the United Kingdom', Technical Report No. 1, September.

UK Treasury (1997), *Appraisal and Evaluation in Central Government: The 'Green Book'*, London, HMSO.

UK Waste (1995), 'Response to the Government's Consultation Document on Landfill Tax', UK Waste Management Ltd, Bucks.

United Nations (1993), *System of National Accounts*, ST/ESA/STAT/SER.F/2/Rev.4., New York, United Nations.

US DoE (1998), (Department of Energy Techline) 'DoE Selects Potential Breakthrough Approaches for Removing Greenhouse Gases from Ecosystem, see http://www.fe.doe.gov/techline/tl_novelseq.html

van den Bergh, J. C. J. M., and Hofkes, M. W. (1998), 'Sustainable Development and Formal Models', in J. C. J. M. van den Bergh and M. W. Hofkes (eds), *Theory and Implementation of Economic Models for Sustainable Development*, Dordrecht, Kluwer Academic Publishers.

Van der Meulen Rodgers, Y. (1993), 'An Economic Analysis of Debt Swaps and Case Study of the Harvard Debt for Education Swap', *World Development*, **21**, 861–7.

Vatn, A. (1998), 'Input versus Emissions Taxes', *Land Economics*, **74**(4) 514–25.

Vermersch, D., Bonnieux, F., and Rainelli, P. (1993), 'Abatement of Agricultural Pollution and Economic Incentives: The Case of Intensive Livestock Farming in France', *Environmental and Resource Economics*, **3**(3) 285–96.

Victor, P., Hanna, S., and Kubusi, A. (1998), 'How Strong Is Weak Sustainability?', in S. Faucheux, M. O'Connor and J. van den Straaten (eds), *Sustainable Development: Concepts, Rationality and Strategies*, Dordrecht, Kluwer Academic Publishers.

Walters, A. (1975), *Noise and Prices*, Oxford, Clarendon Press.

WCED (1987), *Our Common Future*, The Report of the World Commission on Environment and Development, Oxford, Oxford University Press.

Weitzman, M. L. (1974), 'Prices vs Quantities', *Review of Economic Studies*, **41**, 477–91.

—   (1998), 'Why the Far-Distant Future Should Be Discounted at Its Lowest Possible Rate', *Journal of Environmental Economics and Management*, **36**, 201–8.

Weitzman, M. L., and Löfgren, K.-G. (1997), 'On the Welfare Signifi-
    cance of Green Accounting as Taught by Parable', *Journal of
    Environmental Economics and Management*, **32**, 139–53.
Whitby, M. C. (ed.) (1994), *Incentives for Countryside Management: The
    Case of ESAs*, Wallingford, CAB International.
—   (ed.) (1996), *The European Environment and CAP Reform: Policies
    and Prospects for Conservation*, Wallingford, CAB International.
—   Saunders, C. (1996), 'Estimating the Supply of Conservation
    Goods in Britain: A Comparison of the Financial Efficiency of
    Two Policy Instruments', *Land Economics*, **72**(3) 313–25.
Williams, B. (1992), 'Must Concern for the Environment be Centred on
    Human Beings?', reprinted in B. Williams (1995), *Making Sense of
    Humanity*, Cambridge, Cambridge University Press.
Willis, K., and Garrod, G. (1995), 'The Benefits of Alleviating Low
    Flows in Rivers', *Water Resources Development*, **11**, 243–60.
Wilson, O. (1992), *The Diversity of Life*, Penguin.
Winjum, J. K., Dixon, R. K., and Schroeder, P. E. (1992), 'Estimating the
    Global Potential of Forest and Agroforest Management Practices
    to Sequester Carbon', *Water, Air and Soil Pollution*, **64**, 213–27.
Wise Use (1999), 'Trading off Trees for Pollution', *Timber and Wood
    Products*, 6 February, 32.
Woodward, R., and Bishop, R. (1997), 'How to Decide When Experts
    Disagree: Uncertainty-Based Choice Rules in Environmental
    Policy', *Land Economics*, **73**(4), 492–507.
Wootton, H. J., and Poulton, M. L. (1993), *Reducing Carbon Dioxide
    Emissions from Passenger Cars to 1990 Levels*, Report PA 3016/93,
    Transport Research Laboratory, Crowthorne.
World Bank (1997), *Expanding the Measure of Wealth*, Environmentally
    Sustainable Development, ESD Studies and Monographs Series
    No. 17, Washington DC, The World Bank.
World Commission on Environment and Development (1987), *Our
    Common Future*, Oxford, Oxford University Press (the 'Brundtland
    Report').
Wysham, D. (1998), *The World Bank and the G7: Still Changing the Earth's
    Climate for Business*, Washington, DC, Institute of Policy Studies.
Yaeger, P. (1991), *The Limits of the Law: The Public Regulation of Private
    Pollution*, Cambridge, Cambridge University Press.
Zedler, J. B., and Callaway, J. C. (1999), 'Tracking Wetland Restoration:
    Do Mitigation Sites Follow Desired Trajectories?', *Restoration
    Ecology*, **7**, 69–73.

Index